GAY LATTER-DAY SAINT
CROSSROADS
My Journey, Your Journey,
and a Scripture-based Path Forward

EVAN SMITH
Edited by Marci McPhee

(This book was originally released, and remains available, as a free PDF download at www.gayldscrossroads.org. That site also allows readers to easily access the many websites and sources that are referenced throughout this book and to navigate its various chapters and sections online. Readers are invited to freely share this book and that website with others.)

"*Crossroads* offers the reader poignant personal stories, asks engaging questions, and shines a much-needed light to help us - as LGTBQ individuals, as families, and as a church - see our way on this pioneer journey toward a better future."

— **Carol Lynn Pearson**, author of *Goodbye, I Love You* and
No More Goodbyes: Circling the Wagons Around Our Gay Loved Ones,
as well as *I'll Walk With You* (picture book based on her Primary
song by the same name)

"*Crossroads* is a wonderful book from my friend, Evan Smith, an active Latter-day Saint and the father of a gay son, who shares valuable insights into how we can better meet the needs of LGBTQ Latter-day Saints. I encourage parents, local leaders, and our LGBTQ members to read this insightful and thoughtful book to better become the Body of Christ."

— **Richard Ostler**, host of the podcast Listen, Learn and Love,
founder of listenlearnandlove.org, and author of the book
Listen, Learn and Love: Embracing LGBTQ Latter-day Saints

"Evan Smith's book is honest, clear, broad in its reach, and extremely useful. It is very accessible, organized so that the reader can hop around and examine different aspects of the situation depending on the reader's particular interests. As an active church member, a former bishop, and the father of a gay son, Evan is acutely aware of the enormous hurt of LGBTQ church members and their families. He offers very thoughtful paths forward for changes in church policy and culture that are consistent with the foundational doctrines of the gospel and that would, in fact, expand the church's good influence. Very good stuff."

— **Judy Dushku**, co-founder of the magazine *Exponent II*,
former Boston Stake Relief Society President, founder of
THRIVE Gulu in Uganda, former professor of government
at Suffolk University, and mother of a gay son

"This book is a critically important study of how homosexuality is currently thought of in the LDS Church and how we might see it in a different light so as not to leave our LGBT members without a place in our theology. As the loving father of a gay son, Evan Smith has clearly given this topic significant thought over the years and clearly expresses his experience and thinking in a way that invites us to consider how we might do better as a church."

— **Bryce Cook**, author of an influential essay available at www.mormonlgbtquestions.com, founding member of ALL (Arizona LDS LGBT) Friends & Family, and co-director of the annual "ALL Are Alike Unto God" Conference held every April in Mesa, Arizona

"*Gay Latter-day Saint Crossroads* is both highly insightful and inspiring. The book provides excellent clarity of analysis and original insights not previously shared in the relevant literature. Its combination of personal experiences, scriptural analysis, and reference to other works provides a deeply moving and intellectually rigorous picture of LGBTQ and Latter-day Saint experiences and the underlying principles that have, now do, and may yet shape Latter-day Saint approaches to LGBTQ issues. The book will open minds and hearts."

— **Truman Whitney**, gay Harvard law student and returned missionary

"I really appreciated Evan's thorough "no stones left unturned" approach to his examination of the past and current relationship between the church and the LGBTQ community. I loved his suggestions for changes, both big and small, and how many could be justified here and now without new revelation. Read [this book]. Recommend it to your friends and family…It may change your life. It might help you save someone's life... or even your own."

—**Valerie Nicole Green** (she/her), is a co-founder & co-chair of Emmaus LGBTQ Ministry. She is a transgender woman who is active in her church ward in Missouri. Before transitioning, she was married for 34 years and is now widowed. She is the father to five children and grandfather to six grandchildren. Read her full thoughts on *Crossroads* at the Emmaus LGBTQ blog: https://www.emmauslgbtq.org/post/a-journey-leading-to-hope.

"*Crossroads* provides valuable insight into the tough challenges our LGBTQ siblings face as members of the Church of Jesus Christ of Latter-day Saints. It is my hope that many members will read this book so they can better understand the LGBTQ experience and learn to minister to them effectively. I pray that readers will have an open heart and will ponder on ways to help our church be more inclusive. Our LGBTQ members are needed for us to learn how to love as the Savior loves."

— **Christina Dee**, moderator of the Mormons Building Bridges Facebook group, and volunteer at the Utah Pride Center, Encircle, and Affirmation

"Every word in the title of Evan Smith's book is a Christ-like and loving magnet to readers, whether they are queer, allies, or those trying to reconcile their faith with being privileged to learn that a loved one identifies as LGBTQ+. As the title highlights, we are currently at a crossroads. I know of crossroads, having joined The Church of Jesus Christ aware of two things: that I was bisexual, and that the church's history with LGBTQ+ people and gay rights was contentious and less than queer people would hope for. Still, I joined. I am still here, and I intend to stay. So much work on Christ-like love, acceptance, and support remains undone for our LBGTQ+ Saints and their family and friends. Still too often - as Evan details - when LGBTQ+ Saints embrace their sexual and gender identities, they might feel they are at a heart-breaking crossroads - stay in the church and feel inferior or unwanted due to a doctrinal emphasis on heterosexual family ideals, or leave the church and lose connections to family, friends, temples, and saving ordinances. Evan's book gives me hope for our church's future, for my own journey, and for my queer sister and brother Saints."

— **Timothy D.**, a convert who enjoys talking with other converts, listening to the journeys of other LGBTQ+ Saints in-person, on podcasts and in online publications, and spending time with his family

"*Crossroads* approaches LGBTQ issues within the church, exploring potential paths forward in a sensitive manner, with honest assessments and faithful proposals. This nearly encyclopedic work explores previous arguments, declarations and interpretations, calling for a compassionate re-analysis of how Latter-day Saints and leaders relate to their LGBTQ brothers and sisters. Evan Smith explores potential shifts in policy and doctrinal interpretation, that respect the integrity of Latter-day Saint tenets and scripture, which would advance a more welcoming church. His personal odyssey and investigative approach are both analytical and heartwarming."

— **Clair Barrus**, a Mormon historian who manages TodayinMormonHistory.com, blogs at withoutend.org, has published in the *Journal of Mormon History* and most recently in the *John Whitmer Historical Association Journal* ("Religious Authority, Sexuality, and Gender Roles of the Elect Ladies of the Early Republic: Jemima Wilkinson, Ann Lee, and Emma Smith")

"*Crossroads* is an impassioned hope by a father for happiness for his gay son and other LGBTQ church members and their families. Smith poignantly describes the challenges that LGBTQ members face at Church with our current teachings, doctrines and policies. As a father of a gay son, Smith, understands much of the pain, rejection, and challenges of LGBTQ members and gives them voice. Smith recounts personal experiences and his own journey towards allyship and helps us understand how the Church's teachings regarding LGBTQ individuals has changed. But, the high point of Crossroads is how Smith gives us a vision of how believing members can better support our LGBTQ members, regardless of how they choose to live their lives."

— **David Ostler**, author of *Bridges: Ministering to Those Who Question*

"*Crossroads* will take you on a journey of emotions, as Evan shares his family story of how he gained a deeper Christ-like love and acceptance for the LGBTQ+ community, while serving in various positions (bishop, stake presidency, etc.) in the Church of Jesus Christ of Latter-day Saints. This book helps to bring awareness and knowledge to some of the issues we are currently facing within the church. Evan was incredibly thorough in his research. He shares views on church doctrine which are thought provoking, as well as spiritually enlightening. With a prayerful heart, Evan details his personal experience of heartache, forgiveness, love and hope for what's to come. Evan, I am so proud of you for the amazing father, husband, son, and brother you are. My life has been blessed with you as my brother."

— **Sarah Quincy,** affirming aunt and supportive sister

"This book is about hope, love and understanding. It is grounded in the scriptures and prophetic teachings. It has helped me gain more loving insights and compassion regarding our LGBTQ siblings. I highly recommend reading this book."

— **Jason Smith,** affirming uncle and supportive brother

SPECIAL THANKS:

I would like to express sincere thanks to all the individuals who have provided input on this book. Many people reviewed early drafts and provided feedback. You know who you are. Your contributions were incredibly helpful and motivating. Particularly extraordinary levels of assistance were given by Clair Barrus, Bryce Cook, Derek Knox, Kendall Wilcox, and my wife, Cheryl. And indispensable guidance and direction, along with amazing wordsmithing and editing, was provided by Marci McPhee.

DEDICATION:

To Cheryl for showing me how to love; and to Wes for being patient with me

"Remember, it was the questions young Joseph asked that opened the door for the restoration of all things. We can block the growth and knowledge our Heavenly Father intends for us. How often has the Holy Spirit tried to tell us something we needed to know but couldn't get past the massive iron gate of what we thought we already knew?"

— Elder Dieter F. Uchtdorf, Apostle, https://www.thechurchnews.com/
archives/2012-02-11/president-dieter-f-uchtdorf-acting-on-the-truths-of-
the-gospel-of-jesus-christ-53389

"I'm willing to walk by faith in darkness…but the problem comes…when I'm called upon to do something that goes against…the spirit that I am accustomed to hearkening unto, when it's also against what I think is the very heart and soul of the gospel of Jesus Christ and of theology."

— Lowell Bennion (1908-1996), founder of the first food bank and home-less shelters in Utah, "Mormonism's greatest practical philosopher," according to Eugene England (http://eugeneengland.org/wp-content/uploads/sbi/
articles/1996_a_op_002.pdf). From *Lowell L. Bennion: Teacher, Counselor, Humanitarian,* by Mary Lythgoe Bradford, 248 (http://bitly.ws/8E33)

"If you don't love as some people do, Some people think your love's not true. But I won't, I won't!"

— Carol Lynn Pearson, *I'll Walk With You* (picture book based on her song by the same name), 2020 (https://www.amazon.com/
Ill-Walk-Carol-Lynn-Pearson/dp/1423653955)

Transgender issues need more attention than they are getting in the church. However, such issues are not discussed much in this book as the author doesn't have much personal experience with transgender church members. Without excusing that failure, the sincere hope is that any change in the church that benefits lesbian, gay, bisexual or questioning/queer individuals will produce changes that help transgender church members as well.

(Cover design by Owen Smith. Website design and buildout of www.gayldscrossroads.org by Weston Smith.)

CONTENTS

GAY LATTER-DAY SAINT CROSSROADS
My Journey, Your Journey, and a Scripture-based Path Forward

print ISBN: 978-1-09834-233-3
ebook ISBN: 978-1-09834-234-0

EDITOR'S FOREWORD

Jesus' First and Last Message

Come with me to Nazareth. Jesus has just spent forty days alone in the desert, communing with God and preparing for His ministry. He is returning to His hometown, ready to declare to His neighbors that He is the promised Messiah.

This particular Sabbath day, we enter the synagogue along with the rest of the villagers "where he had been brought up." You and I find a place on the stone benches along the walls of the synagogue. Jesus stands, takes the papyrus scroll, and begins to read from Isaiah: "The Spirit of the Lord is upon me, because he hath anointed me to preach the gospel to the poor; he hath sent me to heal the brokenhearted, to preach deliverance to the captives, and recovering of sight to the blind, to set at liberty them that are bruised."

Jesus then makes this astonishing statement that infuriates His hometown neighbors, enough to make them want to "cast him down headlong" over the "hill whereon their city was built." What is the declaration that is a capital offense in His neighbors' eyes? "This day is this scripture fulfilled in your ears."

*   Matthew 4:1, Joseph Smith Translation
**   Luke 4:16
***   Isaiah 61:1-2
****   Luke 4:29
*****   Luke 4:21

From the start, Jesus' ministry is to heal the brokenhearted, deliver the captives, and free them that are bruised. And from the start, the opposition is quick and vicious.

Three years later, come with me to Jerusalem to hear Jesus' last public sermon. We are just outside the city, seated on the hillside on the Mount of Olives, surrounded by a well-tended olive grove with a spectacular view of Jerusalem. It is likely Wednesday, two days before His crucifixion.

What is the message of Jesus' last public discourse? "For I was an hungred, and ye gave me meat: I was thirsty, and ye gave me drink: I was a stranger, and ye took me in: naked and ye clothed me: I was sick, and ye visited me: I was in prison, and ye came unto me."

Towards the end of His mortal ministry, Jesus' last message echoes His first: feed the poor, care for the stranger, the sick, and the captive. How is His final public sermon received? Within days, His followers will take Jesus' lifeless body down from the cross and lay it in a borrowed tomb.

From His first to His final public sermon, Jesus cares a lot about the last, the least, the lost, and the lonely. And Jesus has called us to carry on His work. For some, it may not be much easier for us than it was for Him.

After His resurrection, Jesus appears at the coast of the sea of Galilee. Listen while He calls the apostles to shore from their fishing boats and gives them their final instructions. Did they get it? Did they grasp what His whole ministry was about? Do they understand their charge to leave their nets once again and continue Jesus' work? Here is the lesson in three words, repeated three times for emphasis: "Feed my lambs. Feed my sheep. Feed my sheep." (Notice that Jesus asks us to start with the most vulnerable.)

*   "The Greatest Week in History" by Daniel H. Ludlow
https://www.churchofjesuschrist.org/study/ensign/1972/04/
the-greatest-week-in-history?lang=eng
**   Matthew 25:35-36
***   Mark 2:13-17
****   John 21:15-17

There can be no room in the life of a follower of Christ for un-Christ-like treatment of anyone. Here's Jesus' invitation list: "he inviteth them all to come unto him and partake of his goodness; and he denieth none that come unto him, black and white, bond and free, male and female; and he remembereth the heathen; and all are alike unto God." And what percentage does the word All indicate? One hundred percent. All means All.

Come with me to my family dinner. As we walk around the table, I introduce you to my own close family, including a gay man, a lesbian woman, a transgender person, a pansexual individual, and a sparkling gender-bending sprite of a child who defies all labels and is exuberantly living into their best self, whoever that turns out to be. And a bunch of straight folks, in and out of church, scratching their heads and trying to make sense of us all. This is my family, and I love each one exactly as they are, exactly how God made them. And I'm positive that God loves them too, without exception.

What draws me to this work? Admiration for the strength of character, the creativity and flair that my LGBTQ family, friends and colleagues add to the world.

Like the author, I am a church-going, temple-attending "active member" (some call me a "hyper- active member") of the church. I have long known there must be a way to connect my love for these vibrant people that I love and the teachings of my beloved Church of Jesus Christ of Latter- day Saints. My deep appreciation goes to Evan Smith and his family for this remarkable work, solidly grounded in the scriptures and the teachings of living prophets, as well as their own courageous journey as a family.

Keep reading.

Marci McPhee,
editor marcimcpheewriter.com

---

*　2 Nephi 26:33

WHERE AM I COMING FROM?

In 2013, a 14-year-old teen (who has since given me permission to share this story) came into my office at church to speak with me about something personal. I was serving at the time as their branch president (the volunteer leader of a congregation in The Church of Jesus Christ of Latter- day Saints). I had no idea when they came in that this meeting would be one of the most pivotal experiences in my life.

They were having feelings toward members of the same sex that they had a hard time finding words to describe. I listened without knowing what to say. I ended up simply telling them they were loved by God and that I would like to meet with them again to talk further.

That bought me some time. And I used it to investigate what I had never taken much time to explore before: gay sexual orientation. I spent many hours researching everything I could about what the church, science, and other professionals were teaching on the subject. What I learned opened my mind, changed my heart, and prepared me to embark on a journey I never would have guessed before would turn out to be mine. I eventually became committed to helping that teen and others in their situation in any way I could.

What's my background? From what perspective am I writing?

By way of a little personal background, I grew up near Salt Lake City, Utah. Like many other people raised in Utah, I have been an active and committed participant in the faith and religious practices taught by The Church of Jesus Christ of Latter-day Saints my whole life. My ancestors on both sides of my family tree were pioneers who crossed the American plains and helped establish the state of Utah. My great-great-great grandfather even did so while blind – for real: https://www.churchofjesuschrist.org/study/general-conference/2004/10/where-do-i-make-my-stand. I have always felt support from my family, and a sense of obligation to my ancestors, to be a good person and stay active in my church. (In case you're curious, I am just a run-of-the-mill "Smith" – no family relation to Joseph Smith at all.)

Before college, I dedicated two years of my life to serving a full-time mission for the church. I have had the privilege of serving in many leadership positions in the church, including as the volunteer leader of our local congregation (first as a branch president and later as a bishop) and in a position of regional church leadership as well (as a counselor in a stake presidency). Now, I don't share all that to boast. In fact, it annoys me when people in the church talk about pioneer ancestry or any church assignment (which we refer to as "callings") as badges of honor or a "resume" of sorts. I don't think those things make someone any more special than others. Rather, I share those facts simply to help explain how much the church is a part of my heritage and my life.

I met and married my wife, Cheryl, while attending Brigham Young University (BYU) in Provo, Utah in 1997. Our son, Weston, was born in 1999, the year before Cheryl and I each received our undergraduate degrees together from BYU in 2000. We then moved to Ontario, Canada (where Cheryl grew up) so I could attend law school at the University of Toronto. While in law school, I was accepted to join a large law firm in Boston practicing corporate law. So we moved to Massachusetts when I graduated in 2003. At that point we had added two more kids to our family: Owen (born in 2001) and Laurel (born in 2003). We felt good about moving to Massachusetts even though we didn't know anyone living here at the time. I have had some unusual health issues that we don't think could have been resolved in any other place than Boston's amazing healthcare environment, so we are grateful we felt drawn here.

And we're also grateful for the unique experiences we've had in the church while living here. While we've lived in the very same house in southeastern Massachusetts ever since moving here in 2003, we've actually been a part of two different congregations (congregations in our church are determined by geographical boundaries – you attend church wherever the boundaries dictate). Our congregation changed because, after some growth in the church in our area, a new congregation was formed in 2008 through the realignment of several geographical boundaries of surrounding congregations in our region. By that point we had added a caboose to our family - our daughter, Karissa (born in 2007). When the boundary change happened, we became a part of a congregation that started as a branch (which is a name for a smaller-sized congregation) and grew to become a ward (which is the name for a regular-sized congregation) in 2014. All of us in the new congregation attended church in a local high school building for the first year (from 2008-2009), and then in a rented storefront property for 8 years, until our own standalone chapel was built in 2017.

It has been very rewarding for us to experience the growth of the church while living here. But the thing we love about the church the most in our area is the people. We found amazing friends in the church almost instantly upon moving here. We like to call them our "fr-amily" since we don't have any family living near us and we rely on each other, and love each other, so much.

And even though both Cheryl's and my parents and siblings live far away (near Toronto and Salt Lake City, respectively), we feel close to them and have always appreciated the love and support they have provided us. We couldn't have asked for better families.

How do I feel about the church?
How do I feel about my son's decision to leave it?

My love for the church extends beyond its people and the experiences I have had in it. I also love the divine truths that the church teaches. Those teachings have brought me great joy and a sense of purpose and peace. I could write several books, let alone a book like this, about all the positive, wonderful ways the church has blessed my life.

However, that's not what this book will focus on – because, in addition to being an active member of the church, I am also a "Dragon Dad," which is a colloquial name given to any father of an LGBTQ child who strongly supports them (the motherly equivalent is a "Mama Dragon," which I believe is derived from "Mama Bear" but is specific to mothers of LGBTQ children. Mama Dragons is an organization that was formed many years ago; Dragon Dads was formed afterwards).

Our oldest son, Weston, is gay and has decided to step away from the church because he feels that God's path for him lies in seeking a husband – so he can have the best chance possible for a long-term, stable marriage and family of his own someday (see *"How should I feel about my son leaving the church?"* in Chapter 9 for further explanation of the process Wes went through to receive personal revelation that he should step away the church). Cheryl and I wholeheartedly support him in that decision because we know it is best for his mental, emotional, and spiritual well-being as a gay man. (More about how we came to that decision later.) And, at the same time, I am committed to remaining an active member of the church myself.

For any church members who can't understand why I am supportive of my son's decision to try to find a husband, please consider the following baseline factors of my thinking, each of which will be explored in more depth in other places in this book.

1. The church now teaches that people do <u>not</u> choose to be attracted to someone of their same sex:

"The Church of Jesus Christ of Latter-day Saints believes that the experience of same-sex attraction is a complex reality for many people. The attraction itself is not a sin, but acting on it is. Even though **individuals do not choose to have such attractions**, they do choose how to respond to them." (M. Russell Ballard, Apostle, "Church Leaders," https://www.churchofjesuschrist.org/topics/gay/, 2015)

2. Science has a better understanding of why people are born gay. For a quick primer on the science, you can listen to this excellent lecture given in 2010 by BYU microbiology professor (and former mission president) Dr. William Bradshaw: https://m.youtube.com/watch?v=8I-Hw9DVI3hE (the whole lecture is great, but, if you're rushed for time, you can skip to about the 30-minute mark and listen for 20 minutes to learn about how epigenetics influences sexual orientation). See Chapter 3 for more about the science.

3. Sexual orientation cannot be changed. Even church leaders have acknowledged this fact: "I must say, this son's sexual orientation did not somehow miraculously change—no one assumed it would (Jeffrey R. Holland, Apostle, 2015: https://www.churchofjesuschrist.org/study/general-conference/2015/10/behold-thy-mother). When someone who previously identified as gay says they are now straight, I think that's most often just indicative of their true orientation really being bisexual. My son knows he is gay, not bisexual.

4. The church's teachings, policies and doctrines are fluid and often **do** change (as I'll describe at length throughout this book).

5. Social science evidence indicates that it is risky, from a mental health perspective, for anyone to marry someone to whom they're not attracted, or to proactively suppress the biologically wired mating desire for their entire life. The church teaches straight Latter-day Saint singles to always maintain hope for marriage, not proactively abandon

it. That distinction is important from a mental health perspective because it can mean that straight singles feel like they just have to wait for a spouse. But gay singles in the church tend to feel that a core part of them was created as a mistake that will need to be fixed after this life. I have personally observed that severe mental health damage can be caused by the church's teaching that the only "righteous" paths available for LGBTQ people are marrying someone of the opposite sex or intentional lifelong celibacy.

[Side note: This is consistent with a peer-reviewed 2017 study conducted by Brian Simmons at the University of Georgia on LGBTQ Latter-day Saints, which showed that over 73% of the participants reported trauma and multiple PTSD symptoms (89% reported at least one PTSD symptom) from repeated exposure to basic teachings of the church concerning sexuality, gender, marriage, and family. This stands in contrast to a baseline of 8% experiencing trauma / PTSD from those teachings. Trauma / PTSD was not self-diagnosed but shown through clinical methods derived from the Diagnostic and Statistical Manual of Mental Disorder. The majority of respondents identified as active members with 31% holding current temple recommends. (https://getd.libs.uga.edu/ pdfs/simmons_brian_w_201712_phd.pdf; http://mormonsbuild- ingbridges.org/wp-content/uploads/2019/10/20190928-U-of-U- MBB- Presentation-SIMMONS-FINAL.pptx).

Also, a peer-reviewed 2020 study conducted by James McGraw at Bowling Green State University (BGSU) and his colleagues found that lesbian, gay and bisexual (LGB) Utahns are over 4.5 times more likely to have recently thought about suicide/self-harm and nearly 10 times as likely to have attempted suicide in their lifetimes, when compared to heterosexual Utahns. What's even more alarming is that the rates of suicidal thinking and suicide attempts among LGB Utahns was around three times higher than the rates among LGB non-Utahns living in the U.S., Canada and Europe. The rates of suicidal thinking and suicide attempts among heterosexuals in and out of Utah was not found to be nearly as divergent (https://drive. google.com/file/d/1zNs8K5nNPw4SQxPch0uc_PFH0f0Q3kIq/

view?usp=drivesdk; https://www.tandfonline.com/doi/full/10.10 80/13811118.2020.1806159).

Some people have postulated that Utah's high altitude is a contributing factor to the high suicide rate among LGBTQ people. But I think the fact that the rates for straight folks in and out of Utah were not as different as the rates for LGB folks in and out of Utah suggests that Utah's high altitude is not the primary reason LGB Utahns are so much more prone to suicide. It's important to note that the BGSU study does not propose a reason for its findings or address the influence of religious beliefs at all. But I think when its findings are read in conjunction with those of the above-referenced study from the University of Georgia regarding the traumatic effects of some church teachings on LGBTQ Latter-day Saints, it's not difficult to identify a distinguishing factor about Utah that could be making it harder for LGB people who live there to avoid suicidal thoughts.

The following statistics also underscore how important it is for families and friends of LGBTQ youth to see their role as being supportive and accepting, not prescriptive and condemning:

a. *LGBTQ youth have a much higher suicide rate than the general population (https://en.wikipedia.org/wiki/Suicide_among_LGBT_youth).*

b. *LGB youth who come from highly rejecting families are 8.4 times as likely to have attempted suicide as LGB peers who reported no or low levels of family rejection, 5.9 times more likely to report high levels of depression, 3.4 times more likely to use illegal drugs, and 3.4 times more likely to report having engaged in unprotected sex. (Pediatrics January 2009, Volume 123 / Issue 1).*

c. *LGBTQ youth who experienced someone trying to convince them to change their orientation were 2.5 times more likely to attempt suicide. (The Trevor Project National Survey on LGBTQ Youth Mental Health 2019).*

d. *Families who accept LGBT family members reduce suicide rates of those LGBT family members by 50%. (Journal of Child and Adolescent Psychiatric Nursing 23(4):205-13 · November 2010).*

e. *An LGBT youth who has **just one accepting adult** in their life reduces suicide rates by 40% for the LGBT youth. (The Trevor Project National Survey on LGBTQ Youth Mental Health 2019).]*

What do I hope to achieve in writing this book?

Instead of writing about the happiness I feel in the church, I'm writing this book for some clearly different reasons. First, as *the father of a gay son, I want to explain, and so hopefully do something productive with, the pain I feel from the church's teachings about gay sexual orientation.* Rather than continue to let my hurt fester inside unexpressed, I'm trying to help increase understanding about why the church's position causes intense emotional turmoil for so many people. I want to try to be a voice for many people like me who are suffering. I'm not doing this because I care about what people think of me necessarily, but rather, because I honestly believe there are a significant number of church members who just don't understand (or who don't want to understand) why LGBTQ issues are such a "big deal."

The second reason I'm writing this book: *I want to explore whether the church's current position on gay sexual behavior is more reflective of human prejudice than it is divine truth.* In doing so, I want to acknowledge that only our topmost church leaders, our prophets and apostles, can determine what the church's teachings and practices should be. I don't have that authority. And who knows? Maybe, consistent with the agency God has given us, the church's current position against marriage equality in our doctrine simply reflects God's willingness to let us figure out for ourselves how to love and accept our LGBTQ siblings without prejudice. I wonder if there are lessons to be learned about love and the gospel that we can't learn in any other way than just figuring things out for ourselves as a church. So I'm inclined to assume the prophet won't receive a new revelation for doctrinal marriage equality until most church members feel ashamed about the ways the church treats LGBTQ people differently than cisgender straight individuals. Perhaps at that point the prophet will be desperate for change and so, as he asks with "real intent" (Moroni 10:4), the revelation will come. In any event, I think it's good for all of us to be open-minded to whatever sort of revelation might be received in the future.

[Side note: For those who are unfamiliar with the term "cisgender," it means a person whose sense of gender identity corresponds with the sex they were assigned at birth. It is basically the opposite of "transgender."]

The third reason I'm writing this book is because *I want to try to make amends for any harm I caused in the past as a leader in the church.* While I tried to teach about LGBTQ issues in a loving way in my church leadership roles, I regret not doing more to try to alleviate the pain that our LGBTQ siblings feel from the teachings of the church. I am sorry for the times I taught notions that I now know cause psychological harm to LGBTQ individuals. I am sorry I didn't speak up more in meetings to challenge hurtful ways of thinking. I am sorry I didn't express more love to the gay man (who has since gratefully accepted my apology) who was the subject of a disciplinary council in which I participated as a high councilor. I am sorry I didn't do more to remove any sense of self-doubt and despair from the hearts of the gay and lesbian individuals with whom I counseled as a bishop, many of whom were wondering if they should someday leave the church so they could have the opportunity to find a spouse to whom they were naturally and authentically attracted. I expressed understanding, sympathy, and unconditional love no matter what path they chose – but I felt that, because I was a bishop, I had to always strongly encourage them to stay in the church.

It wasn't until Wes struggled for years to decide what path he should follow that I realized the harm I caused previously. I should have communicated to those ward members the same thing I needed to tell my own son to help him stay mentally healthy: that his decision to find a spouse did not have to be a choice that God only "tolerated." Rather, since he felt God pushing him in that direction, that decision to seek a partner could be viewed as one that God actually preferred and knew was best for him. I was able to tell Wes that I could see how his decision, based on personal revelation, to leave the church could actually be what God wanted – but I didn't ever say that to any other individuals with whom I had previously counseled as a bishop. I'm hoping that writing and sharing this book can help me repent of that "sin of omission" by making it more clear that I honor both paths as ones God could inspire. It all depends on the personal revelation an individual receives (see Chapter 9 for a related insight from the scriptures about Solomon).

I need to do more to end the stigma that often follows LGBTQ individuals if they choose to leave the church. Now, I know I don't have the authority to say what church doctrine should be, but I feel like part of my making amends includes being more open about how I personally feel now, and apologizing for not being more open and honest before.

That's one reason why "crossroads" is used in the title of this book. Writing and sharing this book represents a crossroads for me in my life. Going public like this with my personal thoughts is something I hope helps provide healing for at least one LGBTQ individual who may have had a bad experience with a church leader before. I hope they read my apology here and feel hope that hearts can change as mine did.

I also hope this book can be a crossroads of sorts for straight church members who aren't too familiar with LGBTQ issues. I hope my thoughts serve as a touchpoint for them to learn enough so that they decide to be more loving toward our LGBTQ siblings. I sincerely hope the information, resources, and opinions shared here might serve as a crossroads for at least one more person to commit to becoming an LGBTQ ally.

And finally, the _main_ reason to use the word "crossroads" for this project is because this book will explore the intersection between Latter-day Saint doctrine on gay sexual behavior, on the one hand, and the basic human dignity of (and compassion toward) LGBTQ people, on the other hand. A similar crossroads exists between personal well-being and doctrines on gender identity.

I will not spend much time discussing transgender doctrinal issues in this book as I don't have much personal experience with transgender church members. While the injustices our lesbian, gay and bisexual sisters and brothers face in the church are different from those faced by our transgender siblings, I believe that if the church's doctrine changes to permit same-sex couples to marry and still maintain full church privileges, then changes in our doctrines that cause harm to transgender church members will likely occur at or around the same time as well.

Until all such changes happen, the juncture between church doctrine and personal well-being will remain one that is fraught with tension that can cause intense pain for anyone in the church who is LGBTQ or who has a loved one who is LGBTQ. It forces difficult decisions to be made. So I think we all should take time to explore whether the crosses we see many of our LGBTQ siblings bearing on their roads in life are foisted upon them by the church, not by God.

Is it bad to recognize there is human error in the church?

I hope no fellow church members feel like I am attacking the church or its leaders by asking whether our doctrine opposing marriage equality comes from God. To the contrary, I love the church and am grateful for our leaders' efforts to do what they feel is best for the church as a whole. But also I don't think we should view anyone as an enemy to the church simply because they recognize that it's possible for human frailty to be reflected in church teachings. Multiple prophets in the Book of Mormon acknowledged that their writings could contain both the word of God and their own human mistakes:

> Book of Mormon Title Page (by Moroni) – "And now, **if there are faults they are the mistakes of men**; wherefore, condemn not the things of God, that ye may be found spotless at the judgment-seat of Christ."

> 1 Nephi 19:6 (by Nephi) – "Nevertheless, I do not write anything upon plates save it be that I think it be sacred. And now, **if I do err, even did they err of old; not that I would excuse myself because of other men**, but because of the weakness which is in me, according to the flesh, I would excuse myself."

Mormon 8:12, 17 (by Moroni) – "And whoso receiveth this record, and **shall not condemn it because of the imperfections which are in it… And if there be faults they be the faults of a man**."

Ether 12:23-25 (by Moroni) – "And I said unto him: Lord, the Gentiles will mock at these things, because of our weakness in writing…**wherefore, when we write we behold our weakness, and stumble because of the placing of our words**."

Those scriptures teach us that it is okay to believe that even canonized scripture can contain human error. If we are willing to believe that, I wonder why so many church members bristle when someone asks whether our modern-day non-canonical church teachings might also contain some human error. The hesitancy to admit that our church leaders can make mistakes in teaching doctrine is especially confusing to me because some of our own apostles living today have taught exactly that. They have admitted that mistakes have been made and that nothing God reveals through humans (including through prophets) is perfect:

"And, to be perfectly frank, **there have been times when** members or **leaders in the Church have simply made mistakes**. There may have been things said or done that were **not in harmony with our values, principles, or doctrine**. I suppose the Church would be perfect only if it were run by perfect beings. God is perfect, and His doctrine is pure. But He works through us—His imperfect children—and imperfect people make mistakes." (Dieter F. Uchtdorf, Apostle, https://www. churchofjesuschrist.org/study/general-conference/2013/10/ come-join-with- us?lang=eng, 2013)

"So **be kind regarding human frailty—your own as well as that of those who serve with you in a Church led by volunteer, mortal men and women. Except in the case of His only**

perfect Begotten Son, imperfect people are all God has ever had to work with. That must be terribly frustrating to Him, but He deals with it. So should we. And when you see imperfection, remember that the limitation is not in the divinity of the work. As one gifted writer has suggested, when the infinite fulness is poured forth, it is not the oil's fault if there is some loss because finite vessels can't quite contain it all.

Those finite vessels include you and me, so be patient and kind and forgiving." (Jeffrey R. Holland, Apostle, https://www. churchofjesuschrist.org/study/general- conference/2013/04/ lord-i-believe?lang=eng, 2013)

I don't condemn the Book of Mormon writers for their mistakes and, similarly, I don't condemn our modern-day church leaders for any mistakes they have made or might make in the future. I generally like to focus on the vast amount of divine truth that I believe comes from our prophets and apostles, not on their mistakes. But, as the father of a gay son, I wonder whether the pain that's being caused to our LGBTQ siblings by church teachings on gender, sexuality, marriage, and family is truly necessary. And I think it's okay for faithful church members to ask if pain- inflicting teachings come from God or man.

[Side note: The Book of Mormon teaches that the church as an institution can go astray, even while under the leadership of a prophet. In Alma 4:11 the church, under the leadership of the prophet Alma, is described as wicked. We know that is a description of the church organization itself because just two verses later, in Alma 4:13, the people who were actually following Christ are described as "others." I think that scriptural example is useful in interpreting the following passage of modern-day canon:

> *"The Lord will never permit...any...President of [the] Church to lead you astray. It is not in the programme. It is not in the mind of God. If I were to attempt that, the Lord would remove me out of my place, and so He will any other man who attempts to lead the children of men astray from the oracles of God and from their duty." (Official Declaration 1, Wilford Woodruff, https://www.churchofje-suschrist.org/study/scriptures/dc-testament/od/1?lang=eng, 1890)*

*I do not believe that statement means God will prevent any prophet from making mistakes that negatively affect other people. We do not believe the prophet is infallible. Rather, I think it simply means God will not allow the prophet to do anything that will bring about another general apostasy again. He will not be permitted to do anything that is so egregious that God will deem it necessary to remove priesthood authority from the earth again and start His church all over from scratch once more. Basically, God will not allow the church to go so far astray that it cannot be corrected before it is too late. But that leaves a lot of room for error by the church before that point is reached. For example, it **is** possible for the "example of the church" to lead people to personal iniquity:*

> *"Alma saw the wickedness of the church, and he saw also that the* **example of the church** *began to lead those who were unbelievers on from one piece of iniquity to another." (Alma 4:11)*

So in our own canon, there appears to be a distinction between leading the church "astray" (which I think means leading the church into a situation where it will cease to have authority) vs. leading individuals to personal failings in righteousness. In any event, it seems clear to me that the concept of the Lord not allowing the prophet to "lead [us] astray" should not be interpreted to suggest there is a prohibition on future doctrinal changes. Unfortunately though, I have seen many church members today use the above statement by Wilford Woodruff to suggest that a change from current prophetic teachings is not possible. I find that position to be ironic given that President Woodruff made his statement in the context of changing a doctrinal status quo (the importance of polygamy) that had been stridently taught by multiple prior church presidents as eternal truth.

I recognize that some church leaders have built upon the notion that the prophet will never lead us astray to further teach dogmatic ideas such as "When the prophet speaks, the debate is over" (https://www.churchofjesuschrist.org/study/ensign/1979/08/the-debate-is-over?lang=eng). But most church members are not aware that such line of thought originated with an unauthorized statement that President George Albert Smith privately renounced after it was first published in a church magazine in 1945 (https://www.fairmormon.org/archive/publications/when-the-prophet-speaks-is-the-thinking-done).

Similarly, most church members are not aware that Elder Ezra Taft Benson actually got in trouble for giving his talk titled "Fourteen Fundamentals in Following the Prophet" in 1980 in which he essentially says the living prophet is more important than scripture and should be followed even in political matters because he cannot lead us astray.

President Spencer W. Kimball was so bothered by Elder Benson's talk that he asked Elder Benson to "apologize to the Quorum of the Twelve Apostles, but they 'were dissatisfied with his response.' Kimball required him to explain himself to a combined meeting of all general authorities" as well (http://www.mormonpress. com/ezra-taft-benson-and-politics ; https://archive.sltrib.com/story.php?ref=/lds/ ci_14287116).

In any event, I hope church members will again find comfort in the idea that the prophet cannot lead the church astray when the status quo about what form of marriage is allowed by the church hopefully changes once more in the future to permit marriage between same-gender spouses.]

Many faithful church members have asked a similar question about the church's priesthood/temple ban based on race that ended in 1978. See Chapter 5 for a fuller explanation, but a brief mention here may be useful. In 2013, the church published an essay that denounced certain racist historical teachings from prophets, apostles, and other General Authorities that were spread to justify the ban as being of God. The church's essay now says:

> "Today, the Church disavows the theories advanced in the past that black skin is a sign of divine disfavor or curse, or that it reflects unrighteous actions in a pre-mortal life; that mixed-race marriages are a sin; or that blacks or people of any other race or ethnicity are inferior in any way to anyone else. Church leaders today unequivocally condemn all racism, past and present, in any form" (https://www.churchofjesuschrist.org/study/manual/ gospel-topics-essays/race-and-the- priesthood).

Brigham Young, Bruce R. McConkie, Mark E. Peterson, and many other General Authority church leaders had taught as truth those very ideas that the church now disavows. So it's clear that among the many good, inspired things those leaders taught, there were some mistaken, false teachings as well. That leads me to conclude that it's not a sign of unfaithfulness for church members to ask whether our current church teachings might also include a mix of both inspired truth and human error.

For example, where did the church's ban against marriage between two people of the same gender first come from? Is it possible our church inherited a position against marriage equality from uninspired religious teachings of the other faith traditions from which early Latter-day Saints came? Did we get it from Protestant traditions which church leaders have reinforced with non-canonical teachings ever since? Are we now suffering from a hesitancy to abandon past traditions, despite receiving prophetic warnings against believing too strongly in our traditions before?

> "There has been great difficulty in getting anything into the heads of this generation... Even the Saints are slow to understand. **I have tried** for a number of years **to get the minds of the Saints prepared to receive the things of God, but we frequently see [that] some of them**, after suffering all they have for the work of God, **will fly to pieces like glass as soon as anything comes that is contrary to their traditions**." (Joseph Smith, Prophet, https://www.churchofjesuschrist.org/study/manual/teachings-joseph-smith/chapter-45?lang=eng, 1844)

If so, it wouldn't be the first time false traditions resulted in harmful doctrine in the church. The aforementioned church essay suggests that a similar adoption of uninspired external teachings seems to be what happened with the racial priesthood/temple ban. Because of the church's essay, it is now an orthodox position for Latter-day Saints to assert that there was never any inspired revelation from God saying Black people were inferior because they supposedly descended from Cain or Ham, or that they were ever a cursed race – even though such concepts were widely taught by many General Authorities of the church for decades. Such now-officially-denounced ideas originated from interpretations of the Bible that other Christians in the 1800s and centuries before had maintained. But the church now officially seems to prefer different interpretations of the race-related scriptures that were previously used to justify slavery and inequality. These more modern interpretations are better grounded in historical context and do not promote racism. So I wonder if, similarly, our kids or grandkids will someday see the church allow for an interpretation of the scriptures that seem to discuss gay sexual behavior in ways that might permit monogamous marriage between same-gender partners (see Chapter 5).

I think the following analysis offers a great example from the Bible of how something can be called "divinely inspired" in official teachings at one time and then be disavowed in official teachings as "unrighteousness" by later generations. Trained theologian and Biblical scholar, Derek Knox, taught this in a podcast discussion in March 2020, titled "Khyreauxnah" at www.beyondtheblockpodcast.com.

[Side note: In addition to being a trained theologian and Biblical scholar, Derek also happens to be gay. He is an active and faithful church member. He was baptized into the church in 2015, shortly after the church announced the policy prohibiting the children of gay couples from being baptized, which policy was reversed in 2019. Derek co- hosts one of my favorite church-themed podcasts, "Beyond the Block," along with James C. Jones. James is also an active and faithful church member, raised in the church, and an excellent scriptorian in his own right. He speaks from the perspective of a Black man in the church. Their weekly podcast uses the church's "Come Follow Me" curriculum, examining the scriptures with a focus on marginalized people: www.beyondtheblockpodcast.com.]

"Derek: Do you know about what happened to King David and his choice to do a census of the military powers of Israel?

James: Uh, talk about it. I might.

Derek: Okay. So in 2 Samuel chapter 24, it is said that the Lord prompts King David (one of the anointed leaders of God's people at that time – literally anointed by a prophet of God – and a spiritual leader as well) to census, or to number, the adult men of Israel and Judah – mostly for the purposes of military power. He wanted to brag and see how strong they were. Kind of boast about it - you know, like a "Make Israel Great Again" type of thing. And that was wrong. So what happened was God sent a plague upon Israel and killed 70,000 of the Israelites because of this mistake that David made – because of this arrogant mistake.

Now, what's interesting is the books of Samuel and Kings are an earlier layer of the tradition. Chronicles was written later as a summary and a compendium of a lot of stuff that happened before at a much later date in the tradition. So we have different layers of the tradition saying different things about this. In 2 Samuel 24, it says that God prompted David to undertake this census. But when you read, 1 Chronicles 21, it says, Satan inspired David to take the census. And people say, "Oh, that's a contradiction." And in a sense it is. But what I'm here to say is, look, when later generations tell a story, they're going to tell it differently. And something that an anointed leader of God thought was from God, later generations can say was from Satan.

James: Wow. Very interesting.

Derek: I'm not going to say how this applies to anything going on right now.

James: I mean, do you have to, though?

Derek: But I just want you to know that when later generations tell a story… like how we read [the racist teachings of] Brigham Young up to Mark E. Peterson [and we now say those were] not from God. We throw them under the bus – and we should."

Looking for ways to find hope for that sort of official shift in perspective to occur again, but in the context of full equality for LGBTQ people in the church, is the main purpose of this book.

I hope for a future where there are no longer any painful "crossroads" challenges for LGBTQ church members or their loved ones. I hope for a future where LGBTQ people and their supporters in the church no longer feel any friction between love of family and love of God or between basic human dignity and church teachings.

I hope the reader will remember that I hope for the best for the church. I hope you will remember that I am a lifelong committed member of the church who is just trying to help all our LGBTQ siblings feel truly loved, accepted, and appreciated. I hope you will remember that, rather than intending to hurt the church, I'm simply sincerely wondering if there are reasons to believe that future generations will look back on the way the church has treated its LGBTQ church members as something that was displeasing to God. And I think that's a good question for all faithful church members to ask.

> **"I am not asking that all criticism be silenced. Growth comes of correction**. Strength comes of repentance. **Wise is the man who can acknowledge mistakes pointed out by others and change his course**." (Gordon B. Hinckley, Apostle, https://www.churchofjesuschrist.org/study/new-era/2001/07/ words-of-the-prophet-the-spirit-of-optimism?lang=eng, 1986)

CHAPTER 1:
INTRODUCTION: OUR STORY

Chapter synopsis: I love my gay son. I recognize that my son's sexual orientation cannot be changed. Today I wouldn't want it to be changed, even if that were possible, because it's a core and beautiful part of him - and learning to view gay sexual orientation more appropriately has made me a better person. I also recognize that many important teachings <u>have</u> changed significantly over the course of church history. Therefore, I have quietly hoped for change in the church, to alleviate the pain I feel from the doctrine that my son has to be a lifelong celibate or marry someone to whom he is not attracted in order to be allowed to fully participate in the church. By explaining my pain and my hope, including an exploration of doctrinal concepts, I aim to help people better understand the dilemma facing gay church members and their families.

How do I feel about having a gay son? How does my wife feel? How does my son feel?

Cheryl and I consider ourselves very fortunate to have four amazing kids. None of them has ever given us any real challenges. They have obeyed household rules, done well in school, respected our values, served in their communities, and tried to be good people. I have always tried to teach them that genuine

Christ-like love (i.e., "charity") is the most important thing any of us can learn. Charity is the whole point of true religion, in my opinion. When our kids were little, this just meant "be nice." I honestly can't express how happy I am to see the genuine love and kindness that each of our kids tries to show to other people. They're not perfect, but I couldn't be more pleased with the way each of them is conducting their lives.

That includes my admiration of the maturity, kindness, and grace with which Weston has navigated the spiritual and emotional dichotomies associated with being raised a Latter-day Saint and coming out publicly as a gay man in May 2019. Earlier, Wes came out privately to Cheryl, me, and his siblings when he was a junior in high school in the fall of 2015. As I'll explain further in Chapter 3, I feel like God helped prepare me to be a loving and accepting father for Wes when he came out to us. I was so proud of the courage he showed and felt honored that he trusted me with his feelings – because he knew my views have not always been gay-friendly. It was easy to feel nothing but intense love for Wes when he came out to us because, aside from loving him as my son, I appreciate what an amazing person he is. He is smarter than me and a deeper thinker than me (although maybe a bit more absent-minded too, at times ☺). At every age as he's grown, he has been more spiritually minded, mature, and kinder to others than I ever was at the same age. He is more talented in writing than I can ever hope to be (sorry, readers, I'm sure you'd find this book much more enjoyable to read if Wes were writing it). I am not only supportive of Wes, but I am in awe of him.

[Side note: While I am pleased to write about my love and admiration for Wes, I also want to recognize that the dignity of LGBTQ people does NOT depend on what anyone else thinks of them. Each person has dignity on their own terms. Obviously, families should be supportive, but in the end, outsourcing LGBTQ dignity and self-esteem to the approval of anyone else is not as healthy as encouraging such attributes to develop independently.]

Despite the pain Wes has felt from some religious teachings, he remains firmly rooted in his strong Christian faith. I would still love and support him even if he didn't have faith, but, because I believe in Christ, I am grateful for what I have learned about Christian discipleship in the face of hardship through Wes' example. I am truly, genuinely happy about the choices he has made. I am deeply grateful he is my son. I could say the same thing and describe many other wonderful attributes about each of my other kids as well, including how they each love God and others in their own unique and amazing ways. But because this book is about LGBTQ issues, I'll just stick to providing a picture of Wes.

In addition to all the other things I love about Wes, today I can honestly say I'm happy that he is gay. I know that may surprise some readers here. But I have to say, his being gay has helped open my heart to feel of Christ's love for him, me, everyone in our family, and everyone in the world in ways I never imagined before. And that feels so good. Amazing, even. I feel closer to God because Wes being gay has altered my perspective and has helped me understand better how all people are created in the image of God. I wouldn't change a thing about the journey we've been on together. We've learned to love and support each other as a family with truer charity than I ever knew before. I can't imagine a better way to have witnessed the principle of charity, which I have emphasized with my kids for so long, be put into practice in our family life. And I have learned to recognize similar positive effects of gay sexual orientation on society: gay individuals and couples engender feelings of tolerance, support, and acceptance, and add diversity in thought and opinion, in ways that bless all of us in society at large. I would have been much slower to wholeheartedly embrace that truth were it not for Wes being gay. So basically, I'm grateful his being gay has made me a kinder, more open-minded person – that's something I would never want to trade.

Here is the heartfelt Facebook post that Cheryl made on October 4, 2019:

> *"This is going to be long and I apologize in advance, but I feel like I have a lot I need to say. Thank you in advance to those who take the time to read this all and "listen." I am not an eloquent writer or a very smart person for that matter, but I hope I can adequately portray what I'm trying to.*

Our son, Weston, is gay. He came out to Evan & me when he was 16, after a year of serious depression & suicidal thoughts. He had even tried dating girls and had a girlfriend for a short amount of time. To be totally honest, I knew he was gay from the time he was 8 years old. Certain things he would do or say just made me, as his mom, know. I remember one time he came off the bus in elementary school, clearly upset. One of the boys had called him a faggot. I was so angry. I immediately started driving my kids to and from school. This was just a foreshadowing of the emotional turmoil Wes would have to endure.

I felt lucky that I had grown up with lots of exposure to wonderful LGBTQ people. I knew many were good, loving, kind people & I also knew that they were who they were. Born that way. It was not a choice or a "lifestyle."

Wes didn't want to be "out" in public at that point in life, so we respected his privacy, but assured him of our endless and unconditional love for him. I think it must have been so hard and lonely for him, knowing his sexuality but trying to hide it from his friends & family members. It was hard for Evan & me to keep it from our friends & families. Many would make comments that were hurtful, not realizing they were making comments to us about our own son. We would always try to correct viewpoints or comments that weren't kind in a loving way, but it was and is very hard.

This is when my struggle to balance the love of my child and the love of my church began. Those of you who know me, know I'm a devoted member of the Church of Jesus Christ of Latter-day Saints. Evan and I have sacrificed our time & talents in many ways over the years to serve in many different church positions on the local and for Evan, the regional level. We do our best to be good, kind, faithful people and have taught our children to do the same. The problem I had encountered is that our church teaches that "homosexuality" is a sin. Well, let me rephrase that, they say that ACTING on it is a sin. Now, even before Wes came out to us, this didn't sit well with me. I believe in a loving God. A God who will accept all His children & I just can't fathom that He would send some of us to earth saying we should actively avoid seeking lifelong companionship and that true love & passion that is felt in a committed and loving marriage. Despite my feelings about this doctrine the church teaches, I have remained active in our faith. I wanted to try to be the "voice" in the room when people would make comments that were judgmental or unkind. I would always preach love & acceptance, no matter who you are and how you have chosen to live your life. I wanted to be seen as a "safe" person for any youth or adults struggling with this issue. I was also able to try to focus more on other elements of our doctrine - the doctrine of love, acceptance, repentance & forgiveness.

Weston applied to our church college, BYU, and was accepted there. It was the only school he applied to and was his first choice. He then decided at age 18, just before high school graduation, that he wanted to defer his college acceptance & serve a mission for the church. I pleaded with him not to go. I knew it would be difficult for him to be submersed 24/7 in the church culture. I knew many would say hurtful things. I was worried about his mental health. I was worried about a lot of things. But to his credit, he loves Jesus Christ. He wanted to go to show his devotion. I prayed that people would be kind & that he would be okay. For those of you who are not members of our church, when young men and women serve missions, their families have limited contact with them. Once a week they are allowed to email their families (in February 2019 that policy changed to allow weekly phone/video calls). Before he left on his mission, he opened up to just a few people about his sexuality including our stake president (the man in the church assigned over our region), my sister Lisa & her husband Tagg, & our dear friends,

Gordon & Lauren Laws. I was relieved that we at least now had a few people we could talk to & that I knew he could talk to.

When he got his assignment to the Brazil Curitiba mission, we were so excited for him! He had really wanted to experience a different culture and learn a new language. He was only on his mission for 2 weeks when we got the first email that one of the other missionaries found out he was gay, and the name-calling and chastising began.

[*Side note:* Wes tried to keep his identity to himself, but certain circumstances in the missionary training center in Brazil made that impossible.]

Wes somehow handled it well, throwing himself deeper into learning the language and studying the scriptures. In fact, when he arrived to his mission in Curitiba, the mission president (the man in charge of all missionaries in that area) told my sister-in-law (a former neighbor of his in Utah) that they had never had an English speaking, American missionary arrive there speaking Portuguese so well. I will forever be grateful to that mission president. He is a kind, compassionate & loving man. He helped Wes with his struggles & tried to empathize as best he could.

For the first year of his mission, Wes was pretty happy. He loved the culture & people of Brazil. He was placed with some wonderful companions and when the mission president saw how gifted he was with organizational skills, computer skills & the language, he assigned him to work in the mission office as a liaison for the housing of all the missionaries in their mission. He spent his days finding suitable apartments for the missionaries & managing other housing problems, along with other things the president would assign him to do. He had started to open up to other missionaries about being gay. Some were loving & kind. Others were not. He didn't tell me all of the things said to him. He knew I would worry. He would send long emails to his dad, Lisa & Gordon. They were the ones who heard most of his thoughts & experiences in a non-filtered way. I think Wes knew that my Mom heart just couldn't handle hearing some of the things that he experienced.

Most missionaries serve for a 2-year period. After 18 months on his mission, Wes started struggling with whether he wanted to stay for that whole 2 years. I won't go into all the private details & I know Wes wouldn't want me to share some of the insensitive and totally ludicrous conversations of why he decided he just couldn't do it anymore and what tipped him to a breaking point, but he decided to pray to ask God what he should do. He got the answer to go home, be happy, find a husband & have a family. Now this is the opposite of what the church teaches. They teach to find happiness in a celibate lifestyle and that God will "work it out" in the afterlife. So people questioned whether this answer could really be from God because it would take Wes down a different path in life. Wes still firmly believes that the church is good. He told us he didn't want us to leave on his account. He loves many of its teachings, but just knows there is no place for him in it right now. He still believes in Jesus Christ.

He was finally ready to come home & be out to the world! I was so happy that he didn't have to hide who he really was anymore, but I also prepared myself for what people would do and say. Evan and I spent many sleepless nights worrying about how our church congregation & family members would react when they found out. I'm now ashamed that I even worried. We experienced an outpouring of love like I have never experienced in my whole life. I can't tell you how many texts I received from people that touched my heart. Friends from within the church and friends from our community. I have actually saved many of those texts so when I feel *discouraged, I can go back and read them. Our extended families were loving. Many of them wept when we told them.*

Many of them felt bad Wes had suffered in silence. Some made great effort to travel on short notice to be here for Weston's homecoming.

After Wes came home, he told us he didn't want to attend BYU anymore. This complicated things a bit because now we were past the deadline to apply to other schools he was interested in. He decided to apply to a private college he had never thought of before on a whim (at the suggestion of my brother & brother-in-law), since they had rolling admission. To our delight he received a full academic scholarship & has since been attending there. He has been having a great experience and is loving life as he makes new friends and figures out his path in life. He is finally happy! We have been and always will be 100% supportive of what our son chooses, and he will always be a part of our family. Wes has never asked any of us to leave the church on his behalf & encouraged us to keep going.

Evan, the other kids & myself have been content continuing to attend and serve in church. I was teaching a daily youth Bible study class (known as seminary) in our home every morning & had 12 high school teenagers in my class. Evan continued to serve in his regional calling which he thoroughly enjoyed because it took him to different congregations on a weekly basis & he got to work with many different people. Owen is attending BYU.

Last weekend our regional leadership had to have a change. The stake president (or leader of our region), whom Evan had been working with as a counselor, was moving. Normal protocol is that the church sends in some "higher ups" (an Area Authority and a General Authority of the church) to pick who the new president will be. Evan [and I met with those church Authorities in multiple interviews over the course of the weekend] ...

For personal reasons, and because I do believe everything happens for a reason, I will not go into details here as to what happened or what was said...

[*Side note:* In the church hierarchy, a General Authority is the equivalent of a Cardinal in the Catholic Church. An Area Authority is lower in the church hierarchy and works with assigned General Authorities to oversee a large area of multiple stakes or regions, each with typically 6-12 congregations. I relate the details of this experience with the General Authority and Area Authority in Chapter 9.]

I believe in kindness, empathy & forgiveness, but my soul has literally been crushed. I used to think I could happily attend church, serve & still be a safe place & a voice for the LGBTQ community within our church, but after this weekend I am no longer feeling that way. I have NEVER cried the way I cried last weekend. The pain was so intense I almost fell to the ground, but Evan was there to catch me.

I am beyond distraught, heartbroken and a little angry. For almost a week now I have barely slept or ate. We have sacrificed for years. I was alone many nights with young children while Evan was putting in more than 60 hours every week at work for years, trying to make partner, & still valiantly serving for up to 20 hours a week as the bishop of our local congregation. I could list off 10-20 other positions we have served in over the years. We have both sacrificed. Last weekend, it felt to me that my sacrifices weren't enough because I had a moment of reaction of love & protection for my son. To put it in "horse terms," I needed a gentle pat on the neck and encouragement to keep going & instead I felt like I got a heavy-handed slap from a whip. For the first time, I felt like I had to pick between my faith and my family. And I pick my family.

Evan, I, and each of our kids have had different reactions, responses, and decisions about how they are going to proceed from here. I have personally decided I need a "church break" to heal and process what has happened. I am giving myself until Christmas to regroup and figure out where I can best continue to be a voice and ally of my LGBTQ Latter-day Saint friends. And there are many. Even if they are not "out" yet, they are among us.

[*Side note:* Cheryl has since decided not to return to church at all, other than on special occasions, like to support friends and loved ones. I love and support her in her decision. And she supports me fully in my decision to still attend church. My feelings about attending church alone now are described in Chapter 10.]

I am not pushing for change. Change can only happen when people's hearts and minds are open & I believe that the general population of our church is not ready. I am warning the church though. I'm pretty sure none of the "higher ups" sit in a class with 12 teenagers 6 days a week and listen to what their concerns & thoughts are, whether those kids are gay or straight. This younger generation will be lost if we don't have a better message of love & acceptance for ALL people. They will not only lose younger millennials, but they will also lose long-time faithful members, like me.

Be kind. Be loving. Be a voice for the minority among us. Befriend those who are different than you. Jesus was the greatest example of teaching the undesired & outcasts of His time. I know that if we just follow His example of love we can get there."

Cheryl's post beautifully describes the same conflict that exists in my heart as I try to reconcile the teachings of my church with the love I have for Wes. I admittedly have the emotion of a Dragon Dad – a father who feels protective of his gay son. But, I have also tried to write from the perspective of a lifelong, faithful, and still-believing member of the church, so people reading this can understand better the sincerity behind my words when I say: *I don't intend to alienate any of my fellow Latter-day Saints from the church with what I have to say.* I hope they can draw on their own charitable hearts to feel behind my words my intent to just facilitate greater understanding.

I do not want to reinforce the idea that LGBTQ people are opposed by the church. Instead, I want to help people feel that the more we love the church, and seek to understand its scriptures and doctrines, the more we will be pro-LGBTQ and feel comfortable hoping for change in the church's positions. I don't want anyone reading this book to describe my approach as one that is asking people to "lessen" their devotion to the church in order to accept LGBTQ individuals more fully. Rather, I want church members to see how a greater devotion to Christ's teachings can lead the way to equality in the church for all marginalized groups.

As I share our family's story, I should also acknowledge that Wes does not need me to write any of this. Another complete book could be told from Wes' point of view. He is happy doing his own thing, living his life, and not rocking the boat for anyone else. Wes is a private person and, while he doesn't object to anything I'm saying here, he doesn't like being in the limelight on this issue. And Wes is happy that other people find joy in the church, even though he feels that such joy from the church is not equally available to him as a gay man at this time. Bottom line, he is supportive of me writing this book because he loves me, and he knows it is something I want to do to try to help others. He is supportive of my desire to create better understanding, which will hopefully prevent or minimize church-caused pain for other people – and I pray will also open all of our hearts and minds to the idea that change can still happen in the church. I'm glad Wes is willing to indirectly spend a bit of time in the limelight hoping that someone might be helped by hearing my story. Even if anything I have written in this book only helps one person, I'll be very grateful for that – and grateful for Wes and all other LGBTQ people for tolerating my inadequacy as I share my own story.

What is my despair? What is my hope?

The main ingredient of my present pain is hopelessness – or, better said, near-hopelessness – because I remain optimistic and believe that further change is inevitable. All of my personal story, explanation, doctrinal exposition, and any theological imagination that you'll read here are aimed at helping people understand why I hope that the church and its doctrine will be able to someday offer more joy to LGBTQ individuals and their families.

While I hope the church's position against marriage equality in our doctrine changes as soon as possible, I recognize I don't have the authority to speak for the church. I respect the proper channels of church leadership receiving new revelation for the church as a whole. But I do wonder if a concern about asking the church to "run faster than [it] has strength" (Mosiah 4:27) is impeding revelation. I wonder if the prophet doesn't think church members as a whole are "strong" enough in loving others yet. Maybe, even if just subconsciously, he believes we need to become stronger in loving LGBTQ people before we are trusted to fellowship increased numbers of them. More might start joining (or simply not leaving) the church, once marriage between same-gender spouses is no longer prohibited. Or perhaps the prophet is worried that if marriage equality were doctrinally accepted by the church now, too many homophobic church members would leave.

In any event, assuming God wants to reveal change now, I think it's likely the prophet might always have those kind of thoughts in the back of his mind, preventing him from praying with "real intent" (Moroni 10:4) to know God's will, until more church members' hearts are softened toward their LGBTQ siblings. I say I presume God wants change now because **I don't believe He views protecting the comfort of one group of His children** (cisgender, straight church members) as **being more important than relieving the suffering of another group** (LGBTQ church members). The scriptures teach us, including most powerfully through Christ's ministry, that God's greatest concern rests with helping the marginalized, not in protecting the comforts of the privileged. But, again, I acknowledge I am not authorized to dictate church policy. I am just a regular church member wondering about things and expressing my feelings.

Which is why, even with my hurt, all my prayers for change include the phrase "if it be Thy will." Even our Savior asked His Father in the Garden of Gethsemane if suffering could be avoided, if it was His Father's will. So, while the context is clearly different, I'm praying for God to reveal change if He can – so the suffering of our LGBTQ siblings and their families can end. I want to help more church members recognize that suffering, so that the prophet feels more open to any revelation that might help bring that suffering to an end.

That being said, I'm not trying to force the correctness of my hope on anyone. I respect others' right to disagree with me. But I believe the scriptures and modern-day revelation provide a basis to hope, because they call for love and equality for all people. Christ's core message is love and hope.

[Side note: As of this writing, there are between 154 million to 770 million LGBTQ people in this world (according to estimates that around 2-10% of all humans are LGBTQ: https://en.wikipedia.org/wiki/Demographics_of_sexual_orientation#Denmark). There are 16.5 million Latter-day Saints in total, including all genders and orientations (according to the church's latest statistical report: https://newsroom.churchofjesuschrist.org/article/2019-statistical-report). That means that LGBTQ people outnumber all Latter-day Saints by nearly 10 to 1 at the most conservative estimate, 47 to 1 at the highest estimate.]

I struggle to think that God created so many people as LGBTQ just to condemn them or make them suffer under the doctrine of His relatively tiny church – in other words, I struggle that our doctrine provides so little hope for SO many of God's children who are LGBTQ. It hurts to see how church teachings on LGBTQ issues engender feelings of low self-esteem (and often suicidal thoughts) in LGBTQ people here in this life and a vision of the afterlife that is discouraging, to say the least. I know I fall into a category of ultimate privilege in the church, namely, being a straight, cisgender, white male. So my struggle is not nearly as painful as that experienced by many other church members. However, my pain is still real: it hurts to know that the church I love condemns my son for choosing to try to find companionship that is consistent with the way God created him.

To help you understand my own pain, I'll share in Chapter 9 more details about the experience we had in September 2019 with one of the General Authorities, which Cheryl mentioned in her post. It hurt to have an experience with a respected church leader that resulted in me feeling like I had to choose between being a disingenuously supportive father or being a less-than-ideal church member in his eyes. I choose the latter because I know, no matter what any church leader may say, that God does not want me to feel guilty about the joy I have over my son's well-being. As his father, I know Wes was born gay and I trust his judgment that if he married a woman, that union would not likely be long-lasting. I have seen how negative and depressing it is for Wes to believe he has to pursue a life where he will always have to proactively <u>avoid</u> falling in love ("It is not good that the man should be alone" – Genesis 2:18). I rejoice that he has chosen the path that is best for his mental health and that is most likely to result in him building a long-term, stable family for his future kids. That is not a selfish desire for him to have. But the General Authority we met with basically said none of that justified Wes' decision and that I shouldn't be happy Wes is "sinning." I don't believe the General Authority intended to cause me pain. And he apologized. But, nevertheless, his words were reflective of newly emphasized teachings from our highest church leaders (see Chapter 4), which are the true source of my current sense of near- hopelessness.

I have found a way to stay active and participate fully in the church by privately hoping and praying (again, if it is God's will) that change in church doctrine will come someday. So I don't want pain to be the sole focus of what I'm writing here. Rather, I want hope to be the focus. I can see a path for change that is consistent with existing doctrinal frameworks. I want to show that while teachings from prophets and apostles can sometimes seem to extinguish hope for change in certain areas, that change does still occur – ironically, often shortly after the loudest messages against change are delivered.

Am I trying to attack the church or "steady the ark"?

Some of my fellow Latter-day Saints may think I am sharing the church's historical "dirty laundry" with the public or casting our church leaders in a bad light. But I have no intent to besmirch the church or its leaders. And even though certain teachings of church leaders have caused me heartache, I hold no animosity toward those leaders for such teachings. I know they are good men who are trying their best. I love them and many of the other teachings they have shared over their multiple decades of church service.

I can sustain our prophets and apostles by not expecting them to be perfect – and by explaining clearly exactly why what they say causes me pain. When I was bishop, I appreciated when members of my congregation would tell me when I had said or done something that caused them pain. I even asked regularly in interviews I had with people how I could improve. So I hope my words about the pain I feel from the teachings of our leaders are viewed similarly as productive attempts to improve understanding.

We are all products of our time and place. Many historical church leaders have said things about race or women, etc. that, with the benefit of hindsight, are appalling to our modern ears. But I know they were still good men who sincerely felt that God was in support of their teachings. I don't believe they had intentional malice; I think well-meaning prejudice is a better explanation. I believe the same of our leaders today. Heck, I have said things as a church leader, echoing the church's teachings about gay sexual orientation, that I regret now. While I am sorry I taught those things now, I didn't think I was causing any harm back when I said them. So I don't attribute malice to our current leaders now either (although I would like to see them apologize at some point too – I think that's important to help LGBTQ individuals and their loved ones to heal).

Because I am publicly acknowledging in this book that church teachings cause pain and am pointing out how it's possible for our doctrine to change, some church members who read this book might think I am trying to give instructions about how to improve the church. They may believe I am trying to "steady the ark," which is a phrase that comes from 2 Samuel, chapter 6. It refers to a time when the Ark of the Covenant was being moved over a rough spot and started to topple. A man named Uzzah reached out to try to steady the ark and was struck dead. In commenting on the use of that phrase in Doctrine & Covenants 85:8, a Church Educational System student manual stated: "However well-meaning his intentions, Uzzah approached casually what could only be approached under the strictest conditions. He had no faith in God's power. He assumed that the ark was in danger, forgetting that it was the symbol of the God who has all power. What man can presume to save God and His kingdom through his own efforts?" (https://www.thechurchnews.com/archives/1993-06-12/warning-against-steadying-ark-142325).

I am writing this book to try to help our LGBTQ siblings, not to try to save God or the institutional church. I am not casually trying to correct God or His kingdom, like Uzzah did. Rather than reaching out to steady or correct, I believe I am just crying out to facilitate awareness. I feel compelled to talk about the pain I see being caused by the words of those charged with carrying the ark. But I am not trying to steady it because I acknowledge that only the prophet and apostles are authorized to finally determine what is best for the institutional church. I am not forming protests to try to force them to change the church's doctrine. I am just asking questions and sharing my feelings, trying to help everyone understand better the pain that certain of their teachings cause. And I trust that God has everything under control, including for all LGBTQ people who leave the church and any back-up plans for healing. I am confident God will find ways for His work to be done, with or without me. So I am just focused on trying to keep the promise I made to God when I was baptized to "comfort those who stand in need of comfort" (Mosiah 18:8-9). I am not focused on giving orders to God or to church leaders.

For what it's worth, I think talking openly about the challenges that LGBTQ church members and their supporters are having is actually a positive thing for the church, missionary-wise. Several people reached out to us in response to Cheryl's post, saying they assumed we were anti- gay just because we are "Mormon." Someone else actually said they would have learned more about our church when they met with the missionaries if they had known it was possible to have pro-gay opinions and still be a member. I know people who have actually decided to join our faith after learning church members don't have to be anti-gay. Ultimately, I believe it's better for the growth of the church in the long run for us to confront our complicated issues than to conceal them. (I think it's better for "houseguests" who are exploring whether to join our church "family" to see that we are normal and have some doctrinal "messes" in our home, than it is for them to find out later that we've hid all our messes in proverbial "closets.")

> "If we have truth, [it] cannot be harmed by investigation. If we have not truth, it ought to be harmed." (J. Reuben Clark, Apostle, https://en.wikiquote.org/wiki/J._Reuben_Clark, from his personal journal, 1917)

Why can't I just put my concerns on a shelf and go on with my life?

Some people think I would be better off emotionally and spiritually if I just set my concerns on a proverbial shelf to deal with later. Many people talk about doing that – putting their doubts or concerns with the church or its teachings on a shelf and just moving on with their lives in faith. I don't usually like the idea of placing concerns aside, because I think we grow more personally by continuing to study through and struggle with our doubts ("wrestling with God" as in Genesis 32:24, Enos 1:2 and Alma 8:10). At the same time, I *do* acknowledge the wisdom in being patient while waiting for answers. And I would be patient just quietly waiting if it were solely *my* well-being that was involved. I've already received my answer from God about how to feel personally regarding my son leaving the church and about doctrinal marriage equality in general. If it were just me I was worried about, I would be fine continuing to attend church without ever speaking up about LGBTQ issues or writing this book.

But it's not just me I'm worried about. I feel an obligation – in fact, I made a covenant to God when I was baptized, renewing that covenant weekly at church ever since – to comfort those who stand in need of comfort. I think the parable of the Good Samaritan applies here (Luke 10:25- 37). I don't want to be like the priest or the Levite and simply look away and continue on my way when I see someone in pain. I want to be like the Samaritan and use whatever good fortune I may have to try to help relieve that suffering. If I just put my concerns on a shelf and kept going along quietly with my own worship, I fear I would be like the priest and the Levite.

[*Side note:* *By drawing this analogy to the Good Samaritan parable, I do not intend to make myself look better than fellow church members who are not engaged in LGBTQ allyship efforts. I understand that for most of them, they may not be sufficiently aware of the pain our LGBTQ siblings are feeling to properly see them as the injured traveler fallen on the roadside. I'm hoping this book helps create more awareness of that suffering.*

I also do not intend to compare the church to the robber in the parable. I recognize the robber intended to harm the traveler for selfish gain. But church leaders have acted without such deliberate malice when teaching doctrines that are harmful to LGBTQ church members. So an empathy-building question for all church leaders and members might be: "What would it mean to you to find out that you were unjustifiably hurting someone, robbing them of opportunities to maintain well-being and to experience healthy love and joy – and you didn't even know it?" I think in different contexts, we all have inadvertently been the robber in the parable at one time or another. Once we realize that, I feel that the real test of our discipleship becomes whether we respond by changing roles to act as good Samaritans – to try to fix the harm we have caused.]

One reader of an earlier draft of this book told me they couldn't keep reading all the way through because it was too sad. I acknowledge it's a tough topic, but I've tried to focus on hope as much as I can. And (spoiler alert) this book ends on a high note in the last chapter by talking about how I've learned to reconcile painful church teachings on LGBTQ issues with my love of God and my commitment to stay in the church. I personally feel ecstatic about how my journey has taught me to love better – more like how Christ wants me to love, I feel. I believe I've found a happy ending, due in part to doing the hard work to bring my doubts and concerns to the Lord.

But I don't want to condemn anyone who needs to simply place their concerns aside to maintain their faith. I understand that having a shelf available on which to store our concerns when we're too tired to productively wrestle with them can be important. That being said, for some of us, there simply is no shelf – there's only a bleeding LGBTQ loved one on the road to Jericho.

CHAPTER 2:
HOW CAN WE LISTEN?
WHAT WORDS HELP AND HURT?

Chapter synopsis: I cannot speak for LGBTQ church members. All I can do is share my voice to try to support theirs. Their voices need to be heard more than any others. The church could do better at listening to them and making changes to address their "wants" (Mosiah 4:26). Specific ways that the voices of church members and leaders can hurt or help LGBTQ people and their families are listed.

Am I a qualified voice for my son, other LGBTQ people, or other parents?

Before I go any further, I want to acknowledge that I am an inadequate voice for LGBTQ people, primarily because I am not LGBTQ. Because of my gay son, I may be more familiar than the average church member with the challenges that LGBTQ individuals face in the church – but that does not qualify me to speak on behalf of LGBTQ people in general. Without question, the best voices to listen to on these matters are those expressed by LGBTQ individuals themselves. I hope to simply be an ally to them – someone who uses privilege to help create more awareness. I do not want to supplant their voices. I also acknowledge that, even among the voices of fellow LGBTQ advocates in the Latter-day Saint community, there are many people who are smarter, more eloquent, and more experienced in these matters than I am (several of whom I cite in this book). I encourage readers to check out the LGBTQ voices and ally resources I have listed at the end of this book.

[Side note: My inadequacy as a voice is especially true for our transgender siblings and their families in the church. I am not as familiar with the challenges they face given Wes does not experience gender dysphoria. So I will only touch briefly on a few transgender-related points in this book. I acknowledge the crucial need for more attention to be paid to the pain they feel from church teachings.]

I also know I'm not an authorized voice for all parents of LGBTQ children in the church. I know there are other parents in similar situations who feel differently than I do. That being said, I do know my feelings are shared by many people in the church. Cheryl and I had dozens of church members, from both nearby and far away, privately contact us after her Facebook post saying they were grateful to her for sharing feelings that they felt too. Many (more than we ever would have thought) were closeted gay church members or parents of closeted gay kids in the church. Others were LGBTQ allies who had gay friends or family members, etc. So I feel compelled to at least try to share a bit more about our family's story and my thoughts in case they similarly resonate with them or anyone else.

Shouldn't LGBTQ voices dictate what is best for their own well-being in the church?

When it comes to what's best for LGBTQ well-being, we need to do a better job in the church of listening to the opinions of LGBTQ people themselves. The scriptures teach that we should minister to people "according to their wants" (Mosiah 4:26), not church leader's assessment of their wants or needs. Straight church leaders declare what is best for all church members universally, even though what they decree causes direct psychological trauma for the vast majority of LGBTQ church members. That is the opposite of ministering to LGBTQ church members "according to their wants." I often wonder why I have never heard of a broadcast meeting between leading LGBTQ church members and our prophets and apostles, where the questions, desires, emotions, beliefs, and responses of both sides are aired publicly. We have similar face-to-face meetings with youth, young adults, and with the women's organizational leaders in the church, where questions are invited ahead of time for church leaders' responses. Why not have such meetings with LGBTQ church members too?

My favorite way to hear others' voices is in person. I have greatly enjoyed meeting LGBTQ church members at support group meetings (like those put on by Affirmation.org). I also enjoy hearing their voices on a daily basis through podcasts and in Facebook groups. Some favorite publicly accessible podcasts and groups where LGBTQ Latter-day Saint voices can be heard directly are:

- https://affirmation.org/

- https://beyondtheblockpodcast.com/

- https://lattergaystories.org/

- https://www.listenlearnandlove.org/

- http://mormonsbuildingbridges.org/

- https://www.thepeculiar.org/

- https://podcasts.apple.com/us/podcast/human-stories-with-jill-hazard-rowe/id1468623842

- https://podcasts.apple.com/us/podcast/love-is-spoken-queer/id1491809605

From a doctrinal perspective, the Beyond the Block podcast (linked above) has taught me the most about how a proper interpretation of scripture calls for full LGBTQ equality, and how church culture, policies, and dogma can deviate from what God teaches in the scriptures about loving and caring for the marginalized people in our communities. I recently had the following conversation with James Jones and Derek Knox, co-hosts of Beyond the Block podcast, in an "ask-me-anything" live session on Facebook. (See the Preface for a little more about Derek and James.)

Evan: "How do you respond to people who say the "needs" of the marginalized in the church (LGBTQ people) are best defined by the Brethren because they speak for the Lord (and the Lord knows what we *all* truly need best)?

James: I would start with the fact that that's not what King Benjamin taught. In Mosiah 4:26 he explicitly counsels us to administer to people's relief both spiritually and temporally, according to *their* wants. You also gotta ask them whose needs were being filled when we spiritually dispossessed Black folks for 126 years. That answer will let you know if you should even continue the conversation.

Derek: (1) First, it's not true that they "speak for the Lord" in any simplistic or robotic sense. On the contrary, the Lord can speak THROUGH them, but not everything they do or say is from the Lord. There are plenty of examples among prophets both ancient and modern. And usually in the Bible, when prophets make mistakes, OTHER people die. We should always have a mature perspective on prophets, knowing that they have biases, limitations, weaknesses, etc. We should hold them accountable and insist on transparency in their method. Part of that involves seeing the Church as one body with many members, and we ALL have a role to play to ensure that the body continues to live and grow. The Brethren are our servants, not our masters.

(2) Even taking a simplistic view of prophetic authority, it's quite obvious that they don't know anything (and don't even CLAIM to know anything) about LGBTQ needs. Beyond two claims, which are (a) no gay marriage, and (2) no gay sex, they don't currently claim to have any solid foundational knowledge about LGBTQs. They never claim to know anything about what we SHOULD do, only what we SHOULDN'T do. So, even on their own terms, it is obvious that they don't have ANY comprehensive knowledge or insight from the Lord. They are completely at a loss and admit

they have no idea what to do with LGBTQs. This doesn't sound at all like a connection with the Lord. They have no answers. There is no way anyone can honestly claim that they "know best." They hardly claim to know anything, and what they HAVE claimed about LGBTQs has changed dramatically over the last 40 years. LGBTQs have every right to point that out and supply the answers. And I think the most important tactic in responding to the idea that the Brethren know better than LGBTQs is to have ALLIES speak up often and everywhere. If we LGBTQs are the only ones saying what needs to be said, then some could say that we are biased and trying to justify the "sin" that we have a desire to commit. But when allies take on that burden, it changes the landscape.

(3) I would probably also point out, as in the Second Passover video I did, the numerous times in the scriptures where God's people have pushed back and achieved change. In every case, it was because someone CLOSER to the problem decided to speak up.

[*Side note:* You can see the Second Passover video Derek mentions here: https://www.facebook.com/derek.knox/videos/10107223950567218. It is a great discussion of many scriptural examples where people on the margins in the church were suffering and, after expressing their woes to the prophet/apostles, God revealed a modification to accommodate their concerns EVERY time. It offers sound scriptural support for the role of bottom-up change in the church.]

(4) There's also the Cornelius narrative, where Cornelius the Gentile outsider received a vision that he was included and accepted BEFORE Peter did. And when Peter did, he had to hear the message three times before he got it, because he, even though he was the senior priesthood authority, was so stubbornly clinging to what was comfortable to him and so limited by his biases and prejudices that he didn't believe that kind of change was even POSSIBLE. I'm sure

I could multiply examples like this as well. We've covered things like this in nearly every one of our 50 podcast episodes.

(5) There is also this text, which serves as a great slogan: "For what man knoweth the things of a man, save the spirit of man which is in him?" (1 Corinthians 2:11).

Above all, the most important thing is NOT to be afraid of the Brethren.

(6) One important analytical tool is to ask the question "who bears the cost of getting this wrong?" or "do the Brethren face any personal consequences if they get this wrong?" Those who bear the cost or risk of the decision should ultimately be the ones to make that decision. To put it plainly, if THEY get it wrong, LGBTQs bear all the cost. Alternatively, if WE LGBTQs get it wrong, WE still bear all the cost. It's completely rigged and completely unfair, but that's the way it is right now.

So, because WE shoulder the consequences, WE should be the ones making the decision and taking responsibility for it. I know nothing about the business world, but I DO know that one of the WORST ways of making a decision is to outsource it to decision-makers who have no stake in whether they get it right or wrong.

For example, in the evangelical world, if I marry a dude, and that was wrong and I go to hell — well, the evangelical pastors were right, but I am the one that goes to hell! The pastors don't go to hell if I get it wrong. I do. (In the LDS world, it will be a lower kingdom or something of the sort.)

However, if the Brethren get this wrong, they can still live their life the same way. They can still get married, find love, have sex, enjoy companionship, etc. Their life doesn't change either way, whether they get the LGBTQ question right or wrong. That is not on the line for them as it is for us, so it is so easy for them to get it wrong. Because I bear all the cost, I should be the one to make these decisions about my life.

To use this analytical tool on the dispossession of Black folks until 1978 that James mentioned above — well, the white church leaders bore no personal cost to getting it wrong. THEY could exercise the priesthood, they still had everything. It was Black folks who bore the cost of that decision, so they should have been FIRST at the table making that decision.

(7) Also, one of the most important persuasive tools we have is the narrative of LGBTQs themselves. We have the voices to speak to our own needs and circumstances, and once people get to know us and our stories, they find it hard to believe all those awful things they have been told about us. That's one of the best ways to counter the idea that the Brethren know us better than we know ourselves. Just listen to us speak! People will be blown away by the truth that they recognize in what we are saying.

(8) Another thing, like the experiment of Alma 32, is to look at the fruits of affirming theology vs. the fruits of non-affirming theology. Affirming theology leads to life, to flourishing, to functioning, to righteousness, etc. Non-affirming theology leads to despair, sinfulness, hiding things, hate, contention, etc. The difference is clear. LGBTQ needs are not being met by non-affirming theology."

I love the voice that Derek provides in the church as an astute theologian and a gay man. He is a faithful church member who loves our prophets and apostles and sustains them, even though he recognizes (and publicly discusses) the crucial need for change in the church on LGBTQ matters.

A possible factor in explaining why our church leaders are failing to adequately minister to LGBTQ people according to their wants is because of a phenomenon called "survivorship bias." That bias is aptly described as "the logical error of concentrating on the people or things that made it past some selection process and overlooking those that did not, typically because of their lack of visibility" (https://en.wikipedia.org/wiki/Survivorship_bias). An example of successfully avoiding survivorship bias happened in World War II, when statistician Abraham Wald recommended that planes be fortified against gunfire in the places where returning planes were unscathed, NOT in places where returning planes had bullet holes. His rationale was that the planes that were shot down must have been shot in the spots where surviving planes had no damage. In the church context, survivorship bias might be General Authorities most frequently preaching doctrines and establishing policies based on what has worked in their own lives, as people who have thrived in the church, rather than exploring with sincere and real intent whether the aspects of the church that have worked for them could be the very things that might unintentionally end up "shooting down" the faith of most of our LGBTQ siblings. Without LGBTQ individuals being heard in the highest levels of church leadership, any revelations the Lord may give to the church are likely to reflect elements of survivorship bias to one degree or another.

Elder Bruce R. McConkie echoed the sentiment that decisions by General Authorities, even by prophets on doctrinal matters, may not be consistent with God's will:

> **"Prophets are men and they make mistakes. Sometimes they err in doctrine**. This is one of the reasons the Lord has given us the Standard Works. They become the standards and rules that govern where doctrine and philosophy are concerned. If this were not so, we would believe one thing when one man was president of the Church and another thing in the days of his successors. Truth is eternal and does not vary. Sometimes even wise and good men fall short in the accurate presentation of what is truth. **Sometimes a prophet gives personal views which are not endorsed and approved by the Lord**. (Personal letter to Eugene England, http://www.eugeneengland.org/wp-content/uploads/2012/07/BRM-to-EE-Feb-80-Combined.pdf, 1981)

"Though **General Authorities** are authorities in the sense of having power to administer church affairs, they may or **may not be authorities in the sense of doctrinal knowledge, the intricacies of church procedures or the receipt of the promptings of the Spirit.** A call to an administrative position of itself adds little knowledge or power of discernment to an individual, although every person called to a position in the Church does grow in grace, knowledge, and power by magnifying the calling given him." (*Mormon Doctrine*, p. 284, https://archive.org/stream/MormonDoctrine1966/MormonDoctrine1966 _djvu.txt, 1966)

Derek offers a helpful analogy that might aid more church members in feeling comfortable about recognizing bias and imperfection in the revelations pronounced by our church leaders. (This is a summarized version Derek sent me of a concept he explored more fully on a podcast episode released on February 22, 2020 titled "And He Inviteth Them ALL" at beyondtheblockpodcast.com.)

> *"Our insight into the mind and will of God can be characterized as one of three windows: fundamentalism, skepticism, and critical realism.*
>
> *Imagine three windows.*
>
> *The first is like a pane of perfectly clear glass: we can see into God's mind without any distortion. As long as it's sunny, we have a perfect view of what's outside, and our perspective is exactly the same as reality. That's fundamentalism.*
>
> *The second window is like a mirror. There is no revelation of the outside, only our own reflections. Everything is a subconscious projection of ourselves. This is skepticism.*
>
> *The third window, critical realism, is like a pane of glass that can be a little warped, and a little dirty, and we do see some of our own reflection in it.*

However, we do see some of the reality beyond it as well, and we do have access to some objective truth beyond the window, unlike in the skeptics' window. I think this third window provides the BEST model of prophetic authority, because it explains how ALL of us receive revelation and insight for our own lives or for others. We are all staring at the middle window where we can see some of our own biases and prejudices reflected back, but we can also see the reality that is beyond those. Of the three windows, this is the only realistic approach to revelation.

This very much coheres with what Paul teaches in 1 Corinthians 13 about knowing and prophesying in part, and seeing through a glass darkly. It coheres with what most members experience in their own reception of personal revelation. It coheres with the record of prophets/apostles in the scriptures and in modern times. Basically, it provides MORE faith, durability, and explanatory power than the naive approach to prophetic authority [that our prophets are perfect and they never make mistakes]."

I hope our prophets and apostles sit down at some point <u>publicly</u> with people like Derek: faithful LGBTQ church members who can explain, and back up with scriptures, the need for change in the church. Meetings with leading LGBTQ church members need to happen beyond the local church leadership level – because bishops and stake presidents often do not relay the messages of LGBTQ church members up the chain of command. To help facilitate that sort of public meeting with the Brethren that could benefit all of us, I encourage everyone to listen to, and amplify as allies, the voices of any LGBTQ people we know in the church.

What words are hurtful vs. helpful to LGBTQ people and their families?

As Cheryl and I have tried to become better LGBTQ allies by being more vocal about our desire for change in the church, a lot of people have interacted with us about our situation. Most of those interactions have been wonderful, while others have come from a well-intentioned but still insensitive place (which I understand – I was in that same place for many years).

So in an attempt to create more awareness and sensitivity, I would like to describe some hurtful and helpful things Cheryl and I have heard from fellow church members we know from all over the various places we've lived. I share the hurtful messages here with no sense of anger. But they did cause my heart to ache because I knew people just didn't understand.

[Side note: For a more complete set of ideas about what is harmful vs. helpful to say to LGBTQ church members and their loved ones, please see this amazing list compiled by Emily Nelson: https://www.facebook.com/emily.e.nelson.92/ posts/10219726331658849. Emily is the mother of a gay son and a moderator of the Facebook group called "I'll Walk With You (Supporting Latter-day Saint Parents with LGBTQ+ Children)."]

Based on personal and observed experience, here are some suggestions of things people might want to avoid:

1. *Don't send "scientific" articles about how people "choose" to have gay sexual desires.* As I'll discuss further in Chapter 3 : (i) the current scientific consensus is that having a gay sexual orientation is not a choice; and (ii) the church no longer teaches that having such attractions has to be a choice, or that it comes about because of the acts or omissions of anyone else. Please assume that folks have done a lot of research on the "causes" of sexual orientation. If you still decide to share something, please fact-check and bias- check your source before sending it. There is a bunch of pseudo-science being published by outlets with anti-LGBTQ agendas.

2. *Don't send resources that paint mixed-orientation marriages (i.e., marriages where a gay person marries a straight person) as a solution.* Those might work for some bisexuals or for a tiny percentage of gay people, but, as I will discuss further in Chapter 3, the church no longer recommends that gay people marry straight people. Please assume that

folks have done the necessary research to discover that mixed-orien-tation marriages are 2 to 3 times more likely to end in divorce than uniform-orientation marriages (https://www.huffpost.com/entry/gay-mormon-men-marriage_n_6464848). This may be due to a cor-relation with higher rates of depression and a lower quality of life in mixed- orientation marriages (https://www.tandfonline.com/doi/abs/10.1080/19359705.2014.912970).

3. *Don't compare sexual orientation to anything else.* As I'll describe further in Chapter 7, comparisons to addictions, disabilities, or even language acquisition are harmful and inaccurate. As I'll mention in Chapter 3, sexual orientation develops in a similar way to handedness (i.e., being right or left-handed). That may be an appropriate analogy but only for purposes of discussing similarities in developmental processes of different physical characteristics. Beyond that, it too is an inappropriate analogy because handedness is not as central to human intimacy, life purpose, companionship, mating, belonging, and identity as sexuality is. Being straight is the only appropriate analogy for being gay.

4. *Don't compare the church's expectation that gay people be lifelong celibates to straight singles remaining chaste.* The causes, effects and resolution for straight celibacy and gay celibacy are completely different. Straight singles always have hope, whether in this life or the next, of a loving and attraction-filled marriage. But gay singles in the church are expected to actively avoid marriage in this life. All they have to look forward to in the next life is marriage to someone to whom they are not attracted. If you're straight, put yourself in their shoes: would you look forward to marrying someone of the same sex in the next life or would that cause you dread? Think about that hopelessness for both mortality and eternity. While I recognize that straight singles do have a tough road to walk, their road is not church-prescribed despair that almost always results in poor mental health, which is the road gay people in the church are expected to walk (see Preface).

5. *Don't belittle the psychological harm that gay people in the church feel by comparing their suffering to other marginalized groups in the church.* I'll discuss this at length in Chapter 5. Various people have told me they expect LGBTQ people to stay in the church like some Black people did before they were formally granted full church privileges in 1978. Black people have indeed suffered (and continue to suffer) much from the church and society. But just because one marginalized group has suffered greatly doesn't mean that another marginalized group should also suffer greatly. Nor does the suffering of one marginalized group benefit the other.

While no one can rank suffering except God himself (Doctrine & Covenants 121:10), here are some interesting similarities and differences between gay and Black suffering in the church.

- In both cases, scriptural passages have been interpreted in discriminatory and harmful ways.

- Both gay sexual attraction and skin color are unchosen biological traits, whereas gay and lesbian people are discriminated against based on that plus a *choice* to engage in gay sexual behavior.

- Gay people can choose to stay celibate or marry an opposite sex person and thereby remain in the church with full privileges, which is something Black people never had the option of doing before 1978 – i.e., they could not ignore their skin color to receive the priesthood (for men) or temple blessings (for men and women). In other words, many gay people have been able to "hide" being queer, yet no Black person can "hide" being Black.

- Black church members could get married, have families and still be in the church before 1978. Gay church members cannot without denying their innate, God- created sexuality.

- Black people were told the priesthood/temple ban here on earth would not affect their ultimate status in heaven. So they could look forward to their mortal families being together forever. However, gays and lesbians can't enjoy uniform- orientation marriage and still be in the church, or hope for their mortal families to be together forever.

- Even before 1978, church doctrine gave Black church members hope for equality with non-Black people after this life. Some quotes can be found where church leaders taught that such equality would only come through a mandatory post- mortal change to their race, but it was not settled doctrine that Black people would have to *become* white to be *equal to* whites after this life. However, it *is* current, settled doctrine (for now anyway) that for LGBTQ church members to experience the same joy as cisgender straight people in heaven, they will need to be in a heterosexual marriage after this life (i.e., they will need to repress or have altered for eternity the way they were born to love).

- Black people throughout history have been more widely subject to violence, murder and enslavement. While violence and murder are also risks for LGBTQ people (think about Harvey Milk [1978], Matthew Shepard [1998], Nazis killing gays along with Jews in the Holocaust [1941-45], and many other atrocities against LGBTQ people in the past or even committed today, including in many foreign countries that have anti-LGBTQ laws), suicide appears to be a greater mortal risk than murder presently for LGBTQ church members in the U.S. Statistics show LGBTQ people are more likely to die by suicide than people in other demographic groups in the U.S. In fact, as to LGBTQ church members specifically, studies have shown that church teachings on gender, marriage, sexuality, and family cause suicidal ideation or at least one PTSD symptom in nearly 90% of

LGBTQ church members (http://mormonsbuildingbridges.org/ wp- content/uploads/2019/10/20190928-U-of-U-MBB-Presentation-SIMMONS- FINAL.pptx; https://getd.libs.uga.edu/pdfs/ simmons_brian_w_201712_phd.pdf; https://en.m.wikipedia.org/ wiki/LGBT_Mormon_suicides; https://www.tandfonline.com/ doi/full/10.1080/13811118.2020.1806159; https://drive.google. com/file/d/1zNs8K5nNPw4SQxPch0uc_PFH0f0Q3kIq/view? usp=drivesdk). This is often because of lack of hope (it has been clinically proven that a simple lack of hope can cause depression: https://www.ncbi.nlm.nih.gov/pmc/articles/PMC3721024/).

- More gay people are born into the church than Black people were born into the church before 1978. That is, more gay people are born into a traumatic situation in the church.

- Black children are usually born to at least one Black parent, who can help them learn to navigate Black culture and being Black in the world. Gay people are born into all kinds of families, often to straight parents. That means that many gay people are born to parents that are not like them and may struggle to accept them, or not know how to support their gay children to navigate their lives.

- The racial priesthood/temple ban did not normally create tension within Black families, whereas families with LGBTQ individuals are often torn apart as family members choose different ways to try to reconcile LGBTQ realities with church teachings.

By making the above comparisons, I do not intend to comment on the degree of suffering that different marginalized groups have experienced at large. I just find the differences potentially instructive and empathy-building. I try to remember that if not done with a focus on empathy, comparison can be the thief of compassion.

6. *Don't compare a straight person who decides to leave the church to a gay person who chooses to leave.* The straight person might be choosing to leave the church for reasons they can revisit or repent of later. But a gay person leaving the church often does so as a desperate and difficult way to maintain their mental health. And their sexual orientation will not change, so that conflict (church vs. mental health) will always exist for them. They often do not desire to sin when they leave – rather they just want to avoid trauma from constant exposure to church teachings that the way they were born is inconsistent with the plan of salvation and will need to be fixed in the next life.

   *[Side note: In trying to explain this point to a friend, I once asked them to consider how they would feel if the church said receiving mental health treatment was a sin. This friend has a straight child who struggles with severe depression, so I knew that hypothetical scenario would be meaningful for them. But in drawing that analogy, I also made clear that I was **not** suggesting that gay sexual orientation is a mental illness (I debunk that myth in Chapter 7). Rather, I said I was just trying to help my friend understand better why the church's position against marriage equality in our doctrine causes a dilemma for me as the father of a gay son – because in both the hypothetical situation I drew for them and in my real-life situation, we, as parents, must come to realize that the only way for our children to be mentally healthy is for them to disobey church teachings of today.]*

7. *Don't suggest that a hope for change in church doctrine is a bad thing.* Few church messages have been more consistent than that "the Restoration of the Lord's gospel [is] an unfolding Restoration that continues today." (Russell M. Nelson, Prophet, https://newsroom.churchofjesuschrist. org/article/president-nelson-invites-sharing-gospel- restoration, 2020). Never try to take away the hope for change in the church, because that hope is what allows them to both truly love themselves or their LGBTQ loved one and still believe in the church. As the parent of an LGBTQ child, as I'll describe further in Chapter 5, I think it is

impossible for me to be both a loving parent and a believer in the church without hoping for change.

[Side note: For people who are tempted to condemn the prayers and personal revelations of fellow church members that conflict with current church practices, remember that in Acts chapter 10, the Gentile Cornelius received revelation related to the gospel being preached to the Gentiles before the lead apostle Peter did.

And remember that Peter had to be told three times by the Lord before believing that the change should happen. For a clever enactment of this concept, see James C. Jones' 1-minute video, "Acts 10:10-15 - Jesus Checks Peter's Bigotry" at: https://www.facebook. com/beyondtheblockpodcast/videos/758569211567124]

8. *Don't suggest that a parent of a gay child should always wish their child was still in the church.* Parents of a gay kid need to be allowed to be happy that their child isn't in the church while still being seen as "righteous" church members. That's because if parents are expected to remain sad about their kid leaving the church (again, leaving is often necessary for their kid's mental health), then they end up loving their gay kid in a discriminatory way as compared to how they love their straight kids. All of my children desire to have stable, fulfilling family lives. But one was born with a biological trait that makes it impossible to do so without violating church rules. Parents in the church need to be allowed to publicly say they're proud of their gay children who are pursuing or are in healthy marriages with same-gender partners without being judged. They shouldn't be made to feel bad just for unconditionally loving their child. They shouldn't be made to feel like they need to communicate to church members that they love their LGBTQ child "even though" they are no longer in the church.

[Side note: Consider how silly it would be for a parent to tell their left-handed child that they love them "even though" they write with their left hand, not their right hand. That's how I feel about being asked to consider Wes' potential future gay marriage

any differently than how I consider my other kids' potential future straight marriages.]

9. *Don't say that they should just trust in God to work everything out after this life.* That line of thought has been shown to contribute greatly to suicidal ideation among LGBTQ church members (see Chapter 8). And, as I describe in Chapter 4, a trust-in-the-Lord approach doesn't work for gay church members under current doctrinal constructs anyway. There is no room in our present doctrine for the Lord to work things out for gay church members without heaven seeming like a special kind of hell to most of them.

10. *Don't judge someone just because they publicly disagree with the church's political positions on LGBTQ issues such as conversion therapy and religious liberty.* I'll discuss my views on those matters in Chapter 8. Please remember that the church allows us all to disagree when it comes to politics without losing any church privileges. And many folks view outside pressures as the only thing that might make most church members ready (or make church leaders pray as sincerely as is needed) for change in the church to come about. When you get upset over others' political support for full LGBTQ rights and protections, they may feel that you are indirectly criticizing them or their love for their child.

Here are some positive suggestions that, based on our experience, might be helpful:

1. *Acknowledge that the relevant doctrine causes harm.* You don't have to start disbelieving in the church to simply acknowledge and openly state a proven fact: that core church teachings on gender, marriage, sexuality, and family cause psychological damage to the vast majority of LGBTQ church members. (See the links to studies about PTSD, suicide and depression in point #5 of the above list of things to avoid.)

2. *Tell the families of gay kids in the church that you admire their unconditional love.* Tell them you are happy to see how they are keeping their family circle intact.

3. *Say you wish things were different in the church for LGBTQ people.* Again, you don't have to start disbelieving in the church to make such a statement. The Savior asked if the cup could pass from Him when he was praying in the Garden of Gethsemane (Matthew 26:39), so suffering could be avoided – if it was His Father's will. So I think it's okay for us to similarly ask God if a change in the church can happen, so suffering can be avoided if possible.

4. *Support others' choices, even if they involve leaving (or supporting someone else in leaving) the church.* You are not best suited to know what is best for another's mental health and well-being. Please be supportive of their choices and of the decisions of their loved ones to support those choices. Failing to be supportive of others' choices is especially damaging when you try to counteract parents of gay children when the parents are not around and you have time with the child. Doing that will only cause friction between you and the child's parents and confusion for the child. So just support them in what they say is the best way for them to parent. And for anyone who has the sacred honor of being a person to whom an LGBTQ individual comes out, remember this counsel:

"When a person comes out as LGBTQ, especially a young person to a parent, **they are not looking for you to agree. They are asking if they are still loved.** Assure them that they are." (Debra Oaks Coe, member of the executive committee of the Utah Commission for LGBT Suicide Awareness and Prevention, https://archive.sltrib.com/article.php?id=5117754&itype=CM-SID, 2017)

5. *Acknowledge that someone's choice to leave the church could be one that God actually wants for them.* There are many examples in the scriptures of God making exceptions to commandments given the uniqueness of certain circumstances. None of us, not even our highest church leaders, can know for sure that someone's personal revelation is false. It doesn't hurt church members to acknowledge that an LGBTQ person walking "alongside" the church's prescribed covenant path (as opposed to walking on top of that path, if doing so is hurtful for them) might be what God actually wants for that person. It also doesn't hurt to acknowledge that an LGBTQ person might be walking on their *own* covenant path. Actually, we all are, given the personal nature of our covenants with God. Remember, God doesn't require anyone to run faster than they have strength (Mosiah 4:27).

6. *Say you'll be there as a friend no matter what — even if they leave the church and get angry at it.* Tell LGBTQ people and their loved ones that there is nothing they could do to make you not be their friend. They need that kind of unconditional love to be expressed. Some people they love in the church might feel like they need to distance themselves from them, out of a misplaced sense of needing to avoid condoning sinful behavior. You can be an unconditional friend.

7. *Put that expression of friendship into action by continuing to socialize with them as normal.* LGBTQ people and their families can feel isolated because of their choices. Don't make that worse by not socializing with them anymore.

8. *Let them vent to you about their frustrations with church doctrine and the harshness in attitude of many church members.* You don't need to agree with everything they say, but it will help them feel less alone if you are committed to listening and truly trying to understand how they feel.

9. *Call people out in church meetings when they make any statements that are hurtful to LGBTQ people or their families.* I know that finding

productive ways to help people understand how their statements cause harm can be tricky. And I know from personal experience that doing so is especially difficult while serving in a leadership position in the church, because there's a desire to avoid looking like you endorse something that is not authorized by the church. But finding ways to publicly honor the pain that LGBTQ church members and their families are feeling – and asking people to accordingly be more loving – is extremely comforting. That is a crucial way that you can "comfort those who stand in need of comfort" (Mosiah 18:8-9). And don't wait for parents or outspoken allies of LGBTQ people to speak up first. They can sometimes feel tired or fragile from their efforts and might need the added boost of seeing someone unexpected step in to defend their loved ones with them. If you're not sure of what to say, here are some statements you might store in your memory that could work in almost any situation:

- "Let's try to remember that Jesus spent most of His time ministering to and loving the marginalized and outcast in His society. We should follow His example."

- "Our LGBTQ sisters and brothers in the church walk a road more difficult than most of us can comprehend. Let's keep our comments about them and their lives loving and respectful."

- "There are people in this room who are LGBTQ or have LGBTQ family members. Let's not speak as though they aren't among us."

- "Let's remember the warning in Alma 5:30-31 that says repentance is necessary for anyone who makes 'a mock of his brother, or that heapeth upon him persecutions'."

- "Let's try to be the Good Samaritan when we see people who are beaten down by others, not a robber that helped do the damage."

10. *Become an LGBTQ advocate.* Nothing will help an LGBTQ person or their loved ones feel more loved and supported than if you commit to being an LGBTQ advocate and speak with LGBTQ people about how you can be an ally for them. That means being willing to use whatever privilege you have in your life to further the betterment of LGBTQ lives and well-being. It means you are willing to stick your neck out to help LGBTQ people have full equality in all areas of their lives (including at church). Being willing to act as an ally will allow Christ's love to flow through you to LGBTQ people and their families in the most powerful way possible.

If more church members avoid insensitive comments and proactively say positive things as well, then the pain that LGBTQ church members and their families feel from the doctrine of the church can be softened – and all of that can be done without contradicting the doctrine of the church at all. In fact, I think the most core doctrines of the church relating to true Christ-like discipleship require that we try to soften pain whenever we can and show unconditional love to all.

CHAPTER 3

CAN A CHANGING CHURCH
PROVIDE HOPE?

Chapter synopsis: Positive changes in the church's teachings on gay sexual orientation correspond with greater modern scientific understanding. Both unknowingly helped prepare me for Wes coming out as gay. But painful confusion still exists in the church about how exactly to go about loving and accepting gay people, and gay people still cannot marry (consistent with their sexual orientation anyway) and stay in the church.

How do historical church teachings influence my views?

In order to fully explain my current near-despair about church teachings relating to gay sexual orientation, I need to describe the evolution of my beliefs on the topic. I grew up in Murray, Utah, a wonderful but relatively conservative place. And I grew up in a relatively conservative era as well (the 1980s and 1990s). I remember using gay slurs regularly as a kid (and even in adulthood) in ways to derogatorily tease my friends. I remember playing a made-up game during recess in elementary school that someone started calling "smear the queer," where the guy with the football was the "queer" and the rest of us would just try to chase him down to tackle and pummel him until he gave up the ball. There was no scoring – the whole aim of the game was to tackle the person whose turn it was to be the "queer" and see how much pain he could take before relenting. Now, I should clarify that, despite that horrific game, I wasn't raised to hate.

I'm not even sure I knew what "queer" really meant at the time. I had an amazing upbringing in a loving home - my parents raised me to love and be kind to others. I never thought about actually hurting anyone just because they were gay. No one in my home or in the church ever even suggested that would be okay to do. So I wasn't hateful or violent toward LGBTQ people, but I would definitely say I was ignorant. In hindsight I can say I was intolerant – unintentionally homophobic is probably a good way to describe how I was until my mid-30s.

I think that was in part due to the fact that I have believed in the church's teachings all my life. I haven't been perfect in following all of them all the time (I don't think anyone can be - although I have always had a temple recommend ever since I was old enough to get one). I always tried to be good, and repent to become better at following church teachings. So I accepted the church's views about gay sexual orientation instinctively, without hesitation. I don't remember knowing anyone personally who was openly gay until I was 19 years old and serving a two-year full-time mission for the church in San Francisco (from 1994-1996).

[*Side note:* *Weekly Latter-day Saint church services are open to the public and held each Sunday in chapels. However, access to Latter-day Saint temples (which are much fewer in number than chapels, and are reserved for special ceremonies for church members and their ancestors) is only permitted for church members whom local leaders affirm have sufficient belief and are obeying church standards. Such church members are given cards that are called "temple recommends," which they must show when they go to a temple to be allowed to enter.*]

Growing up, my understanding of official church teachings was that being gay was an evil perversion, and that "same-sex attraction" was a choice and could be altered if someone really wanted to change. Other church teachings and practices during my childhood and youth that I wasn't aware of at the time (but that I have since learned about) included encouraging mixed- sexual orientation marriages as a cure for gay sexual orientation, and abusive conversion/aversion/reparative therapy meant to repress gay sexual desires, including a program at BYU where gay men, as part of their repentance efforts, were shown same-gender erotic materials while having their genitals shocked to try to teach their bodies to not respond with arousal. In the 2017 McMurrin Lecture at the University of Utah, titled "Science vs. Dogma: Biology Challenges the LDS Paradigm," historian and scholar Dr. Gregory A. Prince spoke about these treatments. He wryly notes, "Pornographic pictures of nudes—which he was asked to provide— were... I presume not available in the BYU Bookstore." (https://www.youtube.com/watch?v=gssnz1WZ3dU (this statement is said at the 31:45 minute mark); See also https://abcnews.go.com/Health/mormon-gay-cures-reparative-therapies-shock- today/story?id=13240700; https://en.wikipedia.org/wiki/Brigham_Young_University_LGBT_history).

[Side note: President Dallin H. Oaks, the apostle who is currently next in line to become the prophet and President of the church, was BYU President from 1971 until 1980. The aforementioned electroshock conversion therapy at BYU started in 1959 and lasted until 1983: https://en.wikipedia.org/wiki/Timeline_of_LGBT_Mormon_history_in_the_20th_century.]

Our church wasn't the only church teaching these harmful ideas or engaging in similar abusive practices. Many other conservative churches were doing likewise. But it is still troubling to me to recognize that the highest leaders in our church (including some who are still alive and leading the church today), whom I consider prophets and apostles, were in charge when such practices occurred.

After getting to know some gay people in San Francisco on my mission, I began to research more about our church's doctrine on gay sexual orientation – mostly just out of curiosity though. Because of what I perceived as unwanted sexual advances that a gay church member made toward me while I was on my mission, and a few confrontational interactions I had with gay and transgender people as I was proselytizing on the street, I did not have kind feelings toward LGBTQ people generally while I was on my mission. The church resources

I was able to find on my mission still described gay sexual orientation (not just behavior) as a sinful choice. So it wasn't until years later when I moved to Boston in 2003 that my negative thoughts about people being gay began to slowly soften.

Around that time, marriage equality was a hot political issue. The church was heavily involved around the country in efforts to prevent the legalization of gay marriage, including having local church leaders in California formally instruct their congregation members to oppose marriage equality ballot initiatives with their individual time and money. Church members in California did this especially effectively, becoming what many believe was the primary driver behind the success of defeating the marriage equality initiative in California in 2008: https://www.nytimes.com/2008/11/15/us/politics/15marriage.html. I agreed with the church's political views about gay marriage at the time. But debating marriage equality with my non- Latter-day Saint friends here in Boston who were in favor of it did soften my perspective a bit.

That slight softening turned out to be helpful for me when I served as the volunteer leader of our local congregation (initially as a branch president and later as a bishop) in southeastern Massachusetts from 2011-2016. Some individuals came to me around mid-way through those years seeking guidance about how to approach their attraction to people of their same gender from a spiritual perspective. I honestly didn't know how to help them. So I did some investigating and study.

Does the church say that experiencing gay sexual desire is a choice?

I found in my research that the church had published a website just the year before (in December 2012) called www.mormonsandgays.org (now www. churchofjesuschrist.org/topics/gay/).

[Side note: Some people believe this site was published as a way to counter the intense and extensive negative media attention the church received after marriage equality was defeated in California in 2008. Others think it was created to help high

profile Latter-day Saint political candidates defend against accusations (like some made during Mitt Romney's presidential run) that their church was anti-LGBTQ.]

I learned on the church's website that the church didn't consider being attracted to people of the same gender to be a choice anymore. While the initial version of the site used to have the statement that "same-sex attraction" was not a choice on the lead page (if I remember correctly anyway), you now have to click through a couple pages to find that idea. But the current site still says:

> "The Church of Jesus Christ of Latter-day Saints believes that the experience of same-sex attraction is a complex reality for many people. The attraction itself is not a sin, but acting on it is. Even though **individuals do not choose to have such attractions**, they do choose how to respond to them." (M. Russell Ballard, Apostle, "Church Leaders," https://www.churchofjesuschrist.org/topics/gay/, 2015)

I wish the church would have publicized its original mormonsandgays.org site more when it first came out in 2012. Not many church members knew about it and so held onto false beliefs for many years thereafter, that being attracted to people of one's same gender is a choice. Those beliefs were based on statements made over prior decades by past church leaders – that God would never allow an individual to be born gay because it would contradict the plan of salvation– or that bad parenting could result in a child being gay - both of which are concepts the church no longer teaches are true: https://mormonlgbtquestions.com/. All of those past teachings have now been disavowed by the church. The official teaching of the church now is that gay sexual attraction is not a choice (https://www.churchofjesuschrist.org/topics/gay/).

What does science say about gay sexual orientation?
How common is it in nature?

That new position of the church (that "same-sex attraction" is not a choice) is consistent with what I had just begun to find out about scientific perspectives on the cause of gay sexual orientation as well. Through some reading, I had learned that genetics and developmental environment could both be at play – and neither meant that a person chose to have gay sexual desires. While different studies are continuing to provide more and more details, many have now emerged that suggest that a key to understanding the cause of varying sexual orientations is "epigenetics" (which means "over" or "around" genetics). That is a field of science that studies how environmental factors can actually change how DNA works (i.e., how genes are expressed): https://en.wikipedia. org/wiki/Epigenetic_theories_of_homosexuality.

Specifically, I have learned that researchers have found there are thousands of genes influencing sexual orientation, not a single "gay gene." Scientists also found environmental factors that can actually alter or "hard-wire" the expression of those genes. This can happen with a fetus in the womb (or, as some researchers suggest, with a child after birth, although much less evidence supports post-birth epigenetic changes: https://www.google.com/amp/s/www. telegraph.co.uk/science/2016/03/15/homosexuality-may- be-triggered-by-environment-after-birth/amp/). In utero, brains of fetuses have different levels of exposure to, and different abilities to absorb, testosterone – resulting in interplay of other hormones and steroids (https://www.sciencemag.org/news/2015/10/ homosexuality-may-be-caused-chemical-modifications-dna). It is important to note that in epigenetics, the inherited genetic makeup of the fetus may play a significant role in whether environmental conditions alter DNA. Some inherited genetic makeups may be less affected by environmental conditions than others. So as with most physical traits, both parents play a role biologically in determining the sexual orientation with which their child is born.

All of this can result in a wide spectrum of sexual orientations with which people may be born (just like there are wide spectrums among many other physical characteristics in biology, like eye color, handed-ness (right, ambidextrous, left), etc.). The spectrum of sexuality is often referred to as the Kinsey Scale: https://kinseyinstitute.org/research/publications/kinsey- scale. php). That means that some people who feel gay, bisexual or straight sexual desires may feel them more strongly than others. Even identical twins may feel sexual attractions differently, even though they share the same DNA, because their DNA is expressed differently due to epigenetic factors (i.e., due to different levels of exposure to hormones in utero, because of separate amniotic sacs or otherwise).

Modern science shows that a gay sexual orientation is an unchosen reality for many people. That reality is a biological one by definition, because sexual desires are of the body. I was amazed to learn that both the church and science were now in agreement that having a gay sexual orientation is an unchosen biological trait.

[Side notes:

1. *A BYU microbiology professor, Dr. William Bradshaw, gave a fantastic lecture in 2010 explaining epigenetics and the biological origins and characteristics associated with gay sexual orientation: https://m.youtube.com/ watch?v=8IHw9DVI3hE (the whole lecture is great, but, if you're rushed for time, skip to about the 30-minute mark and listen for 20 minutes to learn about how epigenetics influences sexual orientation). His conclusion is that having a gay sexual orientation is an unchosen biological characteristic. At the 55-minute mark of his presentation, he cites the church's position: "The Church does not have a position on the causes of any of these susceptibilities or inclinations, including those related to same-gender attraction. Those are scientific questions – whether nature or nurture – those are things the Church doesn't have a position on" (https://newsroom.churchofjesuschrist.org/article/interview-oaks-wickman-same-gender-attraction) – and then says: "**I don't think I have tried to hide my conclusion about all of these things. It isn't nurture. It's nature.**" Dr. Bradshaw is a former mission president, former member of a stake presidency, and has written about the biology of gay sexual orientation elsewhere. He is also the host of a short video titled, "Embracing our Homosexual Children" (https://www.youtube.com/watch?v=PyRAueeJNIY).*

2. *Another good explanation of the genetic/epigenetic origins of sexual orientation is given in this lecture by Latter-day Saint scholar/historian, Dr. Gregory A. Prince: https://www.youtube.com/watch?v=gssnz1WZ3dU (again, the whole lecture is great, but if you're in a rush, watch from the 14-minute mark through the 30-minute mark to just learn about epigenetics). This lecture is the best I have heard that summarizes in layman's terms the biological origins of gay sexual orientation. Brother Prince's book*

is also fantastic for summarizing the progression of church doctrine on gay sexual orientation and its political involvement in gay rights: https:// uofupress.lib.utah.edu/gay- rights-and-the-mormon-church/.

3. *A great summary of the science can be found under the section titled "Sexual Orientation is Not a Choice" on the website for Richard Ostler's "Listen, Learn, and Love": https://www.listenlearnandlove.org/articles.*

4. *Some studies have concluded that actual inherited genetics (i.e., normal genetics, not epigenetics) can account for 25-32% of the differences in sexual orientation: https://www.theguardian.com/science/blog/2015/ jul/24/gay- genes-science-is-on-the-right-track-were-born-this-way-lets-deal-with-it; https://www.nytimes.com/2019/08/29/science/gay-gene-sex. html. So the primary determinants for where anyone falls on the spectrum of sexual orientation, including, of course, being gay, may be a mix of inherited genetics and epigenetics, with proportional variation occurring in that mix for each person. Many other biological traits are similarly determined through a mix of inherited genetics and epigenetics, such as being right-handed or left-handed: "[T]win studies indicate that [inherited] genetic factors explain 25% of the variance in handedness, while environmental [or epigenetic] factors [occurring in utero] explain the remaining 75%": https://en.wikipedia.org/wiki/Handedness.*

5. *Scientific research is also showing that there are some observable physiological evidences relating to sexual orientation. I find the following descriptions of such physical observations fascinating:*

"[S]cientists have found that the sexually dimorphic traits [(i.e., those traits that normally differ between the two biological sexes)] of gay men often resemble those of heterosexual females, while those of lesbian women often resemble heterosexual males…

[For example,] beginning with studies in 1991 and later in 2001, ***neuroscientists found that the volume of INAH-3 [which is a part of the hypothalamus in the brain] in homosexual males actually appears closer to that of heterosexual females than it does in heterosexual males…***

And…pheromones; aromatic chemicals produced via hormones by both males and females that induce non- learned, inborn brain activity in members of the opposite sex. For example, the testosterone *found in a male's sweat typically evokes activity in a region of a heterosexual female's hypothalamus that is highly involved in sexual attraction and arousal. But as you might suspect, **homosexuals exhibit this same brain activity and sexual arousal in response to pheromones produced by members of their same sex...***

*[Also,] researchers have been looking at how homosexuals and heterosexuals physiologically experience romantic love. These studies have revealed that the physiological and neurological manifestations of love in the brains of both heterosexuals and homosexuals are the same. Specifically, **brain scans of people in love with opposite sex partners, and individuals in love with same sex partners look the same;** the dopamine reward systems become intensely activated in both heterosexual and homosexual pairs. **This finding confirms that all humans, almost universally, experience romantic love as a basic neurological drive in the brain; energizing and directing our behavior intensely toward acquiring what our brain sees as a basic biological need.***

This drives both heterosexuals and homosexuals towards one of life's greatest prizes: a person to whom they are attracted and with whom they desire to exclusively pair bond, or in more popular terms, fall in love and form a long-term relationship. And unlike mere emotions or "preferences and tendencies," both homosexuals and heterosexuals experience this neurological drive towards romantic love tenaciously, and can experience intense emotional distress and even physiological pain and suffering when it cannot be obtained.

So while we don't yet know definitively how homosexual orientation is formed, it certainly appears to function as a fundamental drive in the same way heterosexual orientation does; meaning it is experienced as a compelling and persistent force with biological causes and profound psychological and physiological impacts."

(These paragraphs come from a public draft of a working article summarizing scientific findings from various sources; resources can be provided upon request: https://docs.google.com/book/d/15Rt-VqRQ5KOeyc6i5BzbNSprMpbJCD6n99VfpKirv_F0/mobilebasic).]

Now, notwithstanding the scientific findings explaining the origins of sexual orientation, a few individuals have told me that since some people have shown "fluidity" in their sexuality over time, sexual orientation can't be just a purely biological thing. They argue that some choice in sexual desire is obviously present because of that demonstrated flexibility. I believe that is a faulty conclusion though. The sexual orientation spectrum is broad because the brains of developing babies absorb wide-ranging levels of hormones while in the womb. Brain development in utero puts most babies on the primarily straight or primarily gay ends of the spectrum. But some people seem to have developed in utero with hormonal absorption levels somewhere in the middle, so they are born with bisexual orientation. They still have an unchosen biological orientation – it just happens to allow for more natural flexibility. Stated differently:

> "Some will argue that our commonsense experiences are full of people who are "fluid" in their sexual orientations or change their sexualities…Change is widely used to argue against biological explanations. Critics will say that if behaviour changes, or is "fluid," then surely it can't have a biological basis? This is false because it is our biology that allows us to learn, respond to socialisation, and helps generate our culture. So showing evidence of change is not an argument against biology. There is indeed some fluidity in sexuality over time, predominantly among women. But there is no "bell shaped curve" to sexual orientation. **People may change the identity labels they use and who they have sex with but sexual attractions seem stable over time**." (https://www.theguardian.com/science/blog/2015/jul/24/gay-genes-science-is-on-the-right-track-were-born-this-way-lets-deal-with-it)

So a biological explanation for sexual orientation is not diminished just because we see someone in a gay relationship at one point and then later observe them to have a straight relationship instead. All that might mean is that they are biologically wired somewhere in the middle of the sexual orientation spectrum

– i.e., their biological orientation doesn't change; it just provides that particular person more fluidity in attractions. This is analogous to the way that an ambidextrous person may alternate between feeling comfortable using their right or left hand in different situations or over the course of their life.

Interestingly, as I continued my research, I also learned that same-sex sexual behavior is widespread in the animal kingdom, occurring in every major animal group. (https://en.wikipedia.org/wiki/Homosexual_behavior_in_animals). I also didn't know that the percentage of animals within many species that exhibit same-sex sexual behavior is about the same as the percentage of humans who are LGBTQ (between around 2-10% of the population, depending on the study and location: https://en.wikipedia.org/wiki/Demographics_of_sexual_orientation#Denmark).

In any event, during the course of my research into all this scientific stuff, I started to realize I was very much behind the curve in understanding the biology behind, and scope of, gay sexual orientation in general.

Finally, I should note that I regret that I required scientific evidence explaining how gay sexual orientation is innate before I believed it could be. I wish I would have believed the testimonies of LGBTQ people, rather than being a Doubting Thomas and requiring evidence. Because straight people are the majority, or heterosexuality is seen as "normal," there are far fewer studies that try to figure out why people are straight. I wish there were no need to have so many studies about why people are gay. I wish we all just loved each other better and understood gay sexual orientation as a helpful and normal occurrence (see Chapter 4 for a discussion about the benefits of gay sexual orientation in nature), not needing evidence to accept each other's lived experiences and realities.

Furthermore, as some LGBTQ rights commentators have noted, relying too much on scientific explanations for LGBTQ realities can actually hurt the cause of equality (https://www.ted.com/talks/dr_lisa_diamond_why_the_born_this_way_argument_does_not_advance_lgbt_equality?language=en). So while I think the scientifically validated middle-spectrum orientations with which some people are born can clearly explain the sexual fluidity that they exhibit over the course of their lives, I nevertheless still wish we all just simply believed each other, without requiring scientific evidence, when we say what our respective sexual orientations or gender identities are, whether LGBTQ or straight/cisgender.

*[Side note: I would love to see the primary question in studies on LGBTQ matters be why people are homophobic or transphobic. How do **they** become that way? What treatments might help them not be that way? Understanding that LGBTQ people are born with their respective sexual orientations and gender identities only gets us to the same starting point as what we see in other contexts where discrimination continues to be problematic: racism and misogyny. People of color are born with darker skin and women are born female. But that doesn't stop racists and misogynists from hurtfully discriminating against them. So understanding that people can be born LGBTQ is not enough to prevent discrimination against them either. We need to do more to understand what motivates homophobia and transphobia and enact policies, and engage in more teaching, to prevent it.]*

Is mixed-orientation marriage encouraged by the church?

Returning to my learnings on the church front, I also discovered that, for quite some time, church leaders had been discouraging gay people from marrying straight people as a cure for having a gay sexual orientation:

> "[M]arriage *should not* be viewed as a therapeutic step to solve problems such as homosexual inclinations or practices" (Gordon B. Hinckley, Apostle, https://www.churchofjesuschrist. org/study/ensign/1987/05/reverence-and-morality, 1987)

> "Marriage should not be viewed as a way to resolve homosexual problems. **The lives of others should not be damaged by entering a marriage where such concerns exist**. Encouraging members to cultivate heterosexual feelings as a way to resolve homosexual problems generally leads them to frustration and discouragement." *Understanding and Helping Those Who Have Homosexual Problems. Suggestions for Ecclesiastical Leaders,*

1992, p. 4. (http://www.qrd.org/qrd/religion/judeochristian/ protestantism/mormon/mormon- homosexuality)

That was different from what I had heard before, and constituted a change in church policy. For decades before the above statement by President Hinckley was made, the church had regularly been promoting mixed-orientation marriages as a cure for someone having a gay sexual orientation. That is, before 1987, informal church policy was for local leaders to advise gay men to marry women.

Some more recent and clear statements by general church leaders saying the church no longer supports mixed-orientation marriage as a cure are as follows:

> "We don't counsel people that heterosexual marriage is a panacea. You'll see in some of these experiences that are related on this site that it has been a successful experience in a few cases, or some have expressed the success they have found in marriage and in raising a family, and in the joy and all that has filled out and blessed their lives as a consequence. But that we know is not always true. And it's not always successful. Sometimes it's been even disastrous. We think it's something that a person can evaluate, and they can discuss, and both with priesthood leaders and family and others, and make decisions. But we simply don't take a uniform position on saying, 'Yes, always,' or 'No, always.'" (D. Todd Christofferson, Apostle, https://www. churchofjesuschrist.org/topics/gay/leaders?lang=eng)

> "[Church leaders] **definitely *do not* recommend marriage as a solution for same- gender feelings**. No, it's not a therapy. In times past, decades ago, there were some practices to that effect. We have eradicated them in the Church now." (Dallin H. Oaks, Apostle, "Elizabeth's Story: Ricardo's Wife," https:// www.churchofjesuschrist.org/topics/gay/videos/elizabeths-story?lang=eng, 2016)

I have heard many accounts of local church leaders, presumably unaware of the church's changed position on mixed-orientation marriage, who still counsel gay church members (who do not express any opposite gender attraction) to earnestly consider marrying someone of the opposite sex. So I think the church's apparent desire to have such advice "eradicated" should be followed up with additional action: more training materials that emphasize the change, and required review on a regular basis by local leaders.

Even some other relatively recent statements by church leaders that seem to encourage mixed- orientation marriage, don't actually do so when they are read closely. Instead, they illustrate that a couple should only marry if there is genuine attraction present between them. I think that means the church's position is that any person who experiences gay sexual desires must be actually <u>bisexual</u> (at least bisexual to a degree sufficient to feel sincerely attracted to their potential spouse) in order to appropriately marry a person of the opposite sex. That's because there has to be genuine attraction present between both parties:

> "We are all thrilled when some who struggle with these feelings are able to marry, raise children, and achieve family happiness… [but] recognize that **marriage is not an all- purpose solution** [and that] same-gender attractions run deep, and **trying to force a heterosexual relationship is not likely to change them**… [Some attempts at marriage] have **resulted in broken hearts and broken homes**" (Jeffrey R. Holland, Apostle, https://www. churchofjesuschrist.org/study/ensign/2007/10/helping-those-who-struggle- with-same-gender-attraction , 2007).

> "**[P]ersons who** have…shown their ability to deal with these feelings or inclinations and put them in the background, and *feel a great attraction* **for a daughter of God** and therefore desire to enter marriage and have children and enjoy the blessings of eternity— **that's a situation when marriage would be appropriate**." (Dallin H. Oaks, Apostle, https://newsroom.

churchofjesuschrist.org/article/interview-oaks-wickman-same-gender- attraction, 2006)

I believe church leaders wisely changed prior teachings on mixed-orientation marriage when statistics in the 1980s and 1990s started showing such marriages had a disproportionately higher rate of divorce. A 2015 study showed such marriages are 2 to 3 times more likely to end in divorce than uniform-orientation marriages: https://www.huffpost.com/entry/gay-mormon-men- marriage_n_6464848. This may be due to a correlation with higher rates of depression and a lower quality of life in mixed-orientation marriages: https://www.tandfonline.com/doi/abs/10.1080/19359705.2014.912970.

[*Side note: Some well-meaning church members have informed us of mixed-orientation couples who seem to be making things work. While we appreciate the intent, we are not supportive of Wes pursuing a mixed-orientation marriage because, on the Kinsey scale (i.e., the spectrum of sexual orientation), he falls squarely on the gay end; he is not bisexual. And, for every couple that seems to be making a mixed-orientation marriage work, we know of many more whose marriages have failed, often after decades of trying. Just because you see a mixed-orientation couple (or even many such couples) that might appear to be happy, that doesn't mean such happiness will be long-lasting.*

As the above study indicates, the divorce rate for such couples is 2 to 3 times higher than it is for straight couples. That doesn't mean NO such couples can make it work and be happy. But it does mean that marital happiness for mixed-orientation couples is very rare. I am happy for everyone who finds joy in their marriage, no matter what types of sexual orientations are involved. I respect the path of mixed-orientation marriage that some people choose. I just also recognize it as a path that carries a much higher risk of failure and pain.

One couple who became somewhat famous within Latter-day Saint circles for their efforts to make a mixed- orientation marriage work was Josh and Lolly Weed. After many years of marriage, they announced their divorce in January 2018. Their blog is instructive for those trying to learn more about the challenges that mixed-orientation marriages face: http://joshweed.com/. I find it interesting that they express regret for inspiring other people to enter into mixed-orientation marriages because so many people who followed their examples ended up divorcing or depressed.

Another example of a high profile mixed-orientation marriage is that of Ed and Lois Smart, the parents of Elizabeth Smart, who was kidnapped for 9 months when she was 14 years old in 2002. Ed and Lois married in 1985, toward the end of the era during which church leaders had been encouraging gay men to marry women to cure being gay. Ed knew he was gay since he was 12 years old. After 34 years of marriage, the Smarts divorced in 2019. Ed has discussed in interviews how church teachings led him to view himself as being "deviant, being abnormal, being mentally sick" just because of his gay sexual orientation. He accordingly hid the fact that he is gay until he decided to come out publicly in the summer of 2019 (which occurred four years after Lois asked him if he was gay): https://www.sltrib. com/news/education/2019/12/08/ed-smart-father/; https://www.nydailynews.com/ news/national/ny-ed-smart-came-out-struggles-gay-acceptance-elizabeth-smart-20191210-qyd6dnbc3vh6fdguwczh3v44pm-story.html.]

Well, after learning of the new positions the church was taking and the science that agreed with such positions, I told the individuals who came to me seeking guidance, to not feel bad about their gay sexual attractions, to try to resist them (because, even though the church had changed its position about the attractions being a choice, acting on them is still considered a sin), and to have faith that God would help them figure out how to stay chaste and be happy going forward. My heart ached in having to provide that counsel, because when I tried to put myself in their shoes, I honestly didn't know how these individuals would be able to obey the church's rule for chastity and also find happiness if they had to repress any hope for a uniform-orientation marriage someday. But, at the very least, I was glad I didn't need to tell them they were sinning in just feeling gay sexual desires, or recommend they pursue a mixed-orientation marriage or go to conversion/reparative therapy, as bishops in the past were instructed to counsel.

I admire church leaders for softening the church's stance. An essay written by Bryce Cook, a faithful, active Latter-day Saint, does a great job summarizing the doctrinal evolution that has occurred within the church: https:// mormonlgbtquestions.com/. This essay also explains the harm that even our improved current doctrine can still have on LGBTQ church members - and possible ideas for how our doctrine could change even more while still staying within existing theological tenets. I'm glad our prophets and apostles became aware of the flawed science that formed the basis of their counsel (and that of so many religious leaders in other churches), and of the harm their positions were causing, and that they changed the official teachings of the church accordingly.

How did the church respond to the legalization of marriage equality?

After observing in private meetings the heartache that the individuals who came to talk to me were experiencing, and seeing their tears and knowing how much they wanted to be happy in the church, I was very encouraged to see the church moving in what I thought was a more kind, loving and Christ-like direction. In fact, in March of 2015, the church was even instrumental in passing groundbreaking LGBTQ rights legislation in Utah, which was great: https://www.nytimes.com/2015/03/12/us/politics/utah-passes-antidiscrimi-nation-bill-backed-by-mormon-leaders.html.

Then the U.S. Supreme Court legalized marriage equality in June of 2015. The following month, the highest governing body of our church gave some instructions in response to the Supreme Court's ruling. That governing body is known as the First Presidency, which is comprised of the President of our church, also referred to as the prophet, and his two counselors. (An analogy to Catholicism would have the prophet being like the Pope, because he holds the highest church position possible.) The First Presidency required that all local church leaders read a statement to their congregation members, to reiterate the church's doctrinal position that gay sexual behavior was still considered a sin.

Because I thought those people I had counseled with in our congregation might be listening especially carefully as I followed that directive from the First Presidency (and because my understanding of gay sexual orientation had expanded greatly and my heart had softened immensely by this point), I decided to read the church's statement in a special meeting where I could try to facilitate a more fulsome discussion. I asked all the adults and teenage youth in our congregation to attend that discussion in lieu of an hour of the

normal Sunday classes. I took only about five minutes in that meeting to follow the church's instruction to clarify that the doctrine forbidding same-sex
sexual behavior had not changed as a result of the Supreme Court ruling. I
then spent almost 40 minutes leading a discussion about two of the church's
other positions that <u>had</u> changed: 1- that gay sexual attraction is not a choice;
and 2- that church members need to do a better job of showing more love and
acceptance toward LGBTQ people.

Many members of my congregation said afterward that they did not
know the church held those positions now. But because of the church's website (https://www.churchofjesuschrist.org/topics/gay/) showing this revised
approach, it was easy for me to stay within orthodox boundaries during that
meeting, while still keeping the focus on gaining greater love and understanding.

How exactly does the church want us to love LGBTQ people?

Unfortunately, I have observed that many church members still aren't aware of
the change in the church's teachings about gay sexual orientation and how we
should increase our efforts to love LGBTQ people. I can understand why that
is. The church's website on same-sex attraction (https://www.churchofjesus-
christ.org/topics/gay/) has not yet been discussed in any General Conference or
publicized much, especially in comparison to marketing efforts the church has
made in other contexts. And there is a long history of many prophets, apostles
and other General Authorities in the church making incredibly homophobic
and hurtful comments, teaching them as church doctrine and God's will (*trig-
ger warning: the quotes contained in this comprehensive history of church leader
statements can be difficult to read*: https://lattergaystories.org/record/). As with
most instances of homophobia, I understand church leaders were speaking from
a position of protecting their own worldview and social/religious dynamics,
not out of hate. But because their statements were taught as doctrine, I think
it will take many years and sustained, increased efforts by church leaders at
new messaging before most church members adopt a new way of thinking.

But while I think much more needs to be done in that regard, I am nonetheless glad that church leaders have been trying in recent years to correct the harmful teachings of the past. Some of my favorite teachings from our current church leaders encouraging more love are as follows:

> **"Hope is very important to everyone involved, but especially to the LGBT individual. Love is the minister of Hope."** (Dallin H. Oaks, Apostle, statement on the original church website mormonsandgays.org)

> **"Young people struggling with any exceptional condition, including same-gender attraction, are particularly vulnerable and need loving understanding – not bullying or ostracism.** With the help of the Lord, we can repent and change and be more loving and helpful to children, our own and those around us." (Dallin H. Oaks, Apostle, https://www.churchofjesuschrist.org/study/general-conference/2012/10/protect-the-children , 2012)

> **"We need to listen to and understand what our LGBT brothers and sisters are feeling and experiencing. Certainly we must do better than we have done in the past** so that all members feel they have a spiritual home where their brothers and sisters **love them and where they have a place to worship and serve the Lord."** (M. Russell Ballard, Apostle, BYU address, https://www.churchofjesuschrist.org/church/news/elder- ballard-tackles-tough-topics-and-gives-timely-advice-to-young-adults , 2017).

> **"…as a Church nobody should be more loving and compassionate. No family who has anybody who has a same-gender issue should exclude them from the family circle.** They need to be part of the family circle…We have a plan of salvation. And having children come into our lives is part of Heavenly

Father's plan. But let us be at the forefront in terms of expressing love, compassion, and outreach to those and **let's not have
families exclude or be disrespectful of those who choose a
different lifestyle as a result of their feelings about their own
gender**…I feel very strongly about this. . .It's a very important
principle." (Quentin L. Cook, Apostle, https://www.fairmor-
mon.org/blog/category/homosexuality#_ednref7).

In addition to those quotes, there have been several other positive statements made by our apostles about generally loving LGBTQ people better than we do. For a good listing of other positive and loving quotes on
LGBTQ matters, see this document compiled by an influential and
active, faithful Latter-day Saint, Richard Ostler: https://drive.google.com/
open?id=1sklAZfBlrG8SnB7B89Cf57gg17PXPQ_Z.

While I love all the teachings that have focused on increasing love, I
think it is still important to clarify what specific acts of love are deemed "okay"
for parents and others to take. Despite all the talk about loving our LGBTQ
church members better, no apostle has stated specifically what sort of acts are
appropriate. I think it would be immensely helpful for someone in the First
Presidency to clarify, in one of our worldwide General Conferences, what
specific acts of inclusion are appropriate (or inappropriate, if there are any).

I know it may sound silly for me to say I want specific instructions about
how to love. But, unfortunately, I know many people in the church worry
about acts of love toward gay people being construed as approval of gay sexual
behavior. So I think we need to get at least some General Authority instruction
on this front that has the same degree of specificity that past statements about
exclusion have had:

> **"Avoid as the plague social interaction with persons who jus-
> tify, encourage or engage in homosexual behavior. Stay away
> from places where those challenged by same-gender attrac-
> tion congregate"** (Alexander B. Morrison, General Authority

https://web.archive.org/web/20120724194315/http://www.
evergreeninternational.org/morrison.htm, 2000).

If parents of a gay son or daughter who has decided to enter into a gay relationship were to follow that teaching precisely, they would have to cut off all contact with their child.

A more recent statement (which has not been retracted or corrected) was made by one of our highest church leaders that parents can be justified in treating their LGBTQ adult children differently from their other kids in several specific ways. The following statement to that effect was made in response to a question about how families should respond to a gay son wanting to attend a family gathering with his same-sex partner:

> "I can imagine some circumstances in which it might be possible to say, "Yes, come, but don't expect to stay overnight. **Don't expect to be a lengthy house guest. Don't expect us to take you out and introduce you to our friends, or to deal with you in a public situation** that would imply our approval of your partnership." (Dallin H. Oaks, Apostle, https://newsroom.churchofjesuschrist.org/article/interview-oaks-wickman-same-gender- attraction, 2006)

Other statements that cause confusion about what sort of interactions are appropriate with LGBTQ individuals include more recent remarks made in 2018 and 2019 by President Dallin H. Oaks, a current member of the First Presidency, that Satan "seeks to confuse gender [and] distort marriage" (https://www.churchofjesuschrist.org/study/general-conference/2018/10/truth-and-the- plan), and that LGBTQ "lifestyles and values" are part of "a culture of evil and personal wickedness" (https://devotional.byuh.edu/node/1788; https://www.sltrib.com/religion/2019/06/20/this-week-mormon-land/). While President Oaks has talked about loving LGBTQ individuals in a few General Conference remarks, he seems to prefer doing so in generalities, and with qualifications (see Chapter 4).

Without clarifying how families should interpret all the above statements, we are left in confusion.

By way of analogy for my fellow Latter-day Saints, can you imagine how we would feel if we heard of nonmember parents who thought our church was evil (and there are people out there who think that) and so told their son who had joined the church and married a Latter-day Saint woman, that their participation in family gatherings would be controlled or limited, and that they wouldn't be introduced to friends, just because he was now a Latter-day Saint or married to one?

President Oaks has talked a lot about "fairness for all" in the religious liberty political context. Shouldn't the same principle apply in our families? In my opinion, it would be helpful for him to publicly clarify how it does specifically. For example, Cheryl and I got that sort of clarification privately when we met with an Area Authority of the church who was in Massachusetts with us in September 2019 (see Chapter 9; note this was <u>not</u> the General Authority discussed in that chapter with whom we had hurtful discussions). He said that if Wes finds a man to marry, we should celebrate at his wedding and welcome his future husband into our family just like we plan to do for any other future spouse of our other kids. While we appreciated hearing that from that Area Authority, until someone in a higher up position (like an apostle or the prophet) says something like that publicly, parents of gay kids in the church will be nervous about having their local leaders revoke their good standing in the church (i.e., take away their temple recommends) because they treat their gay child the same as their other kids. I have heard many stories where that has happened: parents have lost their temple recommends because they paid for a kid's gay wedding or paid for a trans kid's hormone treatments, etc. Without clarification from the top leadership of the church, different local church leaders will interpret things in vastly different ways, with some pointing to past statements by President Oaks and others as justification for being harsh. We shouldn't leave parents questioning how much they can show their love based on a game of local church leadership roulette (i.e., where it all depends on what your local bishop or stake president thinks).

[Side note: In December 2019, a very painful story came to light about a mission president revoking the temple recommend of a young full-time missionary, just because he privately disagreed with the church's stance opposing marriage equality, even though he was willing to sustain the church's leaders notwithstanding his personal disagreement with the position. Fortunately, that mission president's decision was reversed (presumably by higher up authorities in the church). But at that point, the young missionary felt so discouraged he decided to go home early from his mission anyway (https://www.sltrib.com/religion/2019/12/15/can-latter-day-saints/).]

How did my experiences as a bishop prepare me for my son coming out to me?

All that being said, overall, I am happy the church has tried to correct many of the harmful teachings of the past. And I will forever be grateful to the individuals in our congregation who came to talk to me about their gay sexual attractions. They helped me change my views and led me to further research in science and in church policy. I am also glad I spent so much time talking about love and acceptance of gay people in that special meeting our congregation held – because it was only a few months later that Wes finally came out to Cheryl and me. I had no idea my own son was among the members of my congregation toward whom I was trying to be especially (and discreetly) sensitive during that meeting. I'm glad Wes heard me talk about love and acceptance of LGBTQ people in a public setting like that - because I know I had said (and know Wes heard me say) unkind things about gay people in the privacy of our own home over the years.

I believe God was preparing me to appropriately and lovingly respond to Wes when he came out privately to Cheryl and me in the fall of 2015. Without hesitation I told him that I loved him and would support him in any path he chose for his life. In hindsight, I can admit now that I always knew Wes was gay. But I was in involuntary denial. I used to ask Cheryl about once a year or so when he was growing up if she thought Wes was gay. I would see him act a certain way or hear him talk about girls in a way that seemed different to me. Back then, knowing how worried I would have been if I knew Wes was gay, Cheryl would just kindly respond by telling me "No, he's not gay – don't worry about it" (while privately thinking to herself: "I think he actually might be gay"). So I accepted her reassurance and just kept on being oblivious.

Because he is close to his siblings, Wes told them he was gay around the same time he told Cheryl and me. It was good for us all to recognize that his fears about being gay contributed to the depression Wes had been suffering for about 18 months. Cheryl and I tried to help him with his depression to no avail, because he would only partially open up to us, as he was just coming to terms with being gay himself. It finally felt really good for our whole family to be open and honest about everything. And Wes was a bit happier. He was no longer depressed or as scared about being gay because he knew his family accepted him unconditionally. But he did still have worries about finding his place in the church as a gay man.

Overall, we were in a bit of a better place. While we still didn't like the church's position preventing doctrinal marriage equality, we had hope that it would change eventually. But we knew God did not want us to engage in any sort of aggressive public protesting to pressure the church to change its doctrine. I believe only God can know when the membership of the church as a whole is ready for change. Sometimes external pressure can help church leaders pray harder to receive revelation about that, but we didn't feel like it was our role to exert that pressure. I believe that if the time comes, change will be revealed through proper channels (i.e., through the First Presidency and the other apostles). We felt inspired to stay in the church. We felt that God wanted us to encourage more church members to open their hearts to LGBTQ individuals. And we hoped that maybe as more people became increasingly loving and sympathetic, God would deem the time to be right sooner for expanded truth to be revealed. So we had hope for change, even if it was likely decades away still.

[*Side note: Interestingly, during the years before Wes came out to us, when I was learning more and more about gay sexual orientation while counseling with other church members, I kept feeling that I needed to share the information I was learning with my parents and siblings. I began to randomly email them a bunch of information about the church's changed views on gay sexual orientation. I honestly didn't know why I was doing it other than I felt excited about what I was learning and felt like I should share it. Maybe it was because I knew subconsciously that Wes was gay. After Wes came out to us privately in 2015, I continued to have discussions with my family (and now also with Cheryl's family) about my new enlightened views on LGBTQ matters, without letting them know Wes was gay.*

When Wes decided to come home from his mission in May 2019, he gave Cheryl and me permission to call each of our siblings and parents and let them know he was gay. We explained that he was coming home a bit early from his mission because he felt that God's path for him was outside the church. We felt good about making those phone calls for Wes, so all his time wouldn't be spent coming out to everyone over and over again, right when he got home. And the conversations with each of our siblings and our parents went superbly well.

We are so lucky to have such amazingly loving families who have shown their love for Wes in remarkable ways since he publicly came out as gay. Importantly, that includes not treating him any differently. When Wes did eventually get around to speaking with each of his extended family members about being gay, I loved seeing the smile on his face when he relayed that one of his uncles had told him nothing had changed – including that Wes would still be teased by him relentlessly about the same stuff as before (i.e., poor driving skills, video-gaming, etc.). I was happy to see that pity for Wes was not part of the reaction of any of our family members. They are treating Wes the same way they did before – with love. We are very grateful that the circle of love in each of our families remains strongly intact.]

Shifting church policies: How can darkness descend, and hope be rekindled, both so quickly?

In November of 2015, just a few weeks after Wes came out to us, darkness fell like a hammer when the church came out with a new policy that declared that 1) gay couples were apostate (which essentially meant our leaders wanted them all out of the church); 2) the children of gay couples could only be baptized once they turned 18 (instead of at age 8, the normal age for baptism), unless special permission was granted by the First Presidency; and 3) a condition of their baptism was that they needed to disavow their parents' same-sex cohabitation or marriage.

Cheryl and I were on a romantic getaway in Puerto Rico when that news made headlines. I still remember exactly where I was standing in our hotel room when I saw the news on my phone. I honestly felt like my mind and my soul had just been hit by a truck. The policy seemed to go against one of our church's core beliefs that no one should be punished for anyone else's sins, which belief stems from our doctrine that babies are not born into original sin just because of the fall of Adam and Eve. I began to wonder what this new policy might mean for our future grandchildren if Wes eventually married a man and they adopted kids.

The church clarified some days later that the policy was meant to keep kids from being taught things at church that would contradict their parents. While I could recognize that rationale as having a sense of logic to it, I really just couldn't understand why the policy was necessary.

Couldn't gay parents be trusted to decide what sort of mixed messages their children could tolerate, and to help them understand those messages? And what about couples who were in mixed-orientation marriages before divorcing? That is, if the gay ex-spouse remarried a same- sex partner and the straight ex-spouse wanted one of their kids to be baptized, would a termination of shared custody arrangements have to happen first?

[*Side note: Historian and scholar, Clair Barrus, has recorded the numerous stories of families negatively affected by the policy: http://www.withoutend.org/ reactions-the-policy-november-2015/.*]

Nothing about the policy made any sense to me. And I couldn't shake the clear feeling that the church was trying to purge its ranks of anyone who might be raised thinking marriage with same- gender spouses was okay – like this was some kind of preemptive measure to prevent support for doctrinal marriage equality from rising up within the church in the years ahead. But, recognizing that this was just a policy, not a new doctrine canonized in the scriptures, I still clung to my private hope for change and continued serving as a bishop. I think I found it possible to still cling to my hope for change because SO many other church members felt exactly the same way I did about this new policy. It was easy to think it wouldn't last long. Even when an apostle declared a couple of months after the policy's implementation that it was given by divine revelation, I was still guessing the policy wouldn't last more than 10 years.

And it didn't. By way of further divine revelation, the reversal of the policy (dubbed the "Exclusion Policy" by many), was announced on April 4, 2019 after only 3½ years. I was so happy to see it changed. Wes happened to be coming home from his mission in Brazil around the same time. It just gave me such hope that, despite what the prophets and apostles said at any given point in time about God's will for the church, things could change in the future as God gently works on hearts and minds to afford them greater compassion and understanding.

Following the April 2019 announcement regarding the reversal of the Exclusion Policy, the church's handbook of instructions for local and regional leaders was not officially updated to reflect any change until eight months later in December 2019, despite the church having updated several other sections of the handbook in the interim. When the handbook change finally came, the requirement was removed that children of gay parents needed to get First Presidency approval for their kids to be baptized before age 18. Currently, only local church leader approval is needed for any child over the age of 8 to be baptized. Surprisingly though, the December 2019 handbook change also included a brand-new section titled "Church Participation" with this alarming language:

> **"Those who attend should avoid disruptions or distractions** contrary to worship or other purposes of the meeting. All age and behavior requirements of different Church meetings and events should be respected. **That requires refraining from overt romantic behavior** and from dress or grooming that causes distraction. **It also precludes** making political state-ments or **speaking of sexual orientation or other personal characteristics in a way that detracts from meetings focused**

on the Savior." (https://www.churchofjesuschrist.org/study/ manual/general-handbook/38-church- policies-and-guide- lines?lang=eng#title_number3, General Handbook, Section 38.1.1)

While the language "overt romantic behavior" and "sexual orientation" is neutral as to gay vs. straight behavior/orientation, many people are worried that local leaders, given the church's doctrine prohibiting gay sex, will interpret such wording <u>only</u> to the detriment of LGBTQ individuals, and not against similar heteronormative behavior or speech. Many LGBTQ church members and their allies fear this will lead to interpretation by local leaders throughout the church to (i) prevent LGBTQ people from speaking about their sexual orientation at church or at church events and/or (ii) remove from church property gay couples showing any sort of physical affection toward each other, despite frequent physical affection in church being normalized between heterosexual couples, married and unmarried.

Then in February 2020, the church released a new publicly accessible version of a consolidated handbook. This new General Handbook has provisions that no longer categorize someone in a same-sex marriage as apostate. That means that while marriages between same-sex individuals are still considered sinful, local leaders have more discretion about whether or not a member in such a marriage should lose their membership in the church (see Section 32.6.2 here: https://www.churchofjesuschrist.org/study/manual/general-hand- book/32-repentance-and- membership-councils?lang=eng#title_number14).

Concurrent with the release of the new General Handbook in February 2020, BYU changed its Honor Code to remove language saying "homosexual" behavior was prohibited among its students. BYU stated that this change was made to be consistent with the General Handbook's new approach for rules regarding sexual behavior, which is that gay sexual activity (even if within marriage) is now treated the same way as straight extra-marital sexual activity (https://www.sltrib.com/news/education/2020/02/19/byu-appears-remove/). In the days following the change in the language of the Honor Code, hundreds of people made inquiries to multiple officers in the Honor Code Office at BYU, who confirmed that same-sex dating, hand-holding, and kissing would no longer automatically result in Honor Code investigations at BYU. Many gay students came out of the closet publicly following that announcement, saying they finally felt it was safe to do so at BYU.

However, two weeks after the change in the language of the Honor Code, the Church Educational System issued a letter that clarified that nothing had really changed at all, despite previous assurances from Honor Code Office personnel (https://www.thechurchnews.com/leaders-and-ministry/2020-03-04/byu-honor-code-language-clarification-ces-statement-176245). The letter referenced teachings found in the church's 1995 family proclamation, saying that the reason nothing had changed is because "Same-sex romantic behavior cannot lead to eternal marriage and is therefore not compatible with the principles included in the Honor Code."

Many criticisms of that rationale quickly circulated, including that: (i) straight nonmembers at BYU are allowed to date even though their dating is not done with any intention to marry in the temple; (ii) a temple-married widow is allowed to date on campus to try to find a new husband even though under church sealing practices, she can never be sealed to that new husband (because her eternal marriage is deemed to exist only with her first, deceased husband); and (iii) ironically, lifelong celibacy (which is what the church is asking gay students at BYU to embrace) does not lead to eternal marriage either. Perhaps the best criticism is that it undermines the idea that is said to be the basis of the new handbook, namely that heterosexual immorality and homosexual immorality are to be treated equally. Clearly the church does not espouse that idea in practice – because straight non-sexual romantic behavior is not considered immoral but gay non-sexual romantic behavior is considered immoral.

Some people have said that the BYU administration, not the church, was to blame for the confusion over the Honor Code language change. But I find it very hard to believe that someone at BYU would take any action of such a sensitive nature without consulting church headquarters first. That sort of rogue decision is one that would presumably have significant adverse consequences for a person's career at BYU. I strongly suspect that there is a difference of opinion among leaders at BYU and at church headquarters about gay marriage.

In any event, it is a tragic shame that this confusion created false hopes among gay students. And, again, that confusion was not the fault of the students. They were not negligent in letting their hopes rise. They asked clarifying questions of administration officials at BYU and were repeatedly told that same-sex dating was allowed. Parents (including me, because my straight son, Owen, was attending BYU at the time) were also told the same thing by BYU personnel over the phone.

And it wasn't just the students, parents, and administration officials who were confused. A video made by a professor at BYU went viral shortly after the Honor Code language change, explaining why, in his opinion, the allowance for same-sex dating was consistent with the new church handbook. He said that accepting that new allowance on BYU campus was a way for students to follow church leaders. He added that the new policy gave straight students on campus a chance to become better prepared to respond appropriately to gay relationships in the work environment in their future careers (https://www.sltrib.com/news/education/2020/02/26/popular- video-this-byu/).

The church is media savvy and has good public relations firms working for it. There is no excuse for the church to have allowed false hopes to arise among one of the most vulnerable and marginalized groups in the church. The message contained in the clarification letter should have been published at the same time the language of the Honor Code was changed. I wonder why that didn't happen. It's not like it was hard to predict that this action would raise questions.

Because of the harm caused by this misstep in communication, and failure to be sensitive to gay students, it's not surprising that large numbers of BYU students protested the clarification on the same day it was made (https://www.sltrib.com/news/education/2020/03/04/after-byu-honor- code/). Interestingly, I have read in multiple social media accounts that when BYU administration officials approached the group of students who seemed to be leading the largest protest, to explain to them that protests were not allowed on campus without a permit, the officials had in their hands at the time an application for such permit. Ironically, BYU personnel had pre-completed the form for the students. It is clear to me that this opposition to same-sex dating on campus did not come from BYU administration or staff. I think it was directed by the school's governing body, the Church Educational System, whose board is comprised of our church's prophets and apostles.

To help any LGBTQ students who came out as a result of the confusion, and who now feel threatened being on the BYU campus or have now been disowned by their families, a fund was set up to help pay for transfer-related fees. That fund raised over $24,000 from 624 people within hours after being posted online: https://charity.gofundme.com/o/en/campaign/transfer-fund-for-lgbtq-byu-students.

Several months after that BYU Honor Code debacle, in the aftermath of national and worldwide protests about racial injustice sparked by the killing of George Floyd, an additional update to the church's general handbook was released in December 2020. This update included a new instruction for all church members to reject prejudice "of any kind. This includes prejudice based on race, ethnicity, nationality, tribe, gender, age, disability, socioeconomic status, religious belief or nonbelief, and sexual orientation" (https://www.sltrib.com/religion/2020/12/18/lds-handbook-adds-warning/). The reaction to this handbook update that I observed on social media and online generally, among both prominent church supporters and critics alike, was mostly positive. And I think that's appropriate. This update should rightfully be praised. However, I also think it is important to acknowledge the irony that exists in having the church decry prejudice based on sexual orientation. Because when it comes to marriage, current church teachings are, in fact, prejudicial in that regard: they encourage straight church members to marry in a manner that is consistent with their sexual orientation while simultaneously prohibiting gay church members from doing likewise.

If all these changes to the church handbook and BYU Honor Code described above sound confusing, that's because they are. I hope that all this messiness of policy changes, reversals, and hypocritical handbook pronouncements are labor pains, meaning that full equality for all God's children is struggling to be born.

CHAPTER 4:
CAN DOCTRINAL DOUBLING-DOWN CRUSH HOPE?

Chapter synopsis: The fall of 2019 brought my despair to its lowest point as the church's position against church-authorized marriage equality became more firmly entrenched than ever. Two monumental sermons against marriage equality in the church were delivered by our two topmost church leaders in September and October 2019 (the week before and the week after my in-person meeting with the General Authority discussed in Chapter 9).

BYU policy aside, the news of the reversal of the church's 2015 Exclusion Policy for children with gay parents gave me fresh hope. I now wonder though if it might have ironically been one of the worst things to have ever happened for gay church members and their allies. I say that because just a few months after the reversal, it seems like an unprecedented doubling down in doctrinal opposition to marriage equality occurred in new teachings over the pulpit discussed below, coming straight from our prophet and one of his counselors.

I can't help but wonder if they were trying again to prevent support for doctrinal marriage equality from rising up within the church – but this time, they were doing it by preaching more forceful doctrinal messages, rather than by implementing what turned out to be an unworkable policy. Or maybe their aim was to establish a stronger doctrinal position on this issue to bolster the church's legal claims in court battles over religious liberty (e.g., so that the church or any of its affiliated companies or schools can maintain the right to fire employees if they enter into a marriage with someone of their same gender – because religious groups are likely to succeed more in court if their opposition to marriage equality is solidly entrenched doctrinally). Who knows why it's happening? But it is clear that in the fall of 2019, the doctrine opposing marriage equality in the church became more entrenched than ever before.

[Side note: When I refer to doctrine throughout this book, I'm using the dictionary meaning of that word: "a belief or set of beliefs held and taught by a church." I am not using the word doctrine to only mean what I think some church members ascribe to it: a teaching so regularly and universally taught that it is a core, definitional belief (like the concepts that God lives and loves us, Jesus is our Savior, Joseph Smith was a prophet, or other beliefs that fall under any narrow definitions of doctrine described by some church leaders and scholars: https://www.churchofjesuschrist.org/si/questions/what-is-doctrine).

Instead, I'm using a broader definition of doctrine that is based on Doctrine & Covenants 1:38: "whether by [God's] own voice or by the voice of [His] servants, it is the same." While I think that scripture only truly applies when God's spirit actually testifies of the words spoken by leaders (i.e., only then are their words the same as the Lord's voice), I use the word "doctrine" in this book based on a common, broader interpretation of that scripture: that the church should heed the things spoken through church leaders in their capacities as such. In any event, because any policy or position officially maintained by church leaders represents an instruction by the church for how its members should conduct the affairs of their lives, it seems to me that each church policy constitutes a belief about how something should be done – and therefore, policy can be considered doctrine under the above dictionary definition. I think that approach to understanding all policy as a type of doctrine (at least in a sense) is consistent with what one of our apostles and current members of the First Presidency has taught:

> ***"I don't know that it's possible to distinguish between policy and doctrine*** *in a church that believes in continuing revelation and sustains its leader as a prophet." (Dallin H. Oaks, Apostle, https://www.newspapers.com/clip/21138508/partial_transcript_of_ap_interview_with/, 1988)*

For a discussion about how the church's doctrine has always been moving in response to various circumstances and is never static, this podcast episode is great. It features Latter-day Faith host Dan Wotherspoon and Charles R. Harrell, author of the book "This is My Doctrine": The Development of Mormon Theology. http://podcast. latterdayfaith.org/031-what-is-doctrine.]

Have recent prophetic statements further entrenched anti-LGBTQ doctrine?

The first instance of this new doctrinal doubling down against marriage equality in the church happened on September 17, 2019 when our current prophet, President Russell M. Nelson, gave an address at BYU (https://speeches.byu. edu/talks/russell-m-nelson/love-laws-god/). In his remarks, he explained why the Exclusion Policy was modified several months earlier – basically because of compassion and at God's direction. I liked that part of his address. But then he also said prophets and apostles could not change the church's standard that gay sexual behavior is sinful because "truth is truth" and the law of chastity (meaning that sexual relations should only happen between one man and one woman who are legally married) was a divine law. He explained that divine laws are "incontrovertible" and can be compared to unchanging laws of nature, like gravity. While prior church leaders had said before that gay marriage would never be allowed, it was the first time I had heard anyone currently serving as the prophet during the LGBTQ rights era be so blunt. And he went further than any other prophet had before on the topic by comparing the law of chastity to the unvarying laws of nature. He added, "God has not changed *His* definition of marriage."

Now, it was significant to me to hear him say all those things because prior prophets taught repeatedly that God's ideal definition of marriage was polygamy (see Chapter 6). But then subsequent prophets after 1890 taught that polygamy is a sin so severe it is deserving of loss of church membership, which is still the doctrine of the church today.

"If any of our members are found to be practicing plural marriage, they are excommunicated, the most serious penalty the Church can impose. … **More than a century ago God clearly revealed unto His prophet Wilford Woodruff that the practice of plural marriage should be discontinued, which means that it is now against the law of God.** Even in countries where civil or religious law allows polygamy, the Church teaches that marriage must be monogamous and does not accept into its membership those practicing plural marriage" ("What Are People Asking about Us?" Ensign, Nov. 1998, 71–72; https://www. churchofjesuschrist.org/study/general- conference/1998/10/ what-are-people-asking-about-us?lang=eng).

So God's definition of marriage has *in fact* clearly changed at least once already (I'll explain in Chapter 6 how it has actually changed a *few times*). The church has changed other doctrines (stated to have been revealed by, or even spoken in the very voice of, God) many times before. The scriptures teach us that God reveals truth to us "precept upon precept; line upon line...here a little, and there a little" (Isaiah 28:10). I think God gives us further light and knowledge when we are ready for it, but not before. Every doctrine of the church has come to us in that manner:

"If [church members] take the time to read their own history, they will understand that **not a single, significant LDS doctrine has gone unchanged throughout the entire history of the church.**" (Gregory A. Prince, 2017: https://affirmation. org/science-vs-dogma-biology-challenges-the-lds-paradigm/).

Given that history, I don't see <u>any</u> doctrine as being "off the table" when it comes to the possibility for change, which is why the prophet's remarks hurt so much. They seemed inconsistent with the following statements, and many others like them, made by prior church leaders:

"**The canon of scripture is still open; many lines, many precepts, are yet to be added; revelation, surpassing in**

importance and glorious fullness any that has been recorded, is yet to be given to the Church and declared to the world." (James E. Talmage, Apostle, *Articles of Faith*, page 311, 1899; https://www.churchofjesuschrist.org/study/manual/the-pearl-of-great-price-student- manual-2018/the-articles-of-faith/articles-of-faith-1-5-13)

"We need not be surprised if we sometimes find them [our religious predecessors] mistaken in their own conceptions and deductions; **just as the generations who succeed us in unfolding in a larger way some of the yet unlearned truths of the Gospel, will find that we have had some misconceptions and made some wrong deductions in our day and time. The book of knowledge is never a sealed book.** It is never 'completed and forever closed;' rather **it is an eternally open book**, in which one may go on constantly discovering new truths and **modifying our knowledge of old ones.**" (B.H. Roberts, *New Witnesses for God: The Book of Mormon*, pg 503-504, 1909; https://www.churchofjesuschrist.org/study/ensign/1986/03/b-h-roberts-seeker-after- truth?lang=eng).

"**The last word has not been spoken on any subject.** Streams of living water shall yet flow from the Eternal Spring who is the source of all truth. **There are more things we do not know about the doctrines of salvation than there are things we do know.**" (Bruce R. McConkie, "A New Commandment: Save Thyself and Thy Kindred!" *Ensign*, 1976; https://www.churchofjesuschrist.org/study/manual/doctrines-of-the-gospel-student- manual/23-restoration)

But despite the gloom and dread I felt upon hearing the prophet's comments, I was able to interpret them in a way to still keep alive my hope for a change that would eventually allow the church to adopt marriage equality in our doctrine. I wrote these thoughts in my journal shortly after President Nelson's address:

*Maybe the prophet was just saying that God was the source of change, not church leaders – maybe it was just his way of saying "don't shoot the messenger; God hasn't told us to change anything, so we just can't do it on our own." So maybe I could consider the prophet's "truth is truth" teaching to mean that "truth" is just whatever God says it is – period – and, therefore, since I know God has said different things at various times over the centuries, maybe today's "truth" doesn't **have** to be tomorrow's "truth." Maybe, like Jesus defied gravity when He walked on water, and we learned how to defy gravity with planes, God will reveal in the future something to allow the church to defy or expand the current law of chastity? Can even the prophet limit God from expanding upon His truth with us in the future? Teachings from prophets in the scriptures and in our modern era have been reversed later on important stuff. The prophet isn't omniscient, even though God is, so maybe I can still keep hoping?*

Then, a little over a week later, we had an experience with a General Authority here in Massachusetts (see Chapter 9). In our interview together, the General Authority said repeatedly and forcefully that the law of chastity would never change. The strength with which he talked about that suggests to me that there may be a renewed, unified message from top church leadership on that point (or perhaps General Authorities are taking their cues from President Nelson's talk). While other General Authorities with whom I have spoken in the past have never said the law of chastity was something that <u>could</u> change, they also have never shut down the possibility of change in any area of the church. To the contrary, my discussions with them about ongoing change in other areas in the church, and about how we all need to be sensitive about LGBTQ issues, had left me feeling hopeful before. But after speaking with the General Authority on September 28, 2019 I felt chastised for hoping. Because the prophet spoke at BYU with stronger words than any prior prophet on the unchanging definition of the law of chastity, many General Authorities may now be feeling a need to strongly condemn any hope for doctrinal change regarding marriage equality – and I wouldn't doubt if they have been given specific instruction to do so.

Is it fair for us to expect LGBTQ church members to just trust in the Lord to work things out?

My reaction to President Nelson's 2019 talk at BYU might strike some church members as one that is inappropriate – because I ended up still hoping for a change in the law of chastity notwithstanding his suggestion that change is not possible. In fact, several people have told me that hoping for change in our doctrine is not what God wants us to do. Instead, they recommend I simply trust in Christ – that through His mercy, everything will be worked out so that LGBTQ people will be happy in the afterlife. I can understand that thinking. In fact, in many situations, I think it is comforting that a simple trust-in-the-Lord approach to resolve difficult questions is a mainstream teaching of the church: https://www.churchofjesuschrist.org/study/general-conference/2019/10/17oaks. But when the doctrine of the church itself is what is causing pain, as it is in the LGBTQ context, trusting that God will just somehow work things out, without anguished church members also being allowed to freely hope for a change in the harmful doctrine, makes that notion seem very unkind to me.

To understand better why I say that, I need to explain a bit about our religion's belief in the afterlife (for any readers who might not be Latter-day Saints). We believe that all good people will go to heaven. But after final judgement, there will actually be three degrees, or levels, of heaven. To get to the highest degree possible, where the most joy can be found, heterosexual marriage in the temple is required. It is speculated that only heterosexual couples will be allowed in that highest degree because spiritual procreation, where family life and parenting continue forever, will be a fundamental part of eternal life there. Unless there is a change in doctrine that allows for the possibility that gay couples could spiritually procreate too (see Chapter 6 for a discussion of that concept), the church-approved version of the trust-in-the-Lord notion inevitably results in the vast majority of gay people needing to believe that they will be happy having a core part of their identity get stripped away and reversed in heaven (or, if their sexual orientation isn't changed in heaven, they need to believe they will be happy not feeling romantic love toward their spouse for eternity).

Some people say that's okay because everyone will be changed in remarkable ways in that highest degree of heaven. For most of us, that just means envisioning a sort of eternal self- improvement process. But it's different for gay people. A fundamental part of that highest heavenly life is presumably predicated on being in a type of relationship that, for the vast majority of them, feels opposite to their very nature and causes psychological trauma. Their vision of that afterlife is accordingly very bleak. And yet, the way our church leaders are currently teaching the trust-in-the-Lord doctrine requires that gay church members find a way to believe that they will nevertheless be happy in that traumatic vision of heaven. That can make them view their sexuality as something that is fundamentally at odds with heavenly joy. It can make them think they were born defective, which studies have shown frequently results in suicidal ideation (see Chapter 8). Unless church leaders allow the trust-in-the-Lord notion to at least imagine ambiguity about gay couples being in the highest degree of heaven, it unavoidably results in a degrading view of a gay person's state in this life.

[Side note: I think church leaders' current use of the trust-in-the-Lord notion is a sort of theological crutch they rely on, to help them walk a fine line in areas where current doctrines result in similar "sad heaven" outlooks. The doctrine of eternal polygamy is another example of this. While some women may not object to the thought or even welcome it for various reasons, the vast majority of women in the church seem to dread the idea that they might be a plural wife for eternity (https://religionnews. com/2016/07/20/mormon-women-fear-eternal-polygamy-study-shows/).

For me, the trust-in-the-Lord teaching can be a cruel one in that context as well. But in that area, doctrinal ambiguity provides at least some reprieve. Several quotes from past apostles and prophets, and statements in manuals published by the church, indicate that polygamy is not required for exaltation (https://www.fairmormon.org/answers/Mormonism_and_polygamy/

Brigham_Young_said_that_the_only_men_who_ become_gods_are_those_ that_practice_polygamy#Question:_Is_plural_marriage_required_in_order_to_ achieve_e xaltation.3F). And a growing number of mainstream commentators in the church argue that church teachings are clear that no one will be forced to practice polygamy in heaven at all (https://www.gregtrimble.com/what-every- mormon-re-ally-needs-to-know-about-polygamy/). All of that provides at least some semblance of hope for most women in the church.

Unfortunately though, there are no quotes by any top church leader suggesting gay couples will be allowed in heaven. So no helpful ambiguity in doctrine exists to assist gay church members in trusting that the Lord will somehow make heaven a happy place for them.]

The harm caused by applying the current trust-in-the-Lord teaching of the church to gay people became clearest to me when I applied it to my own situation as a father of a gay son and a happily married straight man. It causes anguish to my soul to think about Wes having to always strive to be alone in this life, constantly struggling to avoid thoughts that he might be better off dead – because then he at least wouldn't be broken. And it hurts to think of him potentially finding a husband with whom he builds a lifelong, committed love, just to have that joy ripped away from him in heaven.

[Side note: I realize Wes may not ever find the right man to marry, or that his marriage may start out well but end in divorce, the same as any straight marriage. I plan to love and support him, no matter what. I don't want anyone to interpret my advocacy for gay marriage equality as me pressuring Wes to have a perfect family, any more than I expect my straight children to have perfect heterosexual marriages and families – which I do not.]

I can't imagine heaven as a happy place without picturing Cheryl there with me as my wife. So I find it impossible to hope in any teaching that means Wes will have to view himself as a defective human being in this life or stop being with his future husband in heaven – all so he can instead be with a woman for eternity – someone to whom he was never attracted, and whom he never loved, in this life. With teachings about heaven that are so dismal, even under the trust-in- the-Lord notion, I don't blame Wes for needing to distance himself from the church.

Think about that – especially those of us in happy, heterosexual/uniform-orientation marriages – please stop for a minute and really think about that. Would you be able to devote your life to the church if it taught that you needed to find joy in a rigid, traumatic prospect of heaven? How would you feel about attending, supporting, and serving in a church that taught you that, in the best case scenario for you, inheriting the highest degree of heaven meant you had to end your marriage, switch (or at least ignore) the way you naturally have craved intimate human connection, and then be with a new *same-sex* spouse for the rest of eternity? I don't know of anyone who would feel good about that - even if they believe that they'll understand things differently and feel differently when they're in the next life. No matter what, most happily married straight folks still have gut feelings of fear, worry and despair over separating from their spouses and then being married forever instead to someone of the same sex. I think that is because, when we straight folks are really honest with ourselves, we realize how much of our personal identity relates to how we are wired to love.

[Side note: The idea that LGBTQ identity will be completely wiped out in heaven has been powerfully described as genocide by writer Blaire Ostler: http://www. blaireostler.com/journal/2019/9/19/celestial-genocide.]

Plus, I don't believe any of us will just feel and think completely differently about ourselves or our loved ones in the afterlife anyway. Our scriptures teach that the "same sociality which exists among us here will exist among us there, only it will be coupled with eternal glory" (Doctrine & Covenants 130:2). Now, I don't know if that "same sociality" concept means sexual intimacy will be part of an exalted heterosexual relationship in the highest degree of heaven. To my knowledge, the church has no formal doctrinal position on that. While we do have scriptural passages that discuss marriage being essential to enter the highest degree of heaven (Doctrine & Covenants 131:2 and 132:14-15), there are no verses that discuss exactly what type of intimacy will exist between spouses there – or how spiritual procreation technically occurs. Because our resurrected bodies will have only spirit, not blood, it is hard to imagine procreation occurring in the same way there as it does here. But to me the "same sociality" at least means that the nature of our relationships with people here, and how we ideally should feel about them, won't change in heaven. That concept of the nature of family relationships staying the same is consistent with church teachings and thoughts of church scholars:

> "Latter-day Saints believe [becoming heirs of God] includes eternal family relationships. Latter-day Saint scripture teaches that the 'same sociality which exists among us here will exist among us there [in eternity], only it will be coupled with eternal glory' (Doctrine & Covenants 130:2). The promise of growing to become more like God and ultimately returning to His presence with our families motivates Latter-day Saints to do their best to live according to the teachings of Jesus Christ." (https://newsroom.churchofjesuschrist.org/article/heaven)

> "[Joseph] Smith wrote in a canonized revelation that 'that same sociality which exists among us here will exist among us there, only it will be coupled with eternal glory, which glory we do not now enjoy.'...**Another way of saying this is that for Mormons, heaven is relational, not situational. It is not where you are but in what kind of relationship you find yourself that determines the degree of blessedness or perdition.**" (Terryl L. Givens, *Feeding the Flock: The Foundations of Mormon Thought: Church and Praxis,* 2017)

All of that leads me to think there at least has to be some form of special intimacy that would exist between spouses in eternity – because a unique kind of intimacy that is not found in any other personal relationship is what defines the nature of the spousal relationship in this life.

Without some sort of spousal intimacy, the marriage relationship in heaven wouldn't seem much different from a relationship between two really close friends here (who might also happen to be parents together – like a divorced couple who remain close to make co-parenting easier).

[Side note: While we don't know if spousal intimacy in heaven will be sexual, I believe church teachings maintain that something akin to physical mortal intimacy, that carries similar powers of bonding and procreation, will need to exist among spouses there. But the church also teaches that the biology of resurrected, eternal bodies in heaven will be fundamentally different than the biology of mortal bodies in this life. I don't think anyone can authoritatively say gay couples won't be capable of procreating in heaven too. If we are already finding ways scientifically that might allow two same-sex people to actually reproduce biologically here on earth (https:// medium.com/neodotlife/same-sex-reproduction-artificial-gametes-2739206aa4c0), it doesn't seem like much of a stretch to think that God might know a way that they could spiritually reproduce in heaven, right?

I also want to acknowledge that for some asexual church members, the idea of sexual intimacy being required in heaven can also seem traumatic. To me, that reiterates the importance of us needing to be careful about teaching ideas regarding the intimacy between exalted spouses or about procreation in heaven for which we simply don't have scriptural support. So maybe it would be best if we started teaching that spousal intimacy in heaven and eternal gender are concepts that we just aren't able to understand in mortality – because the nature of our Heavenly Parents' lives and existence is beyond our mortal comprehension. By teaching with an emphasis on the unknown like that, each church member might better find hope in an eternal existence that doesn't frighten them.]

No matter what type of intimacy spouses in heaven might share, happily-married straight church members benefit from believing their feeling of closeness to their spouses will last forever. In happy marriages, physical intimacy is almost always an important part of that sense of closeness (https://journals. sagepub.com/doi/full/10.1177/0956797617691361). So I have found it surprising when some people have told me they believe gay church members should have faith in a trust-in-the-Lord approach, because Christ-like love will permeate eternal marriage, compensating for any lack of marital intimacy between people who are required to be in mixed- orientation marriages there. Or they believe all exalted spouses, including straight ones, will only have Christ-like love in their marriages, not romantic love. I think those lines of thought are inconsistent with church teachings about the importance of romantic love:

> "You [young adults] are old enough now to fall in love – not
> the puppy love of elementary years, not the confused love of

the teens, but the full-blown love of eligible men and women, newly matured, ready for life. **I mean romantic love,** with all the full intense meaning of the word, with all of the power and turbulence and frustration, the yearning, the restraining, and all of the peace and beauty and sublimity of love. **No experience can be more beautiful, no power more compelling, more exquisite.** Or, if misused, no suffering is more excruciating than that connected with love." (Boyd K. Packer, Apostle, *Eternal Love*, Salt Lake City: Deseret Book Co., 1973, p. 6; https://www.churchofjesuschrist.org/study/ensign/1982/10/the-gospel-and-romantic- love?lang=eng)

Church teachings also maintain that marital sex is a sacred act that increases our ability to love our spouse in a unique way (https://speeches.byu.edu/talks/jeffrey-r-holland/souls-symbols- sacraments/). Physical intimacy seems to have the potential to elevate the love between spouses to a special type of love that is uniquely different from any other sort of selfless and pure love we can experience. So I don't think it's fair for gay church members to be expected to trust that heaven will be a happy place for them if marital intimacy there requires a mixed-orientation marriage, or simply not experienced at all. Both of those situational dynamics result in trauma for most gay church members in this life, so we shouldn't expect them to trust that somehow the Lord will make it so such circumstances will bring completely opposite feelings to them in heaven. That seems to contradict the idea that the same sociality we have here will exist there.

[Side note: I have also had people tell me they don't believe gay spousal love can be in heaven because it isn't as powerful or pure as straight spousal love – because the ability to procreate is lacking in gay couples. I think that is too limited a view of the purpose of sex within marriage. While I believe procreation is one of the divine purposes of sex within a heterosexual marriage, I don't think it is the primary purpose of marital sex, even for a heterosexual couple. If I were to think that, I would be suggesting that an infertile heterosexual married couple's physical intimacy is not as meaningful or loving as the intimacy expressed between a husband and wife who are both able to have kids. And I don't think that's right. I think it's better to

view procreation as a wonderful outcome that sometimes occurs from heterosexual married sex than as the primary purpose for it. Take, for example, the situation where an elderly widow and widower who have each already been sealed to their respective deceased spouses decide to marry. They are unable to procreate together in this life (because of old age) and are unable to procreate together in heaven as well (because our doctrine says they will each be with their respective deceased spouse to whom they are sealed, not with each other). The fact that heterosexual marriage is allowed by the church in situations like that, where the spouses will not be pro-creating together either in this life or in the next life, illustrates that marital sex is viewed as a positive thing by the church, even when procreation between spouses will not ever be possible.]

In any event, asking gay people to just trust in the Lord and the power of the Atonement to make everything good for them in the afterlife seems, at first glance, like a hopeful, compassionate doctrinal loophole. But it ironically turns into in a demeaning and cruel sentiment when the implications are fully considered. Under our current doctrine, those unavoidable implications mean, even in the most merciful scenario possible, that they're being asked to believe joy will come for them by having the very way they love and connect intimately be changed or ignored forever. In short, without at least admitting that a trust-in-the-Lord approach might mean God could exalt gay couples too, it will ironically remain a teaching that dehumanizes gay sexual orientation and therefore harms gay church members in this life. And that needs to change if we desire to be a church of Christ's love. As inspiring church scholar and poet, Carol Lynn Pearson, has said:

> "God wants us to be happy in the afterlife, but surely God also wants us to be happy here. **If we see something terrible going on here, it's not our task to say 'Well, that's too bad, but it's going to be all for the best in the afterlife.' We are here on earth to make things better.**" (https://religionnews.com/2016/07/20/ mormon-women-fear- eternal-polygamy-study-shows/)

I hope the church can make things better in this life by, at the very least, allowing for doctrinal ambiguity about whether gay couples can exist in heaven. That would allow a trust-in-the-Lord fallback approach to at least not be harmful.

But my hope doesn't stop there. Because of what I have learned about Christ-like love through having a gay son, my vision of an ideal heaven has expanded beyond the monochromatic heteronormative version of it that is taught by the church. I think that's the power of diversity: to help us learn to love more purely. So I sure hope diversity will continue to exist in ALL its colors and variety in heaven for everyone's sake there. Otherwise, I will mourn the lack of love for others who are different from me (assuming I make it there).

[Side note: It should be noted that our belief in spousal love continuing in heaven arguably makes our doctrine more traumatizing for gay people than the doctrines of many conservative Protestant sects and Catholicism. While same- gender relationships are prohibited in many of those denominations, there are also several honorable paths to celibacy for men and women available. Also, their versions of the afterlife are affirmatively non-sexual and do not contemplate anyone in sealed, eternal marriages. So the despair is worse under our doctrine because, for example, a gay Catholic only has to make it through this life, and then they will be equal with everyone else in the next life – but a gay Latter-day Saint has to make it through this life and somehow also try to find joy in the prospect of continuing to remain unequal with other people after this life as well.]

What can our feelings tell us about doctrine?

When I think of the psychological harm caused to LGBTQ church members by our doctrines on marriage, gender, and family, and when I think of church teachings that exclude loving couples from heaven just because they're loving each other in a way that's consistent with how God created them, I feel sadness, darkness, and hopelessness. In our religion, we place a ton of emphasis on trusting the feelings of God's spirit to tell us what is true (Moroni 10:4-5). We know that God's spirit is one of truth (John 15:26). We also know that the fruit of that spirit is love, joy, peace, gentleness, and goodness (Galatians 5:22).

I have found that God's spirit fills my heart the most when I am focused on loving others. Perhaps that is because simply loving others helps us become less sinful and more like God: "And above all things have fervent charity among yourselves: for charity shall cover the multitude of sins" (1 Peter 4:8). It feels right to me to think of the wide range/multitude of sin as simply anything we do that hurts someone else, because that places us in disharmony with Christ's principal commandment to love one another (John 15:12):

> "The experience of sin is not an unalterable state we inhabit; it is a felt disharmony. The unhappiness of sin is nothing more than our spirit rebelling against a condition alien to its true nature. We have fallen out of alignment with God. The separation from God is not punishment inflicted by God, but the consequence of an existential reality of our own making." (Fiona Givens, *The God Who Weeps*, https://ldsquotations.com/author/terryl-and-fiona-givens/, 2012)

The essence of God is love (1 John 4:8). So as His offspring, we go against our divine nature when we fail to love. *That* is sin. And it's why, if we're humble enough to be aware of being unloving, we usually feel bad about it. I regret how I viewed gay marriage before my heart was softened and my perspective on the issue changed – in other words: before I repented of my hurtful thinking. Now, when I imagine Wes finding the love of his life and being in a fulfilling marital relationship with a man he loves, like how I love his mother, I have joyful feelings that seem in harmony with God's love. But when I think of a loving spousal relationship like that not being allowed to continue in heaven, the feelings of the Spirit are absent. It feels wrong to think I might enjoy the continuation of my marital bliss with Cheryl after this life, but that same joy is not possible for any gay couples.

And so, a simple trust-in-the-Lord approach to solving everything for LGBTQ people without also hoping for a change to our current doctrine produces feelings for me that are the *opposite* of God's spirit. I cannot believe that God wants me to have faith in the status quo. To truly believe Christ will work things out, I have to believe that His true doctrine has yet to be revealed – and that when it is shown, it will provide a way for a gay person to have the same degree of happiness in heaven as a straight person without switching the natural "sociality" they have had their whole mortal lives. Otherwise, our concept of heaven is downright scary for around 2-10% of the earth's population (which is the estimated number of LGBTQ people, depending on the study – see Chapter 1). And it would mean God treats us all differently just based on our biological makeups – which contradicts many scriptures, such as:

> "Of a truth I perceive that **God is no respecter of persons**: but in every nation he that feareth him, and worketh righteousness, is accepted with him" (Acts 10:34-35).

> "[God] inviteth them all to come unto him and partake of his goodness; and he denieth none that come unto him, black and white, bond and free, male and female; and he remembereth the heathen; and **all are alike unto God**." (2 Nephi 26:33).

So, because I don't see any other way to believe that Christ will be fair and loving, I still held onto my hope for change, even after I heard President Nelson's BYU address. I guess I'm a determined optimist and really take God at His word when he says that faith, hope, and love are enduring attributes and that love is paramount (1 Corinthians 13:13). I was so persistent in my optimism that I was emotionally still ready to go back to church without missing a week, even following our family's in-person ordeal with the General Authority that happened the week after President Nelson gave his talk at BYU (see Chapter 9).

[Side note: Despite a family decision to take a "church break" for 9 weeks at the end of 2019 (to try to help one another heal from our experience with the General Authority), I still went to church alone a few times during that period, including when I saw that our ward elders quorum planned to discuss President Oaks' General Conference talk "Two Great Commandments" in class one week (my thoughts on that talk are found in the next section). Our entire family also attended church together again for the Christmas 2019 services at our ward. I expect I will be the only member of my family who attends church with any sort of regularity going forward.]

Since that negative experience, my optimism increases as I study more in depth about what the scriptures teach on the subject of equality. I love how my heart feels when I read the following commentary on the above Book of Mormon verse that states "all are alike unto God:"

"There is no social category of life circumstance that prevents a person from being worthy to sit down at God's table. God invites all. There is no price. No one is excluded...with no strings attached. Biblical scholars point to the use of merism in the story of the creation. **Merism is a rhetorical device in which two ends of the spectrum are named as a way to encompass the entire spectrum in between.** In Genesis, this means that God created the light and the dark, but also every point of dawn and dusk in between. God created the earth and the firmament, but also every place between the seas and the stars. **God created males and females, but also every person who identifies as bi, trans, non-binary, or queer. The two points encompass the spectrum, they don't exclude it. Merism seems to be employed here [2 Nephi 26:33].** God welcomes not just black and white people, but also every shade of pink and brown skin in between. Every social division of Jacob's society is disrupted by God embracing the spectrum of human life. **If modern-day readers were to create their own list of categories used to divide people...we would probably add heterosexual/homosexual, transgender/cis-gender, and immigrant/citizen, among others. Regardless of which groups are named, the message is the same: All are alike unto God.**" Rev. Dr. Fatimah Salleh and Margaret Olsen Hemming, *The Book of Mormon for the Least of These, Volume 1,* 89-90, https://www.amazon.com/Book-Mormon-Least-These/dp/1948218232/ ref=tmm_pap_swatch_0?_encoding=UTF8&qid=&sr=).

Can we keep Christ's two great commandments and still hope for doctrinal marriage equality?

My optimism and hope for change were diminished greatly just six days after that experience with the General Authority when, on October 5, 2019, I listened to

President Oaks deliver a sermon regarding LGBTQ issues in General Conference that church members around the world are encouraged to watch (https://www. churchofjesuschrist.org/study/general- conference/2019/10/35oaks). In his talk "*Two* Great Commandments," (italics in the original) he spoke about what Jesus taught were the two greatest commandments, which are: 1) to love God with full devotion; and 2) to love others as ourselves (Matthew 22:37-39). He said that, when we're trying to show love to others, we should be careful not to forget the importance of everyone still needing to show their love for God by obeying all other commandments as well. He seemed to indicate that the two great commandments can conflict with one another or that there is a ranking, or order of importance, between them. He said:

> "[O]ur zeal to keep [the] second commandment must not cause us to forget the first, to love God with all our heart, soul, and mind. We show that love by keeping His commandments." (https://www.churchofjesuschrist.org/study/ general- conference/2019/10/35oaks)

President Oaks then referenced teachings from President Nelson's BYU talk mentioned above addressing LGBTQ issues, and said that the commandments of the law of chastity and the law of marriage apply with particular significance to LGBTQ individuals specifically. While I don't like how President Oaks singled out LGBTQ people as being more prone to sin than other people, I was grateful to at least hear him use the term *LGBT* instead of *same-sex attracted.* Even though I was nervous about where President Oaks was heading in his talk by ranking the two great commandments as he had, I remember appreciating that shift in terminology in the moment I was listening to his words. I recalled he was not always willing to respect the terms *gay* and *lesbian* as personal identifiers in the past:

> "We should note that the words *homosexual, lesbian,* and *gay* are adjectives to describe particular thoughts, feelings, or behaviors. We should refrain from using these words as nouns to identify particular conditions or specific persons. Our

religious doctrine dictates this usage. It is wrong to use these words to denote a condition, because this implies that a person is consigned by birth to a circumstance in which he or she has no choice in respect to the critically important matter of sexual behavior." (https://www.churchofjesuschrist.org/study/ensign/1995/10/same-gender- attraction?lang=eng, 1995)

Given that past teaching from President Oaks, when I heard him use *LGBT* in his General Conference talk, I started to wonder if that shift might indicate his views on LGBTQ matters in general were also changing. I have since thought that, at the very least, the shift in terminology shows that his prior teaching (that we should refrain from using those terms) was not founded in any sort of divine revelation.

As I continued listening to President Oaks speak, I quickly learned that his views on LGBTQ matters remained mostly unchanged. I was disappointed when I heard him next state that a temple marriage (which, as discussed, the church denies to gay people) was required for the highest degree of heaven, and that "[e]ternal life [there] includes the creative powers inherent in the combination of male and female." While the part about temple marriage being required was not new or disappointing, the line about male and female creative powers was upsetting to me, because I can find no scriptural support for that assertion. Even the scriptures cited in the written version of his talk in support of the combination of male and female eternal procreative powers (Doctrine & Covenants 131:1-4 and 1 Corinthians 11:11) do not talk about the specifics of how spiritual procreation actually occurs at all.

[Side note: Before I go any further, I want to reiterate that my intention in writing this book is not to criticize our church leaders. I know President Oaks is a good, faithful, and loving man who is trying to serve as he feels God desires him to. I sustain him in his calling and don't presume to know more than he does.

In fact, I remember teaching some youth once as a bishop this very idea: that the church may not allow gay marriage because spiritual procreation was only possible through the combined efforts of a male exalted being and a female exalted being. I am sorry for the pain I'm sure I caused in the hearts of the few LGBTQ youth who were in our ward at the time (including my own son, who I didn't know was gay then). I apologize for teaching a non- canonical and speculative concept like that.

If President Oaks reads this book (I have shared it with him), I hope he views my words in this section as just providing feedback, as the parent of a gay child who has learned to open my mind more than it was before, that may possibly help him be more sensitive with his words in the future. And I hope the sharing of my open and honest emotional reactions and thoughts to his talk will help other church members recognize the types of teachings that can cause pain for gay church members and their families – so maybe they can reach out to let them know they are loved if similar teachings are taught again in the future.

Also, I believe that one way we can sustain our leaders is to not expect them to be perfect. Another way is to let them know when something they have said or done has caused us pain. Without giving feedback, I think we are unfairly withholding information that might help our leaders as they seek continued inspiration. By not explaining why their words hurt us, I think we can unfairly leave our church leaders uninformed of our ministering needs. Paul's letter to Timothy helps explain my intent:

> *"Them that sin rebuke before all, that others also may fear. I charge thee before God, and the Lord Jesus Christ, and the elect angels, that thou observe these things without preferring one before another, doing nothing by partiality." (1 Timothy 5:20-21)*

I feel I am simply discussing publicly ("before all") the pain I have felt because of President Oaks' words, without favoring him just because he is a church leader (without "partiality"), in the hopes that other church leaders and church members might perhaps better avoid ("fear") repeating similar teachings that cause pain.]

While I was bothered by those comments from President Oaks about only straight marriages being allowed in heaven, I became even more discouraged as he continued in his remarks, stating how great it is that God loves everyone so much that even people who don't obey the laws of chastity and marriage can still end up happy in one of the two <u>lower</u> kingdoms of heaven.

> "But **there are many we love**, including some who have the restored gospel, **who do not believe in or choose not to follow God's commandments about marriage and the law of**

chastity. What about them? God's doctrine shows that all of us are His children and that He has created us to have joy. Modern revelation teaches that **God has provided a plan for a mortal experience in which all can choose obedience to seek His highest blessings or make choices that lead to one of the less glorious kingdoms.** Because of God's great love for all of His children, **those lesser kingdoms are still more wonderful than mortals can comprehend.**" (https://www.churchofjesuschrist. org/study/general- conference/2019/10/35oaks)

To my ear, President Oaks had basically just taught that we don't need to worry if church doctrine causes mental health issues and emotional turmoil for LGBTQ individuals who try to follow it, because they have the option to disobey and still inherit a happy place in one of the lower kingdoms of heaven anyway. That seemed like a cold and uncharitable teaching to me because it implies many gay people will be satisfactorily happy in heaven even though they won't remain married to their same-sex spouses and even though they will have less joy than people in the highest degree of heaven – all simply because they chose to follow a path that would provide them sound mental health in this life. It sounded to me like President Oaks was viewing the decision of those individuals to maintain good mental health in this temporary, mortal life as a fair trade-off for them having less joy throughout all of eternity.

Besides, one of the lesser kingdoms of happiness will be populated by "honorable men of the earth" (Doctrine & Covenants 76:76). Why the church's extensive missionary effort if not to try to make ALL God's blessings available to ALL God's children? Why not just assume that all those honorable people will likewise be just fine inheriting a lesser kingdom, without our mission-ary-minded interference?

[Side note: Someone visiting my congregation a few weeks after President Oaks gave his talk suggested to me an analogy to help me get comfortable with that line of thought. They said maybe I should be okay with Wes being relegated to a lower kingdom of heaven because parents often see their kids pursue career choices that limit them financially – but those kids are happy anyway. Their son decided to

become a plumber even though they wanted him to be a doctor – but their son is actually happier being a plumber. So the analogy goes that maybe Wes will actually be happier just being an angel in a lesser kingdom of heaven, instead of being an exalted god in the highest degree of heaven, I guess?

*I think that's a faulty comparison because the mental health effects of repressing one's sexual orientation are much more significant than those associated with just being stuck in the wrong career. A gay church member who cannot live with the depression that can come from needing to always **avoid** falling in love, trying to make a mixed-orientation marriage work, or needing to have their sexuality reversed in the afterlife, opts for the only path that will provide them hope and good mental health here and now – leave the church to try to find a same-sex spouse. Many aren't given a fair chance at exaltation under current church doctrine because they have to leave the church to stay healthy. In the analogy, they aren't given a fair or legitimate choice to become a doctor because the path to becoming one is immeasurably more difficult for them than it is for other people. The cards are impossibly stacked against them. Besides, anyone can change their mind and switch careers, but LGBTQ people can't stop being themselves. Those who can't be healthy and stay in the church (which is the vast majority of LGBTQ church members) are essentially forced to become a plumber under our current doctrine.]*

As I listened to President Oaks' talk, I wondered how his teachings would affect the emotional well-being of my family as we hear those teachings taught repeatedly over the next who-knows-how-long until the church's position against doctrinal marriage equality hopefully changes.

General Conference talks are taught as part of Sunday classes or in sermons, so President Oaks' talk will presumably be discussed by people in the church for many years to come. That is hard to consider, as his talk teaches that we can feel justified and derive comfort in thinking that LGBTQ people who aren't obeying church standards will be just fine inheriting a lesser kingdom of glory in heaven. When I think about how such "disobedient" LGBTQ people have almost universally had to choose between maintaining good mental health or following church rules, the notion that we should feel comfortable with them being relegated to a lesser kingdom seems incredibly harsh.

President Oaks did say toward the end of his talk that everyone should be kind and civil toward LGBTQ people, even if they disagree with them. And he ended by praising women for their efforts in helping build up the church.

Those parts of his talk - about being kind and praising women - I liked. But, as noted, many of his other remarks were disturbing to me. Every time a church leader teaches concepts that treat LGBTQ people differently from other people, it's like poking an open wound – a reminder that my son isn't treated fairly in the church, and neither are other gay people I know and love. But I thought President Oaks' words were even more demeaning of gay people than messages on LGBTQ matters that I have heard him or other church leaders deliver before. To my view, he basically had just relieved straight church members from feeling true compassion and empathy, giving them license to feel like they are being adequately loving by just teaching obedience. Sure, he talked about love and civility toward others. But he seemed to qualify that tremendously.

It seemed like President Oaks was giving church members instructions for loving LGBTQ individuals in a way that seems passive-aggressive, certainly not unconditional love. He didn't include much by way of specifics about how to actually show compassion (i.e., his words did not clarify or redact the prior comments he's made about why families might want to treat their adult gay kids and their partners differently on family occasions and not introduce them to their friends, etc.: https://newsroom.churchofjesuschrist.org/article/interview-oaks-wickman-same- gender-attraction). While he talked about being kind and respectful, he also said "Our walk. . . denies support to any who lead people away from the Lord." In my opinion, that is a line that some may use to justify treating LGBTQ people differently from others – if, for example, parents think their gay kid being around the family along with their partner or spouse is leading younger siblings away from the church. I have heard of many examples of parents who have that sort of mentality – who think that just by being themselves and living a "gay lifestyle," their kid is trying to lead others astray.

Since President Oaks' talk, I have seen social media reports of church members using the talk's rationale (that obeying God is more important than loving others) to condemn and distance themselves from LGBTQ family members and friends. And it seems clear that other General Authorities are embracing the construct of a hierarchy that exists between the two great commandments as well. This first became apparent to me two months later, on December 6, 2019. During a news conference to discuss a proposed bill in the U.S. Congress (the Fairness for All Act), which tries to balance religious liberty concerns with LGBTQ rights, Elder Jack N. Gerard said the following:

> "[The Church is supportive of this bill] because it's consistent with the teachings of the Savior. **We aspire to live the two great commandments: to love the Lord by keeping His commandments and *secondarily* to love our neighbor as ourselves.**" (Jack N. Gerard, General Authority Seventy, with Ronald A. Rasband, Apostle, present and presiding at the conference, https://twitter.com/ChurchNewsroom/status/1204232675222908928, 2019)

When I first saw that statement, I was sad to see another General Authority embrace the notion that the first great commandment is superior to the second, rather than that the two commandments are equal and interconnected. I even looked up the definition of "secondarily" to see if perhaps it could just mean "second" – i.e., to simply denote that there is more than one (like how Jesus seemed to use the word "second" when He taught that there are two great commandments, not just one). But to my chagrin, the dictionary says the word "secondarily" only means a "secondary or less important factor" or a "subsequent consequence," not just "more than one."

Four months later, on February 11, 2020, Elder Terence M. Vinson gave an address at BYU that further underscored the influence that President Oaks' talk seems to be having among other General Authorities. In his remarks, Elder Vinson said:

"The **order and emphasis given by the Savior is critical. We cannot supplant the first commandment — the great commandment — with the second…And we cannot disregard the first commandment while purporting to live the second**. We must live both, but we must never allow our love for others to work against our love for God and our desire to keep His commandments…Some interpret a desire to love others with a need to embrace their life choices. There are many today who believe that to love someone means that we cannot disagree with their life choices. This belief is false! … Our first responsibility is to God and to His teachings of absolute truth, and to His commandments." (Terence M. Vinson, General Authority Seventy, https://speeches.byu.edu/speakers/terence-m-vinson/, 2020)

I am truly saddened that these three leaders of our church seem to now teach that the two great commandments should be ranked in importance, or can even be at odds with one another, instead of beautifully completing one another equally. As I'll describe below, I wonder if that is a misinterpretation of the New Testament, which shows how the two great commandments are functionally intertwined: we can't obey one without doing the other.

That being said, two months later, on May 1, 2020, Sister Sandra Rogers, international vice president at BYU and former Relief Society general board member (2012 – 2017), spoke at the general session of the BYU Women's Conference, cosponsored by the Relief Society (https://womensconference. byu.edu/sites/womensconference.ce.byu.edu/files/sandra_rogers_0.p df). Sister Rogers said, "When we are fully obedient to the first commandment, we cannot help but obey the second." She hinted at no prioritization between the two great commandments, contrary to President Oaks and Elders Gerard and Vinson. Her talk was appropriately titled "Gather All Safely in Christ."

President Oaks' talk makes me wonder if he actually thinks that the best way to love LGBTQ people is for us to just tell them they need to keep the law of chastity. But I have to be honest: so long as that means Wes has to always be striving to remain alone or live in a mixed-orientation marriage, my parental instincts can't support that hope. My only hope in order to balance my love for my son with my desire that he can be in full fellowship with me in my religion again someday, is a hope that my church will one day change its doctrine.

[Side note: President Oaks' talk received much criticism online after General Conference, including from many non-LGBTQ people and people without LGBTQ family members. My feelings resonate well with the words of this particular commentator, Jana Riess: https://www.sltrib.com/religion/2019/10/11/jana-riess-oaks-oaks/.]

President Oaks' talk also cut deep wounds in my faith because what he taught about the relationship between the two great commandments is the opposite of what I have been teaching in my home and in my church callings for years. I have taught many times that obedience to church rules (i.e., showing our love for God by obeying His commandments) was important because of the way that can remind us to be more kind and loving to others each day – because charity is the most important thing we can learn in the gospel. Faithfulness without charity is nothing (1 Corinthians 13:1-2). But President Oaks basically said being loving toward others can run the risk of making us forget to love God. So the whole framework of his talk was the opposite of what I had felt the Spirit tell me was true many times before over the years – that we love God the most when we view church rules as a way to help us remember to always be kind and charitable.

President Oaks' talk has honestly made me wonder whether he and I believe differently about the nature of God's divine attributes. The God represented in the framework of his talk seems to worry that too much love and acceptance can be dangerous. But I have long believed that God prefers that if we are going to make a mistake in how we love, that we err on the side of loving others too much, not too little. And I don't believe that the two great commandments somehow conflict with one another. In fact, other scriptures teach that when we are in the service of others, that is exactly how we serve God (Mosiah 2:17). And when Christ said that we show our love for God by keeping His commandments (John 14:15), I suspect the two great commandments were the ones He mostly had in mind. That creates a beautiful circular construct that all points back to loving others as the most important thing we can do. That is, if we love God by keeping His commandments, and the only "great" commandment that doesn't also deal with loving God itself says we should love other people, then that means to me that the most important way we can actually love God is by simply loving other people. I believe any rules God has for us can all be viewed as ways to help us avoid causing harm to others, or inspiring us to help them. In other words, they all relate to loving others, because that is what God cares most about – and that we learn to become perfectly loving like Him.

I have found it comforting to see online that many LGBTQ people and families have had similar reactions to President Oaks' talk. I thought the following comment made a good point (included anonymously to protect privacy):

> "Because Christ said 'The second is like unto it', I am comfortable not treating the second commandment as a subsidiary, especially because Jesus was asked for THE great commandment. **He was specifically asked which ONE commandment was most important and He easily could have just said to love God, but He didn't because 'the second is like unto it'.**"

[Side note: While it has been comforting for me to see comments like this one online, I have been deeply saddened to also see posts from LGBTQ individuals discussing how the teachings in President Oaks' talk have negatively affected them. Many individuals have described increased alienation from family, because family members are using the teachings in President Oaks' talk to justify increased appeals for LGBTQ individuals to repent. They also report higher levels of depression, unsolicited confrontations with church members (including church leaders taking away temple recommends), decisions to step away from church activity, and worsened suicidal ideation – all related to the teachings in President Oaks' talk.]

I think it is very important to remember that "like unto it" is a phrase that denotes equality, not an order or ranking of importance. The idea that the commandment to love God is intertwined with, not superior to, the commandment to love others, is powerfully found elsewhere in the New Testament:

"Those who say, 'I love God,' and hate their brothers or sisters, are liars; for **those who do not love a brother or sister whom they have seen, cannot love God whom they have not seen.**" (1 John 4:20)

"Verily I say unto you, **Inasmuch as ye have done it unto one of the least of these my brethren, ye have done it unto me.**" (Matthew 25:40)

It seems clear to me that by loving our neighbors we in turn love God. That's the construct under which the two great commandments work best (which is interestingly, also the order in which they are presented in Moses 7:33). And it makes sense that Jesus linked them together equally; otherwise, I imagine the Pharisees would have thought that loving God meant keeping all their Mosaic Law rules with the exactness and hollowness they had become accustomed to, rather than seeing beyond their empty rules to view loving others as the <u>true</u> way we love God.

I believe we can best learn what Christ means when he taught how to identify His disciples:

"A new **commandment** I give unto you, That ye love one another; as I have loved you, that ye also love one another. **By this shall all men know that ye are my disciples, if ye have love one to another.**" (John 13:34-35)

Bottom line is, when the Savior's teachings about commandment-keeping are all read together, it seems clear to me that He wanted to remove any sort of order or ranking between the two great commandments. When we show love to others, we are loving God – and to really show love to God, we should be loving others. The two commandments complete each other perfectly without any need for ranking between them.

This is further evidenced by the teachings of the apostles after the Savior's death as well:

"For all **the law is fulfilled in one word**, even in this; **Thou shalt love thy neighbour as thyself**." (Galatians 5:14)

"If **ye fulfil the royal law** according to the scripture, **Thou shalt love thy neighbour as thyself**, ye do well." (James 2:8)

In neither of these scriptures is the first great commandment mentioned. Only the second commandment is discussed even though a description of the fullness of law is being described.

So for me, President Oaks' talk felt like the last straw with respect to me staying quiet in public about the harm I feel the church's teachings about gay sexual orientation are causing. It seemed to me that his talk inadvertently weaponized the Savior's teachings so that intolerant people could use them against LGBTQ people. Because I no longer had a calling as a leader in the church, as of a week before President Oaks delivered his talk (see Chapter 9), I felt more free to finally speak up when I personally felt pain from his talk. Before, I had only tried to mitigate the harm caused by the church's teachings about gay sexual orientation by preaching unconditional love and charity as often as I could. But President Oaks' talk compelled me to do more than just that – because his talk seems to give church members a rationale for stopping their efforts to love at just being kind and civil to LGBTQ individuals who aren't living by church standards. Christ never suggested such a restriction when he taught us how to love the marginalized, no matter how they were living. He didn't say "Go thy way and sin no more – oh, and also, don't expect me to introduce you to my friends if you still keep sinning" (John 8:11).

But President Oaks' talk further justifies that sort of thinking in many people's minds by suggesting that LGBTQ-friendly church members can love LGBTQ individuals <u>too</u> much. As I mentioned in Chapter 3, parents shouldn't have to worry about whether their local bishop or stake president will take away their temple recommends because he thinks they're loving their LGBTQ child too much by supporting their life decisions (and so crossing into the realm of promoting or supporting the "gay lifestyle," which the church opposes). But President Oaks' talk allows church leaders to use the first great commandment to love God as a weapon against people who are just trying to keep Christ's "new commandment" to "love one another" (John 13:34).

I think it's a shame President Oaks hasn't specifically denounced his prior statements about it being okay to exclude gay adult children in family events or not introduce them in public (which statements, by the way, are still easily found on the church's newsroom website by just entering the search term "homosexuality;" in fact, at the time of this writing, the interview in which such statements were made is listed as the second result there). And I think it's a tragedy that he uses his opportunities at the pulpit to further entrench sentiments along those lines rather than talk about love in a manner that is consistent with all of Christ's teachings, and has apparently inspired other General Authorities to use their public speaking opportunities in the same way.

[Side note: One more time, please don't view any of these statements where I express my feelings about President Oaks' talk as me speaking evil of him. I hope you won't hold me to a higher standard than the Apostle Paul who publicly criticized lead-apostle Peter in Galatians, chapter 2. In any event, I think President Oaks has good intentions and is not teaching a framework that is inconsistent with scripture out of a sense of malice. I just suspect he's grasped onto an idea of there being a ranking between the two great commandments as a way to prevent what he sees as wickedness in more and more people supporting concepts like the pro-LGBTQ slogan, "love is love."

*But I find hope in the fact that we've seen this sort of thing happen before – in the context of the Civil Rights Movement. In an October 1967 General Conference talk, Elder Ezra Taft Benson also used a similarly strained argument that pits the first great commandment against the second great commandment. In that talk (in which he criticized the Civil Rights Movement, among other things), Elder Benson argued, "**When we fail to put the love of God first, we are easily deceived by crafty men who profess a great love of humanity, while advocating programs that are not of the Lord.**" (http://www.inspiredconstitution.org/talks/ETB_67oct. html). Thankfully, Elder Benson's argument that the love of God supersedes the love of others failed to prevent church members from eventually fully embracing the Civil Rights Movement.]*

All in all, our family took tough hits three weeks in a row: President Nelson's talk at BYU, our experience with the General Authority, and then

President Oaks' General Conference talk. It was a lot to swallow in three weeks' time.

Why are church teachings inconsistent about gender and post-mortal sexual orientation?

The teachings in President Oaks' talk were not the only declarations that he made in connection with the October 2019 General Conference that caused heartache among the LGBTQ community. In a leadership meeting prior to the conference, he stated that "binary creation is essential to the plan of salvation" and that the church's formal position on the term "gender," including in the church's landmark 1995 document, *The Family: A Proclamation to the World*, is "biological sex at birth" (https://www.sltrib.com/religion/2019/10/02/dark-day-transgender/).

That was a very significant declaration because the family proclamation says, "Gender is an essential characteristic of individual premortal, mortal, and eternal identity and purpose" (https://www.churchofjesuschrist.org/study/manual/the-family-a-proclamation-to-the-world/the- family-a-proclamation-to-the-world). So President Oaks had just declared, on behalf of the church, that, as a matter of doctrine, everyone's biological sex at birth was what their gender was as a spirit before being born and what it would continue to be forever after death as well.

[Side note: This position that biological sex assigned at birth is what constitutes someone's eternal gender was formally codified in the church General Handbook that was released to the public in February 2020. In addition, new provisions were added to the General Handbook that: (i) instruct church members to love and be sensitive toward transgender individuals, (ii) use "transgender" instead of the insensitive word "transsexual" that was in the handbook before, (iii) reference a new church website on the church's gospel topics page titled "Transgender" (https:// www.churchofjesuschrist.org/topics/transgender/?lang=eng), (iv) allow transgender individuals to record their preferred name in church membership directories and be referred to by it in church, and (v) unfortunately, mandate that church membership restrictions will be applied for transgender individuals as a result of any social , medical, or surgical gender transition steps they take, including a name change. The

prior version of the church's handbook only required membership restrictions in the
event surgical transition steps were undertaken (see Section 38.6.23 here: https://
www.churchofjesuschrist.org/study/manual/general-handbook/38-church-poli-
cies-and- guidelines?lang=eng#title_number118).]

I was disappointed when I heard about that new teaching. Not
because it directly affects Wes. He is not transgender; he does not experience gender dysphoria. But rather, I was troubled because I thought it failed
to address science, by: (i) ignoring the clear scientific evidence that shows
that biological sex is not a simple binary construct in humans (https://blogs.
scientificamerican.com/voices/stop-using-phony-science-to-justify-trans-
phobia/; https://m.youtube.com/watch?v=kT0HJkr1jj4&feature=youtu.
be); and (ii) excluding the 1 in every 1,500 babies who are born "so noticeably atypical in terms of genitalia that a specialist in sex differentiation is
called in" (https://isna.org/faq/frequency/) or the 1 in 60 babies born with
perhaps less visible, but still significant, biological characteristics of both
sexes (https://onlinelibrary.wiley.com/doi/abs/10.1002/%28SICI%291520-
6300%28200003/04%2912%3A2%3C151%3A%3AAID-
AJHB1%3E3.0.CO%3B2-F) (which rate of occurrence, by the way, means
there are many, many more intersex people alive on earth than there are members of the church!). Since intersex individuals have biological characteristics
of both sexes at birth, what is their eternal gender?

Also, I continued to wonder about something I have pondered for years,
namely, how to reconcile the church's teaching that gender is eternal for everyone (since 1995 when the family proclamation was published), with what
Joseph Fielding Smith (former prophet and President of the church) taught
in a book published a few years after he passed away in 1972, namely, that no
one in the lower two degrees of heaven will have any gender at all:

> "In the terrestrial and in the telestial kingdoms there will be
> no marriage. Those who enter there will remain 'separately
> and singly' forever. Some of the functions in the celestial body
> will not appear in the terrestrial body, neither in the telestial
> body, and the power of procreation will be removed. I take it

that **men and women will, in these kingdoms, be just what the so-called Christian world expects us all to be — neither man nor woman, merely immortal**." (Joseph Fielding Smith, Prophet, *Doctrines of Salvation, Volume 2*, https://archive.org/stream/Doctrines-of-Salvation-volume-2-joseph- fielding-smith/JFSDoctrinesofSalvationv2_djvu.txt, 1972)

I have always considered this teaching from Joseph Fielding Smith (that people will be genderless in the lower degrees of heaven) to be an oddity to which I didn't need to pay much attention. But I remembered it when President Oaks declared the church's new position on eternal gender being defined by someone's biological sex at birth. And I thought, rather than take a position that seems to both defy science and that continues to conflict with a prior prophet's teaching, I wondered how much more compassionate, loving and consistent it would have been for the church to have simply said we don't always know what someone's eternal gender is or the role that it will play in the afterlife - that sometimes a happenstance of mortal biology might result in someone being born with a biological sex that didn't match their eternal gender – that we just need to look at each situation case-by-case and let God work things out in the afterlife when we can't know for sure. That would have been an approach that is still consistent with the family proclamation's language asserting that "Gender is an essential characteristic of individual premortal, mortal, and eternal identity and purpose."

Also, I thought about how inconsistent the church's new position on eternal gender seems to be with the official church teaching that gays and lesbians will have their intimate "socialities" (the orientations of their desires for intimate connection) switched, or at least turned off, after this life. To explore that official church teaching further, see "*Multiple LDS leaders have taught that same-sex attraction and homosexual desire will not persist beyond death*" at this link: https://www.fairmormon.org/answers/Mormonism_and_gender_issues/Same-sex_attraction. Some authoritative quotes from those listed at that link are:

"As we follow Heavenly Father's plan, **our bodies, feelings, and desires will be perfected in the next life so that every one of God's children may find joy in a family consisting of a husband, a wife, and children.**" (from an official church publication "*God Loveth His Children,*" 2007, https://www. churchofjesuschrist.org/study/manual/god-loveth-his-children/god-loveth- his-children?lang=eng/ - *paste this URL into a browser to make it work*).

"**I do know that this will not be a post-mortal condition. It will not be a post-mortal difficulty.** I have a niece who cannot bear children. That is the sorrow and the tragedy of her life. She who was born to give birth will never give birth, and I cry with her. I just say to her what I say to people struggling with gender identity: 'Hang on, and hope on, and pray on, and this will be resolved in eternity.' **These conditions will not exist post- mortality. I want that to be of some hope to some.**" (Jeffrey R. Holland, Apostle, https://www.pbs.org/mormons/ interviews/holland.html, 2012)

"**There is no fullness of joy in the next life without a family unit, including a husband, a wife, and posterity.** Further, men are that they might have joy. In the eternal perspective, **same-gender activity will only bring sorrow and grief and the loss of eternal opportunities.**" (Dallin H. Oaks, Apostle, https://newsroom.churchofjesuschrist.org/article/interview-oaks-wickman-same-gender- attraction, 2006).

Those teachings about sexual orientation being changed in the eternities confuse me in light of the church's new position on eternal gender identity. If biological sex at birth is indicative of eternal gender, why isn't biological sexual orientation also eternal? I know the church's answer to that is basically that it's just because God says so - but there aren't any scriptures that actually support that point of view (I'll delve more into the scriptural arguments surrounding gay sexual orientation in Chapter 5). Yes, there are scriptures that talk about how heterosexual marriage is necessary to get to the highest degree of heaven and about how men and women complete each other. But such scriptures don't preclude something extra existing there too.

There does not seem to be any logical consistency between the church's positions on gender identity and sexual orientation. The church says mortal biology reflects an eternal characteristic in the former but not the latter. I recognize that the reverse can be said of the position that many people in the LGBTQ community want the church to take instead: that biological sex at birth is not necessarily eternal but that biological sexual orientation can be. So I wonder if a resolution to what appears to be an unsolvable dilemma for both sides, logically at least, might be for everyone to simply admit that no one knows exactly what things will look like in the eternities, focus on fully equal treatment and love for everyone here and now, and just leave it up to God to sort out the afterlife aspects later. (We already do that in numerous other contexts, including ones involving sealing things here on earth that presumably God will have to unseal later, as I'll describe further in Chapter 6.) But unless the church starts teaching that something besides just hetero-sociality might exist between two loving spouses in the highest degree of heaven, that resolution seems impossible because the church isn't allowing God that sort of flexibility.

Can gay sexual orientation in nature provide hope for heaven?

Could we look at nature for an example of how greater flexibility and diversity might actually be beneficial to everyone, even in the afterlife? In nature, hetero-sexuality is clearly essential for the survival of any given species. But, for some reason, nature also allows gay sexual orientation, generation after generation. There are many behaviors in the natural world that are not a good model for heaven, like violence, cannibalism, parasitism, etc. However, I think anything in nature that strengthens, expands, protects, or comforts is something that we can understand as a model for eternal goodness.

There are various theories that ongoing scientific research is exploring that seem to identify gay sexual orientation as something that is good in nature. For example, it may play a crucial role in ensuring genetic diversity to help a species thrive: https://psmag.com/environment/why-are- there-gay-people; https://www.bbc.com/news/magazine-26089486. Or, because sexuality/mating/bonding in general originated in the earliest evolutionary stages of life among cellular creatures that didn't have binary genders, both heterosexuality and homosexuality may persist as simply natural expressions of mating/bonding/intimacy desires: https://www.nytimes.com/2019/11/26/science/same-sex-behavior-animals.html?smid=fb- nytimes&smtyp=cur&f-bclid=IwAR02IcaFSsNayOmcjcwdaaSat2RE_xSqaTEU7uALxBvmg1sA Lw_zUBibvA8. Or, as a BYU microbiology professor concluded, based on multiple studies conducted by other scientists, male gay children apparently produce a higher likelihood for mothers to have more children:

> "How can a trait that tends to lower reproduction maintain itself
> in the population? [Well,] there's a pretty good answer now, and
> it is that in the maternal line of gay men, the mothers, and the
> grandmothers, and the great-grandmothers have more children."
> (Dr. William Bradshaw, BYU Professor, https://m.youtube.com/
> watch?v=8IHw9DVI3hE (starting at 41:00), 2010)

[Side note: I have heard some people argue that gay sexual orientation in nature is an aberration, not an intentional element, because, as this trite and hurtful rhyme conveys: "God created Adam and Eve, not Adam and Steve." However, in conversation with gay theologian and church convert, Derek Knox, I've come to learn that, if we read the creation account in scripture closely, it becomes clear that Eve's gender was not the most important feature that made her a good match for Adam. God followed a careful process in working to pair Adam and Eve and did not want to force an undesirable match. God made sure choice was involved. We can see that in Genesis 2:18-23. Those verses begin with God saying "It isn't good for the man to live alone. I will make a suitable partner for him" (Genesis 2:18, Contemporary English Version). God then creates all the animals and presents them to Adam, but "None of these was the right kind of partner" for him (Genesis 2:20, Contemporary English Version). Only after God then creates Eve from Adam's own body was Adam able to declare his choice for an appropriate match: "Here is

someone like me! She is part of my body, my own flesh and bones" (Genesis 2:23, Contemporary English Version). Too often, casual readers of the creation account assume the most important aspect about Eve is that she was female. But those verses clearly show that the most important reason Eve was a good match for Adam was because she was a fellow human being, not an animal, and choice was involved in the union. Consenting same- gender adults who desire to partner with each other follow the same pattern God established when he helped to pair Adam and Eve.]

I have always thought of heaven as an unimaginably improved version of the majesty and goodness we see in nature here on earth. And if the same sociality that we have here will exist there, wouldn't it make sense that the way nature works to provide joy here will also be reflected there – but in a more glorified and perfected state? I think most members of the church accept the notion that God follows the laws of science and nature, as opposed to just creating rules randomly. So, just like nature allows for gay sexual orientation for some apparent natural benefit, does God want people to be LGBTQ here in mortality to make us all be more open-minded and accepting, like Christ was? Does God know of a spiritual benefit for all of us in having gay couples around in heaven too?

Maybe God knows that perfection isn't everyone being the same - rather, it's pure love and understanding existing among people who are different, right? So maybe exalted beings in heaven need that variety amongst themselves to experience perfection too. Maybe living among exalted gay couples can help everyone else in the highest degree of heaven somehow? And if gay couples are not able to procreate spiritually there, maybe they'll play a different, but important role instead (maybe something similar to the role the Holy Ghost plays as a member of the Godhead; He is not our parent and yet He presumably experiences as much joy as the Father and the Son in eternity. Maybe there are some other roles like that for people to play in exaltation that just haven't been revealed to us yet)? Those are all pretty deep theological and cosmic questions. And I have no idea what the actual truth is about heavenly details like those. But I do wonder whether our collective prejudice is preventing the prophet from sincerely believing God is ready to reveal more knowledge to us about it.

While I don't presume to have the authority to give any answers to questions like those, it makes sense to me that gay couples provide something "extra" that is unique, special, and essential in a different way from what opposite-sex couples provide. Diversity helps enable adaptability, creativity, and compassion, among many other things. Such attributes could be helpful in the job of eternal parenting and of creating spirits that have diversity among themselves as well. And it feels good to me to think that life in the highest degree of heaven may include LGBTQ loved ones and the same-gender spouses that they have come to love deeply here in mortality. Given the negative feelings that I have when I think about someone's intimate "sociality" changing in the afterlife, and about the eradication of spousal gay-sociality entirely in heaven, isn't it reasonable to question whether current church doctrine on this point is of God?

Well, I have found a new way to keep my faith (see Chapter 10). It basically just consists of:

1. never letting the words or actions of anyone (and I mean <u>anyone</u>, even our highest church leaders) diminish my hope for change in the church in any area where I see that church teachings are causing pain to others; and

2. never keeping quiet about my pain and my hope for change ever again.

CHAPTER 5:
IS DOCTRINAL CHANGE STILL POSSIBLE?

_Chapter synopsis: I can't abandon my hope for doctrinal change,
even though recent church teachings make change now unlikely,
or at least push it much further off into the future. This is painful
because I find no scripture or church proclamation that explicitly
forbids marriage equality; significant doctrinal change has happened
before; and we believe church teachings can be improved upon
because prophets aren't perfect._

Is it possible for me to stop hoping for doctrinal change?

To continue to have a positive relationship with the church, I have decided I
have to find the strength to still hope for change, even in the face of the church's
recently expanded and newly entrenched teachings against marriage equality
in our doctrine. Even though such teachings render doctrinal change less likely
or push it off further into the future, I cannot stop hoping for change because
I know these two things: 1) Wes is on the path that God wants for him; and
2) full fellowship in the church can be a good thing for people in this life.

If I stop hoping for change, I inevitably feel like an unloving parent –
because that means I know there is something that would be good for my son
(i.e., his future husband and family, on the one hand, and/or full fellowship

in the church in this life, on the other hand) but I don't want him to have that good thing. So I am committed to never letting anyone, even our highest church leaders, discourage my hope for doctrinal change ever again. I am also committed to never again keep quiet about my pain and hope for change. While I will speak up, I won't protest for change, because only God knows when that will happen for the whole church – and I respect that He'll only tell that to the prophet, not me. But, because of profound personal revelation I have received, I will always hold hope for doctrinal change in my heart and I will always discuss the pain I feel in not seeing the church treat LGBTQ people with full equality. As President Nelson has taught:

> **"Regardless of what others may say or do, no one can ever take away a witness borne to your heart and mind about what is true**." (Russell M. Nelson, Prophet, https://www.churchofjesuschrist.org/study/general-conference/2018/04/revelation-for- the-church-revelation-for-our-lives?lang=eng, 2018)

I have to always believe in the personal revelation I have received that I should never stop hoping for change in the church. Not hoping for change is impossible for me if I want to feel like a good father. Just trusting that the Savior will work things out in the next life is insufficient hope for me because I want the best for my son in this life too. So to be genuine, both as a kind father *and* as a believing Latter-day Saint, the only thing I can do is hope for change.

Some hope that God doesn't actually view it as sin when a gay child leaves the church – because there's an exception for them somehow (which is essentially what we're told to believe by just trusting that the Savior will work things out somehow in the afterlife). I don't believe that is sufficient as the only hope a kind parent of a gay child is allowed to have. Because the parents' stewardship over their gay child is for mortality, I think loving parents also need to hope that their child can be in the church at some point in this life while simultaneously being in a loving marriage with someone of their same gender. If parents are supposed to stop hoping for that, church leaders are basically asking them to give up the hope that their child can one day concurrently have both a happy marriage *and* the positive effects of the church as a faith community.

How can I do that as a mortal parent of Wes when I know that the church's faith community is the most effective and natural spiritual home he can have, because of his upbringing and his family background on both sides? But church leadership is telling me I shouldn't hope for him to ever have that in this life unless he gives up the dream of a naturally affectionate, loving, committed marriage in this life too. As a parent, I can't stop hoping that he can have both things in this life.

Any other straight kids a family may have are likely to feel that same disingenuousness. Those straight kids may be more apt to leave the church because staying feels like a betrayal of their love for their sibling (i.e., it feels mean and selfish to not be allowed to hope that their gay sibling can have both a romantic marriage and the church, as they do). For that reason, the only way I was able to keep my other kids active and believing in the church was to reassure them it's okay to hope that eventually Wes will be able to enjoy the benefits of our faith community in this life again while married to a man – and to explore doctrinally with them how change might happen.

[Side note: Given the doctrinal doubling down against marriage equality in our doctrine that occurred at the end of 2019, these feelings of disingenuousness have become too great for my three straight kids. They have decided to no longer attend church.]

Because of what's best for Wes' mental health, I can't believe that the church is good for everyone in this mortal life - because, in this life, the church is *not* good for gays and lesbians who, like him, can't maintain good mental health while choosing deliberate lifelong celibacy (which is different than being a straight single who hasn't happened to find their spouse yet). That is a fact for gay people whose mental health suffers when they can't engage in a lifelong pursuit of avoiding falling in love and thinking of the darkness that heaven has in store for them - the church *is* bad for them in this life. So I find it incredibly painful and frustrating that church leadership is asking me (over the pulpit in the talks by President Nelson and President Oaks, and in person in my meeting with the General Authority described in Chapter 9) to abandon hope that that could ever change - to abandon hope that church involvement could ever become a positive thing for Wes again in mortality if he's married.

I cannot stop hoping that church leaders provide direction about what gay church members SHOULD do to maintain healthy and happy lives, instead of only basing their guidance on what gay people should NOT do. Decades ago, church leaders used to regularly advise gay church members to marry people of the opposite gender. But they now acknowledge that is not a good course of action (see Chapter 3). And church leaders teach that intentional, lifelong celibacy is _not_ what God wants for straight people. So we are currently in a situation where church leaders' advice about what gay people *should do* (pursue lifelong celibacy) is exactly what they tell straight people *not* to do. I hope for the day when church leaders can give positive advice, not negative proscriptions, to gay Latter-day Saints that will improve their mental health and well- being.

[Side note: When I say poor mental health, I mean risk of suicide and the like, which is documented in many scientific studies (see Preface). Mental health is not just an issue of an optimum quality of life; it's literally a matter of life and death.]

While the changes to doctrine that have already occurred to acknowledge that just being gay is not a sin have been helpful for the mental health of many gay church members, those changes do not go far enough. The current message of "It's okay to be gay, just don't act on it" is still one that causes tremendous psychological harm for the vast majority of church members. And that message also contradicts Jesus' teaching that we should avoid not only sinful acts, but also the desires for those acts (i.e., we should avoid lust in addition to adultery and anger in addition to murder – see Matthew 5:21-30). Saying there is nothing wrong with being gay as long as you aren't in a gay relationship makes no more sense than saying "it's okay to feel greedy as long as you don't steal" (https://wheatandtares.org/2021/02/14/it-is-ok-to-be-gay-just-dont/). So further doctrinal change needs to happen in the church not only because the harmful fruit of psychological trauma should not be attributed to Christ, but also because current church doctrine actually contradicts Christ's teachings.

However, many church members just don't see how it's even possible for church doctrine to change. So I would like to discuss in this chapter some common-sense ideas about how our doctrine could naturally evolve to reflect a more logical and, more importantly, a more kind, inclusive, and loving theology. I can't ignore the call to hope that these ideas scream out to me.

[Side note: Bryce Cook and Dr. Taylor Petrey are among many Latter-day Saint thinkers who have written excellent (and faithful) notions about the conceptual possibilities for doctrinal evolution. Some of my thoughts in multiple chapters of this book come from their articles:

- *Mormon LGBT Questions: https://mormonlgbtquestions.com/*

- *Toward a Post-Heterosexual Mormon Theology: https://www.dialoguejournal.com/wp- content/uploads/sbi/articles/Dialogue_V44N04_420.pdf]*

Do the scriptures prohibit doctrinal marriage equality?

The first place to start for the "change-is-impossible" camp is the scriptures that seem to prohibit gay sexual behavior. But all such scriptures can very easily be interpreted as just prohibiting selfishness, rape, pederasty/pedophilia, sex slavery, fornication, and/or prostitution, not marriage to someone of the same gender. How could ancient writers of the scriptures even be thinking about monogamous gay marriage when almost all societies prohibited that concept until modern times? Sure, they were apostles and prophets, so perhaps they could see our day. But the church interprets a LOT of other ancient scriptural teachings to not apply to our day (like the apostle Paul prohibiting women from speaking in church in 1 Corinthians 14:34-35; instructions that slaves need to obey their masters in Ephesians 6:5 and 1 Peter 2:18-25; and Mormon saying that women lose their virtue when they are raped in Moroni 9:9).

In any event, the Bible is the only book of scripture that Latter-day Saints believe in that might possibly reference gay sexual activity at all. I say "possibly" because the only translations of the Bible that include the word "homosexual" are modern versions. The King James Version does not contain that word. Those other versions have since been shown to have incorrectly used that word rather than translate the pertinent verses to more appropriately communicate sexual abuse (https://www.facebook.com/stan.mitchell.58/posts/3135281313206974; https://www.forgeonline.org/blog/2019/3/8/what-about-romans-124-27). And many Christian churches affirm marriage equality as being consistent with Biblical teachings. Whole books have been written about how all the Biblical scriptures that seem to reference gay sexual behavior, including those found in the New Testament, have been misused to condemn marriage between same-gender partners (https://www.nbcnews.com/feature/nbc-out/ christian-pastor-reframes-scripture-used-against-lgbtq-community-n673471).

[Side note: Other Christian authors who have written books about how the Bible does not prohibit gay marriage include:

- *Matthew Vines- A gay Christian's process and findings of studying biblical texts and meanings to discover more accurate meanings and cultural contexts. (This is the book that seems to be the most known and widely read.)*

- *Karen Keen- Key arguments on the current debate about gay relationships, weighing the context and thought of Old and New Testament laws and ethics, the problem with blanket celibacy subscription, exploring the origins of gay sexual attraction, and ideas for moving forward toward inclusion.*

- *John Tyson- Understanding conservative viewpoints, principles of biblical interpretation, conservative and progressive views and Jesus, biology of gay sexual orientation, and exploring scriptures related to gay sexual relations.*

- *Kathy Baldock- "An examination of the historical, cultural, psychological, medical, social, and religious lenses through which LGBT people have been viewed—with solutions to resolve decades of distortion."*

- *James Brownson- An in-depth study of scriptural origins, translations, and context, and how that translates to our day and the traditionalist/ revisionist disputes.*

- *David Gushee- A leading Christian ethicist writes about his journey to becoming more LGBTQ affirming. He discusses scripture, ethics, and the possibility for change in church stances.*

- *Justin Lee- Justin shares his story of coming to terms with being gay as well as his struggle to reconcile his sexual orientation with his devotion to Christianity. He talks about the roadblocks he found in dealing with other members of his faith and how he navigated finding a balance and cohesion within himself.*

If you're interested in reading some quick arguments online for ways that both the Old Testament and New Testament scriptures that many people say prohibit gay sex can more accurately be interpreted to allow for gay marriage, here are some good sites to check out:

- *https://www.gaychurch.org/homosexuality-and-the-bible/ the-bible-christianity-and-homosexuality/*

- *https://medium.com/@adamnicholasphillips/the-bible-does-not-con-demn-homosexuality- seriously-it-doesn-t-13ae949d6619 ;*

- *http://www.wouldjesusdiscriminate.org/biblical_evidence.html ;*

In addition to Catholic and Protestant authors, some faithful, active Latter-day Saint scholars have opined that there are no scriptures anywhere in the Bible that prohibit marriage equality. I love this podcast episode on that topic that is co-hosted by Derek Knox, an active gay convert to the church who is a Bible scholar/theologian by training: https://beyondtheblockpodcast.com/episodes/the-longest-clobber-passage-s1!0cdef (read more about Derek and his cohost James Jones in the Preface).

Another example is the famous church scholar, Hugh Nibley, who negated the idea that the story of Sodom and Gomorrah is focused on gay sexual activity by teaching that the primary sin of those cities was actually that their people lacked compassion, hospitality, and care for the poor: https://www.reddit.com/r/latterdaysaints/comments/1zdsbd/the_old_testament_doesnt_prohibit_ homosexuality/. That explanation is also consistent with what the Bible itself says was the sin of Sodom:

> "Behold, this was the iniquity of thy sister Sodom, pride, full-ness of bread, and abundance of idleness was in her and in her daughters, neither did she strengthen the hand of the poor and needy." (Ezekiel 16:49)

In short, context matters. Scriptural interpretations that prohibit marriage between same-gender partners don't hold up under honest, contextual scrutiny. Again, many faithful Christians of other denominations also take this approach to the Bible.

Aside from the Bible, other Latter-day Saint books of scripture extol the virtues of heterosexual marriage and of its necessity to enter the highest degree of heaven. But they don't actually say anywhere that gay sexual behavior is prohibited. They don't even mention gay sexual behavior at all – anywhere. Even the Book of Mormon, which Joseph Smith called "the most correct book," doesn't mention gay sexual behavior at all.

A core Latter-day Saint doctrine asserts: "We believe all that God has revealed, all that He does now reveal, and we believe that **He will yet reveal many great and important things pertaining to the Kingdom of God**" (Article of Faith 9). Could our scriptures be added to in the future to expand upon what they teach currently? Allowing for gay marriage doesn't diminish anything the scriptures have said about heterosexual marriage. Could the omission of a specific prohibition on gay sexual behavior in our modern-day scriptures have been something God actually inspired? That way, we wouldn't have to re-interpret any non-Biblical scripture to allow for gay marriage, making it even easier for marriage equality to be affirmed in our doctrine later.

Does the Proclamation on the Family prohibit marriage equality?

Even though the scriptures don't actually prohibit marriage equality, many people view the Church's document "The Family: A Proclamation to the World" as an impenetrable roadblock to doctrinal change (https://www.churchofjesuschrist.org/study/manual/the-family-a-proclamation-to-the-world/the-family-a-proclamation-to-the-world). Issued in 1995, it is widely treated as doctrine in the church (even though it has not been canonized into the scriptures) and is generally thought to explicitly condemn gay marriage.

However, under a close reading, the closest the document comes to prohibiting gay sexual behavior is this: "[T]he sacred **powers of procreation** are to be employed only between man and woman, lawfully wedded as husband and wife." Since two people of the same sex cannot procreate, this statement actually only condemns straight sexual activity outside marriage, not gay sexual activity at all.

[*Side note: This suggests to me that a pressing concern for God might be the frequency of single moms abandoned by deadbeat dads, and the strain that causes to individuals and society. It also suggests to me that marriage between two same-gender partners, which seems to harm no one, is not something God is worried about.*]

Clearer language about procreation is found on the church's website under the topic "birth control" (another area where church doctrine has changed dramatically over the years):

> **"Sexual relations within marriage are not only for the purpose of procreation, but also a means of expressing love** and strengthening emotional and spiritual ties between husband and wife." (https://www.churchofjesuschrist.org/study/manual/gospel-topics/birth-control)

Here church leaders acknowledge that sexual relations can have the purpose of both procreation and expressing love. Unless the church reverses its modern allowance for birth control or forbids infertile straight married couples from having sex, it will always be the case that the church considers non-procreative sex within marriage to be a good thing. Is it possible then that God guided church leaders to use language in the family proclamation that referenced procreation specifically rather than sexual relations in general? Maybe so that, when God finally deems us ready to understand how gay marriage fits into the gospel picture, future church leaders can more easily clarify that the family proclamation doesn't actually prohibit gay sex within marriage?

[*Side note: The church's General Handbook released in February 2020 explicitly condemns gay sexual behavior by using the clear terminology of "sexual relations" rather than "powers of procreation" (see Section 38.6.15 here: https://www.churchofjesuschrist. org/study/manual/general-handbook/38-church-policies-and- guidelines?lang=eng).*]

Elsewhere in the family proclamation, other concepts are presented to support that heterosexual marriage and parenthood are essential to God's plan for His children. But, just like our scriptures, nowhere does it say that gay marriage can't be something "extra" or also "essential" for different reasons. To me, it's like saying trees are essential for a forest - but that doesn't mean other plants and animals can't be important or essential parts of it also, to provide variety and make the whole forest healthier and more beautiful, right? Diversity is a wonderful thing and helps people learn to love more open-mindedly. Perhaps God wants us to have diversity in married couples both here and in heaven, so we can learn to better appreciate one another and <u>all</u> of His creations equally. Could God have inspired the wording of the proclamation to still be flexible for a future, more open-minded interpretation?

[Side note: Some people have postulated that the family proclamation was written for primarily legal reasons to help the church engage in multiple litigations against gay marriage (because, based on just our scriptures alone, it may not have been clear to the courts that opposition to gay marriage was a core doctrine – so having sufficient legal standing to petition the courts could have been lacking). It is interesting to see the timeline of events around when the family proclamation was issued and the church's involvement as an amicus curiae party in an early court case in Hawaii dealing with legalizing gay marriage (https://rationalfaiths. com/from-amici-to-ohana/). If it is true that the initial impetus of the document was mostly to fortify a legal argument, could it make sense that, knowing church leaders were going to use their agency to write the proclamation no matter what (given existing attitudes and biases), God inspired the wording of the proclamation to still be adaptable for the future?]

This might also explain why this document on the family took the form of a proclamation instead of a new revelation in the canonized book, the Doctrine & Covenants. Could God have been guiding the process to help keep the door open for change to happen more easily when the time is right? As mentioned above, gay folks are written out of the family proclamation. Perhaps the current iteration of the family proclamation may come to be known as "The *Heterosexual* Family: A Proclamation to the World." Then, when we are ready to receive it, God might reveal something like "The *Human* Family: A Proclamation to the World," inclusive of our LGBTQ siblings.

[*Side note:* *Evidence that the family proclamation should not be considered a formal new "revelation" from God is found in the words used by President Gordon B. Hinckley when he first presented the proclamation to the church:*

> "[T]he First Presidency and the Council of the Twelve Apostles now issue a proclamation to the Church and to the world **as a declaration and reaffirmation of standards, doctrines, and practices** relative to the family **which the prophets, seers, and revelators of this church have repeatedly stated throughout its history.**" (Gordon B. Hinckley, Prophet, https://www.churchofjesuschrist.org/study/general- conference/1995/10/stand-strong-against-the-wiles-of-the-world?lang=eng, 1995)

We can also see that it is inappropriate to call the family proclamation a "revelation" because President Boyd K. Packer's use of that term to describe the proclamation in a General Conference talk was corrected:

> "In his original talk, Packer said the church's 1995 statement, 'The Family: A Proclamation to the World,' 'qualifies according to scriptural definition as a revelation.' That descriptive phrase has now been omitted, leaving the proclamation simply described as "a guide that members of the church would do well to read and to follow" (https://archive.sltrib.com/article.php?id=50440474&itype=CMSID).]

In the meantime, we should all refrain from using the family proclamation to negatively judge any LGBTQ church member who chooses to date or marry someone of their same gender, or who transitions genders. The proclamation helps us remember to refrain from judging by saying, after discussing gender roles of husband and wife: "other circumstances may necessitate individual adaptation." That simple and direct statement can be a precedent for exceptions to other statements made throughout the proclamation. So we should not use the family proclamation to condemn anyone for their chosen family or gender.

But I think it *is* appropriate to use the family proclamation to chastise parents who put their LGBTQ kids into conversion therapy programs to try to change their sexual orientation or gender identity or who exclude them in any way from their personal lives. The proclamation says, "parents have a sacred duty to rear their children in love" and warns that "individuals who…

abuse...offspring, or who fail to fulfill family responsibilities will one day stand accountable before God." Parents should try to eradicate homophobia and transphobia from their hearts. We should remind parents who subject their LGBTQ children to abusive therapy programs or who reject them in any way, that they are in danger of harsh divine judgment under the proclamation's warnings.

What does the situation with race and the priesthood/temple ban teach us?

Another argument from the change-is-impossible camp is that change is out of church leaders' hands – only God can make a change. I understand that sentiment, but I wonder if God is sometimes disappointed in having to wait to reveal change until church leaders and members are ready to receive it. I have to assume God sometimes wishes we didn't need as much time to grow and learn lessons about love on our own. But I also believe God is pleased when those lessons result in the prophet praying with more fervor about change. In that vein, I find hope for an end to the church's ban on gay marriage by looking at the numerous examples of doctrinal change that have occurred in the church. The church has changed its positions on abortion, birth control, polygamy, slavery, suicide and many other serious issues. Perhaps the most pertinent example of doctrinal change is how the church's racial priesthood/temple ban came to an end. Both that ban and the church's prohibition against gay marriage involve(d) unchosen biological traits, justification by scriptural interpretation, suffering by church members, and statements by church leaders that change was/is out of their control.

[Side note: Official Declaration 2 describes the process of receiving the 1978 revelation that ended the racial priesthood/temple ban in way that supports the idea of change coming about from the bottom up. In fact, it indicates that marginalized groups should not hesitate to voice their hopes and desires to church leaders:

"[W]e have witnessed...that...people of many nations have responded to the message of the restored gospel, and have joined the Church in ever-increasing numbers. This, in turn, has inspired

us with a desire to extend to every worthy member of the Church
all of the privileges and blessings which the gospel affords...[W]
itnessing the faithfulness of those from whom the priesthood has been
withheld, we have pleaded long and earnestly in behalf of these,
our faithful brethren...supplicating the Lord for divine guidance."
(https://www.churchofjesuschrist.org/study/scriptures/dc-testament/
od/2?lang=eng)

Church leaders can only plead earnestly in behalf of the marginalized if they are
aware of their sufferings. We should therefore not hesitate to make our leaders aware
of how church doctrine is causing pain.]

The history of the racial priesthood/temple ban is complex. In short, a few Black men were ordained to the priesthood with the approval of Joseph Smith. But following Joseph's death in 1844, Brigham Young declared in 1849 that no men of Black African descent could hold the priesthood. So, unlike people of any other ancestry, Black men could not perform baptisms, administer the sacrament (i.e., the Lord's supper), or serve as missionaries or leaders in the church. Black men and women were prohibited from receiving sacred temple rites that are necessary to enter the highest degree of heaven and to bind families together for eternity, and they were also restricted from performing any such temple rites on behalf of their ancestors.

During the 129 years of the ban's existence, many church leaders taught that those restrictions were inspired by God, and gave several race-based explanations for the ban. The ban was declared to be a "doctrine" in a letter distributed by the First Presidency in 1949, justified by the notion that Black people were less righteous as spirits before being born. The First Presidency sent a similar letter in 1969 (https://www.fairmormon.org/answers/Mormonism_and_racial_issues/Blacks_and_the_priesthood/Statements).

Just nine years later in 1978, the ban was reversed when President Spencer W. Kimball received a revelation known as Official Declaration 2. This was 10-30 years *after* the civil rights movement in the United States (which occurred during the late 1940s to late 1960s, according to history.com). By 1978, the majority of people in the United States had already gotten comfortable with civil rights for African Americans. Now the church stance is this:

> "Today, the Church disavows the theories advanced in the past that black skin is a sign of divine disfavor or curse, or that it reflects unrighteous actions in a pre-mortal life; that mixed-race marriages are a sin; or that blacks or people of any other race or ethnicity are inferior in any way to anyone else. Church leaders today unequivocally condemn all racism, past and present, in any form" (https://www.churchofjesuschrist.org/study/manual/gospel-topics-essays/race-and-the- priesthood).

I'm deeply grateful the church has denounced the racist teachings of its past. But it took until 2013 (yes, that's right, 2013!) for the church to release that formal denunciation of the former justifications for the racial ban that ended in 1978. We have a history in our church of being so worried about contradicting prior leaders, that positive changes God reveals seem to have been significantly delayed by prejudices engendered through prophetic statements of the past.

[Side note: Some say the crucial difference between the situation with the racial priesthood/temple ban and the ban against marriage between same-gender spouses is that it was always believed that the priesthood/temple ban would end – and no church leader has ever said gay marriage will someday be allowed. I think that argument falls apart when we properly understand when church leaders thought the racial priesthood/temple ban would actually end.

Brigham Young, while prophet in the 1800s, taught that the racial priesthood/temple ban was a position that would not change until after the second coming of Christ (https://en.wikipedia.org/wiki/Black_people_and_Mormon_priesthood). However, the official church essay titled Race and the Priesthood (linked above) says Brigham Young believed Black people would get the priesthood simply at "some future day." Apologists for the church say various statements Brigham made corroborate that overly simplified statement in the church's official essay. They point to statements he made along the lines of: "until Abel's race is satisfied with his blessings, then may the race of Cain receive a fullness of the Priesthood, and the two become as one again" (http://mit.irr.org/brigham-young-it-will-take-time-remove-curse-1852). There is no way to definitively determine what time Brigham is describing with that vague language. Other vague statements made by Brigham on this point were:

"until the times of the restitution shall come" and "That time will come when they will have the privilege of all we have the privilege of and more." However, both of those latter statements were included in the same speech where Brigham seemed to clarify what he meant, by getting very specific:

> *"[T]he Lord told Cain that he should not receive the blessings of the Priesthood, **nor his seed**, until the last of the posterity of Abel had received the Priesthood, **until the redemption of the Earth**."*

> • *see the bottom of page 42 here for this quote: http://bitly.ws/8Egg; and*

> • *compare to the church's essay language here: https://www.missedinsunday.com/memes/race/race-and-the-priesthood/.*

*Brigham Young also stated: **When all the other children of Adam** have had the privilege of receiving the priesthood and of coming into the Kingdom of God and of being redeemed from the four quarters of the earth, and **have received their resurrection from the dead**, then it will be time enough to remove the curse from Cain and his posterity. (Journal of Discourses, v. 2, pp. 142-143, http://bitly.ws/8Uju).*

When all of President Young's statements are taken as a whole, there is no reason to believe he thought the time would come any sooner than after the second coming of Christ.

The timing President Young had in mind can also be understood by looking at what he said about when interracial marriage would be allowed in the eyes of God:

> *"Shall I tell you the law of God in regard to the African race? If the white man who belongs to the chosen seed mixes his blood with the seed of Cain, the penalty, under the law of God, is death on the spot. **This will always be so**." (https://www.fairmormon.org/answers/Question:_Did_Brigham_Young_say_that_race_mixing_was_punis hable_by_death%3F, 1863)*

*From that quote, one could argue that President Young actually thought the priesthood/temple ban would **not** end until blood is no longer involved in procreation – again, until all humankind has been resurrected after Christ's second coming, with bodies quickened by spirit, not blood. The fact that the time for its end came in 1978 instead just means he was wrong, which I don't think is problematic. There were several other things he taught as doctrine that were reversed by the church later. We believe prophets are fallible (see the end of this Chapter 5). They can make mistakes – the prophets in the Bible sure did. Yet that doesn't mean they're* *not prophets. President Young did amazing things in establishing the church in Utah and providing a foundation for it to grow. I think he served in the role God intended for him very well. But he did teach doctrine about Black people that was incorrect and horribly racist. He really messed up on that front, in my opinion.*

So the lack of a statement by church leaders that gay marriage will someday be allowed does not make it inappropriate to compare the situation with the past racial priesthood/temple ban to the current prohibition on gay marriage. Just as church leaders were wrong in their statements about when the priesthood/temple ban would end, it's natural to wonder whether they could also be wrong about not discussing that doctrinal marriage equality will someday be achieved in the church.]

Some people argue that comparing the pre-1978 situation with Black church members to that of LGBTQ church members today is a false equivalency. And I agree that the two situations are very different (see Chapter 2 for a fuller comparison). But despite the differences, I also believe there are some similarities that I think can be instructive. For example, both contexts involve church leaders' interpretation of scripture to discriminate. When a reporter asked President David O. McKay in 1961 about the basis for the policy of restricting Black people from the priesthood, "he replied that it rested solely on the Book of Abraham. 'That is the only reason,' he said. 'It is founded on that.'" ("David O. McKay and Blacks," by Gregory A. Prince, *Dialogue*, Spring 2002, p. 146). Some pertinent scriptures from Abraham are:

> "The land of Egypt being first discovered by a woman, who was the daughter of Ham, and the daughter of Egyptus...; When this woman discovered the land it was under water, who afterward settled her sons in it; **and thus, from Ham, sprang that race which preserved the curse in the land**." (Abraham 1:23-24)

> "Now, Pharaoh **being of that lineage by which he could not have the right of Priesthood**, notwithstanding the Pharaohs would fain claim it from Noah, through Ham, therefore my father was led away by their idolatry." (Abraham 1:27)

Latter-day Saint author Stephen Taggart has also observed:

"With the publication of The Book of Abraham all of the elements for the Church's policy of denying the priesthood to Negroes were present. The curse of Canaan motif borrowed from Southern fundamentalism was being supported with the Church by a foundation of proslavery statements and attitudes which had emerged during the years of crisis in Missouri. (*Mormonism's Negro Policy: Social and Historical Origins*, by Stephen G. Taggart, University of Utah Press, 1970, pp. 62-63).

Other scriptures were also used for over a hundred years to justify racism by many prophets, apostles and other General Authorities of the church, bolstering a view that change was not possible, no matter what church leaders or members desired concerning the racial priesthood/temple ban (http://www.mormonhandbook.com/home/racism.html#top).

I find it interesting to compare this line of thought (that change is out of church leaders' hands) with the following statements that the First Presidency said in that formal letter in 1969 (just 9 years before the church changed its position):

The position of the Church of Jesus Christ of Latter-day Saints affecting those of the Negro race who choose to join the Church falls wholly within the category of religion. It has no bearing upon matters of civil rights. In no case or degree does it deny to the Negro his full privileges as a citizen of the nation...**The seeming discrimination by the Church toward the Negro is not something which originated with man; but goes back into the beginning with God...Revelation assures us that this plan antedates man's mortal existence, extending back to man's pre-existent state...Until God reveals His will in this matter, to him whom we sustain as a prophet, we are bound by that same will.** Priesthood, when it is conferred on any man comes as a blessing from God, not of men...We feel nothing but love, compassion, and the deepest appreciation for the rich talents, endowments, and the earnest strivings of our Negro brothers and sisters… **Were we the leaders of an enterprise created by ourselves and operated only according to our own earthly wisdom, it would be a simple thing to act according to popular will. But we believe that this work is directed by God and that the conferring of the priesthood must await His revelation. To do otherwise would be to deny the very premise on which the Church is established.** (First Presidency letter, https://www.fairmormon.org/answers/ Mormonism_and_racial_issues/Blacks_and_the_priesthood/ Statements#1969, 1969)

The prophetic rhetoric today sounds very much the same as it did back then: that change is not possible because God hasn't said it can happen. But change *did* happen for Black people regardless back then. So I wonder if it can happen for LGBTQ people in the future too – once the prophet is ready to pray with a more sincere desire for change because the general membership of the church is as prepared to embrace our LGBTQ siblings with full equality as church members were in 1978 for Black Latter-day Saints to have full privileges of the priesthood and temple.

[Side note: For a very interesting comparison by historian and scholar, Clair Barrus, between the church's past treatment of Black people and its current treatment of gay people, see here: http://www.withoutend.org/policy-gay- couples-priesthood-ban-comparison/: "In summary, there appears to be a correlation between how homosexuals have been viewed in the modern church, and how Blacks were perceived by Brigham Young, with marriage being the focal point."]

Despite the ending of the racial priesthood/temple ban in 1978, and the denouncement by the church of the racist teachings by church leaders that justified its existence in 2013, racism is still a problem in the church today:

"To this day, churchgoing Mormons report that they hear from their fellow congregants in Sunday meetings that African-Americans are the accursed descendants of Cain whose spirits—due to their lack of spiritual mettle in a premortal existence—were destined to come to earth with a "curse" of black skin. This claim can be made in many Mormon Sunday Schools without fear of contradiction. You are more likely to encounter opposition if you argue that the ban on the ordination of Black Mormons was a product of human racism. Like most difficult subjects in Mormon history and practice, the priest-hood and temple ban on Blacks has been managed carefully in LDS institutional settings with a combination of avoidance, denial, selective truth-telling, and determined silence." Joanna Brooks, *Mormonism and White Supremacy: American Religion and The Problem of Racial Innocence* (https://www.amazon.com/Mormonism-White-Supremacy- American-Innocence-ebook/dp/B08761ZHCP)

Church leaders need to do more to stamp out racism in the church today. Acknowledging that the priesthood/temple ban itself (and not just the teachings that justified it) was a mistake – that it did not come from God – would be an important step. Another step would be for church leaders to apologize, on behalf of the church, to Black church members for the ban. No apology for it has ever been given by the church. Many church members (including several apostles) and other prominent individuals over the course of the ban's existence let church leaders know of the injustices and sufferings being caused by the ban. The ban was not just a product of its times. But for far too long, the church's position did not respond to those cries and align itself with the truth that "all are alike unto God" (2 Nephi 26:33). So I believe an apology needs to be made for that failure.

I also pray that church leaders respond to the cries of LGBTQ suffering sooner than later, so our showing of God's love for all, and the true equality that the scriptures teach He desires us to embrace, are not frustrated any longer than they have been already.

Would allowing marriage equality in our doctrine mean God has changed?

Another argument from the change-is-impossible camp is that no change can happen because God is the same yesterday, today and forever. Yet one of the ways God has consistently stayed the same is that He has always revealed change to prophets for the benefit of His children. From Old Testament times to modern times, the constant element in God's dealings with His children is that He changes certain rules or commandments for us based on the circumstances and times in which we live. For example, animal sacrifice and the Mosaic Law had their time and place in ancient history. And completely abstaining from tobacco, alcohol, coffee and tea is a law that only applies in our modern times. In fact, even within just the history of the modern church, a complete prohibition on such substances was not required for a person to be in good standing in the church until 1921, which was 88 years after Joseph Smith received the revelation in 1833 (https://www.fairmormon.org/answers/ Word_of_Wisdom/History_and_implementation). So, rather than suggest that God changes, I believe the idea of God expanding the law of chastity to allow for marriage between same-gender spouses ironically affirms Him staying the same because He has always revealed era-appropriate adjustments.

As I see it, one reason God needs to make changes little by little (line upon line) over time, rather than just reveal everything to us all at once, is because we are not ready as a people to accept concepts that challenge our prejudices. We have to learn to overcome our biases, become more loving, and open our hearts and minds before He will reveal further light and knowledge.

Ironically, one of the reasons we are often prejudiced is because we think our prophets are not capable of making mistakes. When prophets make racist, sexist, or anti-LGBTQ statements, we let their statements enter our hearts as God's will. But there are many examples of statements made by past prophets that today we find offensive (for example, Brigham Young made many blatantly racist statements: https://www.fairmormon.org/answers/Mormonism_ and_racial_issues/Offensive_statements; https://www.ldsdiscussions.com/

priesthood-ban-quotes). At the time such statements were made, however, many (if not most) people listening to them did not consider them to be offensive at all. And because a prophet made them, people held on to them with a religious fervor that made it harder for God to eventually reveal a change that contradicted such statements. Could that be what is happening currently with the many anti-LGBTQ statements and teachings we keep hearing from our living prophets and apostles?

Would it speed up change if we truly accepted our own belief that prophets aren't perfect?

To diminish the harm being caused by some prophetic statements, I wish more church members would take a minute to think about the following joke that is sometimes told among Latter-day Saints:

> *"Catholic doctrine is that the Pope is infallible, but they don't believe it; Latter-day Saint doctrine is that the Prophet is fallible, but they don't believe it."* (https://www.fairmormon.org/blog/2014/11/25/living-fallibility).

That saying is amusing to us because it seems to be a true reflection of the doctrine of both churches and of the mentalities of their respective church members as well. But I think the damage caused by Latter-day Saints placing too much weight on prophetic statements that are discriminatory in nature is not a laughing matter at all. I wish more church members could get comfortable with the idea that our prophets are human, so we don't get stuck in a paradigm where we think it's bad for prophets to declare doctrinal change.

Many prophets in the Bible exhibited personal failings, including prejudice. As one Bible commentator noted, the Biblical authors were not perfect, and they made errors of expression even in the Biblical record:

> "Though purified and ennobled by the influence of His Holy Spirit; men each with his own peculiarities of manner and disposition—each with his own education or want of education - each

with his own way of looking at things - each influenced differently from another by the different experiences and disciplines of his life. **Their inspiration did not involve a suspension of their natural faculties**; it did not even make them free from earthly passion; **it did not make them into machines—it left them men. Therefore we find their knowledge sometimes no higher than that of their contemporaries**." (James R. Dummelow, *A Commentary on the Holy Bible: Complete in One Volume, with General Articles and Maps* (New York: Macmillan, 1984 [1904]), p. cxxxv.)

Why do we expect our modern-day prophets to be more perfect than scriptural prophets? A helpful chart comparing the flaws of Biblical prophets to those of our latter-day prophets is found under the section "How do Biblical prophets compare to modern prophets?" here: https://www.fairmormon. org/answers/Mormonism_and_doctrine/Prophets_are_not_infallible#Q uestion:_Were_Biblical_prophets_infallible.3F.

I wish more church members could acknowledge that sometimes, even in the prophet's official capacity as the presiding authority, he just teaches according to his own discretion, not divine revelation.

> **"If I do not know the will of my Father**, and what he requires of me in a certain transaction, if I ask him to give me wisdom concerning any requirement in life or **in regard to** my own course, or that of my friends, my family, my children, or **those that I preside over, and get no answer from him, and then do the very best that my judgment will teach me, he is bound to own and honor that transaction**, and he will do so to all intents and purposes." (Brigham Young, Prophet, https://www.goodreads. com/quotes/171150-if-i-do-not-know-the-will-of-my-father)

"Question: Do you believe that the President of the Church, when speaking to the Church in his official capacity is infallible?

Answer: We do not believe in the infallibility of man. When God reveals anything it is truth, and truth is infallible. No President of the Church has claimed infallibility." (Charles W. Penrose, Apostle, https://www.fairmormon.org/answers/ Mormonism_and_doctrine/Prophets_are_not_infall ible)

Consistent with that quote, I think God can sometimes make alternative arrangements to ensure His plan for the church doesn't go off the rails when His prophets act according to their own desires rather than His wishes. The story of the lost 116 pages of the Book of Mormon is a great example of God having a back-up plan already in place, centuries before a future misstep by Joseph Smith (https://en.wikipedia.org/wiki/Lost_116_pages). I think there are individual lives that may be hurt by a prophet's mistakes, which God has to allow because He can't take away a prophet's agency, but He can still take steps to inspire people in other ways to protect the overall trajectory of the church nonetheless.

"Even with the best of intentions, [Church government] does not always work the way it should. Human nature may express itself on occasion, but not to the permanent injury of the work." (Elder Boyd K. Packer, https://www.fairmormon.org/answers/ Mormonism_and_doctrine/Prophets_are_not_infall ible#cite_ note-16, 1991)

"Revelations from God...are not constant. We believe in continuing revelation, not continuous revelation. We are often left to work out problems without the dictation or specific direction of the Spirit. That is part of the experience we must have in mortality. Fortunately, we are never out of our Savior's sight, and if our judgment leads us to actions beyond the limits of what is permissible and if we are listening,...the Lord will restrain us by the promptings of his Spirit." (Elder Dallin H. Oaks, https:// www.fairmormon.org/answers/Mormonism_and_doctrine/ Prophets_are_not_infall ible#cite_note-15, 1997)

All that said, a lot of my fellow Latter-day Saints think that a change to existing doctrine somehow suggests that a prior prophet was wrong. Would it be better if more of us would instead just view the prior prophet to be as correct as he thought the people of his day would allow? That perspective might help more church members be willing to accept future changes without their testimonies of prophets being negatively affected. We cannot expect our prophets to always be as willing to disrupt the status quo as Christ was during His mortal ministry. I think acknowledging that our prophets can sometimes fall short might help more church members remain strong in their testimonies of the gospel, rather than get upset when they learn of the imperfections of our church leaders.

I believe it's good for us to think that as people become more open-minded and more like God over time, then the prophet becomes more confident in asking God to reveal additional information. In that way, I think God's truth can at times be less available to one generation and then expanded and made more accessible when a new generation comes along that is ready to embrace further light. I also assume that sometimes a prophet might fail to get an answer from God about something, and therefore be left to his own devices, because he fears (even if just subconsciously) the people of the church aren't ready for God to reveal the answer. That makes me wonder if revelation might break through any prejudice that a prophet has in his mind if the membership of the church was more ready to welcome (not just nervously accept) change. I wonder if that was maybe why the change with Black church members didn't happen until 1978– because it took decades after the civil rights movement for most church members to affirmatively desire change, rather than just being tacitly okay with it. And that desire of the church members led the prophet to ask about change with more urgency.

Maybe that line of thought could explain why some prophets and apostles actually do directly contradict each other, like when Paul argued with Peter in the second chapter of Galatians. Or in modern times, it might explain why contradictions arise even within relatively short periods of time (for example, whether we should be okay with the nickname "the Mormon Church," instead of the full name of the church: https://www.youtube.com/

watch?v=2lKQrYUE3yc). And it could help explain why official church policies often change to contradict prior positions of the church.

As just one of many examples, consider the church's position on interracial marriage. While no longer viewed as a sin today, the church banned white church members who married Black individuals from entering a temple into at least the 1960s, and recommended against interracial marriage in official publications into the 2000s: https://en.wikipedia.org/wiki/Interracial_marriage_and_The_Church_of_Jesus_Christ_of_Latter-day_Saints. Perhaps this stemmed from Brigham Young's teachings that gruesome death was better than interracial marriages (https://books.google.com/books?id=LkRZGQ-8oO8IC&lpg=PA44&ots=30VXmz65se&pg=PA4 4#v=onepage&q&f=false). Maybe prophets can be wrong sometimes about important things, not because they're bad individuals, but perhaps because God didn't reveal certain truths to them when people of their time were not ready for them.

In any event, it seems like today we're content with our prophets just revealing mostly administrative changes (like ceasing to support the Boy Scout program, changing the mechanics of ministering programs to support each other outside of church services, reorganizing Sunday classes, shortening the length of time we spend at church, etc.). But given how quickly the world is changing nowadays, shouldn't we *desire*, not fear, changes in doctrine as well that appropriately address our times? When a doctrine just doesn't seem rational (based on new scientific discoveries), fair (discriminating based on innate biology), or loving (causing poor mental health and self-loathing), can that be an indication that it's not of Christ? Instead of defending the status quo that produces such darkness and despair, perhaps there is space for us to desire that the prophet might deem us ready for change, which would allow him to more easily receive additional light and knowledge from God to allow gay marriage in the church. Perhaps God could more easily reveal that change because the prophet feels we've progressed in our learning as a society, and because church members have matured generally as well.

My longing is similar to the sentiments recently expressed by Matthew Gong, the gay son of one of our current apostles:

> "The monolithic rigidity of the religion today makes me super sad. **The old school doctrine [in the early years of the church in the 1800s] was…radical. The idea that everyone was an embryonic god? Wild. When they said everyone was worth saving and actually meant it? Unapologetically universalist. The beliefs were molten— shifting and evolving—in fascinating and weird ways. The possibility of change was exciting and hopeful.** But the inertia of tradition quenched the radical spirit as each generation left a patina on the Church. The religion calcified—rigidity replaced flexibility—and the organization became anchored in its conservative position." (https://m.facebook.com/notes/matthew-gong/birthday-letters-27- 28/10158377175735021/, 2019)

I suspect one reason many Latter-day Saints want our prophets, past and present, to be perfect is so we don't feel lost. I think a lot of people are often looking for someone who knows more and has things more figured out so they can just follow along and not figure things out for themselves. We feel safe and secure in that construct. Ironically, our own prophets and apostles have repeatedly taught that we should figure things out for ourselves, not just accept their teachings blindly:

> **"I am more afraid that this people have so much confidence in their leaders that they will not inquire for themselves of God whether they are led by Him**." (Brigham Young, Prophet, https://www.sixteensmallstones.org/debunking-that-quote-about- brigham-youngs-greatest-fear/, 1862)

> **"You may know for yourself what is true and what is not** by learning to discern the whisperings of the Spirit… **Ask your Heavenly Father if we truly are the Lord's apostles and**

prophets. Ask if we have received revelation on this and other matters." (Russell M. Nelson, Prophet, https://speeches.byu. edu/talks/russell-m-nelson/love-laws- god/, 2019)

[Side note: Even Jesus Christ told those He taught to go home and ponder before they just accepted blindly what He said: see 3 Nephi 17:3.]

I think the fallibility of our prophets, and the weakness of the general membership of the church in being unable to love past existing prejudices, are the primary reasons why the restoration of Christ's true gospel is not yet complete. To me, those things explain why we can't just have the fullness of all truth all at once now. So I love what our leaders have taught about the restoration being ongoing – because it gives me hope that change will always continue to happen in the church:

> "Sometimes we think of the Restoration of the gospel as something that is complete, already behind us - Joseph Smith translated the Book of Mormon, he received priesthood keys, the Church was organized. In reality, **the Restoration is an ongoing process; we are living in it right now. It includes 'all that God has revealed, all that He does now reveal,' and the 'many great and important things' that 'He will yet reveal.'** (Dieter F. Uchtdorf, Apostle, https://www.churchofjesuschrist.org/study/ general- conference/2014/04/are-you-sleeping-through-the- restoration , 2014)

> "'We believe all that God has revealed'— that's often the easy part. It takes a special kind of faith to: 'believe that He will yet reveal many great and important things pertaining to the Kingdom,' and then to be ready to accept them, whatever they are. **If we are willing, God will lead us to places we've never dreamed we could go—as lofty as our dreams might already be. His thoughts and His ways are certainly much higher than ours.** In a sense, I suppose we're not unlike those in Kirtland to whom the Prophet Joseph Smith said, 'You know no more concerning

the destinies of this Church and kingdom than a babe upon its mother's lap.'" (Jeffrey R. Holland, Apostle, https://www. churchofjesuschrist.org/study/ensign/2018/12/making-your-life-a-soul- stirring-journey-of-personal-growth, 2018)

I think that quote from Elder Holland is amazing. It makes me wonder if we could still see as much change occur in the church in future years as there has been from the 1830s to now — which would mean some doctrinal refinements, for sure. To be ready, it's good to remember that one of the ways God actually stays the same is by consistently revealing through His prophets doctrine upon doctrine, line upon line, as we, His children, slowly become ready and willing over time to accept further guidance and light. I hope and pray every day that church members will be more accepting so that the prophet will see that and then pray more sincerely about whether it is God's will to allow marriage equality to exist in the church.

CHAPTER 6

IS MARRIAGE TOO FUNDAMENTAL
TO REDEFINE?

Chapter synopsis: It hurts to know that marriage between same-gender spouses is prohibited in the church even though: 1) doctrinal change regarding marriage has happened before, including canonized scripture being changed to redefine marriage; 2) prior statements by prophets and apostles about polygamy did not prevent doctrinal change about marriage; 3) we know very little about spiritual procreation; and 4) temple practices and doctrine do not prohibit doctrinal change. Lack of apostolic unanimity regarding change, and the prophet possibly perceiving church members as not being ready for change, might explain why change has not yet happened.

Despite all the evidence showing our doctrine has evolved many times, and despite statements from our prophets and apostles that change will still come in the future, many members of the church still struggle with the idea that something as fundamental to our beliefs as marriage could be doctrinally redefined. I think part of the reason is because marriage and family are experienced every day, and drive so many of our feelings of purpose and happiness. So when church doctrine discusses marriage and family, many instinctively pay more attention, and those teachings take root more firmly than some other doctrinal teachings.

[Side note: It is interesting that heterosexual monogamous marriage is viewed as "biblical marriage" by so many people when it is actually only one of eight forms of marriage endorsed by God in the Bible: https://www.patheos.com/blogs/ unreasonablefaith/2009/04/the-varieties-of-biblical-marriage/.]

Would allowing marriage equality be a less drastic change than permitting polygamy was?

The church has changed its scriptural canon to redefine marriage before, to first allow for and then rule out polygamy. Starting in 1835, the canonized scripture (known today as the Doctrine & Covenants) contained an explicit prohibition on polygamy in then Section 101 that read as follows:

> "Inasmuch as this church of Christ has been reproached with the crime of fornication, and polygamy: we declare that we believe, that **one man should have one wife; and one woman, but one husband**, except in case of death, when either is at liberty to marry again." (Doctrine & Covenants, Section 101, original wording, 1835) (https://www.fairmormon. org/answers/Mormonism_and_polygamy/1835_Doctrine_ and_ Covenants_denies_polygamy)

41 years later in 1876, this scriptural prohibition *against* polygamy was removed and Section 132 of the Doctrine & Covenants was inserted *endorsing* polygamy in a revelation previously given to Joseph Smith. He received Section 132 "before it was recorded but delayed making it known. The prophet knew the Lord's will on plural marriage within the new and everlasting covenant probably as early as 1831" (https://www.churchofjesuschrist.org/manual/doctrine-and-covenants-student-manual/section-132-marriage-an-eternal-covenant). So Joseph knew that Section 101 contradicted what he understood to be the Lord's will throughout virtually all of his time as the prophet. Section 132 was recorded in 1843 shortly before Joseph was murdered, but it was still not

made public by church leaders until 1852. Even after its public release, it was not canonized until 1876 (shortly before Brigham Young died), which finally allowed church leaders to publicly justify polygamy using modern scripture. However, when a later prophet of the church, Wilford Woodruff, issued a manifesto in 1890 directing the church to abandon polygamy, church leaders had to eventually reinterpret Section 132 as just discussing eternal marriage generally (both monogamous and polygamous), even though the explicit references to polygamy throughout the section are numerous (https://www.templestudies.org/bringhurst- newell-g-section-132-of-the-lds-doctrine-and-covenants-its-complex-contents-and-controversial- legacy/).

That history provides a great example of how the doctrine of the church regarding marriage has been extremely fluid. An unconventional form of marriage was secretly allowed by God despite being publicly (and scripturally) prohibited by the church – then, scripture was changed to remove the prohibition against that unconventional form of marriage, so that additional new scripture facilitating it could be added without contradiction – then that unconventional form of marriage became prohibited once more by prophetic mandate and scripture was reinterpreted.

That's a LOT of doctrinal back-and-forth over marriage and paints a different picture than what I believe many church members understand.

If the church has already changed its scriptural canon and doctrine multiple times to redefine marriage, why couldn't it do so again to allow for gay marriage, especially in light of new scientific discoveries about gay sexual orientation? Couldn't we just say prior prophets didn't have access to such new discoveries and so shouldn't be judged as wrong – that they were instead just insufficiently informed? After all, our current prophet, President Nelson, has said "good inspiration is based upon good information" (https://www.churchofjesuschrist.org/study/general-conference/2018/04/revelation-for-the-church-revelation-for-our-lives). And as a bonus, no current scriptures would even need to be deleted to allow for marriage equality in our doctrine (like

Section 101 had to be deleted to allow for polygamy). Gay marriage would just be an expansion of current doctrine, not a scriptural reversal like polygamy was.

Thinking about gay temple sealings as just an expansion or elucidation of current doctrine, rather than as a change in doctrine, is the way I like best to view a possible adjustment in the church's position. Imagine a world in which everyone was pro-gay when Joseph Smith first revealed the sealing power. In that world, the sealing power would have applied to gay couples automatically unless a revelation said specifically it couldn't. Well, since we have had no formal, canonized revelation in the real world saying gay sealings are NOT allowed, the sealing power is already set up to address gay relationships. I like to think that new revelation on this subject is needed now only because church members require clarification that it is okay for them to abandon past ways of thought that gay couples are evil. It would just involve a new, more open-minded way of thinking about existing doctrine.

Will numerous prophetic statements against marriage equality prevent change?

Now, I have wondered, even though the scriptures allow it, are there just too many statements by prophets and apostles that prohibit gay marriage for it to ever be allowed doctrinally? While I don't know the answer to that question, I find it oddly comforting that multiple prophetic teachings about marriage in the 19th century didn't prevent contradictory doctrinal change from occurring shortly following their utterances. Below are several quotes from church prophets and apostles in the 1800s that stated that polygamy was better than monogamy and/or that polygamy was <u>required</u> in order for someone to enter the highest degree of heaven. Such statements didn't stop the church's position on polygamy from changing.

19th century prophetic/apostolic statements that polygamy is required for the highest degree of heaven and/or is better than monogamy

"From him I learned that the doctrine of plural and celestial marriage is the most holy and important doctrine ever revealed to man on the earth, and that without obedience to that principle no man can ever attain to the fullness of exaltation in celestial glory." (Joseph Smith, cited by William Clayton, in George D. Smith, ed., An Intimate Chronicle: The Journals of William Clayton, (Salt Lake City: Signature Books, 1991), p. 559; also in Andrew Jenson, "Plural Marriage," *The Historical Record*, 6 (July 1887): 226.)

"It is the word of the Lord, and I wish to say to you, and all the world, that if you desire with all your hearts to obtain the blessings which Abraham obtained, you will be polygamists at least in your faith, or you will come short of enjoying the salvation and the glory which Abraham has obtained. This is as true as that God lives... The only men who become Gods, even the Sons of God, are those who enter into polygamy. Others attain unto a glory and may even be permitted to come into the presence of the Father and the Son; but they cannot reign as kings in glory, because they had blessings offered unto them, and they refused to accept them." (Brigham Young, "Remarks by President Brigham Young, in the Bowery, in G.S.L. City," (19 August 1866) *Journal of Discourses* 11:268-269.)

"Some of the nations of Europe who believe in the one wife system have actually forbidden a plurality of wives by their laws; and the consequences are that the whole country among them is overrun with the most abominable practices: adulteries and unlawful connections through all their villages, towns, cities, and country places to a most fearful extent."- Apostle Orson Pratt, *The Seer*, p. 12

"I have noticed that a man who has but one wife, and is inclined to that doctrine, soon begins to wither and dry up, while a man who goes into plurality looks fresh, young, and sprightly. Why is this? Because God loves that man, and because he honors his word. Some of you may not believe this, but I not only believe it but I also know it. For a man of God to be confined to one woman is small business... I do not know what we should do if we had only one wife apiece."- Apostle Heber C. Kimball, *Deseret News*, April 22, 1857

"This law of monogamy, or the monogamic system, laid the foundation for prostitution and the evils and diseases of the most revolting nature and character under which modern Christendom groans..."- Apostle Orson Pratt, *Journal of Discourses*, v. 13, p. 195

"Why do we believe in and practice polygamy? Because the Lord introduced it to his servants in a revelation given to Joseph Smith, and the Lord's servants have always practiced it. 'And is that religion popular in heaven?' It is the only popular religion there..."- Prophet Brigham Young, *Deseret News*, August 6, 1862

"Monogamy, or restrictions by law to one wife, is no part of the economy of heaven among men. Such a system was commenced by the founders of the Roman Empire... Rome became the mistress of the world, and introduced this order of monogamy wherever her sway was acknowledged. Thus this monogamic order of marriage, so esteemed by modern Christians as a hold sacrament and divine institution, is nothing but a system established by a set of robbers."- Prophet Brigham Young, *Deseret News*, August 6, 1862

"We breathe the free air, we have the best looking men and handsomest women, and if they envy our position, well they may, for they are a poor, narrow minded, pinchbacked race of man, who chain themselves down to the law of monogamy and live all their days under the dominion of one wife. They aught to be ashamed of such conduct, and the still fouler channel which flows from their practices."- George A. Smith, Apostle, *Deseret News*, April 16, 1856

"It is a fact worthy of note that the shortest-lived nations of which we have record have been monogamic. Rome, with her arts, sciences and warlike instincts, was once the mistress of the world; but her glory faded. She was a mono-gamic nation, and the numerous evils attending that system early laid the foundation for that ruin which eventually overtook her."- Apostle George Q. Cannon, *Journal of Discourses*, v. 13, p. 202	"Talk about polygamy! There is no true philosopher on the face of the earth but what will admit that such a system, properly carried out according to the order of heaven, is far superior to monogamy for the raising of healthy, robust children!"- Prophet Brigham Young, *Journal of Discourses*, v. 13, p. 317
"[Children of polygamists] besides being equally as bright and brighter intellectually, are much more healthy and strong."- Apostle George Q. Cannon, *Journal of Discourses*, v. 13, p. 207	"A belief in the doctrine of a plurality of wives caused the persecution of Jesus and his followers. We might almost think they were 'Mormons.'"- Apostle Jedediah M. Grant, *Journal of Discourses*, v. 1, p. 346
"To comply with the request of our enemies would be to give up all hope of ever entering into the glory of God, the Father, and Jesus Christ, the Son... So intimately interwoven is this precious doctrine with the exaltation of men and women in the great hereafter that it cannot be given up without giving up at the same time all hope of immortal glory." George Q. Cannon - *Jun. Instructor*, May 1, 1885, Editorial	"Some people have supposed that the doctrine of plural marriage was a sort of superfluity, or nonessential to the salvation or exaltation of mankind. In other words, some of the Saints have said, and believe, that a man with one wife sealed to him by authority of the Priesthood for time and eternity, will receive an exaltation as great and glorious, if he is faithful, as he possibly could with more than one. I want here to enter my solemn protest against this idea, for I know it is false...it is useless to tell me that there is no blessing attached to obedience to the law, or that a man with only one wife can obtain as great a reward, glory, or kingdom as he can with more than one, being equally faithful." (Joseph F. Smith, Apostle, *Journal of Discourses* 20:28-20, 1878)

Some current church scholars try to argue that it was never doctrine that polygamy was required to receive the highest degree of heaven. Since polygamy was practiced by only about 20-30% of church members at its peak, some scholars assert that these quotes are only talking about polygamy being required for those who were actually asked by church leadership specifically to do it. (https://www.fairmormon.org/answers/Mormonism_and_polygamy/Brigham_Young_said_that_t he_only_men_who_become_gods_are_those_that_practice_polygamy#cite_note-10).

Others argue that the above quotes were just hyperbole to bolster the resolve of the people living polygamy, or to enhance sentiment against the U.S. government as it was trying to abolish polygamy. But, as I read the actual quotes, I can only partially accept such explanations.

The sheer number of quotes like these, and the plain meaning of most of such quotes, suggests that church leaders in the 19th century firmly believed that polygamy was a better system than monogamy and that only people who practiced polygamy would inherit the highest level of heaven. That is consistent with what apostle Bruce R. McConkie controversially stated in his 1958 book, *Mormon Doctrine*, that God will "obviously" re-institute polygamy after the second coming of Christ:

> "Obviously **the holy practice [of plural marriage] will commence again after the Second Coming** of the Son of Man and the ushering in of the millennium." (Bruce R. McConkie, *Mormon Doctrine*, 2d ed., Bookcraft, 1966, p. 578) (https://archive.org/stream/MormonDoctrine1966/MormonDoctrine1966_djvu.txt) (https://en.wikipedia.org/wiki/Mormonism_and_polygamy)

That also echoes earlier teachings by Brigham Young that the primary purpose of polygamy was to bring about the second coming (see John Cairncross, *After polygamy was made a sin: the social history of Christian polygamy*, Routledge and Kegan Paul, 1974, ISBN 0-7100-7730-0, p. 181). And it is consistent with the following statement made in 1891 by the First Presidency and all the apostles of the church in a petition to the President of the United States:

> "We formerly taught to our people that **polygamy or celestial marriage** as commanded by God through Joseph Smith was right; that it **was a necessity to man's highest exaltation in the life to come**." (*Reed Smoot Case, Vol. 1*, page 18) (http:// bitly.ws/8HXJ)

All of those teachings are no longer publicly taught as the church's doctrine today. However, some Latter-day Saint scholars have noted that because church leaders haven't actually denounced the idea of polygamy in heaven, current church doctrine is essentially just putting a pause on polygamy, speculating that it will resume in the eternities for everyone in the top degree of heaven: https://www.amazon.com/Ghost-Eternal-Polygamy-Haunting-Hearts/ dp/0997458208.

If our prophets and apostles changed what they were saying about the superiority of one form of marriage before (including statements that only that one form of marriage could allow someone to enter the highest degree of heaven), why can't they likewise change their teachings again now to allow for marriage between same-gender spouses (and allow for the possibility that gay couples might exist in heaven too)? Many think that current church leaders are talking about gay marriage often and strongly today for legal reasons (see Chapter 4). Well, if the forceful nature of the above quotes was intended to bolster pro-polygamy sentiment against the government, then why couldn't all the forceful statements against gay marriage simply become moot in the future as well? I think it's sometimes good to remember that, even if well-intentioned, not <u>all</u> statements from our apostles and prophets stand the test of time:

> "God will not change his law of celestial marriage (polygamy). But the man, the people, the nation, that oppose and fight against this doctrine and the Church of God will be overthrown." Lorenzo Snow (1886, from jail) - *History of Utah*, Whitney, 3:471

Do we know for sure that spiritual procreation requires a man and a woman?

I think the most compelling (while still not actually convincing) reason some people think doctrinal change allowing gay temple marriage will always be impossible is based in the belief that spiritual procreation occurs in the highest degree of heaven. President Oaks said in his October 2019 General Conference talk titled "*Two* Great Commandments" that spiritual procreation will happen through the "creative powers inherent in the combination of male and female." That teaching seems to make sense upon first thought because, if things work in heaven in a similar pattern to how they do here, then only a combination of male and female would be able to reproduce there too. While we don't know very much about how spiritual procreation is actually carried out, existing scripture teaches us just enough about the way spirits are created that we have a decent basis for understanding that it is an entirely different thing than biological procreation. Different rules of nature apply because an eternal spirit is being created, not a mortal body.

Canonized Latter-day Saint scripture, as interpreted by numerous prophets and apostles, teaches that a human spirit is created by shaping or organizing a pre-existing "intelligence" into a spirit (Abraham 3:22; Doctrine & Covenants 93:29, 33-34) (http://emp.byui.edu/satterfieldb/quotes/Intelligence%20 and%20Spirit.html). This is different from the idea of creating a spirit *ex nihilo* (i.e., out of nothing) or through the combination of the essences of a male parent and a female parent, as in mortal biology. In other words, spiritual procreation seems to be more about transforming than conceiving.

President Oaks stated that the transformative process requires the participation of both a male and a female. However, the scriptures mentioned above seem to refute that, referring to organizing instead of conceiving, making no mention of Heavenly Mother in creating spirits. The existence of Heavenly Mother is well grounded in our doctrine since at least 1845, when Eliza R. Snow's hymn "O My Father" was published. In fact, the revised Young Women theme announced in October 2019 includes the mention of

Heavenly Parents, not just Heavenly Father (https://www.churchofjesuschrist. org/church/news/new-young-women-theme-class-name-and-structure-chang- es-announced?lang=eng).

[Side note: The third verse of the hymn "O My Father" reads: "

I had learned to call thee Father,

Thru thy Spirit from on high,

But, until the key of knowledge

Was restored, I knew not why.

In the heav'ns are parents single?

No, the thought makes reason stare!

Truth is reason; truth eternal

Tells me I've a mother there."

Eliza R. Snow (1804-1887), Hymns, *292.]*

I wonder if the truth is that we just don't know what is involved or how that transformative process is actually carried out. Creating a spirit sounds just plain different from creating a body. We know all about the latter, but we know very little about the former. But President Oaks' recent assertion that we do know makes it hard for me to find any sense of peace when I think about this area of church doctrine, especially given how long his teaching will remain in circulation within the church going forward.

Doesn't the idea of spiritual procreation being fundamentally different than biological procreation make more sense than thinking that exalted women will be pregnant throughout all eternity with billions of spirit babies? I person- ally find it comforting to think that spiritual procreation might have all the benefits of parenthood without the physical toil and limitations associated with parenthood here in mortality. Since science is finding ways that might allow gay couples to actually reproduce biologically here on earth (https://medium. com/neodotlife/same-sex-reproduction-artificial-gametes-2739206aa4c0), it doesn't seem hard to think that God might know a way that gay couples could spiritually reproduce in heaven, right?

Even the creation of the earth occurred through the transformation or organization of existing substance, rather than through creation *ex nihilo*. Most Biblical scholars recognize that the idea the earth was created out of nothing was largely the result of intellectual developments in the 2nd and 3rd centuries (https://en.wikipedia.org/wiki/Genesis_1:1), not something the original writers of the Bible proposed. The original text of the Book of Genesis supports Joseph Smith's teaching that the creation of the earth was done through the organizing of existing matter, not *ex nihilo* (https://scholarsarchive.byu.edu/cgi/viewcontent.cgi?article=1626&context=msr). We believe that, under the direction of His Father, Christ organized existing matter from chaos to create the earth. And we believe Christ had other individuals helping in that effort as well: "Elohim [the Father], Jehovah [Christ], Michael [Adam], a host of noble and great ones – all these played their parts" (Bruce R. McConkie, Apostle, https://www.churchofjesuschrist.org/study/ensign/1982/06/christ-and-the-creation , 1982) (Abraham 3:22-24). Notice again that Heavenly Mother's role, if any, is not mentioned at all, making it hard to support the idea that one male and one female are necessary in the eternities.

Based on all those teachings, it appears to me that the process by which a *spirit* is created is more akin to how the *earth* was created (by individuals cooperating to organize existing matter) than it is to how a *human body* is created (by conception, combining the essence of male and female parents). Moreover, we believe that all spirit is matter (Doctrine & Covenants 131:7). So it seems logical to assume that an "intelligence," as just an unorganized spirit, is also an element of matter, and that, therefore, the process of creating a human spirit from that intelligence could occur through the combined effort of persons that are not just one male and one female. As Elder McConkie stated above, we're comfortable with the doctrine that Christ and Adam, two male beings, created the earth. So can we get comfortable with the notion that two exalted men (or two exalted women) could similarly create a human spirit? "Elohim" is just the plural of "God" in Hebrew (the name literally just means "Gods" in Hebrew). Perhaps that's why Elohim is the name used in original Biblical texts for God the Father – kind of as a collective, singular title for both our Heavenly Fathers, both our Heavenly Mothers, or one of each.

Or perhaps, most likely, because biological genders are constructs human-kind only understands through the lens of our limited, mortal experience, the nature of celestial gender is impossible for us to completely understand. Maybe attempting to understand the gender traits of our Heavenly Parents as exalted, perfected, divine beings, is as hard for us to do as imagining what eternity truly means. Perhaps "Elohim" is just a collective phrase for divine parents whose gender and procreative traits are impossible for us to fully fathom at this time.

I don't know the answers to any of those sorts of questions. But I do know that that our doctrine says we are literally children of Heavenly Parents and that we have inherited divine potential from Them (https://www.churchofje-suschrist.org/study/manual/gospel-topics/spirit-children-of- heavenly-parents).

Could temple ceremonies be changed to allow for gay temple marriage?

If we can get comfortable with the idea that gay couples might actually be able to procreate spiritually in heaven, just like straight couples, then the next logical step is to look at whether it's possible for our temple marriage ceremonies to change to allow eternal sealings for gay couples. In Latter-day Saint theology, a husband and wife can be married for eternity, not just "until death do [they] part," provided they are married by an authorized church representative in one of the church's temples.

[Side note: As noted in Chapter 3, Sunday church services are open to the public and held each week in chapels, whereas access to temples is only permitted for people whom local leaders affirm have sufficient belief and are obeying applicable church standards – i.e., people who hold temple recommends. The ritual by which a couple is married for eternity is called a sealing ceremony. The work that goes on inside temples involves the performance of various sacred covenant rituals for church members. Once done for themselves, church members perform the same rituals by proxy on behalf of their deceased ancestors, to give their ancestors the

chance to choose to accept such sacred rituals and commitments if they did not have
an adequate opportunity to do so during this life.]

Temple ceremonies are so sacred that church members promise not to
discuss certain details about them outside the temple. So I will not discuss any
of the ceremonial details associated with a sealing. However, I will mention
that in January 2019, it was publicly reported that extensive changes were
made to the language of various temple ceremonies to make them less sexist.

Specific to temple sealing, it was reported that a change was made to
reflect "gender equality in the language of the sealing ceremony, where the bride
and groom now apparently make the same promises to each other" (https://
religionnews.com/2019/01/03/major-changes-to-mormon- temple-ceremo-
ny-especially-for-women/). (As that article notes, the language of the sealing
ceremony previously did not reflect gender equality; men were implied to
hold a more elevated status.) If the wording of the sealing ceremony and other
temple rites can be changed to accommodate the heartfelt desires of women
in the church for greater equality, I have no doubt that, if our doctrine eventually evolves to allow for marriage between same-gender spouses, the sealing
ceremony could again be updated to accommodate that marriage equality for
our LGBTQ siblings as well.

What about gay marriage for "time only," in or out of the temple?

Short of gay temple sealings, some middle-ground compromises might allow
gay couples to be married in this life only and still stay in the church. Such
compromise solutions have been discussed for years, including the ecclesiastical
equivalent of a civil union, which was proposed by the group Affirmation in
the 1970s, long before marriage between same-gender spouses was legalized
in all 50 U.S. states in 2015 (https://en.wikipedia.org/wiki/Law_of_adop-
tion_(Mormonism)). Now that marriage equality is legally protected in the
U.S., perhaps gay couples could be married civilly and still retain their church
membership, even if they cannot hold temple recommends.

Some people postulate that such a gay-civil-marriage-without-loss-of-church membership compromise might already be a possibility for some gay church members, depending on the views of their local leaders. Under the church's General Handbook released in February 2020, someone who is in a gay marriage is no longer automatically considered to be an apostate (like they were under prior versions of the church's handbook). That means that while gay marriages are still considered sinful, local leaders have more discretion about whether or not a member in a gay marriage should lose their membership in the church (see Section 32.6.2 here: https://www.churchofjesuschrist. org/study/manual/general-handbook/32-repentance-and- membership-councils?lang=eng#title_number14).

While I concede it is possible that some local church leaders may now feel more enabled to NOT to take action to revoke the church membership of someone who has entered into a gay marriage, I am doubtful many local leaders will actually follow that path. I think we may occasionally see such a lack of action to withdraw church membership in cases where the gay person simply stops coming to church anyway. In fact, many inactive straight members of the church engage in conduct (such as living with lovers outside of marriage) that can technically put their church membership in jeopardy. But local leaders do not always seek them out to take action against them (i.e., revoke their church membership) if such church members have simply stopped attending church. So I can see something similar happening (or, better said, NOT happening) with inactive church members who have entered into gay marriages as well. Since the February 2020 handbook update, local leaders may feel like they have permission to leave such people alone, rather than seeking them out to commence withdrawing their church membership.

That being said, I do not think it likely that any local leader will allow a person who is attending church and who enters into a gay marriage, to continue to attend church without having their membership withdrawn or restricted in some way – because even under the updated General Handbook, gay marriage is still defined as sexual immorality for which a membership council may be "necessary" (see Section 38.6.5 here: https://www.churchofjesuschrist.org/study/

manual/general-handbook/38-church-policies-and- guidelines?lang=eng#title_number102).

Another level of compromise is this: in addition to allowing married gay couples to simply retain church membership as discussed above, perhaps gay couples could marry in the temple for "time only" (i.e., just for this life), rather than for "time and all eternity." Temple marriage for "time only" is currently allowed in a situation where a man and a woman are each already sealed to a spouse who is deceased (https://www.churchofjesuschrist.org/study/manual/general- handbook/27-temple-ordinances-for-the-living?lang=eng#title_number32). In that context, a church-approved marriage that will never lead to a temple sealing is allowed – and can be entered into within the walls of a sacred temple. I would weep with joy to see a change like that in the context of gay marriage. Even if gay couples couldn't be married for eternity under current doctrine, it would still be a wonderful progression to see the church formally condone such marriages as healthy relationships for gay people in this life – and to allow those marriages be performed in the temple.

Either of these changes – accepting gay marriage for "time only," in or out of the temple, without loss of church membership – would only require the church to update its General Handbook again to proactively say gay couples are allowed.

However, that's all I want to say about the possibility of church-approved gay marriages for "time-only" – because my heart yearns for full doctrinal equality for *everyone*. I see how much LGBTQ individuals contribute in positive ways to the human race and am in awe of their amazing examples of love and caring here on earth. Heaven just doesn't feel right to me if I have to think of it as a place where gay couples are separated from their spouses. And since this book is all about me expressing my feelings so people can understand better the pain and hope of a Dragon Dad in the church, I feel like shooting for the stars by discussing gay temple sealings.

Do we need to worry about doing a sealing here that shouldn't continue in heaven?

Another reason a change in the church's position against marriage equality in our doctrine may be slow in coming is because church leaders are worried about sealing here on earth something that shouldn't be sealed in heaven. Referring to the sealing power, Jesus said to Peter "whatsoever thou shalt bind on earth shall be bound in heaven" (Matthew 16:19; Doctrine & Covenants 132:7; Helaman 10:7). Without knowing for sure whether gay couples can be present in heaven, or if they will be able to spiritually procreate, church leaders might not want to make a mistake by sealing them here on earth, since, according to that scripture, any such sealing would have eternal effect. However, I wonder if that worry grossly underestimates the sealing power suggested by scripture. I wonder if truly <u>*whatever*</u> we bind on earth through the sealing power, God will honor and keep bound in heaven. Maybe God is telling us through His words in scripture that those who have the sealing power are endowed with broad discretion about who they are allowed to seal – discretion that could be extended to the sealing of gay couples.

In any event, what I don't think many church members realize is that many unrelated men have already been sealed together. Until 1894, many men and women were sealed to General Authorities with whom they shared no biological/familial connection (https://www.dialoguejournal.com/wp- content/uploads/sbi/articles/Dialogue_V34N0102_87.pdf). And many men who were not related to each other in any way were also sealed to one another directly (in a father-son relationship) as well under the "law of adoption" (https://scholarsarchive.byu.edu/cgi/viewcontent.cgi?article=1625&context=byusq). The LGBTQ community tried to use the law of adoption doctrine to further its cause a few decades ago:

> "There is no evidence to suggest that homosexual sex was
> involved as part of the original practice of the law of adoption
> in the 19th century. However, beginning in the 1970s, some
> members of Affirmation: Gay and Lesbian Mormons began to

suggest that the leadership of the church should restore the law of adoption in order to allow same-sex couples to be sealed to each other in the temple in a kind of quasi-celestial marriage. It has been argued that this would preserve the primacy of heterosexual marriage but would allow an ecclesiastical equivalent of homosexual civil unions—a homosexual ecclesiastical union. The church did not respond directly to these suggestions." (https:// en.wikipedia.org/wiki/Law_of_adoption_(Mormonism))

While these are not strong arguments as historical precedents for gay sealings, such past (and now abandoned) sealing practices in the church nevertheless make me wonder whether the doctrine of sealing has more to do with uniting separate families as a whole human family, eventually uniting all of humanity together, through priesthood and sacred covenants, rather than solely binding individuals as romantic couples. Various Latter-day Saint scholars have suggested similar lines of thought (https://interpreterfoundation.org/ news-an-invitation-to-thank-dr-richard- bushman/).

The church itself even recognizes that the way Joseph Smith taught the doctrine of sealing was more expansive than how it is currently taught today – and that might be one of the possible reasons why Joseph Smith was sealed to up to 14 women who were married to other living men. (Note that some of Joseph's marriages were religious in nature without romantic sexual activity; it's not clear whether these sealings were in that category.) The intention of these sealings may have been to create eternal bonds between families, not just between himself and each woman (https://www.churchofjesuschrist.org/ topics/plural-marriage-in-kirtland-and-nauvoo). To me, these historical sealing practices show how a door could be opened to expand current sealing policies to include gay couples in the future. The church wouldn't have to teach something new per se – it could instead just point to what was done in the early days of the church and say that the spirit of the early sealing practices allows us to think about sealing more broadly than we currently do.

[Side note: For those who can't imagine gay sealings being possible, I would invite you to remember that interracial sealings used to be impossible too – and that Brigham Young said that would "always be so" under God's law:

> *"Shall I tell you the law of God in regard to the African race? If the white man who belongs to the chosen seed mixes his blood with the seed of Cain, the penalty, under the law of God, is death on the spot. **This will always be so**." (https://www.fairmormon.org/ answers/Question:_Did_Brigham_Young_say_that_race_mix- ing_was_punis hable_by_death%3F, 1863).]*

An interesting sealing practice that is actually done today could possibly also serve as a door to expand sealing policies for gay couples. When a deceased woman was married to more than one man over the course of her life, and if all the parties are presently deceased, the church's current policy is to seal the woman to _all_ of the men to whom she was married during her life:

> "*Deceased women married more than once.* You may have a deceased woman sealed to all men to whom she was legally married. However, if she was sealed to a husband during her life, all her husbands must be deceased before she can be sealed to a husband to whom she was not sealed during life." (https://www.churchofjesuschrist.org/man- ual/members-guide-to-temple-and-family-history-work/ chapter-7-providing-temple-ordinances)

If each of those sealings has eternal effect, then there will be a situation where one woman will be eternally living in marriage with multiple husbands. But I'm not aware of any church leader who has taught about that heavenly scenario (where a woman has multiple husbands forever) being even remotely possible. In fact, no one actually knows how that situation will play out in heaven.

Why is the church okay with the eternal ambiguity of that situation – just letting God sort it out in the afterlife - but not okay with sealing two men (or two women) in marriage? Why can't we just let God correct that situation too if it turns out gay couples aren't supposed to be sealed? I think the present injustice and pain suffered by a living gay couple not being able to be sealed is more pressing than that of a dead woman being sealed posthumously to her multiple husbands.

Yet church doctrine allows God to undo a sealing for that dead woman if she ends up having a superfluous number of husbands sealed to her - but for some unknown reason, current doctrine can't contemplate God being able to undo the sealings of gay and lesbian couples if those are deemed similarly superfluous as well. I don't think that logical inconsistency in doctrinal reasoning is God's fault. Rather, I suspect that logical failing exists because God can't force us to be more inclusive of LGBTQ people here and now than we want to be. I think God knows we have to overcome our biases on our own, and then He will reveal expanded doctrine that makes more sense.

If doctrinal change is possible, why hasn't it happened?

Because marriage between same-gender spouses is not specifically prohibited in the Bible, in any other book of Latter-day Saint scripture, or by the family proclamation – and because there are ways to imagine doctrinal change occurring within existing theological frameworks and expanded temple practices - I can imagine a future day when God opens the minds and hearts of our prophets and apostles to reveal a doctrinal clarification to them that allows for gay temple marriage. That would be consistent with our beliefs that God continually reveals truth line upon line and that He will "yet reveal many great and important things" pertaining to His kingdom (Article of Faith 9).

Even though change is possible doctrinally, some likely reasons that change hasn't occurred yet might be:

- A change like that may be viewed as a negative reflection on the credibility of our church leaders as prophets and apostles. Our leaders don't want to risk hurting people's faith in them.

- Some of our leaders might have grown accustomed to using the rallying cry against LGBTQ equality as a convenient way to energize church members – inadvertently feeding off of our collective homophobia to unite us in a "just" cause. It may be that the zealousness of such rally-ing efforts is making it harder for those leaders to reverse course now.

- Some of our leaders may be hesitant to lose the support of other conservative churches. Our church is part of a conservative political movement against many LGBTQ rights, and some of our leaders may not want to lose the benefits that come from being part of a large coalition.

For those reasons, I would be incredibly surprised to see such a change hap-pen any time before it is either essentially imposed on the church by outside forces (see Chapter 8), or until the teenagers of today grow up to become the prophets and apostles leading the church in the future.

That doesn't mean I don't suspect some of the apostles who are currently alive might wish gay marriage were allowed in the church (although I would never expect them to say so publicly because church leaders always like to maintain an image of unanimity in public). I actually think it likely there are robust discussions happening about marriage equality among the apostles and the First Presidency. When my parents were called to preside over a couple hundred young missionaries in Tennessee in 1999, our entire family had the opportunity to meet with an apostle when my parents were set apart (a ritual to formally bless a person to carry out a specific calling or responsibility). Our meeting with the apostle occurred in a room in a church office building in Salt Lake City that, upon entering, he described as the "war room" because it was where the apostles and/or First Presidency met regularly when they are not otherwise meeting in the temple together. He explained that there are often intense and vigorous (but respectful) discussions where differences of opinion are debated on many topics in those meetings. He also explained that a decision to take action on any topic wasn't made unless there was unanimity among the First Presidency and all the other apostles.

But we should avoid presuming that unanimity of thought among the apostles exists just because the church has formally declared a position on gay marriage. There are reports in biographies of past apostles of robust debates that transpire among the Quorum of the Twelve and the First Presidency (https://www.google.com/amp/s/www.latimes.com/archives/la-xpm-1988-12-03-me-923-story.html%3f_amp=true). And when apostles are called, they are charged to support whatever the majority of the apostles desire and to publicly portray complete unanimity:

> "Later, **the president gave me what is known as the "charge to the apostles.**" That charge included a commitment to give all that one has, both as to time and means, to the building of the Kingdom of God; to keep himself pure and unspotted from the sins of the world; to be obedient to the authorities of the church; and **to exercise the freedom to speak his mind but always be willing to subjugate his own thoughts and accept the majority opinion—not only to vote for it but to act as though it were his own original opinion after it has been approved by the majority of the Council of the Twelve and the First Presidency.**" (Hugh B. Brown, Apostle, *Hugh B. Brown and Edwin B. Firmage (ed.), An Abundant Life, 2nd ed. (Salt Lake City: Signature Books*, pages 126-127; https://www.google.com/amp/s/prophetsseersandrevelators.wordpress.com/2015/06/01/th e-calling-of-an-apostle/amp/, 1965)

It may be the case that no change in doctrine about it will occur for many, many years, until several of the current apostles – maybe even all of them – pass away. But I could be wrong – because the reversal of the racial priesthood/temple ban happened even though an apostle who had published incredibly racist teachings to justify the ban was still alive at the time. To his credit, he immediately minimized all his prior teachings on the subject:

> "**Forget everything I have said, or what...Brigham Young... or whomsoever has said...that is contrary to the present revelation. We spoke with a limited understanding** and without the light and knowledge that now has come into the world." (Bruce R. McConkie, Apostle, https://www.fairmormon.org/

answers/Criticism_of_Mormonism/Websites/MormonThink/
Blacks_and_the_Priesthood, 1978)

Based on several accounts, it seems clear that the prophet at the time, Spencer W. Kimball, really wanted to make the change (perhaps encouraged by the desires of most church members, outside social pressures or worries over government retribution against the church, as I'll discuss further in Chapter 8). Often, official "unanimity" among church leaders (including at the local levels) is expected (and therefore given) whenever the presiding leader states that his strongly held view is the result of divine revelation. So when President Kimball spoke in those terms, the rest of the apostles quickly fell in line and supported him, even though that meant some of them might face some personal public embarrassment over their past teachings.

However, even if a current apostle who is perhaps LGBTQ-friendly becomes prophet someday, I am not sure whether that alone will be enough for doctrinal change to occur – because I believe the prophet may only have the "real intent" (Moroni 10:4) necessary to receive new revelation on a topic when he is personally confident that the majority of church members are ready to embrace the change. This is different from how Jesus implemented change during His mortal ministry. He did not wait for the majority of the Sadducees and Pharisees to be ready for change when He taught them His radical message of love. And it is different from the way Joseph Smith revealed new doctrines and principles as well. He was constantly revealing adjustments and new, radical thoughts. But ever since Joseph's death, many subsequent prophets in the church have seemed to take on, as their primary responsibility, the role of a reliable steward; someone who protects and encourages deeper living of what has already been revealed, rather than someone who helps facilitate new, radical changes in doctrine. When it comes to the idea of allowing marriage equality in the church, I personally think the general population of the church isn't sufficiently open-minded enough to prevent such a change from "shaking their faith." That may not happen for another generation or two yet, at least. And so until that time comes, whomever is serving as the prophet may be consciously or unconsciously hindered in having sincere intent when asking God about changes in the doctrines affecting our LGBTQ siblings in the church.

I don't know what will happen, obviously. But I do know that it hurts my heart as a father deeply, to be familiar enough with the history, doctrine and theology of the church to be able to imagine a way change could happen, and then hear members of the First Presidency speak words in September and October 2019 that seem almost sure to delay and make change harder to come about, entrenching prejudice more deeply among the general church membership. Nevertheless, I remain committed to speaking up to promote awareness of LGBTQ suffering in the church, to embracing unconditional love instead of prejudice, and to remaining steadfast in my hope that the Lord will someday reveal needed change in the church.

What about countries in which same-sex behavior is still against the law?

Some ask whether the varying legality of gay sexual behavior around the world might be influencing the church's approach to marriage equality under our doctrine, since it is a worldwide church. We continue to see headlines about more and more countries legalizing gay marriage. Pew Forum states that as of October 2019, "30 countries and territories have enacted national laws allowing gays and lesbians to marry, mostly in Europe and the Americas." (https://www.pewforum.org/fact-sheet/gay-marriage-around-the-world/0). But despite the growing acceptance of gay marriage around the world, it still remains prohibited in many countries. As of April 2019, there were 71 countries in the world where same-sex relations are illegal, according to Newsweek: https://www.newsweek.com/73-countries-where-its-illegal-be-gay-1385974. It's a fair question to ask whether church leaders might be worried that acceptance of marriage equality by the church would have a negative effect on the church's image or its missionary work around the globe, or put church members in a difficult position if the laws of the land conflict with church policies.

While that is a fair question, I also believe it has an easy answer. The church has been very capable of convincing leaders of countries with laws that are different from those of the United States that the church believes in "obeying, honoring, and sustaining the law" (Article of Faith 12) wherever the church operates. Under those assurances, the church is able to send volunteers (not calling them missionaries) into countries where certain religious proselytizing is illegal. The church promises government leaders that those volunteers will only do charitable work within their borders, not try to gain religious converts. So I think the church could just as easily tell government leaders around the world that the church will not condone gay marriage among its members in any country where it remains illegal.

At the same time, the church does not condone laws that make gay sex illegal. To the contrary, the church has actively supported non-discrimination laws protecting gay couples (https://www.nytimes.com/2015/03/12/us/politics/utah-passes-antidiscrimination-bill-backed-by-mormon-leaders.html). Church leaders have also taught that showing love and respect for LGBTQ people (including those who are in gay marriages) is a doctrinal teaching that church members should follow (see Chapter 3). So the church's formal doctrine is already more LGBTQ-friendly than the laws of many countries where the church operates. This includes countries in which the church is currently growing rapidly, such as Nigeria and Uganda (https://www.amnesty.org.uk/lgbti-lgbt-gay-human-rights-law-africa-uganda-kenya-nigeria- cameroon; https://en.wikipedia.org/wiki/The_Church_of_Jesus_Christ_of_Latter- day_Saints_in_Nigeria; https://en.wikipedia.org/wiki/The_Church_of_Jesus_Christ_of_Latter- day_Saints_in_Uganda), and other countries in the Americas in which the church has operated for a long time, such as Bolivia and Paraguay (https://en.wikipedia.org/wiki/Recognition_of_same-sex_unions_in_the_Americas).

As long as gay marriages among church members are only condoned by the church in countries where marriage equality is legal, I don't think the church allowing for gay marriage in our theology will have much of a negative effect on the church's image or its missionary work around the globe. Sure, some prospective converts in countries with homophobic laws or cultures may not be interested in learning more about the church if they discovered it supported gay marriage elsewhere. But, based on the fact that many people in those countries are joining the church currently, even though church leaders have supported certain laws that protect the rights of gay couples in the U.S., I don't think those prospective homophobic converts would pay too much attention to the church's position outside their own country. So if the church continued to teach it was a sin to have sexual relations outside of a legal marriage, people who morally oppose gay marriage in any country where it remained illegal could still take comfort in the fact that the church taught that gay marriage was a sin within their borders. I think that is the main thing such prospective converts will care about on this issue.

Thinking of the cruelty of laws in other countries that affect our LGBTQ siblings makes my heart ache. It is a horrible shame that, just for trying to experience loving companionship and natural human intimacy, or just for coming out as LGBTQ, they need to worry about their liberty or physical safety, in addition to worrying about harmful church teachings and their church membership status. I know LGBTQ people in the U.S. and in other countries worry about their safety in certain contexts as well (and I don't want to discount that fear), but I feel a keen sense of sorrow for the LGBTQ people in countries where the law upholds violence or imprisonment against them, just for being who they are. I am grateful the church does not subjugate its doctrine to the imperfect laws of any country, even though we believe in obeying such laws when under their jurisdiction.

CHAPTER 7

COULD EXISTING BELIEFS HELP JUSTIFY CHANGE?

Chapter synopsis: It hurts to hear people compare gay sexual orientation to addictions, disabilities or anything other than straight sexual orientation. Our doctrine and practices allow for compassion and mercy in other difficult circumstances but not for our LGBTQ siblings.

Looking at such other circumstances might be a way the church could find a merciful solution in the future.

If God ever decides that church leaders and church membership as a whole are ready for doctrinal change regarding marriage equality, I have often wondered what the details of such change might look like. I readily admit that my doctrinal imagination is worth even less than two cents, as I am not a theologian or an apostle. But, as I have already written, my mind has still tried to reconcile the idea of gay temple marriage with our existing teachings about eternity. I wonder if the key to any new doctrinal construct allowing gay couples to be sealed in the temple for eternity might be as simple as focusing on the example of Christ. Even if we don't get a new revelation that provides specific details about what all relationships in heaven will look like, perhaps we could still allow for gay temple sealings by simply focusing on His example of going against societal conventions to treat marginalized people with equality – and then just let Him figure out later exactly how things will look for everyone in heaven.

The crucial difference between that hopeful version of a trust-in-the-Lord approach vs. the harmful version that I talked about in Chapter 4 is looking at the nature of what needs to be resolved. The harmful version expects LGBTQ church members to trust that the Lord will redefine *trauma* here as *joy* in heaven. But the hopeful version of trust-in-the-Lord simply expects that spousal and familial happiness will continue there somehow. In the hopeful version, ambiguity about heaven allows equality to exist in this life, consistent with scriptural declarations that "all are alike unto God" (2 Nephi 26:33) and that God is "no respecter of persons" (Acts 10:34-35). It asks us to trust that church policy based on those scriptures will not result in a "sad heaven" later for anyone. But in the harmful version of trust-in-the-Lord, a uniform and rigid notion of heaven based on unnecessary theological assumptions, rather than clear scriptural assertions, forces LGBTQ church members to live with inequality in this life – and to look forward to disparity and pain somehow becoming good things in heaven. Under the harmful version, many LGBTQ church members struggle with psychological trauma as they try to look to the Lord to reconcile their innate, God-given desires for love and intimacy with a contradictory concept of heaven. But under the hopeful version, an increased willingness by the church to allow ambiguity about heaven helps LGBTQ church members maintain optimism and good mental health in this life, as they place the burden on God to reconcile how He created them with what He has in store for them in eternity.

I would be happy (even if not completely satisfied) to see the church simply modify its stance about being sure gay couples won't exist in heaven, so that a trust-in-the-Lord approach might be able to provide comfort for LGBTQ church members like it does for many other people in challenging circumstances. This idea of treating people fairly and lovingly now and just letting God sort out whatever difficulties that might suggest about the afterlife later is not a new notion under church teachings. We already do this in several contexts in the church; I have often thought of these as possible precedents that could be used to provide a path towards acceptance of marriage equality within the church.

Is it appropriate to compare being gay to anything other than being straight?

First, I want to spend some time discussing the inadequacies of analogies made in an effort to justify the church's prohibition of gay marriage. When I discuss contexts that I believe offer precedential value in this chapter, I don't intend to suggest that any of the situations I'll examine are analogous to gay sexual orientation. Rather, I am only suggesting that doctrinal or policy approaches that the church has already adopted to deal with certain other situations might also be helpful in finding a more compassionate approach to our LGBTQ siblings as well.

I want to make sure no one confuses any of the comparisons I'll be drawing in later sections of this chapter to any comparison with gay sexual orientation itself - because I feel it is very important for everyone to understand that there is only one analogy that is appropriate for being gay - and that is being straight. When someone tries to compare being gay to anything other than being straight, the comparison inevitably fails when it is closely scrutinized.

Is alcoholism or any other addiction appropriately analogous?

A common comparison sounds like this: asking gay people to refrain from gay sex is like asking someone born with a predisposition to alcoholism to avoid drinking. Other comparisons are often made to other addictions as well – with the general theme being that keeping gospel commandments may be harder for some because of predispositions that they are born with.

I think any comparison to addiction is wrong for many reasons, including because alcohol, drugs, gambling, and pornography can all lead to disconnection from self and others – whereas LGBTQ identities are about seeking connection with self and others. I believe most comparisons to addiction originate from disproven psychological understandings of gay sexual orientation which were developed decades or even centuries ago, when gay sexual orientation was regarded as psychologically abnormal or unhealthy. In the 1970s, the American Medical Association removed "homosexuality" from its list of mental disorders. That was a long time ago!

Nevertheless, comparing gay sexual orientation to addiction is still a common occurrence, even though being gay is not considered a disease any longer by any reasonable therapist, counselor or doctor, yet addiction has been categorized as a disease by the American Medical Association since 1956 (https://www.hazeldenbettyford.org/articles/why-is-alcoholism-classified-as-a- mental-illness).

Because comparing gay sexual orientation to addiction is so common, I have seen many comments in social media groups for Latter-day Saint allies of LGBTQ individuals where people debunk the comparison. I thought the following three comments were particularly good (included anonymously to protect privacy):

Comment #1:

"Of course, there's truth to the idea that we are all responsible for our decisions no matter what our predispositions are. But one minor but important difference is the avoid-ability factor. Alcoholism and drug addiction are hard to beat, but pretty avoidable if you never partake of either. To develop the addiction, you have to make an initial choice that's already against the Church's teachings. True, this may be coerced, but such coerced cases are rare. In contrast, homosexual desires, gender dysphoria, etc. seem to develop regardless of an initial catalyzing "sin," making them much more difficult to avoid/resist.

To me, though, the more important difference is in the health effects. Even with all the tabloid studies saying that a little alcohol might be good for you, there aren't many experts claiming that a little alcohol is better than no alcohol at all, especially when you factor in the risk of it developing into alcoholism, and there's not really anyone arguing that excessive alcohol drinking isn't bad for you. For drugs, the complete abstinence route is even more widely accepted. Even for more debatable Word of Wisdom substances like coffee and tea, it's pretty clear that you can lead a very healthy life without them, even a much healthier life than one in which they're overused. In these situations, the Church's stance has generally gradually become backed by the science. And helping people overcome associated addictions is a legitimate, even laudable measure to preserve their overall health.

One of the biggest differences for queer people is that the opposite holds. There's a growing consensus among health experts, particularly in the realm of psychology, that the Church's stand on queer people is unhealthy. Lifelong celibacy, mixed-orientation marriage, retaining birth gender in spite of gender dysphoria, and so on—all of these Church-backed choices appear to be associated with significant mental health detriment, leading to increased levels of anxiety, depression, self-harm, and suicide. Whereas in so many other respects following the Church's counsel is seen to lead to greater health and happiness, for queer members following Church guidance, it appears to lead to an overall deterioration of health. Who, then, can blame a queer person who starts to feel that **for them** in the Church, **righteousness never was happiness**?

I believe that we're fortunate to live in a time when the Church can take a more nuanced view than saying that a person who takes their own life has condemned themselves to lesser post-life glory, acknowledging instead that such individuals have fallen prey to issues of mental health often not completely in their control. Unfortunately, however, I feel that we still don't live in a time when the leading voices in the Church fully acknowledge their role in such issues. I feel that there is still some introspection to be done among the Church's leadership, some epiphanies to be had about the uniquely difficult positions into which they put a small percentage of the Church's membership. I still pray that the time will come, and hopefully in the not too distant future, when the people in high-up Church positions will gain real understanding of the plight of these downtrodden within their fold, and the extent to which they have had a hand in that suffering.

Until then, I hope you never just yield yourself to those who would paint you as no more than a recovering addict. For many reasons, including but not limited to the ones mentioned here, you are in a unique and a difficult position. You are a child of God, and I think it's fair to hope that He loves and understands you to a degree not accurately emulated by any of the detracting voices you hear, even those through whom God ostensibly directly reveals His will. I hope that all of us who find ourselves falling victim to people preaching with preconceived prejudices such as these can stand strong. Perhaps we can eventually change some of the hardened hearts that may still cling to these preconceptions."

Comment #2:

"First, the comparisons are categorically not equal. Being LGBTQ is biologically determined and not chosen. This point is not contested by the LDS Church.

Second, the stereotypes displayed here are that being LGBTQ is directly compared to things LDS members consider evil. This is the root of the hate-speech most LDS people aren't even aware is hate-speech. You are classifying a group of people as evil and it is embedded at a theological level.

This doesn't mean there isn't a morality to sexuality or chastity. It just looks the same as a heterosexual person: infidelity, fornication, pornography, adultery, etc. But it is compounded by not allowing same-sex marriage or disrespecting same-sex relationships. LGBTQ people living in committed, monogamous relationships are as moral and rewarding as straight relationships.

Denying that [choice] to them pushes their relationships into the shadows and has more to do with causing the "gay lifestyle" that straight people criticize than anything else. You can't on the one-hand criticize a loose-moral culture while simultaneously denying legitimate marriages to same-sex people. If you truly wanted to reduce the "gay lifestyle" (i.e., homosexual promiscuity), you would be rushing to support same-sex marriages."

Comment #3:

"When I have had these conversations, the person's argument is typically rooted in the "it's not a sin to be gay, just to act on it" mindset. So basically, they're thinking just because you want something, doesn't mean you need to partake, which for some reason gets extrapolated to addiction and incredibly unhealthy pursuits. So, my question back to them is usually to consider the fruits. What are the fruits of pornography? What are the fruits of drugs or alcohol? Or any addiction? And then consider: what are the fruits of a healthy, committed relationship? They absolutely cannot be compared if you consider the fruits. I have had some people say the fruits of a same-sex relationship are that it puts you outside of God's laws. Well...so do a lot of things [like] civil (rather than temple) marriage. There are a lot of things people do every day that are outside the bounds of what we've been taught - do we compare their actions to pornography or addiction? I think we'd be making a lot more enemies if we did (which is why it's easier to look at LGBT people - who tend to already be an "other" to most - this way)."

All of those comments resonate with me. It seems plain to me that comparing gay sexual orientation to any addiction is not only faulty reasoning, but also very insulting to gay people in general.

[Side note: There are dozens of social media groups formed specifically to provide support to people at the crossroads of LGBTQ issues and Latter-day Saint doctrine and culture. In addition to Mama Dragons and Dragon Dads, which I mentioned in the Preface, there are groups like Mormons Building Bridges, Latter-gay Stories, Affirmation, Peculiar, Encircle and numerous others. There are thousands of Latter-day Saints in these groups who are praying for more compassionate treatment of LGBTQ individuals by the church. Cheryl and I belong to many of these groups. It seems like every day I see a post about another Latter-day Saint parent of an LGBTQ child who is joining one or more of those groups. Many days I see multiple posts like that. And the stories we read about in these groups are heartbreaking. It is overwhelming at times to realize how many people are feeling so much pain.]

Is physical or mental disability appropriately analogous?

Another comparison is that gay sexual orientation is like a mental or physical disability. I think the main problem with that analogy is that the vast majority of gay people don't feel they are disabled. And rightly so. The definition of "disability" is "a physical or mental condition that limits a person's movements, senses, or activities" (https://www.lexico.com/en/definition/disability). Nothing about being attracted to someone of the same sex limits anyone's movements, senses, or activities. And gay people are able to love and connect physically and emotionally just as meaningfully in their gay relationships as straight people are in theirs.

I have heard some people say that is not true because gay couples cannot reproduce. Therefore, that biological inability to procreate between them can be loosely viewed as a disability. But that means we must also call infertile heterosexual couples disabled as well. I don't think it's accurate, intellectually or emotionally, to say that a heterosexual couple who doesn't have kids, or one that adopts kids, has a marriage relationship that is limited or not as full or rich as a couple that has reproduced and has biological offspring. There are many examples of couples who have reproduced biologically who are not as closely bonded as other couples who have not done so. And it's also not accurate to say that adoptive parents are limited in comparison to biological parents either. My sister and her husband have adopted three children and I think they are <u>way</u> better parents, and have closer relationships with their kids, than many other couples I know who have biologically reproduced. So I don't think it's right to view gay couples as disabled just because they can't have kids. Their parenting skills are not lacking in any way (and in some situations are clearly better in comparison to heterosexual couples; see Chapter 8).

[<u>Side note:</u> It is important to note that parents can be sealed to their adopted children. If gay temple sealings are ever allowed in the church, opposite gender couples who adopt and same-gender couples who adopt would then be in exactly the same position from an eternal perspective.]

It's also inappropriate to view gay sexual orientation as similar to a disability from a doctrinal/eternal perspective as well. Some believe that a gay person having their sexuality switched in the afterlife shouldn't be thought of more negatively than how we view the removal of a physical or mental disability in the afterlife. But the significant problem with that comparison is that it fails to consider whether the disabled person *wants* to be changed after this life. In most cases, they are looking forward to not being disabled (or, for a person with insufficient mental capacity to understand the concept of such a change, we assume they would look forward to being healed of their disability if they could understand the idea of it). That is not true for all gay people though, especially for those who are in loving relationships with a same-gender spouse. While some individuals who experience gay sexual desires, perhaps especially those in mixed-orientation marriages, may want to be changed after this life, many gay people do not want to be changed. This is especially true for those who are in loving relationships and are learning how to connect intimately and express affection and devotion in ways that are strongly connected to their sexuality. Those are all good things, especially the bond they share with their spouse. Can those of us in loving heterosexual marriages understand how painful it is to imagine being asked to think of our closeness and affection with our spouse as something that doesn't fit anywhere in heaven? Or that it's something we should have faith will be a good thing to lose in the afterlife? For that reason, it is incredibly painful and inappropriate to suggest that a gay person being "fixed" after this life is similar to a disabled person being healed of their disability.

In short, I believe that the resurrection will only "fix" negative things – not take away something positive. And diversity is a positive thing. We should teach that all the things that bring us deep and lasting joy in this life should remain, not be removed. If we start accepting the belief that the resurrection will physically change us in ways that will result in us no longer being able to maintain the loving relationships that bring us the most joy in this life, then our theology becomes quite dark and depressing, not full of the Spirit.

Is the ability to speak a language appropriately analogous?

Perhaps because comparing gay sexual orientation to a disease like addiction or to a physical or mental disability is harmful, some Latter-day Saint thinkers and therapists have tried to compare it to other human behaviors or capacities that do not have negative connotations. Dr. Jeff Robinson, a Utah psychotherapist, espouses a notion that gay sexual orientation is like being able to speak a native language. He argues that having a gay sexual orientation is something someone just "knows how to do" without remembering having learned it. Like native-language acquisition, he teaches that sexual orientations are acquired, not inborn. I first came across Dr. Robinson's teachings in 2018, after he gave a speech at a church apologist conference: https://www.fairmormon.org/conference/august-2018/thinking-differently-about-same-sex- attraction). A few well-intentioned people I know asked me to read Dr. Robinson's lecture, to help me view Wes' sexuality from a different perspective. Unless hearing a presentation that justifies harmful conversion therapy will be emotionally traumatizing for you, I encourage you to take a break from reading here and spend some time to review in full that speech by Dr. Robinson, so you can understand his viewpoint better before you read my thoughts on his teachings.

— Okay. Are you done reading his presentation? Great. ☺

My first reaction when I read Dr. Robinson's speech was that it was harmful to gay individuals because it implies that it is just as possible to learn a different sexual orientation as it is to learn a foreign language. But I have never heard of anyone killing themselves over not being able to learn to speak a different language – yet there are many, many cases where gay people <u>have</u> killed themselves because therapies to help them become straight haven't worked (see Chapter 8). I think his views nonetheless seem to resonate with many of my fellow Latter-day Saints who are trying to understand gay sexual orientation because his ideas allow them to take the position that even though gay sexual desire is not a choice (as the church acknowledges now), it still doesn't have to be something someone is born with. I think that allows church members to feel less bad about the fact that our doctrine treats gay people differently than everyone else.

My main substantive criticism is that Dr. Robinson's notions don't give proper weight to ongoing scientific discovery. Numerous scientific studies have confirmed that genetics and epigenetics play a central role in why people experience gay sexual attraction (see Chapter 3). For each person who experiences gay sexual desire, the primary cause of such attraction (or of any sexual orientation really) is likely a combination of both inherited genetics and epigenetics.

With that in mind, here are some related criticisms I have of Dr. Robinson's notions:

1. Someone being able to speak a particular language has nothing to do with the physiological responses of their body. That is, someone's biological processes don't work differently than another person's just because they speak a different language. But with sexual orientation, physiological response is triggered by different stimuli – which is an

unchosen chemical reaction, not just something the mind "knows how to do." That is not true with language acquisition - speaking Russian vs. English doesn't correlate to varying changed chemical and physiological response.

2. Language deals with the expression of concepts. But sexuality deals with the instinctive drive to mate. Yes, both involve communication I suppose, but they are fundamentally different kinds of communication. One is focused on understanding as the primary goal and the other is focused on innate biological bonding as the primary goal. (Note I didn't say "reproduction" – it is possible to mate biologically without the two lovers being able to reproduce.)

3. Relatedly, if someone tries but finds they are unable to learn how to speak another language, their psychological and emotional pain is limited to just frustration at people not understanding them. But if a gay person wants to "learn" how to feel sexually attracted to the opposite sex but is unable to do so, their frustration cuts to the core of how they mate with another human. Then they end up confirming their fears: that their sexuality is an unchangeable part of them, not just something they unknowingly learned how to do.

4. Speaking another language is not deemed a sin by the church, but acting on gay sexual desires is. There is an element of shame brought into one but not the other, at least for church members.

5. I don't think Dr. Robinson's analogy reflects how most people feel about their sexuality. For example, I wonder if straight church members who find his analogy useful are willing to apply it to themselves, but in reverse. After all, Dr. Robinson says that: "[W]hat I have said about homosexuality, or same-sex attraction, also applies to heterosexuality. I believe that no specific sexual arousal pattern is hardwired at birth." Since most people are presumably able to learn to speak another language, then straight church members should be okay learning to be

gay too, right? If they really think hard about that prospect, I believe most of those straight church members will abandon their support for Dr. Robinson's analogy because they'll realize their sexual orientation has more to do with their body's physiology than it does the heteronormative culture in which they were raised. I imagine they'd agree with what I have already noted from Dr. William Bradshaw, a BYU microbiologist (and former mission president): "I don't think I have tried to hide my conclusion about [the cause of gay sexual orientation]. **It isn't nurture. It's nature**."

I think all of those points make Dr. Robinson's analogy dangerous. I believe he is giving church members a basis on which they can treat gay people in harmful ways by telling them their sexuality isn't a part of them; it's just something they know how to do. When our gay siblings learn that, contrary to Dr. Robinson's views, their sexual orientations are innate, not acquired, their feelings of depression and darkness might become more acute if they are emotionally close to family or church members who believe in his misguided teachings. Many church leaders are aware of FairMormon, the apologetic group that put on the conference at which Dr. Robinson spoke, and they rely on it for church-friendly information about difficult issues. I think it's a shame that some church leaders will rely on this man's well-intentioned but false (and harmful, even dangerous) ideas.

Is pedophilia appropriately analogous?

I unfortunately feel it is necessary to address one final type of false comparison to gay sexual orientation that I've heard people raise: pedophilia. I really want to just type "NO, being gay is NOT like being a pedophile!!" and move on, because I still have a hard time believing someone would ever think pedophilia could be analogous to gay sexual orientation. But, believe it or not, several people have told me they consider the two desires to be comparable. So I feel like I have to at least briefly address this insulting and hurtful comparison.

The argument of those who make this analogy is that, assuming both gay sexual orientation and pedophilia are things people are born with, asking a gay person to refrain from having sex with someone of their same gender is no different than asking a pedophile to refrain from having sex with a child. But the obvious reason why those situations are vastly different is that one involves a request to refrain from engaging in intimacy and companionship with a consenting adult (which are things that have been shown in multiple studies can reduce depression and suicidality among LGBTQ people). The other is a request to refrain from preying on a child who cannot provide consent. Requiring that pedophiles not have sex with minors protects children from harm. But requiring consenting gay adults to avoid intimate relationships with each other *causes* harm.

[*Side note: There are many resources that debunk the myth that gay men are more likely to be pedophiles. The well- respected Southern Poverty Law Center website linked below includes some of those resources as well as others that debunk the following myths too:*

- *Myth #1: Gay men molest children at far higher rates than heterosexuals*

- *Myth #2: Same-sex parents harm children*

- *Myth #3: People become homosexual because they were sexually abused as children or there was a deficiency in sex-role modeling by their parents.*

- *Myth #4: LGBT people don't live nearly as long as heterosexuals.*

- *Myth #5: Gay men controlled the Nazi Party and helped to orchestrate the Holocaust.*

- *Myth #6: Hate crime laws will lead to the jailing of pastors who criticize homosexuality and the legalization of practices like bestiality and necrophilia.*

- *Myth #7: Allowing gay people to serve openly will damage the armed forces.*

- *Myth #8: Gay people are more prone to be mentally ill and to abuse drugs and alcohol.*

- *Myth #9: No one is born gay.*

- *Myth #10: Gay people can choose to leave homosexuality.*
  https://www.splcenter.org/fighting-hate/intelligence-report/2011/
  10-anti-gay-myths-debunked.]

Okay, so to reiterate before proceeding: sexual orientation is only analogous to itself; meaning, the **ONLY** analogy that works for someone having gay sexual desires is someone else having straight sexual desires. The only appropriate analogy to being gay is being straight. Is that clear enough? Okay. Good. I wish more church members would realize (and really think about) that.

Do current doctrinal gaps provide an example for a possible solution?

Now, back to the idea that the church might be able to look at ways it already treats some difficult mortal or post-mortal situations as a model for how it could better handle gay sexual orientation. There are already many situations where we basically just rely on hope without getting too specific on eternal details – where we are comfortable with ambiguity and just letting God eventually fill in any doctrinal gaps:

1. We don't define rigidly when someone has had the chance to accept the gospel in this life; we just say God is the judge of whether they would have accepted it if they could. We perform temple ceremonies (including eternal marriage) for them by proxy so they can be saved just like everyone else.

2. Similarly, we don't tend to hear in General Conference repeatedly (like we do with LGBTQ issues) that non-church member spouses will be left single for eternity, so that their believing member spouse can be married to someone else for eternity. Rather, we tend to mostly acknowledge that we don't know what will happen with that non-member spouse. We just trust God to work things out in a way that will make everyone happy.

3. When a straight person doesn't have the opportunity to get married in this life, we teach that God will work it out so they will find someone to marry after this life.

4. When a widow who has been sealed in the temple remarries, and her second husband is a man who has not yet been sealed in the temple, we don't condemn that man to a lesser degree of heaven just because he cannot also be sealed to her. We just trust God to work things out.

5. For Latter-day Saints like me who believe polygamy will not exist in heaven for anyone (which I believe reflects the strongest doctrinal position on eternal polygamy, based on scripture anyway), we just trust that God will somehow make those plural wives happy with someone else in heaven (which, based on many of their journal entries, might be exactly what they're hoping for now anyway).

6. When a woman is worried about having to live in polygamy for eternity because her widower fiancé has already been sealed to a prior (deceased) wife, we tell her to just trust God to work things out. This specific example was something President Oaks encouraged in another General Conference talk in October 2019 - https://www.churchofjesuschrist.org/study/general-conference/2019/10/17oaks).

7. We don't say someone will inherit a lower kingdom of heaven when they die by suicide. The doctrine of the church used to say that, but it no longer does. Now church doctrine just leaves it up to the judgment of God where a person who has committed suicide will end up in eternity.

[Side note: I wonder if the church's doctrinal evolution on suicide could perhaps offer a precedent for how doctrinal evolution could occur on marriage equality too. Historical statements by church leaders on suicide included the following:

> *"Shortening life is sin. This temple of God is the body that the Lord has given us. It has been given to us to last a long time. **It is a terrible criminal act for a person to go out and shorten**

his life by suicide or by any other method if it is intentional, by shortening it with the things that will create an early death." (Spencer W. Kimball, Prophet – The Teachings of Spencer W. Kimball, p.188; http://www.russellyanderson.com/mormons/basic/doctrines/suicide_eom.htm, 1982)

"Every member of the Church should be made to understand that it is a dreadful sin to take one's own life. It is self-murder." (George Q. Cannon, a member of the First Presidency from 1873- 1901)

But current church teachings leave the eternal effects of suicide ambiguous: https://www.churchofjesuschrist.org/study/manual/doctrine-and-principles/doctrine-and-principles. Maybe someday the church will allow gay people to marry and stay in the church, and just leave the eternal consequences in God's hands as well?]

I could go on and on, listing "work-it-out" scenarios like those. Whenever we bump into a situation in mortality where our theology doesn't seem kind, we just put a pin in things and leave it to God to sort everything out in the afterlife with His perfect mercy – which I think is great. I know of no religion whose theology doesn't have some "mysteries" that need to be handled in that way.

But in order to do that in the context of the difficult situations facing LGBTQ individuals in the church, I think we actually need to have a change in doctrine first – because our current doctrine just doesn't allow for God to work anything out for LGBTQ individuals without them still suffering in eternity. In each of the above examples (and in all other "work-it-out" situations I can think of), current doctrinal constructs allow for us to just leave it to God to judge someone's heart and make appropriate arrangements accordingly, so they can be happy in heaven. But the doctrinal paradigm that heterosexual marriage is the only kind of marriage that can exist in heaven makes the idea of eternal happiness there actually seem miserable to gay people and causes more heartache than what trusting in the Lord to work things out would mean in any other context.

For example, consider scenarios 1 and 2 above: what constitutes a chance to hear the gospel in this life, and non-church member spouses. In those situations, the only difficulty someone might need to face to have things worked out for them is that the non-church members involved will need to change their minds and finally accept the gospel after this life. For scenario 3, the lifelong single straight person, the difficulty is that a single person has to trust that, at some point in the afterlife, they'll find someone they'll love to marry. Similarly, in scenario 4 about the sealed widow who remarries, and scenario 5 about polygamy, spouses here in mortality will need to find someone else to marry after this life. But none of those situations will need to have their sexuality switched also. And, in scenario 6, if polygamy will exist in the afterlife (which I don't believe it will, for anyone – but again, I digress), I feel that sharing the love of your life for eternity in polygamy is not as bleak a prospect as it is to lose them entirely and then have to spend eternity with someone toward whom you had no natural affection. And finally, in scenario 7 about suicide, there is only peace found for everyone in the thought that God will judge someone mercifully and leniently if they take their own life.

Bottom line: in order for a "work-it-out" or "trust-in-the-Lord" approach to function in the context of LGBTQ individuals, I think our doctrine needs to allow at least the imagining of a heaven that offers something appealing to them, which currently, it does not. We need a doctrinal change to at least allow for ambiguity, so that the idea of just trusting God to make things right can really be a viable hope for all people.

Should we prioritize healthy relationships here and now over heavenly unknowns?

Would it be possible to at least just say we don't know if gay marriage can exist in heaven (as opposed to saying we're sure it cannot exist there), allow for equal treatment here on earth, and then just let God sort it all out later? Could we just seal every loving couple who wants a temple marriage, straight or gay, and let God figure out if they can reach the highest degree of heaven and spiritually procreate there later?

The sealing ceremony in the temple currently quotes the Bible in instructing the man and woman to "multiply and replenish the earth" (Genesis 1:28).

But I know several heterosexual couples who can't follow that commandment because they are infertile or marry past childbearing years. If we're comfortable thinking God is okay with us asking sealed couples in this life to obey a commandment they are not physically able to comply with, then why is it so hard for us to think God might also be alright with us sealing a gay couple even though they might or might not be able to reproduce in heaven?

Well, many church members might answer that question by emphasizing the difference between a mortal vs. eternal condition. Or they might worry that we could incorrectly be sealing here on earth something that God doesn't want sealed in heaven. But, as I discussed in Chapter 6, that concern may not need to be viewed as a compelling reason to refrain from sealing gay couples when we recognize (i) that many unrelated men have already been sealed to one another (through the historical practice of the "law of adoption"), (ii) that deceased women are allowed to be sealed to more than one man, (iii) that Joseph Smith taught the doctrine of sealing in a much broader way than we currently practice it today, and (iv) that God may have already promised us in scripture that *whatever* we seal here will be respected by Him as something appropriate to remain sealed in heaven. In other words, we are already trusting God to work out a lot of unusual sealing situations, so why can't we trust Him similarly with gay couples? A lot of deep thought on how the sealing doctrine might be expanded to include gay couples has been written about more extensively here: https://www.dialoguejournal.com/wp- content/uploads/sbi/articles/ Dialogue_V44N04_420.pdf. (This is an article I already shared previously; I'm just providing the link here again because I think it's really great.)

Perhaps ensuring that our religious practices here match what we think we know about the order of heaven results in "putting the cart before the horse," theologically speaking. Jesus didn't teach that a true focus on heaven involved strict rules of procedure in religious worship and a constant obsession with what our station will be in the afterlife. He actually condemned that tendency among the Pharisees repeatedly. Instead, Jesus and his disciples taught that to make it to heaven, we need to believe in Him and care most about the people around us here and now (Matthew 7:21; Matthew 22:37-39; John 6:40; 1 John 3:23).

This concept is also taught beautifully through an introspective question posed by a popular Buddhist teacher and author:

> "Rather than speculating about what happens when we die, what if we could anchor ourselves in the present moment. **What would your world look like if you chose to believe in life before death?**" (Noah Rasheta, https://www.amazon.com/Secular- Buddhism-Noah-Rasheta/dp/1366922735, 2016)

Similarly, what would our doctrine look like if we chose to believe in life before death? Could we focus on just letting gay people find happiness and fulfillment here (and avoid self-loathing and poor mental health), through monogamous, moral, and committed gay marriages, and through full church fellowship as well, and then just trust in God to work out what happens in eternity later somehow? We focus a lot on future events in our theology, like Christ's eventual return and sacred ordinances we perform to allow for a better existence in the afterlife. But during His mortal ministry, Jesus seemed to focus most on how we should love each other in the present.

I believe God cares most that we show true charity to all people in this life, rather than telling them to just wait and hope for better things in the afterlife. Even though I don't like the current doctrine that gay couples can't be together forever in heaven, my soul could tolerate it much better if the church simply allowed married gay couples to maintain their membership in the church in this life. If the prophets and apostles of our church feel like their hands are tied doctrinally because God hasn't revealed that gay couplehood can last in eternity, then perhaps they could at least just make a policy change applicable to this life only – to allow gay individuals to marry each other civilly and still stay in the church? Many straight members of the church worry about polygamy in heaven, but we tolerate that possibility (horrible to some) because we don't have to actually live it here. The prophets and apostles may feel their hands are tied doctrinally about polygamy too, because God may not have revealed to them whether it will be required in heaven. Maybe the church could take a similar approach to gay people: let them have good and healthy marriages here, and worry about heaven later.

I don't know for sure, but perhaps such an approach has not been implemented yet because some of our prophets and apostles believe that gay relationships are actually counterproductive to eternal progression. I have heard various religious leaders teach that because men and women are so different from one another, the way they learn to love each other requires more compromise, communication, and effort than what gay spouses do in their marriages. Therefore, the straight couple learns to become more loving and compassionate than the gay couple can. I don't believe that is true though. From what I have gathered, gay spouses face unique challenges in dealing with bigotry from others, in trying to bring children into their family, and in affirming one another in their respective roles in their marriage. These challenges are equally (if not more) difficult than the challenges a husband and a wife face in learning to understand one another as opposite-sex persons.

Both types of couples provide opportunities for individuals to learn selflessness, compromise, loyalty, sacrifice, devotion, kindness, tenderness, and a million other amazing things that marriage can teach. But, sadly, because of the church's teaching that gay sex is a sin worthy of loss of church membership, there is one wonderful thing a gay married couple cannot learn that a straight couple can: the exciting sense of discipleship and unity that can come from serving together as a family in our church. Different lessons of discipleship and unity can be learned outside of the church, for sure. But because gay couples are denied membership in the church, anything that straight couples can learn uniquely from being involved in church service are lessons that are, by default, denied to gay couples. I personally cherish each of the unique lessons I have learned from my years of church service. So it hurts my heart to know those lessons are withheld from <u>anyone</u> who is otherwise willing and ready to serve in the church simply because someone wants to have a uniform-orientation marriage and family.

At the very least, I hope our church leaders might someday allow married gay couples to stay in the church as a compassionate exception to church rules, even if they affirmatively say such exception has no implications for eternity (i.e., so even if only gay *civil* marriage is viewed as a tolerated exception by the church while gay *temple* marriage remains prohibited). I would consider that tolerable progress that is at least partially consistent with the Dalia Lama's teaching:

> "Our prime purpose in this life is to help others. If you can't help them, at least don't hurt them." (https://www.inuth.com/india/ happy-birthday-dalai-lama-11-quotes-from- the-tibetan-spiri-tual-leader-that-would-inspire-every-millennial/)

Could gay marriage be seen as an exception to the commandment to marry straight?

In my heart of hearts, I don't want to just hope for non-temple gay marriage to be viewed as tolerable. That would result in gay couples being treated as second-class members of the church (i.e., not as "good" as straight couples who have been sealed), just because they're gay. So I aim my hope at the stars and keep dreaming that gay temple marriage will someday be allowed.

However, many church leaders have stated their belief that even just gay civil marriage (let alone gay temple marriage) goes against the family proclamation's teaching that heterosexual marriage is "ordained of God" and against the scriptural teaching that heterosexual marriage is necessary to enter the highest degree of heaven (Doctrine & Covenants 132) (https://www.chur-chofjesuschrist.org/study/manual/gospel-topics/marriage). But such teachings do not need to be diminished simply because gay temple marriage is added as something extra that could also work (see Chapter 5).

Even if that idea of gay marriage being an extra and harmless thing is accepted, another problem still arises to prevent gay marriage: apostles and prophets have interpreted scripture to teach that heterosexual marriage is actually an affirmative commandment:

"Scriptures declare that 'it is lawful that [a man] should have one wife, and they twain shall be one flesh, and all this that the earth might answer the end of its creation' (Doctrine & Covenants 49:16). Another affirms that 'the man [is not] without the woman, neither the woman without the man, in the Lord' (1 Corinthians 11:11). **Thus, marriage is not only an exalting principle of the gospel; it is a divine commandment.**" (Russell M. Nelson, Apostle, https://www.churchofjesuschrist.org/study/general-conference/2008/10/celestial-marriage, 2008)

If heterosexual marriage is a commandment, some might wonder how the church could ever allow gay marriage, because that would seem to condone a choice that would close the door on a gay person obeying the commandment to enter into a straight marriage. Well, I think we might gain some insight by looking at a situation where this commandment is not deemed applicable: people with physical or mental disabilities are not expected to marry (nor do they even need to be baptized, for that matter: https://www.churchofjesus-christ.org/study/ensign/1976/04/i-have-a- question/should-mentally-retard-ed-children-be-baptized). Now, I want to make clear that I am not suggesting that having a gay sexual orientation should be considered a disability. I have already debunked that analogy at the outset of this chapter. Rather, I am just raising this example where an aspect of someone's physical makeup or biology renders a commandment inapplicable to them. Can we imagine the problems that would arise if we tried to force everyone with a mental disability to get married? Well, while not as extreme a situation, the church's doctrine currently seems to expect gays and lesbians to conform to rules that are not healthy for them mentally or emotionally either. Is it possible God might not expect the same rules to apply for gays and lesbians? Instead of commanding that they marry someone of the opposite sex or abstain from lifelong companionship altogether, could God be okay with them marrying someone of the same sex, especially now that society has progressed sufficiently that marriage equality is legally protected?

There may be scriptural support for the idea that different rules apply for gay people. In Matthew chapter 19, Jesus teaches about marriage and says divorce should not be allowed for "every cause" – that it shouldn't be as easy to "put away" a wife under His gospel construct as it had been for a man to do so under the law of Moses. His disciples then wondered whether it would be better for a man to just not get married at all then, to which Jesus said:

> "But he said unto them, **All men cannot receive this saying, save they to whom it is given. For there are some eunuchs, which were so born from their mother's womb**, and there are some eunuchs, which were made eunuchs of men: and there be eunuchs, which have made themselves eunuchs for the kingdom of heaven's sake. He that is able to receive it, let him receive it." (Matthew 19:12)

Based on the frequent usage of the term "born eunuch" in other ancient writings (including in the Talmud) to refer to gay males, many Bible scholars have said that the first class of eunuchs Jesus described in the above scripture were gay men. Such an interpretation results in the following understanding of this scripture (with some of my own commentary in brackets):

> "Here Jesus identifies three classes of men who should not marry women. Taking his categories in reverse order, first, there are those who have made themselves eunuchs for the kingdom of heaven, i.e., those who foreswear marriage to better serve God *[think of our young full-time missionaries, for example]*. Second, he mentions those who have been made eunuchs by others, an apparent reference to castrated males *[this was done to slaves in ancient times]*. **But Jesus mentions a third category: eunuchs who were born that way. Some might argue that Jesus was referring to males born without testicles, but this would be extremely rare. Moreover, this interpretation ignores how the term 'born eunuchs' was used in other literature of the time.**" (http://www.goodhopemcc.org/spirituality/

would-jesus-discriminate/456-jesus-said-some-are-born-gay-
matthew-1910-12.html)

So, Jesus seems to teach in Matthew 19 that being gay is a valid reason to not
enter into a straight marriage.

Another scripture that might be interpreted to teach that the commandment to enter into straight marriage does not apply to gay people is in
the Book of Mormon:

> "I know that the Lord **giveth no commandments** unto the
> children of men, **save he shall prepare a way** for them that
> they may accomplish the thing which he commandeth them."
> (1 Nephi 3:7)

I have wondered if that scripture means that God doesn't actually even *give*
commandments in the first place to people who He knows won't be able to
keep them.

Most Latter-day Saints interpret that scripture to mean God will prepare
a way for each one of us to follow *all* the commandments, no matter what they
are. And I think that is a correct interpretation, applicable to the vast majority
of people and situations. But I wonder if there is an additional way to read that
verse too: maybe God doesn't actually even give certain commandments in
the first place at all to particular people because He knows there is no way for
them to ever accomplish what He would command. Maybe God gives some
commandments only according to someone's individualized capacity to obey.
For example, for those of us who are given a way to accomplish the command
to marry heterosexually and multiply and replenish the earth, we are required to
receive and obey – and trust that God will "prepare a way." But for gay couples
or infertile couples who do not have a way to comply with God's command
regarding procreation, can we assume that perhaps God has not actually even
given them that commandment at all – and they are therefore not required to
"receive" it (since it's never even been offered to them)?

Another way of saying this could be that if God doesn't prepare a way to accomplish something, then it shouldn't be seen as a commandment. Joseph Smith seemed to favor such an interpretation:

"[T]he first and fundamental principle of our holy religion is, that we believe that we have a right to embrace all, and every item of truth, without limitation or without being circumscribed or prohibited by the creeds or superstitious notions of men, or by the dominations of one another, when that truth is clearly demonstrated to our minds, and we have the highest degree of evidence of the same; we feel ourselves bound by the laws of God, to observe and do strictly, with all our hearts, all things whatsoever is manifest unto us by the highest degree of testimony that God has committed us, as written in the old and new Testament, or any where else, by any manifestation, whereof we know that it has come from God: **and has application to us, being adapted to our situation and circumstances**; age, and generation of life; and that we have a perfect, and indefeasible right, to embrace all such commandments, and do them; **knowing, that God will not command any thing, but what is peculiarly adapted in itself, to ameliorate the condition of every man under whatever circumstances it may find him**, it matters not what kingdom or country he may be in. And again, we believe that it is our privilege to reject all things, whatsoever is clearly manifested to us that they do not have a bearing upon us. Such as, for instance, **it is not binding on us to build an Ark, because God commanded Noah to build one.— It would not be applicable to our case**; we are not looking for a flood. It is not binding on us to lead the children of Israel out of the land of Egypt, because God commanded Moses. The children of Israel are not in bondage to the Egyptians, as they were then; our circumstances are very different." (Joseph Smith, Prophet, Letter to Isaac Galland, 1839. Featured version published in Times and Seasons, Feb. 1840, p. 54., https://www.josephsmithpapers. org/paper-summary/letter-to-isaac-galland-22-march-1839/4)

With that expanded scriptural understanding, maybe we could transition from viewing gay couples as "disobedient" for marrying, to instead just reserving judgment – and give them the benefit of the doubt – presuming that they must have assessed the possibility of heterosexual marriage and determined that that particular commandment did not apply to them. I know many church members who just read that last sentence might worry about a slippery slope from such a construct: that anyone could just start justifying their way around commandments by saying they don't apply to them personally. I don't worry about that concern though. I think any exceptions could be limited to just circumstances that can't be contrived, such as all the exceptional situations I describe in this chapter. So I'm not worried about that slippery slope - I don't think anyone "fakes" their sexual orientation just to marry someone of the same sex.

Can we learn something from the church's approach to abortion?

With great caution and sensitivity, I would like to briefly discuss another context in which an unchosen biological condition can allow an exception to a commandment: abortion when the pregnancy results from rape. Now, before I go any further with this line of thought, I want to say upfront that I understand there is a <u>HUGE</u> and fundamental difference between someone having gay sexual desires they didn't choose, and a woman becoming pregnant against her will. In the former case, a person is simply born that way; but in the latter case, a woman is violently assaulted. Someone being gay is a circumstance that I think represents beautiful biological diversity and something that can help other people learn to love more openly and be better humans. However, a woman being pregnant from rape is a circumstance resulting from horrific violence that causes physical, mental, and emotional pain. So I understand they are vastly different contexts. All that being said, my lawyer's mind can't help but still draw a narrow analogy between the two situations as follows: both circumstances represent someone having a biological condition that is not of their choosing, and yet the church allows an exception to a commandment in one case (abortion) but not the other (gay marriage).

As I write about that analogy here, I pray I have done so with the sensitivity and care that any rape victim reading this is owed. I in no way desire to belittle your suffering or, if you became pregnant as a result of rape and decided to have an abortion, draw any comparison that diminishes in any way the agony I'm sure you endured in making that decision. I know such a choice is completely different in its nature than the one that two people of the same sex make when they decide to get married. The abortion is a traumatic experience, whereas the marriage is joyful. So I hope I do not offend anyone by discussing abortion and marriage in an analogous way like I do here. My analogy is intentionally very limited in scope (just two unchosen biological conditions) because I know they are fundamentally different things.

The church's position on abortion is as follows:

"Church leaders have said that some exceptional circumstances may justify an abortion, such as when pregnancy is the result of incest or rape, when the life or health of the mother is judged by competent medical authority to be in serious jeopardy, or when the fetus is known by competent medical authority to have severe defects that will not allow the baby to survive beyond birth. But even these circumstances do not automatically justify an abortion. **Those who face such circumstances should consider abortion only after consulting with their local Church leaders and receiving a confirmation through earnest prayer**." (https://www.churchofjesuschrist. org/study/manual/gospel-topics/abortion)

The narrow parallel I have drawn above focuses on how the church's position on abortion allows for a context-driven exception to a serious commandment. In the case of abortion, that commandment is: "Thou shalt not ... kill, *nor do anything like unto it*" (Doctrine & Covenants 59:6). The church teaches that killing is a more severe sin than breaking the law of chastity, which makes obvious sense. But I completely support the church's position that abortion in the case of rape is not a sin at all. No one should feel guilt or shame for having an abortion in that context. One reason for this particular abortion exception seems based on the fact that the pregnant woman did not make a choice that resulted in her becoming pregnant. The circumstance was forced upon her.

Given that both science and the church agree that gay sexual desires are not chosen, I wonder if church leaders could view permitting abortion in the circumstance of rape as a conceptual precedent to allow for gay marriage – because both situations could view an unchosen biological condition as justification for an exception to a commandment. Could such an idea be used to help adopt a policy whereby gay church members are allowed to enter into a gay marriage after they have consulted with their local leaders and received confirmation through earnest prayer as well?

Again, I recognize it's problematic to compare the feelings of despair felt by Latter-day Saint LGBTQ people with those of a woman who is pregnant with her attacker's child. They are very different contexts and it's meaningless to try to compare their respective pains. I definitely do not intend to do so here. I simply wish to point out that there seems to be a precedent where the church allows an exception to a serious commandment so that suffering can be relieved in a circumstance where someone's biological condition is not of their choosing. Christ is all about hope, so I think it would be wonderful to see the church extend His mercy in *all* such situations, including allowing gays and lesbians to have uniform-orientation marriages and still stay in the church, whether or not the church allows them to be sealed. Even if no revelation is forthcoming on gay couples being allowed to exist in heaven, could an analogy to the church's position on abortion be useful in providing relief to gay couples here and now at least?

[Side note: I want to clarify that, in making this analogy to the church's position on abortion, I don't think that gay relationships should be seen as an exception to a serious commandment to prevent harm. Allowing them only as an exception reinforces the problematic doctrine about eternal exaltation being solely available

to straight couples that I believe is mostly responsible for currently prohibiting gay relationships in the church. So, as I've stated elsewhere in this book, I would prefer to see revelation received that formally changes the law of chastity. But in the absence of that revelation, I see the church's approach to abortion as a precedent that could justify gay marriage being allowed today simply on the basis of fairness and compassion alone – without any revelation being required.

I also want to acknowledge that I know this analogy does not properly consider bisexual church members. In making the comparison, I do not want to suggest that bisexual people should be forced to marry someone of the opposite gender, because it's feasible for them to find attraction there, and gay people should be allowed to "sin" because there is no opposite gender attraction possible biologically. Rather, I believe true justice and equality will be achieved when we treat same-gender couples (including bisexual individuals in a same-gender marriage) the same as opposite-gender couples.

It is also important to explain that this analogy should not in any way be extended to justify pedophilia. As mentioned earlier in this chapter, protecting a child who cannot consent to sexual activity is a compelling reason to not allow an unchosen, biological attraction to minors to justify any exception being made for pedophiles. In the case of abortion, the church's position reflects the fact that we simply do not know when the spirit actually enters the body in the womb. We do not know if the fetus being aborted is yet "alive". But, in the case of pedophilia, we clearly know a living child is being harmed without their consent.

Ideally, because two consenting same-gender individuals marrying one another causes no harm to anyone, gay couples should be included in the church as equals with straight couples, and not just as exceptions to a commandment. A gay couple should be included at the center, on the same terms as a straight couple, because both simply reflect an arrangement between consenting adults that doesn't hurt anyone else at all.]

Can we sustain our leaders if we disagree with them and empathize with LGBTQ people?

Now, despite my musings here, I honestly have no idea where the church's doctrine regarding marriage equality might go, or even if it will ever progress or change at all. But hopefully my doctrinal imaginings will at least help some people better understand LGBTQ church members and their supporters so that more love and understanding can be expressed to them.

I think asking introspective questions is the best way to engender understanding. That is what helped me change my mind the most - questions I would ask myself regarding how I would feel about things as a man who falls on the straight end of the sexual orientation spectrum. Church doctrine has a history of changing only when questions are asked; in fact, the whole restoration began with a question (see Joseph Smith History 1:10-20). I hope that if enough people learn to have sincere sympathy (or even empathy if possible), the prophet will ask more intently to receive revelation effecting a change. To really try to relate to gay church members, I would challenge each of us to ask questions like these ones I have asked myself:

- How would I feel about being told my sexual relationship with my spouse was sinful?

- How would I feel about my sexual desires for my spouse needing to be reversed or at least turned off in order for me to enter the highest degree of heaven?

- Would I be able to give up sex, intimacy, loving companionship, and never have children for my whole life so I could stay in the church?

- Straight singles in the church can embrace love if it comes their way. How would I feel about having to actively turn my back on love if it came my way?

- As a straight man, if my situation were reversed, how would I feel about the idea that marrying another man was the only "righteous" way I could have a sexual relationship?

When I answer all those questions honestly, despair is my universal response to each of them. I ache at the lack of hope for LGBTQ individuals in this life and the next, and the fact that First Presidency members dug in over the pulpit in the fall of 2019 with a stronger emphasis than ever before, to snuff out any spark of hope that applicable doctrine will ever change.

However, because I believe in Christ, I continue to have faith and hope, despite what any church leaders at any level are saying over the pulpit or to me in person, that love can bring further light to shine on our depressing LGBTQ doctrine – perhaps when a prophet believes most church members are ready for that to happen. And until that change comes (and I can't help but imagine it will come someday), I'll keep sustaining the prophet and other church leaders as good men who are trying sincerely to do what's right, within their mental frameworks and given their respective backgrounds and implicit biases. I sustain them in the same way the scriptures teach that God sustains us: with love and hope for good decisions, while recognizing that sometimes poor use of agency results in disappointment for oneself and others. I believe sustaining is a public expression that is separate from personal opinion. In the words of Patrick Mason, head of Mormon studies at Utah State University, sustaining is "a public act, which is distinct from conscience which is personal" and respecting church leaders while holding a different perspective than they do "is a generous act, *the epitome of sustaining*" (https://www.sltrib.com/religion/2019/12/15/can-latter-day-saints/).

So even if I hold a different personal perspective than my church leaders, I can still sustain them by refusing to protest against them or besmirch their character. The only time the word "sustain" is used in any of our books of scripture is in reference to our belief that we are "bound to sustain and uphold the respective governments in which [we] reside" (Doctrine & Covenants 134:5).

That verse cannot mean we are bound to publicly agree with everything our elected government leaders say and do. Rather, it seems to mean we are supposed to be respectful in how we interact with our systems of government. I think we should apply that same meaning of the word "sustain" to our relationships with the church and our church leaders: sustaining them is about respect, not a duty to publicly agree.

Accordingly, I will be respectful while I wait for them to declare that the time is right for change. In the meantime, I will refuse to believe any teachings that make me feel despair and darkness.

Unless God's spirit of love, peace, and hope testify to me of a difficult teaching I hear and pray about, I will not accept it. I don't think that will render me apostate because, again, I can sustain my leaders and not believe everything they say. This is explained in the following excerpt from an article included on the church's own website under the topic "What is Doctrine?" (with my commentary in brackets):

> "The Prophet can add to the scriptures, but such new additions are presented by the First Presidency to the body of the Church and are accepted by common consent (by sustaining vote) as binding doctrine of the Church (See D&C 26:2; 107:27-31). **Until such doctrines or opinions are sustained by vote in conference, however, they are 'neither binding nor the official doctrine of the Church.'** *[I believe it is noteworthy that the church's position against gay marriage has never been submitted to a vote by the church.]* **How can we know if teachings, which have not been voted upon, are true?**
>
> **J. Reuben Clark explains that when 'we, ourselves, are 'moved by the Holy Ghost,"' then we know that the speakers are teaching true doctrine.** 'In a way, this completely shifts the responsibility from them to us to determine when they so speak.' **It is likely that the Lord has allowed (and will continue to allow) his servants to make mistakes—it's all part of progression and the growing process. We are not forced to accept teachings with which we disagree. We're supposed to receive confirmation from the spirit if what is taught is the doctrine of God,** and of course we're the one who put ourselves in jeopardy if we fail to accept things which will

bless us." (https://www.churchofjesuschrist.org/si/questions/
what-is-doctrine ; https://www.fairmormon.org/wp- content/
uploads/2012/02/What_is_Mormon_Doctrine.pdf)

*[Side note: Some other great quotes that indicate it is crucial to not rely on the
prophets and apostles over the Spirit are as follows:*

*"**Do not, brethren, put your trust in man though he be a
bishop; an apostle, or a president;** if you do, **they will fail
you at some time or place, they will do wrong** or seem to, and
your support be gone; but if we lean on God, He never will fail us.
When men and women depend on God alone, and trust in Him
alone, their faith will not be shaken if the highest in the Church
should step aside. They could still see that He is just and true, that
truth is lovely in His sight, and the pure in heart are dear to Him.
**Perhaps it is His own design that faults and weaknesses
should appear in high places in order that His Saints may
learn to trust in Him and not in any man or men. Therefore,
my brethren and sisters, seek after the Holy Spirit and His
unfailing testimony of God and His work upon the earth."**
(George Q. Cannon, Apostle, 1891; https://www.fairmormon.org/
answers/Mormonism_and_doctrine/Prophets_are_not_infallible/
Quotations)*

*"And **none are required to tamely and blindly submit to a
man because he has a portion of the Priesthood**. We have
heard men who hold the Priesthood remark, that they would do
any thing they were told to do by those who presided over them, if
they knew it was wrong: but such obedience as this is worse than
folly to us; it is slavery in the extreme; and the man who would
thus willingly degrade himself, should not claim a rank among
intelligent beings, until he turns from his folly. A man of God,
who seeks for the redemption of his fellows, would despise the idea
of seeing another become his slave, who had an equal right with
himself to the favour of God...**Others, in the extreme exercise
of their almighty authority, have taught that such obedience
was necessary, and that no matter what the Saints were told
to do by their Presidents, they should do it without asking
any questions. When the Elders of Israel will so far indulge***

in these extreme notions of obedience, as to teach them to the people, it is generally because they have it in their hearts to do wrong themselves. *(Charles W. Penrose, Apostle, Millennial Star, 1852; https://contentdm.lib.byu.edu/digital/collection/MStar/ id/37806)]*

CHAPTER 8

WHAT MIGHT PROMPT
DOCTRINAL CHANGE?

Chapter synopsis: It hurts to see much of society express more compassion toward LGBTQ individuals than our church does, and to see that our church's policy and doctrine may allow harmful therapeutic practices to continue. The suicides of LGBTQ church members are incredibly painful to observe. I wonder if governmental or societal pressure will end up being the only way the church changes. The church allows for disagreement on marriage equality, but LGBTQ activists in the church should still be careful – because alienation of church members is counterproductive.

Will science, normality of LGBTQ families, or guilt over psychological harm help?

I think there are several factors that could help prompt a change in the church's stance on doctrinal marriage equality. The first is science. As the fact becomes more widely known and accepted that gay sexual orientation is not a choice, the more quickly change may come. Many people still don't know about the general consensus within the scientific community, endorsed by the church, that experiencing gay sexual attraction is not a choice. As the genetic and epigenetic causes of gay sexual orientation become more understood by the general population, the general church membership will likewise become more aware as well (https://www.sciencemag.org/news/2015/10/homosexuality-may-be-caused-chemical-modifications-dna ; Also see Chapter 3). That being said, I doubt that widespread knowledge of the science about gay sexual orientation will ever be the main reason to prompt doctrinal change, because church leaders already acknowledge that experiencing gay sexual attraction is not a choice and yet the church still prohibits marriage equality in our doctrine.

A second factor that may spur change eventually is a more widely held understanding that gay couples are not causing any harm to society. I suspect that the longer gay marriages are an ordinary part of our societal makeup, the more people will realize that all the fears were unfounded about the societal ills gay marriage would cause. In fact, people may start to see the societal benefits of gay marriage, such as a decrease in suicide rates, among other benefits: https://www.theguardian.com/world/2019/nov/14/suicide-rates-fall-after-gay-marriage-laws-in-sweden-and-denmark; https://www.upworthy.com/legalizing-gay-marriage-has-caused-a-dramatic-drop-in-lgbt-suicide-rates.

[Side note: I loved the following reasons a friend shared about why gay marriage doesn't hurt people and is good for society (included anonymously to protect privacy):

1. *Gay marriage does nothing to hurt my straight marriage.*

2. *I am grateful that I have a gay couple in my neighborhood where I have the chance to show my children kindness to people that are different than me.*

3. *Both of these men's families are better off because the men aren't alone, lonely, depressed, or suicidal, which is so often the case with those choosing celibacy. Their families are happy that their sons are happy to have a companion to share their daily lives with. Suicide hurts families. Depression hurts families. Happiness and connection blesses families.*

4. *Society is better off when a person gets sick and their spouse can care for them, pay the bills, take him/her to the doctor, and keep their family life going. Society has to step in with government assistance when a person gets sick and can't pay the bills, especially if the gay person has been shunned by parents.*

5. *Gay marriage is a MUCH better option than promiscuity. Fidelity, monogamy and commitment are much better for society at large than promiscuity. When people don't feel safe to come out or live in a monogamous, healthy relationship, sometimes they seek fleeting intimate experiences in dangerous places.*

6. *FAMILY is good for society.*

7. *Compared with times when a gay couple has no rights to help a partner who is hospitalized, like making serious medical decisions when the partner is unconscious, or having access to medical records, it just makes sense that the person most qualified to make those decisions is the one the ill person has chosen to spend his/her life with. If a gay person has lived with a partner for 20 years, does it make any sense to contact the aging parents about those decisions? In a heterosexual marriage, that would seem ludicrous. Same thing. Gay marriage takes care of this.*

8. *I believe our church and members would be much better off to allow gay marriage as part of the gospel, so these good, compassionate people can be blessed by and contribute in the gospel, their local congregations, and the plan of salvation. It's painful for so many of these people to be forced to choose between two important parts of their identity - being Latter-day Saint, and being gay and desiring marriage and family like their upbringing instilled in them.*

9. *Another benefit I see if the church would embrace gay marriage is that morality standards could truly be the same for both gay and straight people. I often see really good gay young people who have graduated from seminary and served missions, leave the church and leave their moral compass of chastity before marriage, since gay marriage isn't respected within the church.]*

Also, as society witnesses more children of parents in gay marriages grow up to be just like all other adults, I believe worries will diminish and hearts will soften. I think it will take time to see that happen, because a lot of people already ignore existing consensus that kids raised by LGBTQ people are no different:

> "Taken together, this research forms an overwhelming scholarly consensus, based on over three decades of peer-reviewed research, that having a gay or lesbian parent does not harm

children." (https://whatweknow.inequality.cornell.edu/topics/
lgbt-equality/what- does-the-scholarly-research-say-about-the-
wellbeing-of-children-with-gay-or-lesbian- parents/)

Rarely is there as much consensus in any area of social science as in the case of gay parenting. This is why the American Academy of Pediatrics and all of the major professional organizations with expertise in child welfare have issued reports and resolutions in support of LGBTQ parental rights (https://en.wikipedia.org/wiki/LGBT_parenting). Similarly, a scholarly consensus seems to be forming that kids raised by gay couples are not more likely to self-identify as LGBTQ (although they are more open-minded about sexuality, and, if LGBTQ, such kids may be more likely to come out of the closet sooner). Most of them identify as heterosexual, and they do not have any differences in their gender role behaviors in comparison to those observed in heterosexual family structures (https://en.wikipedia.org/wiki/LGBT_parenting#cite_note- Stacey_Biblarz-33).

But again, I don't think widespread knowledge of the normalcy of gay marriage and gay parenting will be the primary impetus for doctrinal change either. I say that because, by reversing the November 2015 Exclusion Policy, our prophets and apostles have already acknowledged that gay parents might be good at parenting, because the policy change implicitly acknowledges that gay parents are able to raise kids who want to be in the church. Yet the church still prohibits gay marriage.

A third factor that could help facilitate eventual change might be if it becomes more widely known how intense the harm is that certain religious teachings can cause LGBTQ people. I saw a powerful public post online about this topic in response to President Nelson's talk at BYU on September 17, 2019 (in which he said the law of chastity was a divine law, comparable to unchanging laws of nature: https://speeches.byu.edu/talks/russell-m-nelson/love-laws-god/).

Because the post in response was so eloquent, I am just going to let it speak for itself on this point (included anonymously to protect privacy):

"*A Response to President Nelson's BYU Address*: What makes a heart beat and what makes a heart stop? As a physician, that's what President Nelson shared learning about in his talk. Learning which eventually enabled him to perform successful open heart operations. He went on to share, 'The same can be said of the law of gravity, and the laws of foil and lift that allow airplanes to fly. Each is an absolute truth. Doctors or pilots do not have the power to change those laws, but their understanding of them safeguards lives.'

As a mental health therapist, I too completed my graduate work with a focus on the heart, but in my case, on an aspect more specific and sometimes harder to see: What makes a LGBTQ heart beat and what makes it stop. Or in other words, what makes a LGBTQ heart want to live and what makes a LGBTQ heart want to die. As I am tasked with safeguarding LGBTQ lives against suicide, learning the principles that govern positive mental health outcomes for LGBTQ people has been imperative. Presently, I work with suicidal LGBTQ Mormons on a daily basis and I feel God with me in my work.

President Nelson cites looking to research and new experimentation in his graduate years as the foundation of his learning. My graduate learning about the LGBTQ heart took a similar focus. A growing body of research indicated that sexual orientation had a biological origin and that decades of trying to change people's orientation or gender identity via reparative therapies not only didn't work, in countless cases it caused considerable harm. Research had also begun to point to the incredible power of Family Acceptance of their LGBTQ children — that accepting families reduced risk of LGBTQ suicide attempts by 8 times.

Perhaps one of the most moving studies I learned about was MRI brain scans of people falling in love: Whether someone falls in love with someone of the opposite gender, or falls in love with someone of the same gender, the same parts of the brain bursting with dopamine light up. Recently, brain scans of transgender people have also shown their brains to be more similar to the gender identity they feel within themselves than their biological sex. Science is fantastically eye opening and these are all things we didn't know a generation ago.

Two studies specific to LGBTQ Mormons also had a significant impact on my learning. One found that LGBTQ Mormons who took a single celibate or mixed-orientation marriage path frequently had poor mental health while those who dated a same sex partner had significantly better mental health. **The most eye opening part though was this: that LGBTQ Mormons who were able to integrate and live into both their queer identities and their spiritual identities as Latter-day Saints had the best mental health outcomes of all!** In the second study (a study that took place in the year following the implementation of the November 2015 policy) it was found that stunningly, **73.4% of LGBTQ Mormon participants had [multiple] symptoms of Post-Traumatic Stress Disorder in connection to their religious experiences [89.2% reported at least one symptom]** (http://mormonsbuildingbridges.org/wp- content/uploads/2019/10/20190928-U-of-U-MBB-Presentation-SIMMONS-FINAL.pptx; https://getd.libs.uga.edu/pdfs/simmons_brian_w_201712_phd.pdf). The same symptoms most often associated with soldiers returning from war, refugees fleeing persecution or victims escaping domestic violence or sexual assault, were showing up in both post and still practicing LGBTQ Mormons at a rate 10 times the general population. That was mind blowing. In simplified summary, research was indicating that LGBTQ Mormons did best when they were able to healthily live into both their queer and religious identities at the same time, however this outcome was quite rare, and instead, an astronomical amount were suffering with symptoms of PTSD.

What makes a LGBTQ heart beat and what makes it want to stop? As I sit with LGBTQ Mormons and post Mormons whose hearts are suicidal as an outgrowth of spiritual trauma, they get better as they are able to shed the negative messages they have internalized about being LGBTQ from both religion and society. They get better when their families come to shed these negative ideas as well and embrace them with open arms. They get better when their agency on how to move forward in their life path is honored as sacred ground and are celebrated in communities that affirm their choices. They get better when they distance themselves from negative messages or rejecting spaces while they are still healing. They get better when their family members and friends speak up in their behalf when they are being put down, left out or marginalized, no matter who the speaker is. They get better when their psychological trauma is treated with trauma specific therapies. They get better when they are able to build life partnerships and families that have the same meaningful bonds that every human heart seeks to form and nurture. They get better when they know they can take this journey with their God, not being told or internalizing that they will be cut off from God if they do so. They get better when they are able to lay hold on every good thing — the part of them that is LGBTQ and the part of them that is spiritual; the part of them that wants to connect and the part of them that wants to contribute their many gifts.

Like doctors and pilots, I didn't make up the principles that govern LGBTQ mental health — we have merely discovered them and now use it daily to safeguard lives. I pray with my feet

every day that Latter-day Saints will come to fully understand
these discoveries too. We are all part of one body in Christ. May
we see that each part however different is equally needed by us."

In President Nelson's talk, he also said one of the reasons the Exclusion Policy
was modified was because he and the other apostles wept over the pain the
policy had caused. I'm hopeful that sort of empathy will prompt future doctrinal
change that allows marriage equality to exist in the church as well. But, again,
based on past history in the church with discriminatory issues, I unfortunately
don't think it will be the primary force behind a change, given the focus church
leaders place on eternity over mortality.

What about the church's political stance on conversion therapy?

Examining the church's position on the advisability of reparative therapies
mentioned in Chapter 3 (which are also called "conversion" or "aversion"
therapies) is indicative of how far away from doctrinal change we may still be.

*[Side note: I will be more directly critical of the church in this section than in other
areas of this book because this is a topic in the political, not just the doctrinal,
arena. I speak in large part in this section as just a concerned citizen (who grew up
in Utah), not a church member. Plus, church leaders have given church members
substantial freedom to disagree with the church's political positions without facing
negative church consequences anyway.]*

In October 2019, the church objected to a proposed new licensing rule
in Utah that would have banned reparative therapies for minors. When the
church's objection to the proposed licensing rule received a lot of negative
national press, the church clarified that it does not support such abusive therapies but nevertheless objected to the proposed rule. The church explained the
rationale behind its objection in this Deseret News article: https://www.google.
com/amp/s/www.deseret.com/platform/amp/utah/2019/10/23/20929351/lds-
mormon-church-conversion-therapy-opposition-jesus-christ-latter-day-saints
(you'll need to actually read this article to understand what I'm going to say
below about the church's position on conversion therapy).

A revised version of the licensing rule was endorsed by the governor of Utah some weeks later, but only after making the changes that the church requested (https://www.sltrib.com/news/politics/2019/11/27/gov-herbert-announces/). A good history of the full legislative and rule-making process is found here: https://www.kuer.org/post/how-bill-became-rule-journey-utahs-conversion-therapy-ban#stream/0. The updated version of the licensing rule has now been implemented in Utah, effectively banning most forms of conversion therapy for minors in the state. This is a very positive thing and I'm glad the church supported the adoption of this new rule condemning what it considers to be abusive therapeutic practices.

However, all that being said, I must say that I disagree with the church's position that the initial version of the new licensing rule would have been problematic from a religious liberty perspective. From what I understand, the professional therapist licensing board in Utah felt that there was no risk at all that a parent, grandparent, bishop, etc., who is a licensed therapist would lose their license for just discussing religious beliefs in a context where they have not been engaged to serve as a person's professional therapist. In other words, despite the church's concern, a therapist parent talking to their kid at home or a therapist bishop talking to a ward member at church would not be problematic under the first version of the proposed rule. Even in a professional therapy context, existing professional guidelines require a therapist to discuss with a patient their religious values (and in the case of a patient who is a minor, the religious values of that patient's family) when providing counseling (e.g., https://societyforpsychotherapy.org/integrating-spirituality-religion-psychotherapy-practice/).

Similar religious exemptions already existed in other laws governing the practice of mental health therapy in Utah anyway. So if existing professional guidelines already require a patient's pertinent religious values to be discussed in actual therapy sessions, and Utah's existing laws already allowed for religious discussion by family and clergy who are therapists as well, it's hard to see how the church could have imagined a therapist losing their license for talking about religious values with their own children or ward members outside the context of a professional therapy session. If I'm giving church representatives the benefit of the doubt, they seemed to be worried about an extremely far-fetched slippery slope situation.

But to be totally honest, I suspect the church was trying to get (and ultimately succeeded in getting) language added to the proposed rule that would allow what I consider to be "light" conversion therapy to continue: where undue emphasis is placed on having someone try to live according to church standards than according to what is best for their own mental health and well-being. Now, I don't mean to suggest that the church wants counselors to intentionally provide guidance that is harmful from a mental health perspective. However, I do think the church wants to maintain a situation where minors are allowed to be brought to a therapist who will place more emphasis than is normal (per professional guidelines) on religious beliefs.

I think the church is trying to keep a situation that allows religious values to have more weight in the counseling of a minor patient than existing professional guidelines say they should. That can be a harmful thing to a kid who falls somewhere on the spectrum of sexuality where lifelong abstinence or mixed-orientation marriage will be more likely to result in depression than it might with some other patients. I think the therapist's role should be to try to assess where on the sexual orientation spectrum a patient thinks they are (knowing that can change as a kid matures and figures out more about their sexuality), then assess how the religiosity of that patient and their family might affect the patient's mental health if they conform or fail to conform to the applicable religious values.

With the religious exception that the church successfully requested, therapists can continue to recommend that a minor patient conform to the religious values of their parents, even if doing so may not be in the best interests of that minor's own mental health. In my opinion, that is "light" conversion therapy. Religious values should be weighed, but not more than what professional psychology boards recommend. If a therapist parent or bishop emphasizes religion more than professional guidelines suggest, maybe they should lose their license, right? Shouldn't we all be interested in preventing religion from being used in a way that can cause mental illness? By way of analogy, how would we feel if the church opposed a licensing rule meant to prevent doctors from prescribing harmful medications?

I understand from friends that prior to the updated rule, there were kids in Utah undergoing abusive conversion therapy (of the type I presume the church opposes) at the behest of their misguided parents. So when the church's weak slippery slope concern (which I suspect might be a desire to still allow conversion therapy "light") is weighed against the abuse that was ongoing at the time of the church's objection, I don't see the church's position in opposing the initial version of the licensing rule to be praiseworthy. But I am thankful a version of the rule got approved and implemented that seems likely to prevent that most severe type of conversion therapy with minors from continuing in Utah.

Not all parents of gay kids share even that simple feeling of gratitude though. While the following is more bluntly stated than I prefer, I can nevertheless understand the pain in this comment from a self-described "father of a gay son and former bishop of a large single student ward of the LDS church who ultimately asked to be released, left the LDS church, and began to speak out publicly on this issue twenty years ago" (included anonymously to protect privacy):

> "While the LDS church and its institutions may no longer be involved in the more overtly-barbaric forms of conversion therapy (commonly known as 'aversion' or 'reparative' therapy), it remains ever involved in what I believe to be the more fundamentally and psychologically damaging practice of instilling in LGBTQ youth and their families the core belief that the words underlying the acronym LGBTQ are merely adjectives describing sinful sexual behavior rather than nouns identifying people. This is a doctrine that in reality relegates LGBTQ youth (and adults) to a recognized status within the Mormon church and broader community as broken and defective 'second class

citizens' to be at best pitied ('Loved'), and at worst avoided. Until recently, public pronouncements and writings by church leaders preached the doctrine that 'same-sex attraction' was a conscious, aberrant lifestyle choice. Less of that now, and more 'OK, maybe God did make you that way, tough luck - but no marriage or the deep emotional and sexual intimacy that heterosexuals are permitted as part of God's plan – EVER (unless, of course, you change).' How would it affect you to be reduced to 'collateral damage' in God's eternal plan? By your parents, grandparents, neighbors, friends, and church leaders. This is the most powerful and damaging conversion therapy imaginable. What does your heart tell you about your son or daughter, grandson or granddaughter, family member or friend?"

In all of this, I think it is helpful to remember that the church is not always right on these sorts of things. For example, as I mentioned in Chapter 3, in the 1970s, when President Oaks was BYU President, gay men at BYU, as part of their "repentance" process, received electroshock treatment to their genitals while being shown erotic same-gender images (so their bodies could be "trained" to not be aroused). Again, I'm glad the church doesn't support that sort of conversion therapy anymore, but I think, given that the church did encourage different types of abusive conversion therapy for decades, the onus should be on the church to prove why the revised rule is better for the mental health of gay kids than the initial recommendations of a board of professional counselors in Utah (who are well aware of church values and religious liberty concerns). All parties involved in the bargaining have said they can't discuss what was said in the negotiations process. So I don't think we will ever hear the church give such an explanation. Unfortunately, the church has some trust to earn back in this area, to say the least, and I don't see that happening by insisting that the new licensing rule in Utah had to contain a religious exception to conversion therapy.

Should the church do more to denounce conversion therapy?

Although the church's position opposing what it considers to be conversion therapy is clear, their position is still confusing because the church has not affirmatively denounced former teachings by General Authorities supporting conversion therapy. When I wrote a first draft of this book in October 2019, I visited www.newsroom.churchofjesuschrist.org, searched for "homosexuality," and found a link to a talk that a General Authority named Elder Bruce C. Hafen gave in 2009 at Evergreen International, an organization that provided conversion therapy for many years. The link to his talk has since been removed (which I think happened some weeks after the *Deseret News* article was published, linked above). Many people have pointed to Elder Hafen's talk as an example of teachings that contradict what the church is trying to say now about its opposition to conversion therapy. Summaries of the talk, with some pertinent excerpts can still be seen here: https://religion.wikia.org/wiki/Bruce_C._Hafen; and here: https://www.mormonwiki.com/Bruce_C._Hafen#2009_Talk_on_Gay_Rights_and_Same_Gende r_Attraction. The talk stated very clearly that sexual orientation could be willingly changed.

While those summaries available online don't show it, Elder Hafen quoted a study by Dr. Robert Spitzer that the researcher himself retracted in later years. Dr. Spitzer said,

> "I believe **I owe the gay community an apology for my study making unproven claims of the efficacy of reparative therapy**. I also apologize to any gay person who wasted time and energy undergoing some form of reparative therapy because they believed that I had proven that reparative therapy works with some 'highly motivated' individuals." (https://psychnews.psychiatryonline.org/doi/full/10.1176/pn.47.12.psychnews_47_12_1- b)

[Side note: Many practitioners of conversion therapy have abandoned their teachings to lead lives of openly gay men themselves, often pursuing same-gender romantic relationships. This includes Latter-day Saint David Matheson,

who was formally associated with the conversion therapy organization Evergreen International and who was a founder of ex-gay program Journey into Manhood: https://www.splcenter.org/fighting-hate/intelligence- report/2019/ out-darkness-conversion-therapist-quits-ex-gay-movement.]

I'm glad the church removed Elder Hafen's talk from its website. But I think it would have been better for the church to have actually kept the talk on its site and included a disclaimer that the talk no longer represented church teachings. Just taking the talk down is insufficient because, without a label saying the talk has been denounced or without a different General Authority giving a new talk that specifically renounces all past teachings endorsing conversion therapy, the implication still exists that the church might be okay with statements made in similar talks made by other General Authorities endorsing conversion therapy as well (https://en.wikipedia.org/wiki/Evergreen_ International), like this one:

> **"Can individuals struggling with some same-gender attraction be cured? 'With God nothing should be impossible'** (Luke 1:37) ... The right course of action remains the same: eliminate or diminish same-sex attraction…**Feelings of attraction toward someone of the same gender should be eliminated if possible or controlled.**" (James O. Mason, General Authority Seventy, https://web.archive.org/web/20120724194231/http:// www.evergreeninternational.org/200 5%20Mason.pdf, 2005)

Unless the church does more to affirmatively denounce all prior teachings made by General Authorities about changing sexual orientation with enough faith, mixed understandings about the church's views on gay sexual orientation and conversion therapy will continue to persist.

The First Presidency said the following in 2016: "The Church denounces any therapy that subjects an individual to abusive practices" (https://newsroom.churchofjesuschrist.org/article/statement-proposed-rule-sexual-orientation-gender-identity-change). While I appreciate that statement, it does not constitute a denunciation of conversion therapy because it leaves the word "abusive" open to interpretation and also implies that changing sexual orientation is possible through "non-abusive" therapeutic practices. The closest thing I have seen to a denunciation of conversion therapy by one of our apostles is the following from a General Conference talk in 2015:

> "And, I must say, **this son's sexual orientation did not somehow miraculously change—no one assumed it would.**" (Jeffrey R. Holland, Apostle, https://www.churchofjesuschrist.org/study/general-conference/2015/10/behold-thy- mother, 2015)

Indeed, based on what the church's own professional counseling affiliate, Family Services, offers by way of counseling for individuals who experience gay sexual desire, it still seems quite unclear to me whether the church truly opposes conversion therapy in all forms:

> "We assist individuals and families as they respond to same-sex attraction. Our therapists do not provide what is commonly referred to as 'reparative therapy' or 'sexual orientation change efforts.' However, **when clients self-determine** to seek assistance for individual and family issues associated with same-sex attraction, we help them strengthen and develop healthy patterns of living. We assist clients who desire to reconcile same-sex attraction with their religious beliefs. Our services are consistent with applicable legal and ethical standards, **which allow self-determined clients to receive assistance with faith-based or religious goals.**" (https://www.deseret.com/2018/2/7/20639656/the- weeds-story-is-one-of-many-stories-of-lgbt-latter-day-saints-that-continue-to-be-written)

Similar statements about self-determination being respected in therapy can be found on the church's "Same-Sex Attraction" website as well: https://www.churchofjesuschrist.org/topics/gay/leaders?lang=eng.

I wonder how much a minor child brought to a Latter-day Saint therapist by their religious parents is really able to "self-determine" the degree to which they want to receive the "regular" or the "religious" version of counseling. It seems to me like the religiosity of the parents and of the therapist may do more of the determining in that situation than the kid does. I have heard stories about kids who felt forced to try to stop having gay sexual desires by their parents and Latter-day Saint therapists. I think the church should not be involved in determining the licensing rules for professional therapists and it is sad that the church succeeded in getting a religious exception put into the final version of the new rule in Utah.

When it comes to conversion therapy, I wish the church would follow the example of Allen Bergin, a former BYU professor, bishop, stake president, and member of the General Sunday School Presidency, who apologized in July 2020 for his past endorsement of conversion therapy. Brother Bergin was a psychotherapist and was often quoted by church leaders in the late 20th century as an authority on gay sexual orientation. His teachings included that "homosexuality was a compulsion, it led to bondage...label[ed] homosexuals as bizarre...[that] the average gay man had between 500-1000 partners... [and he] taught that self-discipline and a mixed orientation marriage would successfully overcome the problem of homosexuality." His July 2020 apology is sincere and far-reaching, completely reversing his prior teachings and expressing anguish over the harm he caused. It is worth reading as an example of sincere contrition: https://lattergaystories.org/bergin/; https://religionnews. com/2020/08/07/a-prominent-mormon- therapist-apologized-for-anti-lgbt-activism-whats-the-next-step/.)

Are church teachings contributing to more suicides?

Is there a need for doctrinal change in the church to prevent parents and therapists from contributing, intentionally or unintentionally, to kids feeling depressed about their sexuality? That seems like an effective solution to me, but I leave that up to God and the prophets and apostles to answer. However, in the meantime, I think there is a pressing need to do something now to change how lonely and unwanted most LGBTQ youth in the church feel.

Because Utah has a higher suicide rate than the national average, with suicide being the leading cause of death among Utah youth, and with LGBTQ individuals having a higher suicide rate in general, a debate has been ongoing in recent years about the causality between suicide and church teachings regarding gay sexual orientation (https://www.kuer.org/post/can-lds-church-be- blamed-utah-s-lgbt-suicides#stream/0; https://en.wikipedia.org/wiki/Suicide_among_LGBT_youth). Some strongly believe that church teachings play a role in high suicide rates in states with high Latter-day Saint populations (https://www.mrm.org/suicide-and-mormonism).

The following social media post from May 2020 is written by Thomas Palani Montgomery, a fellow Dragon Dad and an excellent LGBTQ ally writer and commentator. It provides useful resources assessing the reality that church teachings are a contributing factor in suicides of LGBTQ church members:

> "*Meridian Magazine* has once again published an article protecting the LDS Church in any/every way possible regarding harm the LDS Church causes its own LGBTQ youth and adult members. The article meanders through many arguments without actually presenting anything new and attempting to put out many fires. https://latterdaysaintmag.com/is-latter-day-saint-theology-responsible-for-lgbt- suicides/?fbclid=IwAR0F5ErowdnEgoX-QSPkLAmZFEIIxVsAgNLVyQMdnP4A18lapw 3gxcShBNp8
>
> It challenges John Dehlin's study saying that "most studies" say something else - except for the fact that there are no "other studies" that either contradict or challenge John's study. John's study is published and peer-reviewed (9 studies across 7 different journals have published the findings of his studies: http://www.johndehlin.com/research/). https://www.youtube.com/watch?v=0MxCXjfAunk
>
> It ignores that John's study is fully consistent with Brian Simmons's study on PTSD among LDS-LGBTQ Mormons.

Brian's study is published and peer-reviewed. https://athenaeum.
libs.uga.edu/handle/10724/38227

It ignores that John's study is fully consistent with the Family
Acceptance Project's research on the harm of rejection from
orthodox religiosity. The Family Acceptance Project is published
and peer-reviewed. https://familyproject.sfsu.edu/

It ignores the spike of suicides from 2008 in Utah while saying
Utah is comparable to other states in the region. Except for the
past twelve years... years in which the LDS Church's political
activism against LGBTQ people also spiked. From Prop 8 in
California onward, the LDS Church has been actively, politi-
cally hostile to LGBTQ people. The only notable exception is
the Utah work and housing bill extending rights to LGBTQ
persons (with the notable exemption of the LDS Church to the
rights outlined in the bill.) To think that this doesn't seep into
the minds of LDS members is significantly naive - even if they
were not homophobic to begin with. https://rationalfaiths.com/
utahs-escalating-suicide-crisis-lds-lgbtq-despair/

Saying that suicide is complex and multi-faceted, which is true,
does not remove the demonstrable fact that several of those
facets are (1) exclusively heterosexual/patriarchal theology, (2)
Mormon anti-LGBTQ culture, (3) homophobic members and
leaders, (4) continuous political activism against LGBTQ people, and (5) extensive history of harmful rhetoric and actions
from LDS Church leaders.

For active members, ignorance is a shield, and articles (like this
one) are taken as fact in the vacuum of that ignorance. In order
to maintain this ignorance, no mention can be made of Greg
Prince's comprehensive book *Gay Rights and the Mormon Church:
Intended Actions, Unintended Consequences.* You can't read this

book and remain ignorant. Its final chapter is about the current suicide epidemic in Utah. https://www.amazon.com/Gay-Rights-Mormon-Church-Consequences-ebook/dp/B07QNGYBM6/ref=sr_1_1?crid=5OE44JWCO0BV&dchild=1&keywords=greg+prince+books&qid=1589475689&sprefix=greg+prince%-2Caps%2C195&sr=8-1

To all this, I would add my own writing on the subject. Eight years immersed in the pain and harm the LDS Church causes its LGBTQ members and through its political activism, the LGBTQ community at large:

What Can't Be Said (November 2018) - http://www.nomore-strangers.org/what-cant-be-said/

The Safe Way (September 2018) – http://www.nomorestrang-ers.org/the-safe-way/SacredSpaces (October 2017) – http://www.nomorestrangers.org/sacred-spaces/ Grace (July 2017) – http://www.nomorestrangers.org/grace/

Rejection and the Family (March 2017) – http://www.nomor-estrangers.org/rejection-and- the-family/

Anger (November 2016) – http://www.nomorestrangers.org/anger/

A Tale of Two Weddings (September 2016) – http://www.nomorestrangers.org/a-tale-of- two-weddings/

Clarity (July 2016) – http://www.nomorestrangers.org/clarity/

Emotional Distance (May 2016) – http://www.nomore-strangers.org/emotional-distance/ The Scarlet Letter: Apostasy (December 2015) – http://nomorestranger.wpengine.com/the-scarlet-letter-apostasy/

Sadness (October 2015) – http://nomorestranger.wpengine.com/sadness/ Trust (August 2015) – http://nomorestranger.wpengine.com/trust/

Seeing Through My Tears (January 2015) – http://nomorestranger.wpengine.com/seeing- through-my-tears/

Doctrine of Celibacy (October 2014) – http://nomorestranger.wpengine.com/the-doctrine- of-celibacy/

What Words Can't Define (August 2014) – http://nomorestranger.wpengine.com/what-words-cant-define/

A Difference of Opinion (June 2014) – http://nomorestranger.wpengine.com/a-difference-of-opinion/

Shame and Affirmation (June 2014) – http://nomorestranger.wpengine.com/shame-and-affirmation/

Cool Tolerance (March 2013) – http://nomorestranger.wpengine.com/cool-tolerance/ It's Complex (August 2013) – http://nomorestranger.wpengine.com/its-complex/ Christmas Cards (January 2014) – http://nomorestranger.wpengine.com/christmas-cards/ What the Heck is Traditional Marriage? (July 2013) – http://nomorestranger.wpengine.com/what-the-heck-is-traditional-marriage/

Defending Marriage (May 2013) – http://nomorestranger.wpengine.com/defending-marriage/

Why Does the Lord Allow His Covenant People to Err? (April 2013) – http://nomorestranger.wpengine.com/why-does-the-lord-allow-his-covenant-people-to-err/

The Catalyst (January 2013) – http://nomorestranger.wpengine.com/the-catalyst/

The Victoria Theater (June 2013) – http://nomorestranger.
wpengine.com/the-victoria-theater/

Of Pain and the Journey (September 2013) – http://nomore-
stranger.wpengine.com/of- pain-and-the-journey/

I See the Image of Christ in My Gay Son, Lord (August 2012)
– http://mitchmayne.blogspot.com/2012/08/a-fathers-poem-
to-his-gay-son-from.html

It is odd that the author of the Meridian article cites his own
study, but doesn't source his study. The LDS Church's theology
and culture harm LGBTQ youth and members. It may not
harm every LDS/LGBTQ member, but it harms enough of
them to be demonstrable.

I think I have provided ample sources." (https://www.facebook.
com/thomas.p.montgomery/posts/10218664665300613)

On the topic of LGBTQ Latter-day Saint suicide, I also want to highlight the
peer-reviewed August 2020 study conducted by James McGraw at Bowling
Green State University (BGSU) and his colleagues. They found that lesbian,
gay and bisexual (LGB) Utahns are over 4.5 times more likely to have recently
thought about suicide/self-harm and nearly 10 times as likely to have attempted
suicide in their lifetimes, when compared to heterosexual Utahns. What's
even more alarming is that the rates of suicidal thinking and suicide attempts
among LGB Utahns was around three times higher than the rates among LGB
non-Utahns living in the U.S., Canada and Europe. The rates of suicidal
thinking and suicide attempts among heterosexuals in and out of Utah was not
found to be nearly as divergent (https://drive.google.com/file/d/1zNs8K5nN-
Pw4SQxPch0uc_PFH0f0Q3kIq/view?usp=drivesdk; https://www.tandfonline.
com/doi/full/10.1080/13811118.2020.1806159).

Some people have postulated that Utah's high altitude is a contributing
factor to the high suicide rate among LGBTQ people. But I think the fact that
the rates for straight folks in and out of Utah were not as different as the rates

for LGB folks in and out of Utah suggests that Utah's high altitude is not the primary reason LGB Utahns are so much more prone to suicide. It's important to note that the BGSU study does not propose a reason for its findings or address the influence of religious beliefs at all. But I think when its findings are read in conjunction with those of the previously referenced study by Brian Simmons at the University of Georgia regarding the traumatic effects of some church teachings on LGBTQ Latter-day Saints, it's not difficult to identify a distinguishing factor about Utah that could be making it harder for LGB people who live there to avoid suicidal thoughts.

[Side note: In August 2020, James McGraw and his colleagues also released a compilation of all the published and non-published empirical research on Latter-day Saint LGBTQ psychological and interpersonal functioning and synthesized the results together. This is a useful reference to see all the research that has been conducted on the topic (https://www.tandfonline.com/doi/abs/10.1080/1550428X.2020.1800545?-journalCode=wgfs20; https://drive.google.com/file/d/18nKkeahLsuNXA56lYoy95r-fLPtzVG0aB/view?usp=drivesdk).]"

Notwithstanding the debate over the degree of causality in LGBTQ suicides, research has at the very least shown that church teachings that gay sexual orientation will be "cured" in the afterlife have led many gay Latter-day Saints to engage in suicidal ideation or attempt or die by suicide (https://en.m.wikipedia.org/wiki/LGBT_Mormon_suicides). Many LGBTQ individuals have said that statements like the following ones made by General Authorities contribute to such thoughts:

> "The good news for somebody who is struggling with same-gender attraction is this: 1) It is that '**I'm not stuck with it forever.' It's just now**. Admittedly, for each one of us, it's hard to look beyond the 'now' sometimes. But nonetheless, if you see mortality as now, it's only during this season. 2) If I can keep myself worthy here, if I can be true to gospel commandments, if I can keep covenants that I have made, the blessings of exaltation and eternal life that Heavenly Father holds out to all of His children apply to me." (Lance B. Wickman, Seventy, https://

newsroom.churchofjesuschrist.org/article/interview-oaks- wick-
man-same-gender-attraction, 2006)

**"If you are faithful, on resurrection morning—and maybe
even before then—you will rise with normal attractions
for the opposite sex.** Some of you may wonder if that doctrine is too good to be true. But Elder Dallin H. Oaks has
said it MUST be true, because 'there is no fullness of joy in
the next life without a family unit, including a husband and
wife, and posterity.' And 'men (and women) are that they
might have joy.'" (Bruce C. Hafen, General Authority Seventy,
2009, https://religion.wikia.org/wiki/Bruce_C._Hafen;
https://www.mormondialogue.org/topic/59228-church-mak-
ing-further-movements- toward-respect-for-gay-members/
page/2/?tab=comments)

Cheryl and I have personally communicated with gay church members who
have said they felt like Latter-day Saint therapists were not able to sufficiently
invalidate their thoughts that it would be easier for them if they committed
suicide (so God could switch their sexuality) than it would be to live a celibate life. There are thousands of stories of individuals who have felt harmed
from a mental health perspective because of the church's teachings about gay
sexual orientation (https://www.sltrib.com/opinion/commentary/2019/11/02/
justin-utley-darkness-is/).

Notwithstanding the documented harm that can be caused to a gay person's mental health by church teachings and their continued church activity, I
regrettably don't think concerns over such hurt will ever be the primary cause
for any change in church doctrine – because church leaders instinctively place
more emphasis on future eternal blessings than they do on relieving mortal
suffering. If not essentially compelled to change by outside forces, I suspect
the church will always take the view that any suffering experienced by LGBTQ
individuals who try to live according to church standards here in mortality will
be worth the pain they endure, from an eternal perspective.

Will outside forces again influence doctrinal change?

That pattern of only making a change to relieve mortal suffering if forced to do so is what some people argue occurred in the contexts of both the church's abandonment of polygamy and the priesthood/temple ban for Black people. Even if that's true, I don't think external pressure means revelation was absent. To the contrary, I think church leaders can sometimes become closer to God when external pressures require them to confront an "emergency" for the church. That happens to us as individuals when we face trials too; we pray harder and often become closer to God as a result.

In the case of polygamy, the U.S. government "had disincorporated the church, escheated its assets to the U.S. federal government, and imprisoned many prominent polygamist Mormons" (https://en.wikipedia.org/wiki/1890_Manifesto). Were it not for those steps by the government, it's hard to know whether polygamy would have still been abandoned by the church.

In the case of Black people and the priesthood/temple ban, some say a worry over the church potentially losing its tax exempt status may have contributed to the positive change made by the church in 1978: http://www.lds-mormon.com/taxes_priesthood.shtml. The threat of losing revenue from BYU sports programs may have also played a role:

> "African-American athletes protested against LDS Church policies by boycotting several sporting events with Brigham Young University. In 1968, after the assassination of Martin Luther King, black members of the UTEP track team approached their coach and expressed their desire not to compete against BYU in an upcoming meet. When the coach disregarded the athletes' complaint, the athletes boycotted the meet. Also in 1968, the San Jose State basketball and football teams refused to play against Brigham Young. In 1969, 14 members of the University of Wyoming football team were removed from the team for planning to protest the discriminatory treatment they had received in their previous match with Brigham Young. In

their 1968 match against University of Wyoming, BYU football players refused the customary post-game handshakes after their loss and went straight to the locker rooms. They turned on the sprinklers, soaking the University of Wyoming football players. Additionally, a 'caricature of an ape and a black man' awaited them in the visitors' locker room, and a local paper reported 'BYU cleanses field of evil.' In November 1969, Stanford University President Kenneth Pitzer suspended athletic relations with BYU. Athletes protested Mormon racial policies at Arizona State University, San Jose State University, the University of New Mexico, and others." (https://en.wikipedia.org/wiki/ Civil_rights_and_Mormonism#NAACP_involvement)

Certainly, embarrassment about public perceptions of the church was a factor as well. I wonder if outside forces (governmental or otherwise) that threaten financial harm against the church, its institutions, or its members might likewise be what primarily motivates a doctrinal change on marriage equality as well.

One way that may manifest itself in coming years is through the threat of BYU once again being ostracized by the inter-collegiate athletic and academic associations it depends on for competitive, reputational, or financial partnerships. Or BYU students may suffer from a lack of competitive recruitment on campus as a result of increasing numbers of employers and professional organizations boycotting the school for recruitment purposes (which is something that has already occurred in certain areas of study at BYU: https://www.sltrib. com/news/education/2019/11/11/two-science-societies/). As BYU continues to prohibit gay dating on campus, academic professionals predict that the university and its students will become more and more alienated from the associations that they have traditionally relied upon for success in many areas. (An excellent discussion of this possibility is included in a podcast interview given by Michael Austin, BYU alumnus and executive vice president for academic affairs at the University of Evansville, which is a Methodist school in Indiana: https://soundcloud.com/mormonland/college-administrator-examines-byus-honor-code-reversal- on-lgbtq-issues-episode-129).

[Side note: In January 2020, news outlets reported that BYU gave in to external pressure to allow same-sex couples to participate in a championship ballroom dancing competition. "To host the coveted showcase, which it has every year since at least 1997, BYU was required to lift its ban keeping same-sex couples from competing." https://www.sltrib.com/news/education/2020/01/21/first-time-ever-byu-will/.]

And if BYU ever truly does permit gay dating among its students, many believe it is only a matter of time before the injustice of seeing happy gay couples at BYU not be allowed to get married results in the church modifying its prohibition on gay marriage.

In saying all that, I feel it important to reiterate that I don't mean to imply that divine revelation would not be involved in such a process as well. In fact, I believe divine revelation was involved in the changes that occurred with respect to both polygamy and Black people. Just because a prophet is compelled by outside forces to pray harder or be more open-minded about a particular issue than he ever has before, doesn't mean the resulting revelation is not genuinely from God.

I think most, if not all, of the revelations prophets receive come as a result of petitioning God about a mortal situation that is causing angst. Joseph Smith received the church's revelation about health practices because he felt compelled to pray after his wife, Emma, complained about cleaning up spitting tobacco following church meetings (https://www.churchofjesuschrist.org/manual/doctrine-and-covenants-stories/chapter-31-the- word-of-wisdom-february-1833). Moses was compelled to pray because of a political hardship (slavery) facing his people. Just like all the rest of us, prophets often become closest to God when the church or the people they lead are forced to endure hardships. And the church facing threats to its financial well-being has previously been a prophetic hardship resulting in divine guidance and surprising doctrinal change. I suppose it could once again.

I believe the church is worried that the government will eventually require it to provide equal treatment in all respects, including access to temple sealings, for LGBTQ individuals. While the church was instrumental in one instance in passing pro-LGBTQ rights legislation in Utah (https://www.nytimes.com/2015/03/12/us/politics/utah-passes-antidiscrimi-nation-bill-backed-by-mormon-leaders.html), it is more often on the side of litigants seeking to limit LGBTQ rights.

The church often unites with other faiths to file amicus briefs in cases dealing with LGBTQ rights. It did so to try to prevent the legalization of marriage equality in many states and then ultimately at the U.S. Supreme Court as well (https://newsroom.churchofjesuschrist.org/article/faiths-file-amicus-brief-on-marriage-cases- before-tenth-circuit-court; https://www.churchofjesuschrist.org/church/news/church-signs-amicus-brief-filed-on-marriage).

The church also filed an amicus brief in the LGBTQ employment case that was before the U.S. Supreme Court 2019, arguing that religious employers should be allowed to fire someone for being in a gay marriage or for openly transitioning to match their gender (https://www.usatoday.com/story/news/nation/2019/10/08/lgbt-supreme-court-cases-workplace- discrimination-civ-il-rights/3844832002/) (https://www.supremecourt.gov/DocketPDF/18/18-107/113604/20190826131230679_Harris%20Amicus%20Brief%20Final%20Version.pdf). The Supreme Court ended up ruling on the case in June 2020. The court said employers could not fire someone for actions that, if taken by someone of a different sex, would have been protected by law (https://www.cnn.com/2020/06/15/politics/supreme-court-lgbtq-employ-ment- case/index.html). That ruling resulted in landmark legal protections for LGBTQ people from employment discrimination in general, but the court specifically left open the question about whether religious employers were exempted (https://www.washingtonpost.com/politics/2020/06/16/supreme-court-closed-door-lgbtq- employment-discrimination-it-opened-window/). Then, in another case decided just a few weeks later, the Supreme Court confirmed that a religious employer is in fact allowed to discriminate against LGBTQ people in ways that secular employers no longer can (https://www.deseret.com/indepth/2020/7/8/21302953/supreme-court-employment- dis-crimination-catholic-schools-ministers-hiring-firing-ruling). The church filed an amicus brief in this later case as well, arguing that religious employers should be allowed to discriminate against LGBTQ people (https://www.supremecourt.

gov/DocketPDF/19/19-267/132581/20200210172618740_19-267%20 Amici%20Curiae.pdf). So, after these two court decisions, this is now the law of the land in the United States: secular employers cannot discriminate against someone for being LGBTQ, but religious employers can.

[Side note: Here is some further background on this issue, as presented by Latter Gay Stories (https://lattergaystories.org/):

> *"In 1984, newly minted Apostle, Dallin H. Oaks, former BYU President, and judge for the Utah Supreme Court wrote a confidential and secret memorandum for the leaders of the Church of Jesus Christ of Latter-day Saints supporting homosexual discrimination in society and the workplace. The memorandum titled, "Principles to Govern Possible Public Statement on Legislation Affecting Rights of Homosexuals," has been the guiding light for Latter- Day leaders in promoting the Church's discriminatory agenda towards LGBTQ people.*

> *Supported by the First Presidency and Quorum of Twelve Apostles, the memo includes the following statements:*

> *"... arguments for job discrimination against homosexuals are strongest in those types of employment and activities that provide teaching association and role models for young people. This would include school teachers (especially at the elementary and secondary levels), and youth leaders and counselors (such as scoutmasters , coaches, etc.)…The best strategy to oppose further anti-discrimination legislation protecting homosexuals is to propose well- reasoned exceptions rather than to oppose such legislation across the board. Total opposition (that is, opposition to all non-discrimination legislation benefiting homosexuals would look like a religious effort to use secular law to penalize one kind of sinner without comparable efforts to penalize persons guilty of other grievous sexual sins (adultery for example)…I recommend that if an anti-job-discrimination law is proposed to protect homosexuals, the Church should oppose the Law if it did not contain a youth protection exception.*

> *I recommend that the Church tailor its communications on this subject to take account of the formal difference between the condition*

or tendency of so-called homosexual persons on the one hand and homosexual practices on the other." (Pages 4-7)

"Take no position on laws changing the extent to which there are greater criminal penalties for homosexual behavior than for illicit heterosexual behavior." (Pages 8-10)

"Oppose job discrimination laws protecting homosexuals, unless such laws contain exceptions permitting employers to exclude homosexuals from employment that involves teaching of or other intimate association with young people." (Pages 10-17)

"Take no position on laws barring other types of discrimination against homosexuals, unless there is a secular basis (persuasive public policy) to justify such discrimination." (Page 15)

"Vigorously oppose the legalization of homosexual marriages." (Page 17) https://lattergaystories.org/wp-content/uploads/2020/02/Principles-to-Govern.pdf.]

Can a church member be in good standing if they support LGBTQ political causes?

Many church members wonder whether they can support civil marriage equality and other LGBTQ political causes and still be a member of the church in good standing. When one of our current apostles, Elder D. Todd Christofferson, was asked by a reporter back in 2015 whether Latter-day Saints would risk losing their church membership or temple privileges if they supported gay marriage privately among family and friends or publicly on social media, marched in pride parades, or belonged to gay-friendly organizations such as Affirmation or Mormons Building Bridges, he responded as follows:

> "We have individual members in the church with a variety of different opinions, beliefs and positions on these issues and other issues...In our view, **it doesn't really become a problem unless someone is** out attacking the church and its leaders — if that's a deliberate and persistent effort and trying to get

others to follow them, trying to draw others away, **trying to pull people, if you will, out of the church or away from its teachings and doctrines**." (https://archive.sltrib.com/article. php?id=2301174&itype=CMSID).

So, given that latitude allowed by the church, and now that I am no longer in any church leadership position, I am more open about my political support for LGBTQ rights and about laws affecting the LGBTQ community (like the Utah conversion therapy licensing rule). I was hesitant to do so before because I didn't want to risk confusing someone who perceived me as a representative of the church. But in being more open about my support for LGBTQ equality, I am not trying to pull people out of the church. I myself am deciding to stay in the church.

[Side note: I do not support the Fairness for All Act (FAA) that the church endorses: https://www.deseret.com/indepth/2019/12/6/20995260/mormon-utah-chris-stew-art-latter-day-saint-leaders-lgbtq- lds-civil-rights-gay-religious-freedom. In short, I don't think a religious institution/college should be allowed to keep its tax-exempt status and continue to receive federal aid money if it fires someone just because they're in a gay marriage. As a hypothetical situation, if a white supremacist religious organization had tax exempt status and fired an employee for being in an interracial marriage, should the government still allow that organization to not pay taxes? Many believe that true religious liberty means we should answer yes to that question. But I don't believe that. While our government should not make it illegal for any religion to maintain racist or homophobic beliefs, I do not believe tax exempt status or taxpayer dollars should be given by the government to any religious institution that discriminates in employment based on biological traits unrelated to job performance.]

In fact, even in postulating publicly ways the doctrine of the church could possibly change, I don't intend to attack the church. Rather, as I stated in the Preface, my intention is to help facilitate greater understanding of the pain that many LGBTQ church members and their families feel. I don't see how I can do that without sharing my thoughts about church doctrine and my hope for how it could possibly change – because the way that hope has been affected by ongoing teachings from church leaders on LGBTQ matters gets at the root of my pain. I don't want anyone to leave the church because of what I have shared. I haven't left the church myself.

That being said, I don't believe that makes me a better person than anyone who decides to leave the church. Everyone can have a unique path they feel inspired to follow. And I am now in a place in my life where I can say I honor and respect as equally valid all paths people choose to find love or to express love to others. While it's not the path I feel called to pursue, I think it's possible for God to want some people to leave the church to find what He wants for them in their own personal lives, or so they can do His will in ways there that they wouldn't be able to if they remained inside the church.

In any event, I don't think I have crossed any line to be at risk of losing good standing status (i.e., losing my temple recommend). One of the temple recommend interview questions asks: "Do you support or promote any teachings, practices, or doctrine contrary to those of The Church of Jesus Christ of Latter-day Saints?" I don't believe I am supporting or promoting any contrary teachings or doctrine – because all I'm doing is asking questions about current and past doctrines and teachings, not organizing protests for change, etc. I'm just trying to ask whether church members as a whole should be open to the idea that we might be wrong about gay marriage – so we're better prepared to receive any future revelation about how gay couples fit into God's plan. But many LGBTQ-friendly church members are worried about how local and regional church leaders will apply the wording of that question (https://www.sltrib.com/religion/2019/10/22/jana-riess-new-lds-temple/). I am grateful my ward and stake leaders understand I'm just trying to help church members better relate to people like me and that they don't feel inclined to revoke my temple privileges just because I have publicly written my thoughts here.

And I also hope my opposition to some of the political positions the church is taking on LGBTQ rights won't alienate me from any of my church friends. Hopefully we can disagree and still be close friends, even if we're at odds over the church's politics. I have tried to remain close friends with many church members who I feel don't follow the church's teachings on other political issues.

[Side note: An example is immigration. I'm pretty liberal-minded about immigration – and so is the church. If you'd like to see a good collection of statements from church leaders on immigration and refugees (including the church's view that undocumented status is akin to civil trespass and "there's nothing wrong with that"), check out a post made on November 5, 2019 on the public Facebook page "Progressive Mormon Teachings": https://www.facebook.com/ProgressiveMormonTeachings/ posts/2138582373112536].

So I hope my friends can remain close with me even though I choose to disagree with the church's political stance on LGBTQ rights.

Should scripture and history teach the church to stay out of LGBTQ politics?

One of the reasons I feel comfortable being a believer but still not liking the church's involvement in politics is, ironically, based in scripture. When the church argues against LGBTQ rights, I have wondered whether it is violating its own scripture:

> "We believe that religion is instituted of God; and that men are amenable to him, and to him only, for the exercise of it, unless their religious opinions prompt them to infringe upon the rights and liberties of others…**We do not believe it just to mingle religious influence with civil government, whereby one religious society is fostered and another proscribed in its spiritual privileges**, and the individual rights of its members, as citizens, denied." (Doctrine & Covenants 134:4, 9)

I often wonder whether the church is inappropriately mingling religious influence with government, and whether the church's efforts are actually resulting in something that the above scripture says we don't believe in: the favoring of one religion over another to the detriment of individual rights of citizens who are members of the disfavored religion. Specifically, because some churches support full LGBTQ equality in civil rights as a tenet of their religious belief to love everyone as Jesus did, could our church's involvement in anti-LGBTQ rights issues promote a situation where <u>one set of religious beliefs</u> gets favored by the government over others? When religious beliefs of different groups conflict in the area of civil rights, should we interpret the above scripture as instruction for us to back off and just let civil government sort things out without religion being mingled in at all? One of our past apostles taught as much as follows:

> **"Anything that persons profess to do under the name of religion, which interferes with the rights of others is wrong**, and the secular law may step in and protect the citizens and restrain or punish those people who attempt to do this under the plea of religion." (Charles W. Penrose, Apostle, *Journal of Discourses*, Volume 25, Discourse 27, https://bycommoncon-sent.com/2016/07/11/stop-skipping-the-establishment-clause/)

I also feel comfortable not agreeing with the church's position on certain political issues because I draw a distinction between religious belief and political opinion. For example, just because I'm okay with a religious belief that prohibits drinking alcohol, that doesn't mean I am in favor of reinsti-tuting Prohibition. Also, the church has sometimes been on the immoral side of political issues and has changed its political positions repeatedly (including five times about slavery: https://gregkofford.com/blogs/news/five-times-mormons-changed-their-position-on-slavery).

One of the reasons I wish the church would stay out of politics is because I fear it will be embarrassed if doctrinal change occurs again in the future. This hap-pened not only about slavery but also interracial marriage. For many decades, the church supported laws making interracial marriage illegal and taught that it was a sin (https://en.wikipedia.org/wiki/Interracial_marriage_and_The_Church_of_Jesus_Christ_of_Latter-day_Saints). In a speech to the Utah legislature in 1852 in connection with a proposed pro- slavery law in Utah, Brigham Young even taught, while prophet, that it would be better from an eternal salvation perspective if an interracial couple and their children were decapitated or killed than be together as a family (https://books.google.com/books?id=LkRZGQ-8oO8IC&lpg=PA49&ots=30VXmz65se&pg=PA4 9#v=onepage&q&f=false)

(https://www.fairmormon.org/answers/Question:_Did_Brigham_Young_say_ that_race_mixing_ was_punishable_by_death%3F).

If the church was wrong about its politics with respect to marriage and civil rights before, is it possible the church is wrong about its politics again today? Will we someday look back on the church's legal efforts today to allow religious employers to fire their employees just because they are in a gay marriage with a similar sort of horror that we do when we look back on the church's support of laws prohibiting interracial marriage? If so, wouldn't it have been better if the church hadn't got involved in LGBTQ politics at all?

How careful should LGBTQ political activists in the church be?

All that being said, I am not aggressive in communicating any political opinions I have that might diverge from the church's political efforts. I want to keep good relationships with my church friends. So while I will be vocal (including on social media), I will not be combative because I love my fellow Latter-day Saints. Plus, I don't want to be part of stoking any flames that would prompt church leaders to harden their positions doctrinally. I believe church leaders started to double down over the pulpit like never before against gay marriage in the fall of 2019 in response to pressure from general church membership to reverse the Exclusion Policy.

If I'm right in that supposition, it wouldn't be the first time doctrinal "tightening" has happened to try to change the sentiments of church members. Our health code, which was initially revealed in 1833 as just a recommendation (i.e., a "word of wisdom"), became a rigid rule in 1921 in part because the prophet at the time didn't want alcohol consumption to be legal. When most church members in Utah voted to repeal Prohibition more than 10 years later, the prophet expressed his disappointment in them (https://en.wikipedia.org/ wiki/The_Church_of_Jesus_Christ_of_Latter- day_Saints_and_politics_in_ the_United_States). So to avoid the risk of even further doctrinal "tightening" on LGBTQ issues, I think pro-LGBTQ church members might need to be circumspect in how loudly we object to the church's political endeavors when speaking within church circles.

There is a fine balance we need to strike to lovingly educate church members about the harm we feel is being caused by the church's position on LGBTQ issues, without arguing so forcefully that church leaders feel they need to act with haste doctrinally to tamp down any growing sympathies. At the same time, I do speak up about political issues affecting LGBTQ people, because it is abundantly clear to me that not granting them equal rights in all areas of life is harmful (https://www.washingtonpost.com/outlook/2019/12/19/ anti-lgbt-discrimination-has- huge-human-toll-research-proves-it/) and not justified by any sort of religious liberty arguments.

CHAPTER 9:
CAN A PAINFUL EXPERIENCE WITH A LEADER RESULT IN GOOD?

Chapter synopsis: Church doctrine alone is painful for LGBTQ church members and their families, but their pain is often made worse by the statements and actions of other church members. For several reasons listed in this chapter, I think it is actually good for the church that I share the details of a painful experience we had with a General Authority. It hurt when that General Authority discussed my son being gay with harshness, suggested that emotional loyalty to church doctrine should be placed above emotional loyalty to family, and repeatedly warned that I would lose my family if I didn't believe in the church's doctrine. That was especially painful because God previously confirmed to us through powerful personal revelation that we could be faithful believers and still be genuinely happy about our son's decision to step away from the church.

As described in Cheryl's Facebook post on October 4, 2019 (see Chapter 1), she and I met with two higher-up church leaders here in Massachusetts over the weekend of September 28-29, 2019. These two men hold the ecclesiastical office of Seventy in our church. One of them is referred to as a General Authority and the other is referred to as an Area Authority. Out of respect for them and the love they said they had for my family and me, I have decided not to use their names anywhere in this book. I have simply referred to them by those titles (or together as the Authorities). They were visiting our area to reorganize our regional church leadership (our stake presidency) on behalf of global church headquarters in Salt Lake City. At that point, I had been serving as first counselor in the stake presidency for two years. The visiting Authorities had arrived to go through a process during which they would determine who would continue serving in the stake presidency, because the man to whom I had been a counselor for those two years (the stake president) was moving.

Before I go any further in sharing the experience we had with the General Authority, I want to acknowledge that mine is just one side of the story. I'm sure the General Authority could share a different version that clarified his intentions. But all I can do is share what I perceived. I have tried to do so here with as much objectivity as I can. It would bother me to know that anyone reading this book held negative views of these Authorities just because of what I will share in this chapter. And it would upset me greatly if anyone took steps to contact them. Both Authorities (especially the Area Authority) communicated what I believe were sincere expressions of love toward us. And, as I'll describe below, the General Authority (who was the only one who said hurtful things) sincerely apologized. I believe he was well-meaning but just not very sensitive to the mindset of parents of a gay child. I can't blame the General Authority for his insensitivity because (as you can read more about in Chapter 3) I was once quite insensitive to LGBTQ issues as well.

Why am I sharing details of my private conversation with a General Authority?

Before I get into telling the story, I feel like it's important for me to provide some explanation about why I feel it's actually helpful to the church for me to do so. While ecclesiastical duties of confidentiality only run in one direction (from the presiding church leader to the regular lay congregant), I know some people reading this book might feel like I am betraying the General Authority by sharing publicly some of the things he said to me in private. I can understand those feelings. However, I don't see any other way to communicate these points, which I think actually help the church, if I don't share some of the details of our conversations. (For what it's worth, there are in fact many details I have omitted from the story that I share in this chapter out of respect for the privacy of the General Authority.)

I think sharing the details of our experience with the General Authority is good for the church because:

1. Unfortunately, the experience itself unfolded in a very public way in front of hundreds of people who were aware that something was going on but didn't know the details. I want to clarify for those people that I was not released from my calling as some sort of punishment. Just a few months before, I had taught publicly in a stake conference that we should be more loving to our LGBTQ siblings in the church, and not judge anyone who hopes for change in the church. As you'll read in this chapter, the General Authority actually praised that talk after I emailed him a copy of it (which you can read here as well if you're curious: https://drive.google.com/open?id=1YwAV5rPRmx1bI9CLDhBLgAcueAQ8fH7n).

2. I want to clarify that the church does not have a policy that prohibits parents of gay kids from serving as leaders in the church. After our experience, many people asked us if that was the case. Many people who *haven't* asked us that might falsely continue to believe that the church does have some sort of rule like that, unless I share the circumstances under which I was released from my calling (as I do in this chapter).

3. I think it's good for people to know that the General Authority apologized to us. Even before Cheryl made her Facebook post, dozens of people expressed to us that they felt bad that we had a negative experience with a General Authority. Our experience was that public in nature; it was impossible to hide from the hundreds of church

members who were present the fact that something painful happened to us that weekend. I don't know how to help those people (many of whom love and respect us) feel kindly toward the General Authority without sharing the details of our conversations with him and his eventual apology. When they or others have a negative experience with a church leader, it may help them to know that sometimes that leader may apologize.

4. To summarize the above three points generally: in situations like ours where misunderstandings exist, I think that full and complete transparency is the best approach to protect the church's well-being and reputation.

5. I want any other church leaders to have a better idea of what is helpful vs. harmful to say when meeting with LGBTQ church members or their families. I know from various Facebook groups for people seeking support in the crossroads of LGBTQ and church issues, that there are many local church leaders and other church members around the world who are insensitive and say things that are very similar to what the General Authority said to me. And because most leaders in our church are cycled in and out of their positions fairly frequently (every several years), any sensitivity training that the church might conduct now for its leaders in this regard would largely become unknown among their successors fairly quickly. That is what happens with protocol training unless it is published in the church's General Handbook of instructions. And since there is no passage in the General Handbook that specifically says what sort of statements are hurtful or helpful to LGBTQ church members and their families, I'm hoping any reader who is a current or future leader in the church will remember some of the details I'll share in this chapter and maybe come back to read them again when dealing with LGBTQ-related situations in the future.

6. I think it's good for church members to occasionally see the human side of our leaders. For example, I know my testimony and commitment to the church were strengthened when I read the biography *Joseph Smith: Rough Stone Rolling,* written by active church member Richard Bushman. That book relates many stories of the mistakes, frailties, and failings of the prophet. I found it uplifting to know that a great man like Joseph was still human. That gave me hope that, if I just try to be the best person I can be, I might be remembered in a positive light despite my weaknesses too. Today's General Authorities in the church are also revered by many active church members. So I'm hoping that by sharing our experience, church members can similarly take comfort in knowing that even General Authorities sometimes make missteps – and I hope local church leaders can learn from the example of the General Authority's gracious apology to us.

7. Finally, I think it's good for the church to have its members become aware of more people who have experienced church-inflicted pain and yet still decide to stay in the church. Now, that's not to say that, in writing this book, I'm trying to hold myself out as an austere example of righteousness. Not by any means. But I think my explanations for why I'm staying in the church (see Chapter 10) may be more meaningful – and may help people who are thinking of leaving the church over similar pain they have felt – if the details of the hurtful experience are shared. I respect others for making different choices about their church activity, including members of my own family. My ability to stay engaged with the church while openly discussing my frustrations with its doctrines that affect LGBTQ people does not make me a better person than anyone else. It just means I feel called to something different. I hope anyone who feels similarly called to stay in the church, despite being hurt by it, will find something about my experience that resonates with them.

I hope all of those reasons make sense to church members who might question why I would share specific details of a negative experience with a General Authority. I don't believe I am speaking evil of him because I know he didn't mean to cause harm – and he apologized. Besides, I have been in his shoes. I know I messed up on occasion as a local church leader, and if someone I counseled with felt it would benefit the church as a whole to publicly discuss what I did to hurt them, I honestly invite them to go public with my missteps as well, so that I and others can learn to do better. I talked about a few of my mistakes on the LGBTQ front while serving in church leadership in the Preface. In short, I hope no reader imagines anything but benevolent intent as my motivation for sharing my story.

What did the General Authority say to us?

And with that introduction and background, here is what happened from my perspective.

After a preliminary interview on Saturday morning, which was the first day of the Authorities' visit that weekend, the General Authority asked me to return with Cheryl to meet with him again that afternoon – so he could extend the assignment to me to continue serving as a counselor to the man who would be called as the new stake president.

[Side note: I know that was the calling he was going to extend to me because there were only three callings to fill that day: a new president and his two counselors. The General Authority told me at the beginning of this second interview that the new stake president had already been called. I also know that I was being interviewed for a counselor position because we discussed that fact the next day with the new stake president and the Authorities in the Sunday follow-up meeting I describe below.]

Near the outset of this second interview that afternoon, the General Authority said he learned from a discussion he had with someone else that day, about Wes' decisions to leave his mission and to step away from the church because he is gay. Instead of simply attending to the business of extending the calling to me, it was clear he wanted to explore this topic with me. Over the course of our conversation, I told the General Authority I was comfortable with Wes' decision to leave the church because I thought it was best for his mental health and emotional well-being. I told him that I privately hoped for the church to change its position on gay marriage but that I never advocated for that publicly, and that I tried to always be careful to only teach authorized church positions in my capacity as a leader in the church.

Here are some of the views the General Authority shared in response to my sentiments (each of which was communicated in a cordial manner; I believe we were both trying to express our feelings in as kind and loving a way as possible):

- He said I shouldn't be happy that Wes decided to leave the church – because sin of any kind is not justified. Basically, sinning is sinning. I told him I felt, as Wes' father who knows him well and am aware of what he's gone through over the past few years, like Wes had the choice to either stay in the church and be depressed (possibly suicidal) or leave the church and be mentally healthy. The General Authority said he didn't believe those were the only options – because other gay people have chosen to be lifelong celibates and are happy as such in the church. I told him that solution didn't work for most gay people since the vast majority of them leave the church and feel traumatized by church teachings. Regardless of whether it worked for others, it wasn't working for Wes.

- He drew an analogy between the feelings a parent can have when a child leaves the church to commit crimes and the feelings he imagined I might be having because Wes had left the church to date other men. I think he was trying to help me understand that many parents have kids who leave the church for a variety of reasons. When I said (as politely as I could) that the difference between those two situations was that gay relationships didn't cause harm to any third parties, he said that wasn't always the case because gay couples can cause harm by raising children in their homes. I told him that studies showed no meaningful difference in the well-being of children raised by gay parents vs. those raised by straight parents (and no greater likelihood to be LGBTQ than other kids either). He said he knew of studies that showed otherwise, so it was an open question.

[Side note: See Chapter 8 for the overwhelming scholarly consensus, based on over three decades of peer- reviewed research, that having a gay or lesbian parent does not harm children (https://whatweknow. inequality.cornell.edu/topics/lgbt-equality/what-does-the-scholarly-research-say- about-the-wellbeing-of-children-with-gay-or-lesbian-parents/).]

- When I asked if it was possible that God directed Wes through personal revelation to pursue his own path, as a unique exception to the church's prohibition against gay marriage, he said he doubted Wes received such direction because people can often feel as if they have received divine revelation for whatever they want, if they want it badly enough. He also said he didn't believe Wes could have received direction like that because God doesn't give conflicting commandments. I questioned that rationale by discussing examples of God giving conflicting commandments to various people in the scriptures (I specifically mentioned Nephi and Laban, but was also thinking of Adam and Eve, Abraham and Isaac, etc.). He wouldn't admit the possibility of an exception – but he did concede that there are times when God allows circumstances that only He can understand.

- He postulated that God may not condemn some gay people for choosing to be in gay relationships because they may not have complete control over their behavior – and speculated that they could have diminished individual agency, similar to a long-time abuse victim who may have instinctive physical defense responses they can't control when placed in triggering situations. He acknowledged that was not a perfect analogy because gay sexual orientation isn't a mental illness or a result of abuse, but he thought it was still helpful to explain that only God can know someone's capacity to live in a certain way – and that we therefore need to just have hope that the Savior will work everything out somehow.

- He said many times over the course of our conversation that the law of chastity (i.e., the church's rule that sex is only allowed within straight, monogamous marriage) won't ever change, and that church leaders can't change it because it is of God. I asked him what he thought about prior changes in the law of chastity in the church, from monogamy to polygamy and back to monogamy. He said that line of thought (that the law of chastity changed before and so could change again) was the argument of the LGBTQ rights movement as the "opposition," used to confuse people. I told him I didn't like saying "opposition" in reference to the LGBTQ rights movement.

- He randomly mentioned at one point that the church is expecting to be pressured by the government and other forces to do gay marriages in temples and to allow gay couples to show affection on church property. He said the church will spend resources to fight legal battles to prevent all of that. I didn't vocally respond to that statement as I was surprised he would mention something like that to me, as a tithe-paying father of a gay son. It seemed like a provocative and challenging thing to say to me, not a loving one – something that had nothing to do with me.

- I asked him if it was okay that I hoped for a change in the church's position on gay marriage, even though I didn't agitate for it and even though I always stayed within bounds when teaching publicly or speaking with anyone in the capacity of my calling. I told him that the Savior may have provided an example of it being okay to ask if suffering can be avoided, by asking if the cup could pass from Him so His suffering didn't have to happen. So I asked if maybe I don't need to feel guilty for asking if it's possible that a change occur in our doctrine so the suffering of LGBTQ church members can stop, sometime before God just "works it all out" after they're dead. I asked if it was okay for me to hope and pray that such a change will come quickly so people's suffering can stop sooner, IF it's God's will, that is. He told me it was better to just have hope that the Savior will work things out somehow on a case-by-case basis after this life, not to hope that the church will ever change.

- I mentioned I was always very careful about how and what I taught on the LGBTQ topic. I said I didn't want to be prideful and damage my spirit by trying to get out ahead of the Lord's will for all the church collectively, which I recognized was only given through the topmost church leaders. I said I wasn't authorized to know when the appropriate number of church members were ready for a change in doctrine to occur. He said Cheryl and I were perhaps called by God to be Wes' parents because we are strong enough to handle the dichotomy of believing while still loving him without reservation. But other people may not be as strong. So I needed to be careful about how I talk about things, so I don't give anyone any reason to doubt the church.

[Side note: That idea of us being stronger than other people was the General Authority's suggestion, and is not a notion with which I agree. Personally, I believe we often find God most effectively by turning challenges in our lives into opportunities to love others. But it has always been super easy for us to love Wes. I know other people who face challenges in which it is difficult to show love. So I view having a gay child to be a special blessing for us, not a challenge by which our strength should be measured. I think we got lucky to learn more of God's love in such a naturally caring role as parents.]

- He promised me very intensely at least four times at various points during our conversation (scooting forward in his chair and staring into my eyes, inches away) that I would lose Cheryl as my wife and that my family would fall apart in this life if I "lost my faith." He later explained in a follow-up meeting that he said this would happen because he thought if I left the church I would become a greater target for Satan than other people are, because I have made temple covenants and served as a leader in the church. After one of the times he gave me that warning, he said that people who leave the church aren't happy. They say they are (and feel relief and happiness initially) but most of them eventually end up breaking major commandments that bring them misery. I told him I felt at times like, rather than lose my family because of lack of faith in the church, it seemed like the opposite was happening to me. I had to struggle harder to keep my family united because of the dichotomy for each of us between loving Wes and our respective decisions whether to stay in the church. Even though Wes has never asked any of us to leave the church, it still sometimes feels like a betrayal of our love for him to keep attending. I told the General Authority that hope for change sometimes seemed like the only thing I could offer to my other kids to keep them in the church because they loved their brother so much.

- At the end of the interview when we were standing, he shook my hand and stated, looking me in the eyes, that everything he told me in our conversation was said by him as a "special witness for Christ," which is one of the titles for someone in his position.

As we ended the interview, he said he felt good about still issuing me the calling, because he felt comfortable that I would "protect" the doctrine of the church. And I felt okay about continuing to serve in the calling while continuing to support Wes' decisions – because while the General Authority clearly thought my feelings weren't ideal, he didn't insist I change my mind to be able to keep serving in the calling. He just warned that I would lose Cheryl if I didn't have proper faith, which I knew would not ever happen, no matter what I did or did not believe. I knew this from prior discussions with her and multiple strong experiences of personal revelation. As long as I still kept my feelings private, he seemed fine with me continuing to serve (even though he clearly thought I needed to change how I felt, in order to be a more faithful church member).

Per church practice, the next official step to formally receiving a calling like the one I was being given was to make sure Cheryl was supportive. That is what happened two years before when a different General Authority first called me into the stake presidency: he met with me first and then he met with both Cheryl and me together.

So Cheryl was then asked to join the General Authority and me. At this point, she had been waiting in the hall to meet with us for around 70 minutes. This was extremely worrying for her because it was normal to expect my interview to last only a few minutes before she would be invited to join. It was also worrying because halfway into my conversation with the General Authority, a separate leadership meeting had already started where the General Authority and I were supposed to be giving talks to over 100 people that Saturday afternoon. It was very odd for the two of us to be announced as speakers in that meeting and then for us to just not go into it. So when Cheryl joined us, she naturally asked what took so long. When she found out it was because we were talking about Wes, she started crying and asked why Wes needed to be discussed at all - that she didn't think it was fair we were being treated differently just because we had a son who was born gay and is doing what he needs to for his mental health and overall well-being.

The General Authority didn't stay in the room to discuss Cheryl's concerns. Because he saw that this would take some time and that he needed to get to the other meeting, he left after Cheryl had only been in the room for a minute or so. As he was leaving, he asked me if I thought it would be best if I spoke with Cheryl first to "calm her down" and relay what he and I had discussed – and then he would finish extending the calling to us after the afternoon meeting ended and he could return. He said he felt like he was sent to Massachusetts to minister to us and our family, even more than to reorganize the stake presidency.

When he left, we were in no shape to join the meeting. Cheryl said I looked upset when she had first come into the room. I am so grateful for how well Cheryl knows me – because I was very hurt and upset, but I was trying to bury my feelings and convince myself that they didn't matter, so I could continue being a voice for increased love in the church in an official capacity as a leader. I knew that, like it or not, most church members give more credence to things church leaders say than what other people in the church say. And I wanted to continue to serve as a church leader to be able to help more people feel the need to love unconditionally.

I discussed with Cheryl the things the General Authority had said, and told her I really didn't like how he had warned me as a witness for Christ that I would lose my family if I didn't hold to certain beliefs. Cheryl then said she couldn't continue to feel that her unhindered love for Wes and what we know is best for him had to be so carefully expressed (almost like it had to be hidden) all the time. She didn't want to talk to the General Authority about anything further because she was upset and didn't want to say anything she'd regret. So we decided to leave the church building and go home to process things.

Right when we got outside, even before we made it to our car to drive home, Cheryl broke down crying harder than I have ever seen her cry in my life. She was sobbing and almost couldn't stand up. She asked if she was condemning our family because she loved and supported Wes in his decision to leave the church. I told her she wasn't condemning us and that I KNEW we were fine in the Lord's eyes – because I had felt His Spirit confirm that to me. I said I knew she felt exactly how God wanted her to feel – and that I thought we were just ahead of our time in the church. I say this with no sense of pride, just echoing Paul's words, "as of one born out of due time" (1 Corinthians 15:8). We then went home, and I wrote down my memories of my conversation with the General Authority while they were still fresh.

After being home with Cheryl for an hour or so, I felt like I needed to further express my feelings to the General Authority. So, with Cheryl's encouragement (because she recognized it's a rare opportunity for anyone to be able to sit with a General Authority of the church, let alone someone like me who wanted to explain why the church's doctrine was painful to us), I drove back to the church building that night. The evening session of a few hundred people had ended by that point. Again I was noticeably absent as I was supposed to be sitting on the stand in front of the congregation. When the General Authority and the Area Authority came out of that meeting, they stayed with me to talk until late in the evening.

What did I say to the General Authority?

I started that new conversation with the Authorities by telling them that I had never seen Cheryl weep so hard in my life. I told them of the strong connection that Cheryl and I had – that she made me happier than anything else in my life. And I was very upset she was hurt. I told them I came back to talk further because I needed them to understand the pain that families like ours feel from the doctrine of the church on LGBTQ matters. Interestingly, now that the General Authority was not alone with me, his demeanor and the tone of the discussion was very different. Instead of the feeling being ominous and challenging like before, there was a feeling of sorrow and compassion I felt from both Authorities. I attribute this to something the General Authority said at the beginning of this new meeting: that he had had an opportunity to think things over and discuss our prior conversation with the Area Authority.

So I asked them in this new conversation if I should feel bad about being happy for Wes, or guilty for hoping for change in the church. They said I didn't need to feel bad – because any loving dad would think like that – but that it would be better if I didn't hope for change (I'm still not sure how to reconcile their words).

I then discussed with them, at a high level, the fact that no scripture or proclamation of the church actually prohibits gay marriage (see Chapter 5) and some of the other possibilities I have wondered about for doctrinal change (like how gay temple marriage could fit into our theology – see Chapter 6). I also discussed with them what science now knows about how sexual orientation is determined (see Chapter 3).

I told them more about Wes' personal revelation on his mission about what to do with his life (as I describe below in this chapter). I told them how religious Wes is and how converted he is to the Savior – about how he was studying the Bible intensely now. In fact, since Wes had a new hobby of writing a series of novels himself, he was examining Jesus as a character and concluded that no author or group of authors could have made Him up because His responses and teachings are always so perfect. I discussed how Wes is visiting different churches now to try to find a Christian denomination or congregation that he liked and that allowed gay marriage so he could be more fully involved in church (rather than just listen from the pews) if he finds a man to marry.

At the end of our conversation, they informed me that they felt it necessary to extend the counselor calling to someone else instead – because Cheryl and I had left the church building that afternoon. Early the following morning they asked to meet with another man and his wife to extend the calling to him (who, I should say, is an amazing guy - I'm very happy he's the person who was chosen).

Before I left, we discussed whether Cheryl would want to meet with them as well the next day. I said I would ask her. When I got home that night, she said that would be fine. So we woke up the next morning (after getting very little sleep) and went to the general Sunday morning meeting.

Several hundred people were in attendance. Since I was part of the out-going stake presidency, I was allocated a few minutes to share some thoughts and feelings. I took that opportunity to publicly apologize for missing the conference meetings the day before (citing "personal family reasons"), thank everyone with whom I had served, explain that Wes came home from his mission a bit early a few months previously because he is gay (something Wes was fine with me publicly announcing like that at this point in his journey), encourage everyone to love better those who are marginalized in our church, and declare that I loved, and that I knew that God loved, Wes exactly as he was. I closed my brief remarks with these words from a text earlier that morning from a friend who was concerned about me (because he, like many other people, suspected I missed the public meetings the day before due to a clash with the General Authority relating to my support for LGTBQ people). I said, *"In the words of a text I got from a friend this morning: "Unconditional love, man. That's the Savior's way. Full stop."*

What did Cheryl say to the General Authority?

Following that general meeting, on Sunday afternoon, Cheryl and I met with both visiting Authorities together. I asked for both the outgoing and incoming stake presidents to also be present during this meeting, so that everyone could be familiar first-hand with our story, for any future ecclesiastical interactions with us after the Authorities left. Before we went into this next meeting, Cheryl prayed with me privately and asked God for strength to help her appropriately represent each person we knew of from our local congregation who was LGBTQ. She mentioned all of them (mostly youth) by name in her prayer.

We then went into the room for the meeting and Cheryl started the conversation. She told everyone present for almost 40 straight minutes how she felt. She was awesome. The Authorities courteously and intently listened.

Cheryl talked about how much it hurt to have the church treat our family differently just because we have a gay son – and how that was especially painful given all we've sacrificed in the name of church service over the years (which I describe a bit further in Chapter 10). She discussed how there is a double standard because other leaders of the church in our area have straight children who are not living according to church standards, but they don't get spoken to in the same way I did when they are being interviewed for church callings.

She told them (without sharing any names) about the many LGBTQ church members we know just in our local congregation alone and how that percentage (around 8% of the active members) is almost definitely similar stake-wide and church-wide globally (because studies estimate that around 2-10% of the population at large is somewhere on the LGBTQ spectrum). She said she heard questions about LGBTQ issues from gay kids AND straight kids almost every week in the early morning scripture study class she taught before school every day. She said all the General Authorities need to get on the same page about being more loving and accepting on LGBTQ issues or the vast majority of the rising generation will leave the church. We talked about how much different our experiences and interviews had been before with other

General Authorities of the church – that they seemed more compassionate about LGBTQ issues.

She asked all of us men in the room to consider how we would feel if we were told that the physical desires we have for our wives were not allowed to be expressed, and that we instead were only allowed to be intimate with a man.

She talked about how Wes is incredibly spiritual – how she begged him not to go on a mission (because she was worried for his mental health), but he wanted to go anyway. She discussed how we worried every week during the 19 months he was on his mission and hoped he wasn't having suicidal thoughts like he had had in high school. He had a kind mission president but many other people on his mission said horrific things to him.

Cheryl talked about how most of her family (after years of similar sacrificing for the church as well) had stepped away from the church over this issue. We discussed how Cheryl's sister, who no longer attends church, is donating her time and resources to help with the Toronto chapter of Affirmation (a support organization for LGBTQ Latter-day Saints and their allies). We said that she's a living example that many people aren't leaving the church over this issue because they no longer want to serve others or because they want to "sin," but because they don't feel love in the church at all on this front, and that's not how Jesus teaches us to be.

I won't share publicly here the many other things we discussed in this meeting and in the other conversations I had with the Authorities the day before. We want to respect at least a certain amount of privacy. But Cheryl and I feel it is important to share what I <u>have</u> described here because we suspect many of the General Authority's statements to us represent sentiments that other church leaders might be inclined to echo, as they counsel with LGBTQ individuals and their loved ones. By openly talking about how his words hurt us, we are risking the ire of many of our friends and loved ones in the church, who feel it is bad to ever say anything negative in public like this about a General Authority. We do so because we want to make clear to any other church leaders that the statements he made were not helpful to us. We had already figured out how to love Wes completely while still showing respect for the church's doctrines about LGBTQ issues publicly. We had figured out how to balance that dichotomy. We were ready and willing to continue serving in the church for years to come. But the inappropriate analogies, insensitive arguments, and harsh warnings from the General Authority made us feel despair and anger in a way we hadn't anticipated.

To his credit, the General Authority apologized after listening to everything Cheryl had to say. He said he regretted how he had spoken to me the day before. And he said he had suffered a mostly sleepless night because he was worrying about how things transpired the day before. He told us he messed up, saying he should not have been so ominous or harsh. He said he admired us as parents. He discussed how his not having an LGBTQ child made it impossible for him to know how we felt (and I do expect some of his insensitivity stemmed from his lack of experience as a parent in our situation). And he said we should focus any anger or frustration about what was said on him, not on the church.

[Side note: Please recall here what I mentioned in the Preface that I am not trying to attack the church by writing this. While I would appreciate the church, through its leaders, apologizing for the trauma suffered by LGBTQ individuals as a result of church teachings on marriage, gender, and sexuality, I am not sharing my pain publicly to shame the institution. My ultimate aim is not to embarrass the church, but rather, to hopefully help any church members or leaders more effectively minister to LGBTQ individuals and their loved ones going forward. I want to help prevent as many people as possible from experiencing similar church-related pain. While prompting an apology is not my objective, I do hope that at some point, greater sensitivity among church members and leaders does lead to an apology from the church to the LGBTQ community.]

The General Authority's personal apology was sincere, and I do not have any hard feelings toward him now. However, I will admit that, in a way, his apology ironically has since caused me more pain – because it wasn't accompanied by any action by him to remedy the pain he caused to my family and me – even though he said he felt God sent him to Massachusetts to minister to us more than any other official reason he was there. There has been no ministering or outreach by him to my family or me since. Other church leaders have contacted us and have gone to great lengths to minister to us, but we haven't heard from that particular General Authority by way of follow-up since. But that doesn't really matter - I'm not too bothered about the lack of follow-up. Maybe he thinks we would be upset if he contacted us again? I also realize that he is a busy man with many responsibilities. Regardless, for me, going to church is about connecting with God and helping others – so I have never viewed just being offended by someone as a good reason to stop attending church.

Why did the General Authority's words hurt so much?

Our initial reaction to this whole experience was that it felt like the General Authority wanted us to choose between being happy for Wes and his choices vs. being truly faithful in the gospel. And that felt like an impossible choice for us to make as parents. We know Wes was born gay and that he is doing what is needed for his mental health and emotional well-being – so it's impossible for us to be sad about that. But the multiple warnings he gave made us feel like we were being told we weren't good parents in God's eyes because we supported Wes in our hearts – and that everything we had done to serve in the church and raise our family in the gospel was now at risk, just because we loved our son and were pleased he was finally healthy and happy.

It was all very confusing though – because the General Authority had said he was fine still proceeding with me serving in the stake presidency calling even though he knew my private views. At the time, I suspected he was ready to still proceed because I had convinced him that his views vs. mine came down mostly to just a matter of semantics and feelings, not actions. I didn't tell him I would love or support Wes any differently. I just truthfully and genuinely told him that, notwithstanding my feelings, I would be very careful not to cross any lines in performing the responsibilities of my calling, where I might be seen by others to endorse teachings that were unauthorized by the church. It seemed like the General Authority was trying to make sure I understood that I needed to seem sad in public about Wes' decision to leave the church, even if I privately believed it was the best thing for him. And that implicit expectation hurt.

I also still feel pain from the experience stemming from how Cheryl was treated in all of it. I have come to deeply regret not inviting her into our interview earlier. In the context of extending a calling to someone, it is standard protocol for a church leader to meet with the person alone first, to assess their worthiness, and then, assuming they are worthy, to invite their spouse to join the meeting when actually asking them to serve in the calling. So those dynamics of our interview made me feel like I couldn't invite Cheryl to participate – because I personally was being assessed for my worthiness. But when we started discussing Wes, I regret not insisting that she join us. At that point, a typical worthiness interview was no longer being conducted and I believe it would have been more appropriate to have Wes' mother be a part of our discussion, especially since we both were planning on Cheryl joining us next anyway. Both the General Authority and I were very experienced with interviews and personal counseling, so I have come to wonder how we could have we left Cheryl out in the hall worrying for so long. I assume the General Authority just didn't realize she would be upset. But I was worried about what Cheryl would think when our lengthy interview finally ended – especially once she found out what we had been discussing. So I blame myself for not having the presence of mind to ask that she join our conversation.

I can't help but think the General Authority felt stuck with me in the calling, uneasy about my circumstance, and relieved to have Cheryl's reaction as an excuse to not have me continue to serve. Those thoughts come to my mind in part because when I was first asked to serve in the stake presidency two years before, I was told I would likely be in the assignment for a period of 9 years. That is a customary expectation throughout the church for time of service for someone in a stake presidency, and I had only served 2 years. So I'm sure the General Authority was not surprised when the new stake president asked for me to continue to serve as one of his counselors (especially since I was the only member of the outgoing stake presidency who was not moving out of state). I can't help but wonder sometimes if the General Authority was relieved to have an excuse to overrule the new stake president's preference for me to keep serving. I try not to focus on that thought though, as I want to be charitable to the General Authority.

[Side note: I am positive that it is not a secret church requirement that General Authorities try to keep people with gay kids out of leadership callings. The General Authority who first called me to be in the stake presidency two years earlier in 2017 was very kind and sensitive with Cheryl and me. We're pretty sure he knew about Wes being gay because Wes had just left on his mission a month earlier and had told the then stake president about his sexual orientation before he left. That other General Authority didn't mention Wes' sexuality at all (which was appropriate because it is irrelevant to me being considered for any church calling). He did say I was being called into the stake presidency then partly because of how Cheryl and I had loved and raised our kids. I have also heard of other General Authorities who have expressed support for the idea that gay church members shouldn't be looked down on if they decide to leave the church. Views about LGBTQ issues seem to vary among the General Authorities.]

I think this may have been the first time or two that the relatively new General Authority had ever been in charge of re-organizing a stake presidency. So I can imagine he was trying to be super cautious – that maybe he just didn't want to take a risk on anyone who had any "issues" to continue serving in a prominent leadership position. But, again, I try not to focus on that line of thought too much though – because I want to be charitable toward the General Authority and give him the benefit of the doubt. I want to accept him at his word and believe what he said when he apologized to us: that he simply messed up.

I find it easy to accept that explanation for what happened when I remember that, while church leaders are called of God, they're still just normal people. They make mistakes just like all the rest of us do. Church leadership callings that are higher up in the ecclesiastical hierarchy are not a reward for superior righteousness. And callings to look after toddlers on Sunday are not a punishment. So going into that weekend, Cheryl and I were trying to be ready for any outcome or calling. I didn't want to feel entitled to continue to serve in the stake presidency, even though it seemed like a logical choice that I would do so for purposes of continuity and even though I felt called (and still feel called) to be a voice for marginalized people in the church.

I have noticed that logical choices are not always the ones the Lord wants made. And that's fine. Love should be the focus of the church, and love is not always logical. No matter where any of us serve (whether in an official calling or not), we are all just trying to do our best to love and help one another. Without a leadership calling, I actually feel more free now to discuss my views on love. And I'm sure the General Authority aims to have love as the focus of his service as well. Just like church doctrine must be revealed through fallible leaders, God can only administer His church through imperfect people, whose human side can sometimes get in the way of everything being done perfectly, even though the best of intentions might underly our efforts.

Does any of this mean that what I taught before on LGBTQ matters is wrong?

A few days after the General Authority had left Massachusetts, at his prior request, I emailed him a copy of a talk I had given several months earlier in our last stake conference, in which I discussed LGBTQ acceptance and inclusion at length. I told him it represented the most LGBTQ-friendly statements I had ever made in the capacity of my calling in the stake presidency. A few days later, he responded with a message that praised the love he felt from the talk and he said I was "valiant" in my service to the Lord. (A copy of my talk can be found here: https://drive.google.com/open?id=1YwAV5rPRmx1bI9CLDhBLgAcueAQ8fH7n).

Now, I don't share any of that to boast or anything like that. Rather, I feel it's important to clarify that I wasn't relieved of my calling because of anything I had taught previously about all of us needing to love, accept, and include LGBTQ individuals better. Unfortunately, I know some people have assumed that I got "fired" because I did something wrong, and that they are therefore justified in maintaining LGBTQ views that are less-than-kind. And I don't want any progress that I perhaps helped facilitate in softening anyone's heart to go to waste. So please understand that what I taught in my calling about how we need to show more compassion toward LGBTQ people has been approved of by a General Authority of the church – so there's no "excuse" to disagree with what I taught. ☺

That's actually the main reason I am sharing these details about our experience with the General Authority – because I don't want church members in our area (or anywhere else in the church) to think it is bad to talk about how we need to love LGBTQ individuals better. Unless I share these details of our experience, I fear many people may make the false assumption that it is not good to talk about showing more love to our LGBTQ siblings. So hopefully readers here can view my sharing of our experience with the General Authority as a positive thing for the church, which is what I intend.

Can parents of gay kids be church leaders?

To be fair in my telling of this whole experience, I also want to clarify once more that, despite what happened to us, Latter-day Saint parents who have gay kids are not automatically disqualified from serving in leadership positions in the church. One of the highest-up leaders in our church (one of our apostles) has a gay son (see the mention of his son in the latter half of this article: https://www.sltrib.com/religion/local/2018/06/29/mormon-churchs-newest/). And we were told by the visiting Authorities that other general and regional leaders throughout the church have LGBTQ kids too.

[Side note: Another apostle has a gay brother, but brothers are not "held responsible" in the same way that parents of gay kids are (https://www.deseret.com/2017/9/13/20619341/gay-brother-of-mormon-apostle-shares-his-spiritual-journey).]

Now, I don't know how the church's position on LGBTQ matters affects other leaders' kids personally. That might depend on where their kids fall on the spectrum of sexual orientation and gender identity, or how traumatic church teachings are to their kids. I also don't know if those other parents have ever felt like a General Authority wanted them to view as sin something they knew was necessary for their child's mental health and emotional well-being. If so, I can't help but wonder if those other parents are just better suited to deal with that sort of cognitive dissonance than Cheryl and I are. (That ironically hurts to think about too – because it makes me wonder if I'm not as faithful as those other parents because I can't hold those conflicting thoughts and emotions in my head and heart at the same time as well as they can.) I simply don't know. But I did get the feeling in my interview with the General Authority that anyone holding a prominent church leadership position that has a gay child who has left the church should feel an obligation to demonstrate both a sufficient level of disappointment about them having left and complete comfort in the current doctrine of the church.

Upon subsequent reflection, I think that's what made me feel most uncomfortable with the General Authority's words: the implication that it would be best, from a gospel devotion perspective, for me to change or sacrifice (or at least hide) my feelings of support for my son. In hindsight, maybe I shouldn't have been surprised by that perceived expectation, because Joseph Smith taught that "a religion that does not require the sacrifice of <u>all</u> things never has the power sufficient to produce the faith necessary unto life and salvation." Some related church teachings say that when someone is committed enough in their heart to sacrifice everything for God, then they can know here and now that their eternal salvation is assured:

> "When faith is sufficient to sacrifice all earthly things, **even life itself if necessary**, it is possible for a person to know that he is accepted of the Lord for what he has done, and with this strong faith he may eventually receive eternal life." (https://www.churchofjesuschrist.org/study/ensign/1976/07/accepted-of-the-lord-the- doctrine-of-making-your-calling-and-election-sure)

So maybe I should have been more prepared for the possibility that a time would come in my church experience where it might be suggested I should make a sacrifice like that, rather than merely promise that I would be willing to do so in the future. I guess I just didn't anticipate that such a high bar was required for simply serving in a stake presidency, especially one I would already been serving in for two years. And it's one thing to consider sacrificing my own life; it's another to think that I might be encouraged to sacrifice my adult son's life (through hammering him with doctrine that encourages his suicide).

I never expected that any such required sacrifice would involve me distancing myself emotionally from my son over a choice he made to seek some of the same things in his life that have brought me joy in mine: spousal love and healthy family life. I know Luke 12:53 teaches that because of the gospel, "the father shall be divided against the son; the mother against the daughter," etc. But given my lived experience of seeing Wes diligently strive for righteousness and his desire to be a father who is a stable and regular presence in his future kids' lives (rather than just being around every other weekend if a marriage to a woman didn't work out – which happens with the vast majority of marriages between a gay person and a straight person), it feels like the church, not the gospel, is what wants me to be divided from my son. It would be different if Wes were choosing something that was selfish or unkind. Then the gospel could be expected to divide us. But he's not. He's just choosing family. So I don't think that scripture applies to our situation. I don't believe God wants me to be sad about Wes' decision to date men to hopefully find a husband who loves him and with whom he can build a family.

How should I feel about my son leaving the church?

As his father, I have prayed and felt God's Spirit confirm to me that Wes trying to always be alone or trying to make a marriage to a woman work are not good options for him. His particular biological makeup means he wouldn't be able to have natural attraction toward a woman. (Current church teachings say that without genuine attraction, a gay person should not marry a straight person: see Chapter 3.) So marriage to a woman will not work, and is not advisable, for him.

And affirmatively striving to be alone forever is not good for him either. Many gay church members talk about feeling deep despair because they think something about their personal makeup goes against God's eternal plan for all of us. And even those gay church members who are able to see past that falsehood and affirm their infinite value in God's eyes, often still feel pain at being "pitied" by their fellow church members. It breaks my heart to know that Wes ever thought something was wrong with him – and it frustrates me that church teachings result in many church members feeling sorry for my amazing son – all just because of how his body is naturally wired for intimacy and love.

[Side note: There is a great scriptural analogy (for which I give credit to Derek Knox, a gay theologian and convert to the church), which I'll repeat with more commentary in the following chapter because I find it so powerful. It compares a parent's decision to joyfully embrace their gay child leaving the church to the decision that was made in the story of Solomon and the baby, found in 1 Kings 3:16-28. Just like the true mother in that story was willing to let her baby be raised by a woman in a different home so the baby wouldn't be cut in half, parents of gay kids in the church may be willing to let them find different spiritual homes so they avoid experiencing trauma and the real risk of suicide.]

I'm also not sad about Wes' decision to leave the church because he got an answer to his prayers. After many years (years!) of sincere and repeated petitions, he felt that God did not want him to spend his life trying to avoid falling in love and having a family. When he told me about his answer, I was comfortable with it, because I had seen the process Wes had gone through to get it. He was humble, willing to do whatever might be required of him. He was patient, always willing to wait until God deemed fit to answer questions on His timeline. Wes had counseled with Cheryl and me, some close friends, and church leaders extensively. The answer to his prayer came as he was finally, truly ready to offer up lifelong celibacy to God, knowing how hard that would be for him, if that was what God wanted. This was not a case of someone praying and wanting something so badly that they fooled themselves into getting an answer they preferred. I accepted that Wes had received divine personal revelation for his life. I was glad his personal answer was consistent with the scripture that says, "it is not good that...man should be alone" (Genesis 2:18). But I also recognized that his answer was unique to him. And Wes recognized that too. Not everyone in a situation similar to his will get the same divine direction (although over 70% of same-gender attracted church members do feel it necessary to leave the church: https://www.huffpost.com/entry/gay-mormon-men-marriage_n_6464848). God deals with each of us individually and many personal facts and circumstances can result in different answers for different people. Some church members who feel gay sexual desires feel prompted by God to stay in the church and remain celibate. While that is a hard and lonely road that often results in depression and mental health struggles, I still respect their stated inspiration and admire their desires to be obedient. But that wasn't what God told Wes to do – and I equally respect his inspiration and admire his desire to be obedient to God's clear will for him as well.

[Side note: The idea that it is not good for man (or woman) to be alone is foundational in our understanding of eternal families. People who enforce celibacy and want some of God's children to be alone in this life (or who teach LGBTQ people will be happy enough being alone in the lower kingdoms of heaven) are therefore asking for something that is "not good" according to the scriptures. As Elder Bruce R. McConkie taught: "Celibacy is not of God, whose law is that 'marriage is honourable in all' (Hebrews 13:4)" (Bruce R. McConkie, Apostle, https://archive.org/stream/MormonDoctrine1966/MormonDoctrine1966_djvu.txt, 1966). I find it perplexing that church leaders today are asking gay Latter-day Saints, who do not feel an attraction to anyone of the opposite gender, to remain celibate their entire lives, contrary to what the scriptures teach is "good" for people.]

For my fellow Latter-day Saints reading this who are perplexed at how God could give Wes direction that contradicts what the church teaches is a commandment from God, it might be helpful for us all to remember that there are examples in our scriptures where prophets were commanded by God to do things that would normally be considered sins but that God still wanted them to do because a higher cause was to be served. One example of this is the story with Nephi and Laban in the Book of Mormon – but I don't love that one because that involved a sin that causes actual harm – killing; I prefer instead the example of Adam choosing to partake of the forbidden fruit in Eden so he could obey the commandment to have a family with Eve. Now, yes, I will admit Wes is not a prophet (in the sense in which we most frequently use that term in the church anyway). ☺ But, regardless, he is still entitled to receive personal revelation as to the affairs of his own life, as we all are. So when Wes told me he finally got his answer, I soon felt from my own subsequent personal prayers that even if the church says gay marriage is a sin, Wes is still on the path God wants for him, and God wants me to support him. Given the wholesome goals that Wes has (to find lifelong monogamous marriage, continue worshipping Christ, and serving others), I think his path is right alongside the covenant path that the church offers, and represents his own covenant path that is as equally valid as the unique covenant path any other church member walks. But the visiting General Authority seemed to want to reprimand me for having that perspective.

Am I struggling because I was personally offended?

Regardless, at this point, I'm no longer offended and am absolutely fine not being in the stake presidency. In fact, since my release I have received inspired feelings, confirming for me that things happened exactly as they did for a special reason: so I can relate just a tiny bit better to Wes and catch a fleeting glimpse into what he felt, in needing to choose between church loyalty vs. family loyalty. I wrote the following to a friend to describe that impression, just a few days following the experience with the General Authority:

> I'm glad this experience happened because I think I can now better empathize with Wes, even if just slightly; so I could understand a little bit better how painful it was for him to have to choose between having a stable future family vs. having full fellowship in the church. In the moment I had this epiphany, I felt comfort me and I seemed to catch a glimpse of the empathy that Christ has for Wes - and of His ability to love and console him so much more than I can. And I saw how important it is for me to always try to show that same type of pure love, without mixed emotions or qualifications, to my family.
>
> I'm so thankful God blessed me with a gay son. My understanding of the comforting power of Christ's Atonement and of His matchless

love and empathy have been deeply enriched because of the challenges Wes has faced. Because of his belief in Christ, he has forgiven so many people who have said hurtful things to him. The Atonement has similarly helped me forgive the General Authority who met with me. I have accepted his apology completely. I know his words aren't reflective of the Savior's views (or even of the views of some other General Authorities I have spoken with, to be honest). And I'm eternally thankful for the Atonement's ability to alleviate my pain and to teach me how to best support Wes by loving him as Christ loves me.

So in a way, I'm grateful for the General Authority and how he helped me come to relate to Wes a tiny bit better. Yes, I was offended at the time by what the General Authority said and how he said it. But I am over that now. I know some people reading this may not believe that. But, seriously, I am no longer upset or offended by what happened that weekend in late September 2019 with the General Authority.

Any enduring pain I feel relating to the church has nothing to do with a personal affront or conflict of personalities. Rather, it has only to do with the doctrine of the church regarding gender, marriage, sexuality, and family and the harm (sometimes fatal harm) that it causes in the lives of LGBTQ church members and their families. In any event, I love the people in my local congregation and wouldn't want to separate myself from them just because of a bad experience with someone from church headquarters.

But I know there is a strong tendency in our church culture to assume that people struggle with the church simply because they were offended. So I hope all the doctrinal analysis and opinion in this book will help get that notion out of the way. I am committed to frequent church attendance going forward, so I hope it is clear that I am not just stuck brooding over how his words and actions were painful. I have moved on from the experience and am trying to now focus on the informal calling I feel God wants me to do: that of being a vocal ally within the church to our LGBTQ siblings, naming their pain without hesitation and emphasizing the Christ-like hope for change and full equality that I see possible for them within the scriptures and church doctrine.

Strong messages deeply embedded in our theology and new teachings from our highest-up global church leaders have made it even harder than ever to endure the emotional and spiritual dichotomy that families like mine already experience. I hope you will understand why my family's hope was hanging on by just a thread for years - and why I feel like that thread was cut over the course of a few weeks in September and October 2019 – and how hard it is going to be to try to reestablish the same type of commitment to the church in a mentally healthy way going forward. But I am committed to re-weaving that thread, staying active in the church, and trying to find a way to serve and love others with the lessons I have learned.

CHAPTER 10:
CAN WE STAY IN CHURCH & AVOID THE "DARK CLOUD"?

Chapter synopsis: I'm committed to a new approach to my church membership. I know it won't be easy to continue because of the pain caused by church doctrine. But God's allowance for variation among faithful disciples and a focus on love for LGBTQ church members – and, admittedly, the protection I feel from mental harm myself, due in part I believe to my relative privilege as a straight, white male in the church – allow me to stay.

Well, after so much discussion, it's time to answer the final question: How exactly am I managing to stay in the church if the doctrine on LGBTQ issues hurts so much? Well, because of the doctrinal doubling down against LGBTQ people (see Chapter 4) and the meeting I had in person with the General Authority (see Chapter 9), I need to approach the church differently going forward to make sure that church culture and anti-LGBTQ doctrines don't make my church experience painful. Over the years, when something about church doctrine or culture has caused Cheryl angst, she has often referred to those negative feelings as the church's "dark cloud" (whether it's over LGBTQ issues, the unequal treatment of men vs. women in the church, feelings of inadequacy next to the long list of church expectations, confusion about the relationship between blessings and obedience, not being able to relate to a

Heavenly Mother because we don't know hardly anything about Her at all, the fact that there seems to be more judgment than love at times at church, etc.). In the past, we were able to avoid the church's dark cloud from becoming too overwhelming by focusing on hope for change and just teaching love amongst our fellow Latter-day Saints. Our feelings closely mirrored this statement from a gay son of one of our apostles:

> "A truth behind any power structure is that the power of the system is proportional to peoples' belief or adherence to the system. As much as the organization appears to be top-down, **meaningful changes in the lives of individuals start from the bottom up. This gives me hope that even while the organization and religion remain unyielding, the culture can be the impetus for change.**" (Matthew Gong, https://m. facebook.com/notes/matthew-gong/birthday-letters-27- 28/10158377175735021/, 2019)

But, given how much more acute the pain over LGBTQ issues has gotten just recently, and how much more intractable the current doctrine seems to be now, Cheryl and I aren't sure how to avoid the dark cloud and remain members of the church unless we take steps to guard ourselves that are different from what we tried before.

Church should make us happy and Christ should give us hope, right?

It's disappointing that we feel we need to protect ourselves from the influence of the church because the idea of any religion is that it's supposed to generally make people feel happy, right? This is something our leaders have taught us repeatedly about the church:

> "In the days and years ahead, you may suffer some discourage-ment and disappointment. On occasion, you may feel genuine despair, either for yourself or your children or the plight and

conditions of others. You may even make a personal mistake or two—serious mistakes, perhaps, though I hope not—and you may worry that any chance to be happy and secure in life has eluded you forever. When such times come, I ask you to remember this: **This is the church of the happy endings**." (Jeffrey R. Holland, Apostle, http://www.ldsliving.com/-This-Is-the-Church-of-Happy-Endings-Elder-Holland-Gives- Powerful-Message-to-Graduates/s/88339, 2018)

While I love that idea – that happy endings are what the church is about – I feel hurt when I recognize that such an idea has little applicability to LGBTQ church members.

[Side note: Remember, research shows that the only ending they can hope for in eternity, under current doctrine anyway (i.e., that they will be "cured" of having a gay sexual orientation in the afterlife), has led many gay Latter- day Saints to engage in suicidal ideation or to attempt or die by suicide, to bring the "cure" sooner, rather than endure being stuck in what feels like an impossible situation in this life. And in a 2017 study, 89% of LGBTQ Latter- day Saint participants reported one or more symptoms (with over 73% having multiple symptoms) likely to warrant a PTSD diagnosis – with all such symptoms specifically relating to their religious experiences in the church (https://getd.libs.uga.edu/pdfs/simmons_brian_w_201712_phd.pdf; http://mormonsbuildingbridges.org/wp- content/uploads/2019/10/20190928-U-of-U-MBB-Presentation-SIMMONS-FINAL.pptx).

At the time of this writing, I am aware of a couple of new peer-reviewed studies that are currently being conducted. Initial results from one of them is consistent in showing that religious teachings that define gay sexual behavior as sinful result in psychological damage and depression: https://www.facebook.com/groups/mormonsbuildingbridges/permalink/2517990774968435/.]

While I don't feel their same pain personally (because, like it or not, deserved or not, I have cisgender straight privilege in the church), the limitation of church doctrine to provide a sense of happiness for LGBTQ people does make me very sad, especially as the father of a gay son.

[Side note: Besides PTSD, another psychological category of harm is called "traumatic invalidation." Studies show that LGBTQ individuals experience this type of harm when exposed to non-affirming ideologies (https://bostonchildstudycenter.

com/ptsd/?fbclid=IwAR1W7K83a0UWkPUzRkm7ftAJx6mIcWzyZdRawcwm-
51jXlroq 7FwxZKZJ9a0).]

Now, don't get me wrong, I personally have felt immense love, fellowship, support, spiritual goodness, and faith-promoting joy from my involvement with the church and my belief in its core doctrines. I believe in the power of love to make people happy. And I have felt that in my associations with my fellow church members on many, many occasions. I agree with this quote from an amazing Latter-day Saint author:

> "**[M]y theology comes down to 'God is love,'** as illustrated in the little song that we sing, '**Where love is, there God is also.' To me this means wherever in a straight or a gay relationship there is genuine caring and devotion—there God is.** And where in Islam, in Catholicism, in Buddhism, in Mormonism there is genuine caring and devotion—there God is. **The fact of the matter is that in Mormonism I find a great deal of love—and therefore a great deal of God.**" (Carol Lynn Pearson, https://www.sunstonemagazine.com/ why-i-stay-2/, 2014)

Cheryl and I have spent literally countless hours in unpaid church service over our lives. I spent two years on a full-time mission before college at my own family's expense. Until late 2019, I doubt we've ever spent less than 20 hours a week collectively on average on church service and devotion since the beginning of our marriage. We've taken time off work to go on many youth camps. For many years when our three oldest kids were little, we woke them up early Sunday morning to bring them to church with us more than an hour earlier than the rest of the congregation, because Cheryl and I were both serving in congregational leadership roles and had council meetings to attend. We've taught early morning scripture study classes to teenagers every day before school for years. We even paid for babysitting once a week for a year so we could go together to teach college students a weekly scripture class at night as well. And we found joy in all of that service. We love the people with whom we served, and we love the Lord.

But unfortunately, ever since I first counseled with people as a bishop about their gay sexual orientations several years ago, and especially since Wes subsequently came out to us as gay in 2015, the doctrine against marriage equality makes it feel at times like church depletes, rather than replenishes, my spiritual cup - because of the despair I feel when I'm reminded of painful church teachings. While I know my feelings are not as intense because I am not gay, the following statement resonates with me nonetheless for how it expresses a similar duality:

> **"The religion [teaches] me to be intentional, patient, compassionate, forgiving, repentant, and to strive to better myself. I believe at the religion's core is an immensely powerful set of values that drive human progression.** In that core, I see an elegance that is beyond human intention. **[But] I have also seen the human intentions in the history of weaponizing the religion. The religion also taught me that queerness, is a mental illness, is vile, or simply does not exist.** I learned this explicitly from the pulpit." (Matthew Gong, https://m.facebook.com/notes/matthew-gong/birthday-letters-27-28/10158377175735021/, 2019)

And as much as I believe in the power of the Savior's love, just hoping that the love of Christ will "work things out" for gay church members after this life is still a very sad and depressing thought if that means abandoning their same-sex spouses and altering their sexuality in order to be in the highest degree of heaven. For me, part of trusting in Christ to "work things out" means believing that the church's doctrinal teaching in this area is incomplete and more will be revealed. I can't separate my belief in Christ and His mercy from a belief that the doctrine will change – because Christ is hope, not despair.

So I am no longer hesitant to use words like "incomplete," "deficient," "painful," "dark," "hurtful," "un-Christ-like," etc., when referring to doctrines on LGBTQ issues in the church. I may need to moderate my exposure to some church members and some messages from here on out, in order to ensure that church is an uplifting, rather than a painful, experience for me. The members of my local congregation are great, so hopefully that challenge won't prove too difficult.

Some people have reached out to Cheryl and me, encouraging our family to have faith like other marginalized or traumatized groups in our church's history have had historically. But, as I have mentioned in Chapter 2, and with as much sympathy and sensitivity as I can imagine expressing to individuals in such groups, I think LGBTQ people in the church face a different situation. In addition to the examples about Blacks and polygamy mentioned elsewhere in this book, here are others:

- Many people feel that women in the church do not have an equal voice. But their voice is heard more loudly than that of gays and lesbians who are in uniform- orientation marriages (because they are kicked out of church callings entirely for being in such marriages).

- Parents of straight children who have left the church have hope that such children will nevertheless be saved in the highest degree of heaven with them (https://www.churchofjesuschrist.org/study/ensign/2002/09/hope-for-parents-of-wayward-children). But parents of gay children can only have such hope if it also involves having their kids' sexuality changed, which is a depressing thought.

- Parents of deceased young children have the assurance that their kids will automatically make it to the highest degree of heaven (https://www.churchofjesuschrist.org/study/ensign/1981/06/i-have-a-question/will-those-who-died-as-little-children-have-to-receive-baptism-at-some-future-time). While I would never want to trade places with any parent who has lost a child, the *eternal* hope provided to parents of inactive gay and lesbian children is much more bleak.

- Straight singles in the church can have hope for uniform-orientation love someday, even if only in the afterlife. But gay singles are supposed to avoid uniform- orientation love here. And because of the church's teachings, many gay singles struggle with feelings that something about their physical makeup offends God – because uniform-orientation love can't exist for them in heaven either, without rewiring.

- And lastly, Mormon pioneers who died crossing the plains had the hope of being together forever as families. But gay and lesbian couples are told there is no way they can be with their same-sex mortal spouses after this life.

So, when mortal circumstances and eternal prospects are viewed collectively, there is much to despair about for our LGBTQ siblings.

That realization clearly negatively affects the parents and family members of LGBTQ individuals as well. Under current doctrine, Cheryl and I are stuck with church teachings that relegate our son to either a lesser kingdom of heaven or requires a change to how he loves to be in the highest degree of heaven, which engenders feeling of anguish as well. And that is the prospect he faces simply because he wants to eventually marry someone with whom he can raise a family in a stable marriage filled with love, intimacy, and lifelong companionship, just like the rest of us. That desire is good and selfless. So the dichotomy the church is asking us to endure is incredibly hard to bear as parents.

[Side note: I am grateful for older families with LGBTQ children who paved the way in the church years ago, through their efforts to increase awareness and understanding among church leaders and church members. They make the journey that our family has to endure less painful. I recognize that many families have suffered more than we have. One situation I recently learned about with the David and Carlie Hardy family has made me reflect on how much improvement is still needed in the church. Their story happened over two decades before ours, but still resonates for many reasons: https://www.thenation.com/article/archive/mormon-family-values/ (I am glad conversion therapy was never encouraged by our church leaders for Wes). Even though written decades ago, this letter by Brother Hardy to Elder Boyd K. Packer does an excellent job of outlining the still pertinent reasons why the church is not good at providing happy endings for families like ours: https://sites.google.

com/site/breakawayfrommormonism/Downhome/mormonism/mormon-history/
aterrificlettertoboydkpacker. The church pamphlet authored by Elder Packer referred
to in that letter can be found here: https://blakeclan.org/jon/to-the-one/. Over 20
years later, the fact that families like ours are still feeling pain in the church over
this issue means we still have a lot more progress to make.]

Are there different ways to endure to the end?

Each member of our family has had their own unique reaction to this whole
situation. We're learning that each of us has a different ability to ignore others'
views that we should feel guilty about hoping for a change or to hold up under
the pain of the constant pokes to our wounds brought about by demeaning
General Conference talks on LGBTQ matters (which then get discussed during
church lessons on Sundays). Ironically, we have never felt closer as a family, as
we've united to express love to each other and talk about each of our respective
capacities to tolerate the emotional pain and the "dark cloud" that the church's
doctrine on this topic produces.

As I have thought about our situation recently, the word "endure" has
come to mind often. How much church can we endure? It's interesting that
one of the commandments we have in the church is to "endure to the end,"
which means to basically always stay active in the church until death (https://
www.churchofjesuschrist.org/study/ensign/1977/03/i-have-a-question/what-
does-it-mean-to-endure-to-the-end-and-why-is-it-necessary). With that being
a commandment, I have wondered how guilty I should feel if I fail to serve in
the church in the same ways I have been up until now in my life. But I had
an epiphany come to my mind one day some time ago while thinking about
why the church is okay with some people being exempt from following certain commandments. I wrote the following in my journal when the thought
came to me:

> *Jesus taught that the first great commandment is to love God*
> *(Matthew 22:35–40). He also taught that the way we love Him is*
> *by keeping His commandments (John 14:15). But what's interesting*

*is that when he taught the commandment to love God, he used subjective wording: "Thou shalt love the Lord thy God with all **thy** heart, and with all **thy** soul, and with all **thy** strength, and with all **thy** mind" (Luke 10:27). So maybe that's why, if someone's mind can't comprehend the importance of a commandment, it makes sense that they're not expected to obey it. And if someone's heart and soul would be broken by keeping a commandment, maybe that commandment just doesn't apply to them. And if someone doesn't have the strength to keep a commandment in full, maybe God only sees it as a commandment for them to the extent their strength allows it to be. We love God by keeping His commandments, but maybe Christ said we only need to love Him with our own respective hearts, souls, strengths, and minds for a reason – so we understand that obedience is a personal, subjective matter – just between us and God – not something about which we should be compared to others.*

So, with that understanding, maybe I should view the commandment to endure to the end a bit differently. Maybe God will understand if I (or members of my family) are not able to keep serving in the church as actively as we have before. While I don't agree with most of what Elder Hafen taught in his talk about conversion therapy (as I noted in Chapter 7), I do like an analogy he gave in that talk about the way God judges us (https://religion.wikia.org/wiki/Bruce_C._Hafen). He referred to Olympic diving, in which a diver is judged not only by his technical execution of a dive, but also on the difficulty of the dive. (Maybe I just like that analogy because I was a diver in high school!) I like remembering that the Lord judges us not only on our thoughts, desires, and behaviors, but also on the difficulties we face, which are unique to us, or in other words, on the difficulty of our varying dives. Because my family is being asked to perform a more difficult dive than some families in the church, maybe we can still get just as good of an overall score, even if we aren't as involved in the church as some other families? All of that seems consistent with what the Book of Mormon teaches about how "it is not requisite that a man should run faster than he has strength" (Mosiah 4:27). Because LGBTQ-related church doctrines result in us being asked to essentially run uphill in the church, I think God might view us just as favorably as He does some other church members who might only be running on a flat incline, even if we are less involved in church service than they are. Our strength is no less than theirs, but it is depleted more quickly inside the church because our circumstances there are harder. So I am comfortable with anyone in my family who feels their strength is best spent serving others outside the church, where their strength can last longer. In my view, that decision is just as worthy (and in some ways more selfless) as a decision to stay and serve within the church.

I personally will *strive* to attend church as often as I can to renew my personal commitment to God, including to comfort others who are struggling as well and to help be a voice for increased love. But I know my family members may not all be with me every time I go to church because we all have to take care of our own respective mental health too. My family is basically trying to figure out how to keep the good things we've felt from the church in our lives, including continuing to serve and help others, while better managing how to avoid the things that cause us to hurt and despair. That means each of us may end up walking our own unique path, which is consistent with the scriptural teaching that the righteous path is entered into by a strait (i.e., narrow) gate and then continues on a narrow way (Matthew 7:14). I think that suggests a path that is unique to each of us, because the narrowness of both the gate and the path doesn't allow anyone else to be on it. That makes sense given that our covenants are unique to each of us too – so the same should hold true for our respective covenant paths. But, notwithstanding our unique paths, we will always support each other on our individual journeys.

I am coming to appreciate more and more how my family members' strengths may be needed outside the church, to be with and comfort those who are leaving church activity. My path inside the church is not better than theirs – it is just different. And their strengths are just different from (not less than) mine too, which is why I am sure they can faithfully endure to the end utilizing their strengths outside church activity on the path of service God has revealed to them.

Is it okay if no one else in my family comes back to church with me?

For various reasons, Cheryl has decided that her church involvement will be more limited than mine. And I support her 100% in that decision. While Wes has not asked that anyone in our family leave the church with him, I am personally glad that he has his mother's company as he walks "alongside" the church-prescribed covenant path, on his own valid and worthwhile covenant path outside the church. For our three other children (all younger than Wes), the dichotomy is confusing and causes anxiety and guilt, either way they turn. They like the relationships they have with people at church, but they don't like how church doctrine against marriage equality makes them feel – at all. So at the time of this writing, they have each decided to stop attending church regularly.

Some less active adult church friends have said that when they were kids, they felt their parents loved the church more than them – or at least that their parents prioritized church service over them. We do not want to alienate any of our kids from us, regardless of their chosen level of activity in the church. We don't want to make the mistake that one of our past prophets made with his inactive son:

> "Over the years **Spencer's repeated, anguished efforts to call his son to repentance only widened the gap between them.** The son believed he should not be expected to profess faith and live his life in a way inconsistent with his convictions. The father kept hoping that perhaps one more appeal would make the difference. Even if it did not, he felt it his responsibility as a parent to make the effort." (https://www.millennialstar.org/ president-kimball-and-his-inactive-son/)

I never want a lack of unity between any members of our family. So I have given my kids more freedom to decide for themselves about church than ever before – because things are more intense and difficult church-wise for all of us now. All of our kids love many things about the church – especially the people. They might have decided to remain active in the church were it not for the pain caused by the newly entrenched doctrine on LGBTQ issues. (They each also don't like the inequality between men and women in the church, but they were able to ignore that concern for years and still participate fully.)

Interestingly, giving my children more space to choose what to do is consistent with an impression I had when I went to the temple on September 20, 2019, after President Nelson's BYU sermon but before my meeting with the General Authority. I wrote the following down in my journal when I came out of the temple:

> *I had a spiritual witness in the temple today that I need to trust the Lord when it comes to my kids. I need to avoid pressuring them.* **Teach them, yes. Testify to them, yes. Love them, absolutely. But pressure them about the church, no. God can guide them more effectively and wisely than I can, and He knows what paths will be best for them.**

I heard an interesting analogy on a podcast (which I already shared briefly in a side note in Chapter 9 and which, as noted, I believe was originally taught by Derek Knox) that relates to that sentiment as well. At a conference for LGBTQ-supportive parents in the church, a mother was expressing anguish. She was upset about the desires of her teenage daughter to no longer attend church because she was a lesbian. Going to church and related activities made the daughter feel bad about herself and think about suicide. The conference presenter thought for a minute and then answered the mother's question by relaying the Bible story of Solomon and the baby: two women are fighting over the baby, and Solomon says he could just chop the baby in half so they could share (1 Kings 3:16-28). One woman was okay with that solution; she was apparently most interested in winning the argument. But the other woman was more concerned for the baby's well-being and so was willing to let the baby go to a different home to be raised in safety and peace. The presenter then asked the mother if she was willing to let her lesbian daughter be raised in a different spiritual home so she could likewise be safe and at peace – so she wouldn't want to kill herself. That story resonates with me and I am trying now to focus more on the emotional and spiritual well-being of each one of my kids, based on their unique personalities and needs, than I am on just keeping them active in the church – because I'm realizing now that the church may not be a healthy place for everyone right now.

On that note, I'm glad that in 2018 the church adopted a new approach that emphasizes the integration of gospel study at home. The catchphrase is "home-centered, church-supported." I think that means the primary responsibility for gospel instruction, learning, and commitment should come from the home, not from time spent at church. The word "support" means holding up a part of the weight of something. I think the church is saying that each family needs to make sure that it is holding up the primary weight of gospel learning and living, not the church. So while I will strive to attend church often, I will also not hesitate to stay home on Sundays when I feel that I need to be with my family, to circle our wagons and heal from any hurtful messages or attitudes church teachings might be bringing into our lives. I believe that approach is consistent with the teaching that personal revelation for our families is no less important than revelation received by church leaders for the church:

> "As General Authorities of the Church, we are just the same as you are, and you are just the same as we are. **You have the same access to the powers of revelation for your families and for your work and for your callings as we do.**" (Boyd K. Packer, Apostle, https://www.churchofjesuschrist.org/study/general-conference/2007/10/the-weak-and- the-simple-of-the-church, 2007)

I believe that when prayerful guidance is sought from God by parents regarding what is best for their children, the answers they receive carry as much weight in that relationship as any amount of church authority. I believe God stands eager and ready to reveal and give authority to Cheryl and me in how we support, love, teach, guide, and celebrate our gay son and each of our other kids.

We hope no one will judge us negatively for not being as heavily involved as before. I think that's one of the most serious cultural problems within our church - a notion of perfectionism that leads to judgment of others. Many people are so insecure about their ability to be "enough" that they compare themselves to others to make themselves feel better. And we tend to look down on questioning and on hopes or thoughts that are against orthodoxy, thereby making each other feel guilty for that too. For example, I have wondered at times why I should ever feel bad for not being able to think about Wes the way the General Authority seemed to want me to. I have wondered whether other families in the church can balance serving in the church and having a gay son better than we can. But that line of thought just causes more feelings of darkness about attending church. Like we are never good enough. So to avoid that vicious circle of thought, I think it's important for everyone in my family to decide on their own what they can tolerate church-wise while still staying mentally healthy – enduring to the end based on where they feel God wants them to devote their strength, not on what others think is necessary (Matthew 24:13, 2 Nephi 31:17, Doctrine & Covenants 53:7). All that really matters in the end is if we each know we're good with God. In that vein, I love the following quote from one of the former general worldwide women's leaders in our church:

> "Be spiritually independent enough that your relationship with the Savior doesn't depend on your circumstances or on what other people say and do. **Have the spiritual independence to be a Mormon—the best Mormon you can—in your own way. Not the bishop's way. Not the Relief Society president's way. Your way.**" — Chieko N. Okazaki, Former Counselor in the General Relief Society Presidency; from her book *Lighten Up* (https://mormonquotes.wordpress.com/2014/10/02/be-spiritually- independent/)

Why am I committed to staying in the church?

I think it's appropriate to begin to wrap up now by stating the main reasons I am staying in the church:

1. Because it is my spiritual home since childhood: Author Carol Lynn Pearson quoted the Dalai Lama: "'Grow Where You Are Planted.' I expect that is what the Dalai Lama meant when he said that whenever possible we should stay in the religion we were born to." (Carol Lynn Pearson, https://www.sunstonemagazine.com/why-i-stay-2/, 2014)

2. Because I believe in what I consider to be its truly core teachings about Christ-like love and His gospel.

3. Because I love many of the unique doctrines and theological concepts that the church teaches, such as: the idea that everyone who has ever lived will have an equal and fair opportunity, whether in this life or the next, to make it to the highest degree of heaven; the idea that we have a Heavenly Mother; the idea that our Heavenly Parents want us to become like Them after this life; the idea that the heavens are never closed to further revelation because there are prophets and apostles walking the earth today just like they did anciently; the way the Book of Mormon clarifies the power and scope of Christ's Atonement; the Book of Mormon's teaching that this life is not a mistake that came about because of the fall of Adam and Eve, but that, rather, it is part of God's plan for us and a time for us to be tested and to grow; and many others.

4. Because I love the associations I have with my fellow Latter-day Saints; and

5. Because I made a promise to God when I was baptized that I would "comfort those who stand in need of comfort" (Mosiah 18:8-9). LGBTQ Latter-day Saints need and deserve plenty of comfort.

I feel like I'm in a somewhat unique position to help comfort others in the church who are struggling with the church's LGBTQ doctrines, given the combination of me having a gay son and my experience growing up in the church and serving in many church leadership capacities as an adult. I'm also staying because Wes wants me to - although he would be fine if I didn't stay too. He just wants me to be true to myself (and that's what this whole book is about - me being true to myself). And part of being true to myself means striving with my fellow Latter-day Saints to make the world a better place. I guess I believe that:

> **"...distilled to its essence the Church is its members, striving for meaning and a better life. Beautiful in their attempts, terrifying in their potential, and human in their efforts."** (Matthew Gong, https://m.facebook.com/notes/matthew-gong/ birthday- letters-27-28/10158377175735021/, 2019)

I am going to try to help the marginalized members of the church – the ones who feel like they're on the fringes – feel like they belong, because they do. I love what Peter teaches us in the New Testament about making sure we don't reject the marginalized people among us:

> "You are followers of the Lord, and this stone is precious to you. But it isn't precious to those who refuse to follow him. They are the builders who tossed aside the stone that turned out to be the most important one of all." (1 Peter 2:7, Contemporary English Version)

Christ lived His mortal life on the margins of society in His day. I think we reject Christ, the most important stone in the structure of the gospel, if we fail to find a way to help people who don't seem to fit the typical mold know that they are important to the church too. So I will stay in the church to try to ensure that fewer precious stones get cast away. Meanwhile, my approach to doing so, again, is going to be more guarded going forward - to protect the mental health and well-being of myself and that of my family. To be honest, for the first time in my life, I sometimes wish I didn't have a strong testimony and belief in the church. It would be a lot easier to just leave the church than it is going to be for me to stay and try to keep it a safe place.

I'm going to take up the challenge to stay and be a vocal proponent for increased love and charity (as I was before), to be more open about my thoughts on LGBTQ political issues, and to no longer be hesitant to say that I am praying with all my heart, every day, that the church's doctrines about LGBTQ issues change. I don't think that means I'm sustaining or promoting teachings that are contrary to the church's doctrine – to do that, I think I would have to be demanding that the church change its positions (instead of just expressing the pain that is caused by them) or be trying to convince people to leave the church. I'm not trying to do that. Rather, I'm just being honest about the desires of my heart and mind, so people understand the sentiments of a father of a gay son better than perhaps they did before – which will hopefully help church members minister better to such people going forward.

While I'm staying, I will also need to hope differently by accepting church teachings in a more selective way. To be able to put up with what I anticipate will be many future decades of teachings that feel hostile to our LGBTQ siblings, I have decided to pick and choose what church teachings I decide to have faith in. One Latter-day Saint author described this sentiment perfectly for me as follows:

> **"I also believe an important reason that I am able to stay is that in some ways I do not stay. I do not stay in concepts that I do not accept. I do not stay in traditions that I do not believe in. I move, in my own very imperfect way, toward the horizon that truly calls to me.** I believe the best thing I received from my pioneer ancestors was not a destination, but an invitation. They gave me the model of being a pioneer and encouraged me to follow in their footsteps." (Carol Lynn Pearson, https://www.sunstonemagazine.com/why-i-stay-2/, 2014)

And I think there is prophetic support for me to take this sort of selective-acceptance approach to church teachings:

> "I never thought it was right to call up a man and try him because he erred in doctrine; it looks too much like Methodism and not like Latter-day Saintism. **Methodists have creeds which a man must believe or be kicked out of their church.**

I want the liberty of believing as I please. It feels so good not to be trammeled." (The Prophet Joseph Smith, https://www.josephsmithpapers.org/paper-summary/discourse-8-april-1843-as-reported-by-william-clayton-b/3, 1843, spelling and capitalization modernized)

"The first and fundamental principle of our holy religion is, that **we believe that we have a right to embrace all, and every item of truth, without...being circumscribed or prohibited by the creeds...of men...when that truth is clearly demonstrated to our minds,** and we have the highest degree of evidence of the same." (The Prophet Joseph Smith, https://www.churchofjesuschrist.org/study/manual/teachings-joseph-smith/chapter-22?lang=eng, 1839)

"...**if a man rejects a message that I may give to him but is still moral and believes in the main principles of the gospel and desires to continue in his membership in the Church, he is permitted to remain**...so long as a man believe in God and has a little faith in the Church organization, we nurture and aid that person to continue faithfully as a member of the Church **though he may not believe all that is revealed.**" (President Joseph F. Smith, *Reed Smoot Hearings, US Congress, 1903-1907*, pg 97) (https://bit.ly/2TksPK9)

I think selectively choosing which church doctrines I will have hope and faith in is a good thing for me as I start what feels like a new spiritual journey. To that end, I really like this quote from Brigham Young:

"**I do not even believe that there is a single revelation,** among the many God has given to the Church, **that is perfect in its fullness.** The revelations of God contain correct doctrine and principles so far as they go; but it is impossible for the poor, weak, low, groveling, sinful inhabitants of the earth to receive a revelation from the Almighty in all its perfections" (Discourses of Brigham Young, Deseret Book, 1977, p. 40) (https://www.fairmormon.org/answers/Doctrine_and_Covenants/Textual_changes/Why_ did_Joseph_Smith_edit_revelations#Brigham_Young_.281855.29:_.22I_do_not_even_believe_that_there_is_a_single_revelation.2C_among_the_many_God_has_given_to_the_Church.2C_that_is_perfect_in_its_fulness.22)

The importance of taking a selective approach to accepting church teachings is powerfully described as follows:

> It seems to me we must not accept any interpretation or scripture, or any statement by a Church leader or teaching in a Church meeting or Church school class that denies or diminishes the clear, central doctrine that all are alike unto God, black and white, male and female. **It is more reasonable, as well as ethical, to give up racist and sexist and (homophobic) theology than to cling to every statement by every Church leader as authoritative.** (Jody England Hansen, Author and Mama Dragon, https://affirmation.org/lgbtqia-mormons-families-friends-reactions-general-conference/, 2017)

I will try to promote growth and healing in the church by worshipping God in the way I see most worthwhile: through creating love wherever I can. So ironically, the current doctrine of the church provides me a great opportunity to worship more meaningfully than I perhaps could anywhere else:

> **"We have the privilege in our day of doing something of historical importance for our gay loved ones** just as our ancestors did when they gave up the slave trade, when they banned segregation, when they decided women had souls and even gave them the vote. They knew there was no love in what they had been doing and also knew that for there to be love things had to change. **You and I have the privilege of seeing the sad places and creating more love – more goodness...Our**

church provides a perfect opportunity for me to create love in places where it appears to be lacking. I think creating more love in the world is the only reason to try to change anything." (Carol Lynn Pearson, https://www.sunstonemagazine.com/why-i-stay-2/, 2014)

I will make it a matter of sincere devotion as I stay in the church to encourage Latter-day Saints to see the beauty that is present in the love that gay couples share. And how they contribute in a positive way to the kaleidoscope of diversity that enriches our society and our souls. And I'll try to help people see how I can imagine that gay couples being in highest degree of heaven could enrich everyone's collective experience there as well. I wonder if the following words from one of our apostles might apply as much to our relationships in the church here in mortality as they will to our relationships in heaven:

> "[W]hile the Atonement is meant to help us all become more like Christ, it is not meant to make us all the same. Sometimes we confuse differences in personality with sin. **We can even make the mistake of thinking that because someone is different from us, it must mean they are not pleasing to God.** This line of thinking leads some to believe that the Church wants to create every member from a single mold—that each one should look, feel, think, and behave like every other. This would contradict the genius of God, who created every man different from his brother, every son different from his father. Even identical twins are not identical in their personalities and spiritual identities.
>
> It also contradicts the intent and purpose of the Church of Jesus Christ, which acknowledges and protects the moral agency—with all its far-reaching consequences—of each and every one of God's children. As disciples of Jesus Christ, we are united in our testimony of the restored gospel and our commitment to

keep God's commandments. But we are diverse in our cultural, social, and political preferences.

The Church thrives when we take advantage of this diversity and encourage each other to develop and use our talents to lift and strengthen our fellow disciples." (Dieter F. Uchtdorf, Apostle, https://www.churchofjesuschrist.org/study/general-conference/2013/04/four-titles, 2013)

As I continue in my covenant path in the church, I'll also make sure to continue to sustain our general, regional, and local church leaders as they strive to do what they feel is God's will. I will sustain them by not expecting them to be perfect, and by letting them know when something they do or say causes me or others pain – so they have more information with which to continue to seek ongoing inspiration. I will acknowledge that their priesthood authority is worldwide and mine is just with respect to my family.

For that reason, I won't aggressively agitate for change in the church, as I believe there needs to be order in the church for it to function properly. That being said, I will continue to vocalize my questions, concerns and pain, so we, as members of the church as a whole, can open our minds to the possibility that the church's position against marriage equality in our doctrine might not reflect the fullness of the gospel that the Lord wants to reveal to us. I think keeping an open mind in that respect is important. As I have said, I believe change may only come about when we have learned on our own certain lessons about love that will make most members' hearts become excited about having gay couples with us in the pews, not nervous about it.

As I try to do all this, I'm hopeful I can find a sense of purpose and meaning in the church as I have otherwise felt throughout my life. I recognize that in order to feel that again, I will need to be more vigilant and stoic in dodging the dark cloud of doctrinal despair in the days, years, or decades ahead, until change comes.

And I do believe change is inevitable. As soon as church leaders acknowledged (around 2010) that experiencing gay sexual desires is not a choice, I think the train to "Doctrinal Change Town" left the station. While I acknowledge that train has had some fits and starts, and that in September and October 2019 it was slowed down drastically by the talks given by President Nelson and President Oaks, I don't think that majestic train will ever be stopped entirely. The LGBTQ-friendly sentiment is growing in society and that will either continue to stoke the church train's engine or it will result in a government train pushing from behind to encourage doctrinal change to happen in the decades ahead. I hope I'm still alive and in the church to hear an apostle someday say something like this:

> "Forget everything I have said…or whomsoever has said… that is contrary to the present revelation. **We spoke with a limited understanding and without the light and knowledge that now has come into the world.**" (Bruce R. McConkie, Apostle, speaking in 1978 about a change in doctrine to let Black church members have equal status in the church, https://www. fairmormon.org/answers/Criticism_of_Mormonism/Websites/ MormonThink/Blacks_and_the_Priesthood, 1978)

Even if change doesn't ever happen, I hope the love I might be fortunate enough to create along the way will be worthwhile in and of itself. I think hoping for a better reality, even when it seems unlikely, can be an important way to create love.

But because pure love, justice, and mercy all demand doctrinal change, I do believe it will happen. I can't believe otherwise - because I refuse to accept that God adversely discriminates on the basis of unchosen biological traits. I believe He will relieve suffering in the next life from <u>unwanted</u> biological conditions, but I can't believe He will take away a trait we are all taught we should want to keep: how we love genuinely and connect intimately in marriage.

If parents of gay children in the church can't hope for their kids to have true love here on earth that continues forever in heaven, then maintaining faith is impossible. And *faith dies if there is no hope.* I think there is profound truth in learning that faith, hope, and charity are each dependent on one another. So I choose to focus my faith and hope on Christ and His love, not on the teachings of anyone in His church (as well-intentioned as they may be) that are hurtful and cause despair and darkness. I don't know where exactly that will take me, but as a popular Christian writer has taught, that's not the point of faith anyway:

> "...faith isn't about having everything figured out ahead of time; **faith is about following the quiet voice of God without having everything figured out ahead of time**." (Rachel Held Evans, https://www.goodreads.com/quotes/655971-faith-isn-t-about-having-everything-figured-out-ahead-of-time)

I think the key to all of this – to everything in life <u>and</u> eternity – is charity: the pure love of Christ. When I was a bishop, the youth in our ward started calling me "Bishop Charity" after a while because that was all I ever talked about (not that I necessarily exemplified it any better than others). I believe that in every gospel topic we are ever asked to teach about in church, there is always room within that area to improve how we love others. And I think if we were to ask God in person if we're forgetting the first great commandment (to love Him) because we're worried so much about the second great commandment (to love others), He'd laugh at us and say we're being silly. He might remind us that when we are kind "unto the least" of our fellow humans, we are being kind to Him (Matthew 25:40). I suspect He might also point us to the formula that is perfect in its simplicity and that will always produce results that are best for everyone: "*Charity never faileth*" (1 Corinthians 3:8). In that vein, I agree wholeheartedly with this apostolic teaching:

> "Religion without morality, **professions of godliness without charity**, church- membership without adequate responsibility as to individual conduct in daily life, **are but as sounding brass and tinkling cymbals**. ... Honesty of purpose, integrity of soul, individual purity, freedom of conscience, willingness to do good to all men even enemies, *pure benevolence* **– these are some of the fruits by which the religion of Christ**

may be known, far exceeding in importance and value the promulgation of dogmas and the enunciation of theories" (James E. Talmage, Apostle, *Articles of Faith*, page 429, 1899) (https://www.churchofjesuschrist.org/study/manual/the-pearl-of-great-price-student-manual-2018/the-articles-of-faith/articles-of-faith-1-5-13?lang=eng)

As I said earlier, I have found a new way to keep my faith in spite of the hurtful dogmas that some church leaders perpetuate. It is driven by a desire to show and feel of that *pure benevolence* that should be the core of all religious devotion. My new way to maintain my faith basically just consists of:

1. never letting the words or actions of anyone (and I mean anyone, even our highest church leaders) diminish my hope for change in the church's positions that are hurting people; and

2. never keeping quiet about my pain and my hope for change ever again.

I hope and pray that as church members go about giving talks and teaching lessons in church and at home, they will remember to have pure benevolence toward all, especially our LGBTQ siblings. You might realize someday that, as you spoke, you were unknowingly helping rekindle faith in the heart of an LGBTQ person or their friend or loved one as they felt the hope and love of Christ from your words. And if you're as fortunate as I was with the lesson I taught as a bishop on loving our LGBTQ siblings, that person will turn out to be your own child.

I love you, Wes – exactly as you are. And I know Christ loves you – exactly as you are. That gives me hope – which helps me keep my faith alive.

"And now these three remain: faith, hope, and love. But the greatest of these is love." 1 Corinthians 13:13, New English Translation

A PATH FORWARD

Summary of Choices for Individuals and the Church

Same-sex attraction occurs in 2-10% of all humans across culture and time. It is also widespread at around the same rate in the animal kingdom, occurring in every major animal group (see Chapter 3). LGBTQ beings are part of God's creation and part of His plan.

Same-sex attraction is not a choice but is inborn (agreed by science and The Church of Jesus Christ of Latter-day Saints - see Chapter 3).

Current choices for LGBQ* Latter-day Saints

1. Remain celibate and stay in the church	2. Enter a mixed- orientation marriage and stay in the church	3. Leave the church, with or without a gay legal marriage
This is a joyful choice for some. For nearly 90%, teachings about this choice result in increased depression, trauma and suicidality (see Chapter 2 and Chapter 10).	This is a joyful choice for some but generally correlates with a higher rate of depression and lower reported quality of life. For nearly 70%, this results in divorce (see Chapter 3).	Some find a joyful spiritual home outside the church. Others keenly feel the loss of church blessings for self, parents, children and ancestors
"Every Sunday for one whole year, every Sunday I went into my bishop's office and he gave me a blessing. All that happened during that year was that I pretty much succeeded in feeling nothing for anyone. My emotions were dead. At the end of the year, I thought, I am never going to change. I'm destined to go to the lowest place in God's kingdom, and I'd just as well go now." **	"I have a friend who will commit suicide very soon. He has a beautiful wife and six wonderful children. They were married in the temple and are active in the Church. He has served as a bishop and has never acted on his same sex attraction. He is empty inside. He has sought professional counseling. He does not draw strength and hope and the will to go on from his relationships." **	"Jo had to decide to give up the Church or to end her own life, so she gave up the Church. But there is still a 'huge ache' there for all the things she loves so much and still believes." ** "The Mormons have got to stop being so rejecting. To be rejected by something so wonderful as the Mormon Church is nearly more than a person can bear." **

*Lesbian, gay, bisexual and questioning/queer. Absent from this acronym is T for transgender. Issues for our transgender siblings may be different from these in this chart.

** from *No More Goodbyes: Circling the Wagons around Our Gay Loved Ones,* by Carol Lynn Pearson. Page numbers are 43, 36, 38, 44-45.

Institutional church choices regarding LGBQ* Latter-day Saints

1. Insist on celibacy or mixed-orientation marriage for church worthiness	Status quo
2. Same worthiness standards but (i) formally acknowledge doctrinal ambiguity about gay couples in heaven and/or (ii) formally allow LGBQ* members to leave the church without guilt if needed to protect mental health.	These changes could be done simply through a General Conference talk by the prophet or an apostle. They would allow LGBQ* church members to better trust in God and avoid needing to believe in a traumatic or sad heaven (see Chapter 4).
3. Accept gay civil marriage for church worthiness but not temple worthiness (i.e., the individuals can be members of the church but not hold temple recommends)	For this change to be universally applied in all congregations where gay civil marriage is legal, it would likely require a policy change to the Handbook (see Chapters 6 and 7).
4. Accept gay civil marriage in the temple for time only. This would make the individuals temple worthy but would not change the status of their marriage after death	This change would require a policy change to the Handbook and likely a re-interpretation of the 1995 family proclamation as only addressing the heterosexual family (see Chapters 5, 6 and 7).
5. Full equality for LGBQ* church members, including gay temple sealing and full church and temple participation	This change would require a doctrinal clarification through revelation from God (Official Declaration 3?) (see Chapter 6).

FAVORITE CHURCH-RELATED
LGBTQ AND ALLY RESOURCES

Essays and Books:

- Mormon LGBT Questions – Essay by Bryce Cook – <u>https://mor-monlgbtquestions.com/</u>

- Faith, Hope, Charity and My Son's Marriage — Essay by Jack Hadley — <u>https://www.jackhadley.com/faith-hope-charity-and-my-sons-marriage/</u>

- *Listen, Learn and Love – Embracing LGBTQ Latter-day Saints –* Book by Richard Ostler – <u>https://www.amazon.com/Listen-Learn-Love-Embracing-Latter-day/dp/1462135773</u>

- *Goodbye I Love You –* Book by Carol Lynn Pearson - <u>https://www.amazon.com/Goodbye-Love-Carol-Lynn-Pearson/dp/1555179843</u>

- *No More Goodbyes: Circling the Wagons around our Gay Loved Ones –* Book by Carol Lynn Pearson- <u>https://www.amazon.com/No-More-Goodbyes-Circling-Wagons/dp/0963885243</u>

- Toward a Post-Heterosexual Mormon Theology – Essay by Taylor Petrey – https://www.dialoguejournal.com/wp-content/uploads/sbi/articles/Dialogue_V44N04_420.pdf

- *Tabernacles of Clay – Sexuality and Gender in Modern Mormonism –* Book by Taylor Petrey - https://www.amazon.com/Tabernacles-Clay-Sexuality-Gender-Mormonism/dp/1469656213

- *Gay Rights and the Mormon Church* – Book by Gregory A. Prince – https://uofupress.lib.utah.edu/gay-rights-and-the-mormon-church/

Websites, Podcasts and Blogs:

- https://affirmation.org – **Affirmation** - A non-profit organization working to connect, uplift, and empower lesbian, gay, bisexual, transgender, and queer Mormons and their allies around the world from all along the spectrums of sexual orientation, gender identity, faith, and involvement with the church.

- https://beyondtheblockpodcast.com – **Beyond the Block** – Weekly podcast where James C. Jones and Derek Knox, a Black life-long member and queer convert, respectively, discuss the scriptures as staunch advocates for the theology and harsh critics of the culture of the church, maintaining that the inner thrust for justice, love, and salvation for all people, regardless of color, sex, orientation, and other identities is not only consistent with the message of Christ, but it *is* the message of Christ.

- http://www.blaireostler.com/ – **Blaire Ostler** is a philosopher who is specialized in queer studies, and is a leading voice at the intersection of queer, Mormon, and transhumanist thought.

- https://encircletogether.org – **Encircle** seeks to deepen and enrich the conversation among communities of faith and LGBTQ+ people.

By teaching individuals to love themselves and empowering families, Encircle helps cultivate an environment where LGBTQ+ individuals can thrive.

- https://podcasts.apple.com/us/podcast/human-stories-with-jill-hazard-rowe/id1468623842 – **Human Stories Podcast** where Jill Hazard Rowe goes in depth with some of today's most inspiring and touching LGBTQ stories.

- https://lattergaystories.org – **Latter Gay Stories** - A podcast and resource center with a simple and organized approach to understanding the intersection of sexuality and reality. An amazing collection of all quotes on LGBTQ matters from church General Authorities since the time of Joseph Smith was compiled by Kyle Ashworth, who manages Latter-Gay Stories. It can be a triggering history to read, but it is crucial to understanding church history and efforts to avoid the mistakes of the past: https://lattergaystories.org/record/.

- https://listenlearnandlove.org – **Listen, Learn & Love** - Resource site and podcast hosted by Richard Ostler. Fully committed to the success of The Church of Jesus Christ of Latter-day Saints. Not proposing or advocating for changes in the church's policies or doctrines. But committed to facilitating meaningful, loving, and productive dialogue. LGBTQ guests are frequently interviewed on the podcast.

- https://podcasts.apple.com/us/podcast/love-is-spoken-queer/id1491809605 - **Love is Spoken Queer Podcast** - Join Dustin Larsen (an active gay church member), Hayden Davis, René Hernandez and their guests each week as they discuss a new gospel topic through a queer perspective.

- https://mormonsbuildingbridges.org – **Mormons Building Bridges** - The MBB ministry is about making every congregation welcoming to LGBTQIA+ people. The MBB community does not center itself around a single leader or organizational body; instead MBB is a movement centered around a sense of ministry and mission. It is not a formal organization and there are no formal members. The MBB ministry embraces and amplifies all thoughtful innovation and collaboration that helps LGBTQIA+ people to thrive.

- https://thepeculiar.org – **Peculiar** - Resource and networking to inspire and empower parents and families to unconditionally love and embrace their LGBTQ+ children.

- https://podcasts.apple.com/us/podcast/questions-from-the-closet/id1504990147 - **Questions from the Closet** – Podcast where two gay, active Latter-day Saints, Charlie Bird and Ben Schilaty, are joined each week by a guest to discuss common questions from LGBTQ/SSA members of the church. Also check out Ben's book (https://deseretbook.com/p/walk-in-my-shoes-questions-im-often-asked-as-a-gay-latterday-saint?variant_id=190022-paperback) and Charlie's book (https://deseretbook.com/p/without-the-mask-coming-out-and-coming-into-gods-light-ppr?variant_id=186572-paperback)

TOPICAL INDEX OF
REFERENCED WEBSITES

(websites of particular significance are **bolded**)

2019 First Presidency Teachings (and related teachings/commentary)

Referenced site	Summary	Location used
https://speeches.byu. edu/talks/ru ssell-m-nel-son/love-laws-god/	As Prophet, President Russell M. Nelson, compares the church's current formulation of the law of chastity to the unchanging laws of nature.	Chapter 4
https://www.chur-chofjesuschrist. org/ study/general- confer-ence/2019/10/35oaks	President Dallin H. Oaks says church members should not love LGBTQ people so much that they forget to remind them to obey the church's law of chastity – and that LGBTQ members who don't obey that law can be happy enough in the lower degrees of heaven.	Chapter 4
https://www.chur-chofjesuschrist.org/ study/general-confer-ence/2019/10/17oaks	President Dallin H. Oaks teaches that we should just trust in the Lord to work out difficult situations - after this life.	Chapter 4 Chapter 7

*   Visit www.gayldscrossroads.org/topical-index for active hyperlinks to these sources

https://twitter.com/ Church Newsroom / status/ 120423 2675 22290 8928	Elder Jack N. Gerard said: "We aspire to live the two great commandments: to love the Lord by keeping His commandments and secondarily to love our neighbor as ourselves."	Chapter 4
https://speeches.byu.edu/ speakers/t erence-m-vin-son/	Elder Terence M. Vinson said "The order and emphasis given by the Savior is critical. We cannot supplant the first commandment — the great commandment — with the second… And we cannot disregard the first commandment while purporting to live the second."	Chapter 4
https://womensconfer-ence.byu.edu/sites/wom-ensconference.ce.byu.ed u/files/sandra_rogers_0. pdf	Sister Sandra Rogers, international vice president at BYU and former Relief Society general board member (2012 – 2017), speaking at the general session of the BYU Women's Conference, said: "When we are fully obedient to the first commandment, we cannot help but obey the second."	Chapter 4
https://www.sltrib.com/ religion/20 19/10/11/ jana-riess-oaks-oaks/	Review by commentator and researcher, Jana Riess, of President Oaks' talk "Two Great Commandments."	Chapter 4
https://www.sltrib.com/ religion/2019/10/02/ dark-day-transgender/	News article reporting on church's formal position that eternal "gender" is determined by biological sex at birth.	Chapter 4

* Visit www.gayldscrossroads.org/topical-index for active hyperlinks to these sources

| http://www.inspired-constitution.org/talks/ETB_67oct.html | Elder Ezra Taft Benson said in October 1967 General Conference that "When we fail to put the love of God first, we are easily deceived by crafty men who profess a great love of humanity, while advocating programs that are not of the Lord." His talk referenced the Civil Rights Movement. | Chapter 4 |

Abortion

Referenced site	Summary	Location used
https://www.churchofjesuschrist.org/study/manual/gospel-topics/abortion	The church allows its members to have abortions in the case of rape, incest, or risk to the health of the mother, and still remain in good standing.	Chapter 7

Anti-LGBTQ church teachings/practices

Referenced site	Summary	Location used
https://abcnews.go.com/Health/mormon-gay-cures-reparative-therapies-shock-today/story?id=13240700 https://en.wikipedia.org/wiki/Brigham_Young_University_LGBT_history	Church-sanctioned genital electroshock conversion therapy took place at BYU	Chapter 3

* Visit www.gayldscrossroads.org/topical-index for active hyperlinks to these sources

https://en.wikipedia.org/ wiki/Timeline_of_LGBT_ Mormon_history_i n_the_20th_century	Timeline that shows electroshock conversion therapy was going on during the entire duration of President Dallin H. Oaks serving as president of BYU.	Chapter 3
https://web.archive.org/ web/20120 724194315/http://www. evergreeni nternational.org/ morrison.htm	Elder Alexander B. Morrison said church members should avoid gay people and their allies like the plague.	Chapter 3
https://newsroom.chur- chofjesuschr ist.org/ article/interview-oaks- wick- man-same-gender-attraction	Elder Dallin H. Oaks said parents might be justified in not letting their adult gay children meet their friends or participate in family events in the same way as their other children.	Chapter 3
https://www.churchofje- suschrist.org/study/gen- eral-conference/2018/10/ truth-and-the-plan	Elder Dallin H. Oaks said Satan "seeks to confuse gender [and] dis- tort marriage."	Chapter 3
https://devotional. byuh.edu/node/1 788; https://www.sltrib.com/ religion/20 19/06/20/ this-week-mormon-land/	Elder Dallin H. Oaks said in 2019 that LGBTQ "lifestyles and values" are part of "a culture of evil and per- sonal wickedness."	Chapter 3
http://www.blaireostler. com/journal/2019/9/19/ celestial-genocide.	The idea that LGBTQ identity will be completely wiped out in heaven has been powerfully described as geno- cide by writer Blaire Ostler.	Chapter 4
https://blakeclan.org/jon/ to-the- one/	Church pamphlet *To The One* in which Elder Boyd K. Packer says, "some forms of these treatments [reparative therapy] are of substan- tial help in about 25 percent of the cases" without offering any authority for this statistic.	Chapter 10

* Visit www.gayldscrossroads.org/topical-index for active hyperlinks to these sources

Black African race-based priesthood/temple ban

Referenced site	Summary	Location used
https://www.churchofje-suschrist.org/study/man-ual/gospel-topics-essays/race-and-the-priesthood	The church's current essay disavowing prior racist teachings.	Chapter 5
https://www.fairmormon.org/answers/Mormon-ism_and_racial_issues/Blacks_and_the_priest-hood/Statements	The First Presidency issued state-ments in 1949 and 1969 saying the priesthood/temple ban against Black people was a doctrine from God, not a policy.	Chapter 5
https://en.wikipedia.org/wiki/Black_people_and_Mormon_priesthood http://bitly.ws/8Egg (see the bottom of page 42)	Brigham Young said the priesthood ban against Black people would not end until after the second coming of Christ (i.e., "until the redemption of the Earth").	Chapter 5
http://mit.irr.org/brigham-young-it- will-take-time-remove-curse-1852	Brigham Young said the priesthood/temple ban against Black people would last "until Abel's race is satisfied with his blessings."	Chapter 5
http://bitly.ws/8Uju	Brigham Young said Blacks would not receive the priesthood until all other people were resurrected.	Chapter 5
https://www.missedinsun-day.com/memes/race/race-and-the-priesthood/	The church's current essay discussing the priesthood/temple ban against Black people arguably misrepresents when Brigham Young said the ban would end.	Chapter 5

* Visit www.gayldscrossroads.org/topical-index for active hyperlinks to these sources

https://www.fairmormon. org/answers/Question:_ Did_Brigham_Young_ say_that_race_mix- ing_was_punishable_by_ death%3F	Brigham Young said the penalty for interracial marriage was death and that it would "always be so."	. Chapter 5 Chapter 6
https://www.fairmormon. org/answers/Mormon- ism_and_racial_issues/ Blacks_and_the_priest- hood/Statements#1969	The First Presidency said in 1969 that they couldn't get rid of the priesthood/ temple ban because it was of God and that "[r]evelation assures...[it] extend[s]...back to man's pre-exis- tent state."	Chapter 5
http://www.mormon- handbook.com/home/ racism.html#top	List of scriptures used by many leaders of the church for over a hundred years to justify racism.	Chapter 5
http://www.withou- tend.org/policy- gay- couples-priesthood- ban- comparison/	Historian, Clair Barrus, compares the church's historical treatment of Black people and its current treatment of gay people.	Chapter 5
https://www.fairmormon. org/answers/Mormon- ism_and_racial_issues/ Offensive_statements https://www.ldsdiscus- sions.com/priesthood- ban-quotes	Collections of racist statements by church leaders.	Chapter 5

*   Visit www.gayldscrossroads.org/topical-index for active hyperlinks to these sources

https://en.wikipedia.org/ wiki/Interr acial_mar- riage_and_The_Church_ of_Jesus_Christ_of_Lat- ter- day_Saints	The church banned white church members who married Black indi- viduals from entering a temple into at least the 1960s and recommended against any interracial marriages in official publications into the 2000s.	Chapter 5
https://books.google. com/books?id =LkRZ GQ8oO8IC&lpg=P A49&ot s=30VX- mz65se&pg=PA49#v=o- nepage&q&f=false https://books.google. com/books ?id=LkRZGQ8oO8IC& lpg=PA44&ot s=30VX- mz65se&pg=PA44#v=one page&q&f =false https://www.fairmormon. org/answers/Question:_ Did_Brigham_Young_ say_that_race_mix- ing_was_punishable_by_ death%3F	Brigham Young said it would be better from an eternal salvation perspective if an interracial couple (and their children) were decapitated than be together as a family.	Chapter 5 Chapter 8
https://gregkofford.com/ blogs/new s/five-times- mormons-changed- their-position-on-slavery	The church changed its political posi- tions five times in respect of slavery.	Chapter 8

---

*   Visit www.gayldscrossroads.org/topical-index for active hyperlinks to these sources

https://en.wikipedia.org/wiki/Interr acial_marriage_and_The_Church_of_Jesus_Christ_of_Latter- day_Saints	The church supported laws making interracial marriage illegal and taught that it was a sin.	Chapter 8
https://www.amazon.com/Mormonism-White-Supremacy-American-Innocence-ebook/dp/B08761ZHCP	Book published in 2020, written by Joanna Brooks, that discusses the pervasiveness of racism still in the church today, its relation to the church's past priesthood/temple ban and related teachings by church leaders, and the many calls for change that were made by church members (including some apostles) over the course of the ban's existence.	Chapter 5

Celibacy

Referenced site	Summary	Location used
https://archive.org/stream/Mormon Doctrine1966/Mormon-Doctrine19 66_djvu.txt	Elder Bruce R. McConkie taught: "Celibacy is not of God, whose law is that 'marriage is honourable in all' (Hebrews 13:4)."	Chapter 9
Genesis 2:18	"And the Lord God said, It is not good that the man should be alone"	Chapter 4 Chapter 9

*   Visit www.gayldscrossroads.org/topical-index for active hyperlinks to these sources

Church membership/participation
(including temple recommend)

Referenced site	Summary	Location used
https://www.chur-chofjesuschrist.org/study/manual/gener-al-handbook/32-re-pentance-and-mem-bership-coun-cils?lang=eng#title_num-ber14 (See Section 32.6.2)	Church updated General Handbook of instructions that no longer classi-fies entering into a same-sex marriage as "apostasy" and makes the taking of action by local leaders to restrict or remove the church membership of any individual in a gay marriage something that is discretionary (deter-mined by local leaders), not manda-tory (as it was previously).	Chapter 3 Chapter 6
https://www.sltrib.com/news/educa tion/2020/02/19/byu-ap-pears- remove/	BYU removed language prohibit-ing "homosexual" behavior from its Honor Code for students, to be consistent with the church's updated General Handbook.	Chapter 3
https://www.sltrib.com/news/educa tion/2020/02/26/popu-lar-video- this-byu/	News article about a viral video made by a BYU professor who explains why the Honor Code change that ostensi-bly allowed same-sex dating was real, from the prophet and apostles, and good for all BYU students.	Chapter 3
https://www.thechurchnews.com/le aders-and-minis-try/2020-03- 04/byu-honor-code- language-clarification- ces- state-ment-176245	Church Educational System letter, issued two weeks after the Honor Code language change, clarifying that the change in language does not mean same-sex dating is allowed at BYU.	Chapter 3

*   Visit www.gayldscrossroads.org/topical-index for active hyperlinks to these sources

https://www.sltrib.com/news/education/2020/03/04/after-byu-honor- code/	News article reporting on large student protests occurring at BYU in response to the clarification that same-sex dating is still prohibited at BYU.	Chapter 3
https://charity.gofundme.com/o/en/ campaign/transfer-fund-for-lgbtq-byu-students	GoFundMe campaign to help gay BYU students pay to transfer to different schools.	Chapter 3
https://www.sltrib.com/religion/20 19/12/15/can-latter-day-saints/	News article about a young missionary (who has a lesbian mom) who got his temple recommend taken away for privately supporting marriage equality.	Chapter 3
https://www.sltrib.com/religion/2020/12/18/lds-handbook-adds-warning/	News article about a December 2020 update the to the church's General Handbook of instructions that asks all church members to reject prejudice "of any kind", including (ironically) prejudice based on sexual orientation.	Chapter 3
https://www.churchofjesuschrist.org/study/manual/general-handbook/38-church-policies-and-guidelines?lang=eng#title_number3	Church handbook section (released in December 2019) that says sexual orientation should not be discussed in church "in a way" that detracts from a focus on the Savior.	Chapter 3
https://www.churchofjesuschrist.org/study/manual/general-handbook/38-church-policies-and-guidelines?lang=eng#title_number102 (see Section 38.6.5)	Church updated General Handbook of instructions says gay marriage is sexual immorality for which a membership council may be "necessary."	Chapter 6

* Visit www.gayldscrossroads.org/topical-index for active hyperlinks to these sources

https://www.churchofje-suschrist.org/study/manual/general-hand-book/27-temple-or-dinances-for-the-liv-ing?lang=eng#title_num-ber32	Temple marriage for "time only" is currently allowed in a situation where a man and a woman are each already sealed to a spouse who is deceased.	Chapter 6
https://archive.sltrib.com/article.ph p?id=2301174&i-type=CMSID	Elder D. Todd Christofferson said church members can support gay marriage publicly, march in pride parades, and belong to gay-friendly organizations without losing their temple recommends.	Chapter 8
https://www.sltrib.com/religion/2019/10/22/jana-riess-new-lds- temple/	Article about how LGBTQ-friendly church members are worried about how local and regional church leaders will apply the new wording of temple recommend questions.	Chapter 8
https://www.huffpost.com/entry/gay -mormon- men- mar-riage_ n_ 6464848	Study that shows more than 70% of same-gender attracted church members leave the church.	Chapter 9
https://drive.google.com/open?id= 1YwAV 5rPR mx1bI9C LDhBLgAc ueAQ8f H7n	Talk I gave on LGBTQ love and acceptance in a stake conference in May 2019.	Chapter 9

* Visit www.gayldscrossroads.org/topical-index for active hyperlinks to these sources

https://www.sltrib.com/religion/local/2018/06/29/mormon-churchs-newest/	News article referencing the fact that Elder Gerrit W. Gong has a gay son.	Chapter 9
https://www.deseret.com/2017/9/13/20619341/gay-brother-of-mormon-apostle-shares-his-spiritual-journey	News article referencing the fact that Elder D. Todd Christofferson has a brother who is gay.	Chapter 9
https://www.churchofjesuschrist.org/study/ensign/1976/07/accepted-of-the-lord-the-doctrine-of-making-your-calling-and-election-sure	Church teaching that being willing to sacrifice everything (including your own life) for your faith is necessary if you want to be assured of exaltation while still living here on Earth.	Chapter 9
https://www.churchofjesuschrist.org/study/ensign/1977/03/i-have-a-question/what-does-it-mean-to-endure-to-the-end-and-why-is-it-necessary	The church teaches that the commandment to "endure to the end" means to basically always stay active in the church until death.	Chapter 10

Civil rights/Politics

Referenced site	Summary	Location used
https://uofupress.lib.utah.edu/gay- rights-and-the-mormon-church/	Great book by Dr. Gregory A. Prince that summarizes the progression of church doctrine and its political involvement in gay rights.	Chapter 3

* Visit www.gayldscrossroads.org/topical-index for active hyperlinks to these sources

https://www.nytimes.com/2008/11/ 15/us/politics/15marriage.html	Many people believe Latter-day Saint efforts were the primary driver behind the success of defeating the marriage equality initiative in California in 2008.	Chapter 3
https://www.nytimes.com/2015/03/12/us/politics/utah-passes-antidiscrimination-bill-backed-by-mormon-leaders.html	The church has been involved in passing some LGBTQ rights legislation.	Chapter 3 Chapter 6 Chapter 8
https://twitter.com / Church Newsroo m/status/ 12042 32675222908 928	The church supports the Fairness for All Act.	Chapter 4
https://www.pewforum.org/fact- sheet/gay-marriage-around-the-world/0	Pew Forum states that as of October 2019, "30 countries and territories have enacted national laws allowing gays and lesbians to marry, mostly in Europe and the Americas."	Chapter 6
https://www.newsweek.com/73-countries-where-its-illegal-be-gay-1385974	As of April 2019, there were 71 countries in the world where same-sex relations are illegal, according to Newsweek.	Chapter 6

*   Visit www.gayldscrossroads.org/topical-index for active hyperlinks to these sources

https://www.amnesty. org.uk/lgbti-lgbt-gay-hu- man-rights-law-afri- ca-uganda-kenya-nige- ria-cameroon https://en.wikipedia. org /wiki/The_ Church_ of_ Jesus_Christ _of_Latter -day_Saints_in_Nigeria https://en.wikipedia.org / wiki/The_ Church_ of_ Jesus_ Christ_of_Latter -day_Saints_in_ Uganda https://en.wikipedia. org/ wiki/ Reco gnition_ of_ same- sex_unions_ in_the _Americas	The church's formal doctrinal posi- tion about showing love and respect to gay couples is more LGBTQ- friendly than what the laws of many countries where the church operates reflect, including countries where the church is growing.	Chapter 6

https://newsroom. churchofjesuschr ist.org/ article/faiths-file-amicus-brief-on-marriage-cases-before- tenth-circuit-court https://www.churchofje-suschrist.org/church/ news/church-signs-amic-us-brief-filed-on-marriage https://www.usato-day.com/story/news/ nation/2019/10/08/ lgbt-supreme-court-cas-es-workplace-dis-crimination-civ-il-rights/3844832002/ https://www.supreme-court.gov/Docket-PDF/18/18-107/113604/ 20190826131230679_ Harris%20Amicus%20 Brief%20Final%20Ver-sion.pdf https://www.cnn. com/2020/06/15/ pol-itics/ supreme-court-lgbtq- employment-case / index.html https://www.wash-ingtonpost.com/ politics/ 2020/06/16/ supreme- court-closed-door-lgbtq-em-ployment- discrimina-tion-it-opened-window/	The church spends money on lawyers to fight against LGBTQ rights. It united with other faiths to file amicus briefs to prevent the legaliza-tion of gay marriage in many states and then ultimately at the U.S. Supreme Court as well. It did likewise in the more recent cases before the U.S. Supreme Court about whether someone can be fired for being gay or transgender, arguing that religious employers should be able to fire someone for being in a gay marriage or for openly transitioning. The U.S. Supreme Court ruled in June and July 2020 that secu-lar employers cannot discriminate against someone for being LGBTQ but religious employers can engage in such discrimination.	Chapter 8

---

* Visit www.gayldscrossroads.org/topical-index for active hyperlinks to these sources

https://www.deseret.com/indepth/2020/7/8/21302953/supreme-court- employment-discrimination-catholic-schools-ministers-hiring- firing-ruling https://www.supremecourt.gov/DocketPDF/19/19-267/132581/20200210172618740_19-267%20Amici%20Curiae.pdf		
https://lattergaystories.org/wp- content/uploads/2020/02/Principles-to-Govern.pdf	In 1984, Elder Dallin H. Oaks (who was a newly called apostle at the time) wrote a confidential memorandum for the First Presidency and Quorum of the Twelve Apostles in which he outlines how the church could effectively oppose employment anti-discrimination laws protecting LGBTQ people.	Chapter 8
https://www.deseret.com/indepth/2019/12/6/20995260/mormon-utah- chris-stewart-latter-day-saint-leaders-lgbtq-lds-civil-rights-gay- religious-freedom	The church supports religious liberty legislation so it can continue to be allowed to not employ people in gay marriages.	Chapter 8

*   Visit www.gayldscrossroads.org/topical-index for active hyperlinks to these sources

https://bycommoncon-sent.com/201 6/07/11/ stop-skipping-the- estab-lishment-clause/	Elder Charles W. Penrose said "Anything that persons profess to do under the name of religion, which interferes with the rights of others is wrong."	Chapter 8
https://gregkofford.com/ blogs/new s/five-times-mormons-changed-their-position-on-slavery	The church changed its political position five times in respect of slavery.	Chapter 8
https://en.wikipedia.org/ wiki/Interr acial_mar-riage_and_The_Church_ of_Jesus_Christ_of_Lat-ter- day_Saints	The church supported laws making interracial marriage illegal and taught that it was a sin.	Chapter 8
https://en.wikipedia.org/ wiki/The_ Church _of_ Jesus_ Christ_of_ Latter-day_Saints_ and_politics _in_the_ United_States	Most church members in Utah voted to repeal Prohibition even though President Heber J. Grant didn't want them to.	Chapter 8
https://www.facebook. com/Progressive-MormonTeachings/ posts/21385823731125 36	Collection of statements from church leaders on immigration and refu-gees (including that "there's nothing wrong" with undocumented status).	Chapter 8

* Visit www.gayldscrossroads.org/topical-index for active hyperlinks to these sources

Conversion therapy; church's past
(and limited present) endorsement of

Referenced site	Summary	Location used
https://en.wikipedia.org/wiki/Evergreen _International	Church leaders historically taught that gay sexual orientation could be "treated" or "cured."	Chapter 8
https://religion.wikia.org/wiki/Bru ce_C._Hafen https://www.mormonwiki.com/Bruce_C._Hafen#2009_Talk_on_Gay _Rights_and_Same_Gender_Attra ction	Elder Bruce C. Hafen taught that same-sex attractions can be replaced with opposite-sex attractions in this life (and after it) if gay people are faithful enough. He also taught we are judged on the degree of difficulty of lives' challenges, not just our thoughts and actions.	Chapter 8 Chapter 10
https://psychnews.psychiatryonline.org/doi/full/10.1176/pn.47.12.psyc hnews_47_12_1-b	Dr. Robert Spitzer (who was quoted by Elder Bruce C. Hafen as a professional who said conversion therapy could work to make someone no longer be gay) apologizes for his "unproven claims of the efficacy of reparative therapy."	Chapter 8
https://lattergaystories.org/bergin/ https://religionnews.com/2020/08/07/a-prominent-mormon-therapist- apologized-for-anti-lgbt-activism- whats-the-next-step/	Allen Bergin, a former BYU professor, bishop, stake president, and member of the General Sunday School Presidency, who was a psychotherapist often quoted by church leaders in the late 20th century as an authority on gay sexual orientation, apologized in July 2020 for his past endorsement of conversion therapy, among other things.	Chapter 8

*   Visit www.gayldscrossroads.org/topical-index for active hyperlinks to these sources

https://web.archive.org/ web/20120 724194231/ http://www.ever-greeni nternational. org/2005%20Mason.pdf	Elder James O. Mason taught that same-gender attraction could be cured.	Chapter 8
https://www.deseret. com/2018/2/7/ 20639656/the-weeds-story-is-one-of-many-stories-of-lgbt-latter-day-saints-that-continue-to-be-written	Church therapists still provide a form of conversion therapy for patients who "self-determine" that they want to stop experiencing gay sexual attraction.	Chapter 8
https://www.churchofje-suschrist.org/topics/gay/ leaders?lang=eng	Similar statements about self-determi-nation being respected in therapy can be found on the church's "Same-Sex Attraction" website as well.	Chapter 8
https://www.splcenter. org/fighting-hate/intel-ligence-report/2019/ out-darkness-conversion-therapist-quits-ex-gay-movement	Article describing many former con-version therapists who have abandoned their teachings to lead lives of openly gay men, including Latter-day Saint David Matheson, who was formally associated with Evergreen International and who was a founder of ex-gay pro-gram Journey into Manhood.	Chapter 8
https://blakeclan.org/ jon/to-the- one/	Church pamphlet *To The One* in which Elder Boyd K. Packer says, "some forms of these treatments [reparative therapy] are of substantial help in about 25 per-cent of the cases" without offering any authority for this statistic.	Chapter 10

*   Visit www.gayldscrossroads.org/topical-index for active hyperlinks to these sources

Conversion therapy; Utah's ban on (church's view of)

Referenced site	Summary	Location used
https://www.google.com/ amp/s/ www. deseret. com/ plat-form/ amp /uta h /2019/ 10/ 23/ 20929351/ lds- mormon- church - conversion- therapy- opposition- jesus-christ- latter-day- saints	News article wherein the church explains why it opposed a ban on conversion therapy for minors in Utah.	Chapter 8
https://www.sltrib. com/news/poli-tics/2019/11/27/gov-her-bert-announces/	The church was able to get changes made to a proposed ban on conversion therapy for minors in Utah.	Chapter 8
https://www.kuer.org/ post/how-bill-became-rule-journey-utahs-conversion-therapy-ban#stream/0	History of the full legislative and rule-making process for the ban on conversion therapy for minors in Utah.	Chapter 8
https://societyforpsy-chotherapy.org/integrat-ing-spirituality-religion-psychotherapy-practice/	Professional guidelines require a therapist to discuss with a patient their religious values when provid-ing counseling.	Chapter 8

Demographics

Referenced site	Summary	Location used
https://en.wikipedia.org/wiki/Demog raph-ics_of_sexual_orienta-tion#Denm ark	Around 2-10% of the human popu-lation is LGBTQ, depending on the study/location.	Chapter 3
https://en.wikipedia.org/wiki/ The_ Church_ of_ Jesus_ Christ_ of_ Latter- day_ Saints_ membership_ history	All living members of the church rep-resent less than ¼ of one percent of the earth's present 7.7 billion people.	Chapter 10

Diversity; benefit of (to the church)

Referenced site	Summary	Location used
https://www.chur-chofjesuschrist.org/study/general- confer-ence/2013/04/four-titles	President Dieter F. Uchtdorf said the church thrives when we take advantage of diversity.	Chapter 10

Doctrinal summaries (re LGBTQ issues)

Referenced site	Summary	Location used
https://www.chur-chofjesuschrist.org/topics/gay/	Church's current positions on LGBTQ matters, including a quote in the "Church Leaders" section by Elder M. Russell Ballard that same-sex attractions are not a choice.	Chapter 3

* Visit www.gayldscrossroads.org/topical-index for active hyperlinks to these sources

https://mormon-lgbtquestions.com/	Excellent source for seeing the evolution of the church's doctrine on LGBTQ matters. Great arguments for why change is still needed. Exploring this site is a must for anyone seeking to understand LGBTQ issues in the church.	Chapter 3
https://drive.google.com/open?id =1 sklAZfBlr G8SnB7 B89Cf57 gg17PX PQ_Z	Compilation by Richard Ostler, an influential LGBTQ ally and active/faithful Latter-day Saint, of positive and loving quotes from church leaders on LGBTQ matters.	Chapter 3
https://lattergaystories.org/record/	Compilation by Kyle Ashworth, host at Latter Gay Stories podcast, of all statements made by church leaders regarding LGBTQ matters since the time of Joseph Smith. This is a triggering list of quotes to read through, but it is a crucial document to aid in helping avoid any repetition of past mistakes and harm.	Chapter 3
https://www.churchofjesuschrist. org/ study/manual/ the-family-a- proclamation-to-the-world/ the- family-a-proclamation-to-the-world	The church's Proclamation on the Family.	Chapter 4

* Visit www.gayldscrossroads.org/topical-index for active hyperlinks to these sources

Doctrine; evolving nature of

Referenced site	Summary	Location used
https://www. thechurchnews.com/ archives/2012-02-11/ president-dieter-f-ucht-dorf-acting-on-the-truths-of-the-gospel-of-jesus-christ-53389	Elder Dieter F. Uchtdorf taught that questions have been the foundation of the restoration and asked: "How often has the Holy Spirit tried to tell us something we needed to know but couldn't get past the massive iron gate of what we thought we already knew?"	Dedication page
https://www.facebook. com/ derek.knox/ videos/ 1010 7223 950567 218	Video where Biblical scholar and theologian, Derek Knox, discusses scriptural examples of God revealing change to ease suffering of marginalized groups who ask for relief. Sound scriptural support for the role of bottom-up change in the church.	Chapter 2
https://affirmation. org/science-vs- dog-ma-biology-challeng-es-the-lds- paradigm/	Historian and scholar, Dr. Greg Prince, says no significant doctrine of the church has gone unchanged over time.	Chapter 4
https://www.chur-chofjesuschrist.org/ study/manual/the-pearl-of-great-price-student-manual-2018/ the-articles-of-faith/ articles-of-faith-1-5-13	Elder James E. Talmage said in 1899 that canon is still open and that "revelation, surpassing in importance and glorious fulness any that has been recorded, is yet to be given to the Church."	Chapter 4
https://www.chur-chofjesuschrist. org/study/manual/ doctrines-of-the-gos-pel-student-manu-al/23-restoration	Elder Bruce R. McConkie said the "last word has not been spoken on any subject" and that "There are more things we do not know about the doctrines of salvation than there are things we do know."	Chapter 4

*   Visit www.gayldscrossroads.org/topical-index for active hyperlinks to these sources

https://www.chur-chofjesuschrist.org/study/ensign/1986/03/b-h-roberts-seeker-after-truth?lang=eng	Elder B.H. Roberts taught that future "generations…will find that we have had some misconceptions and made some wrong deductions in our day and time. The book of knowledge is… an eternally open book, in which one may go on constantly discovering new truths and modifying our knowledge of old ones."	Chapter 4
https://www.fairmormon.org/answers/Mormonism_and_racial_issues/Blacks_and_the_priesthood/Statements#1969	The First Presidency said in 1969 that they couldn't get rid of the priesthood/temple ban because it was of God and that "[r]evelation assures… [it] extend[s]…back to man's pre-existent state."	Chapter 5
https://www.fairmormon.org/answers/Word_of_Wisdom/History_and_implementation	Complete prohibition from tobacco, alcohol, coffee and tea was not required of church members until 1921.	Chapter 5
https://newsroom.churchofjesuschrist.org/article/president-nelson- invites-sharing-gospel-restoration	President Russell M. Nelson teaches that "the Restoration of the Lord's gospel [is] an unfolding Restoration that continues today."	Chapter 2
https://www.churchofjesuschrist.org/study/general-conference/2014/04/are-you-sleeping-through-the-restoration	President Dieter F. Uchtdorf said the restoration of the gospel is ongoing and includes great things yet to be revealed.	Chapter 5

* Visit www.gayldscrossroads.org/topical-index for active hyperlinks to these sources

https://www.chur-chofjesuschrist.org/study/ensign/2018/12/making-your-life-a-soul-stirring-journey-of-personal-growth	Elder Jeffrey R. Holland said many great things are yet to be revealed to the church, similar to what has been revealed from the early days of the church up through modern times.	Chapter 5
https://m.facebook.com/ notes/matthew-gong/ birthday -letters-27- 28/ 10158377 17573 5021/	Matthew Gong, gay son of Elder Gerrit W. Gong, says that "culture can be the impetus for change" and that the religion of the church teaches many good things but has also been weaponized to hurt people.	Chapter 10
https://www.fairmor-mon.org/answers/Doctrine_and_Cove-nants/Textual_changes/Why_did_Joseph_Smith_edit_reve-lations#Brigham_Young_.281855.29:_.22 I_do_not_even_ believe_that_there_ is_a_single_revela-tion.2C_among_the_ many_God_has_given_ to_the_Church.2C_ that_is_perfect_in_its_ fulness.22	Brigham Young said there was no revelation given that was complete in its fullness.	Chapter 10

*   Visit www.gayldscrossroads.org/topical-index for active hyperlinks to these sources

https://affirmation.org/ lgbtqia- mormons-fam- ilies-friends- reac- tions-general-confer- ence/	Author Jody England Hansen teaches "It is more reasonable, as well as eth- ical, to give up racist and sexist and (homophobic) theology than to cling to every statement by every Church leader as authoritative."	Chapter 10
https://www.chur- chofjesuschrist.org/ study/manual/teach- ings-joseph-smith/ chapter-45?lang=eng	Joseph Smith taught that the "minds of the Saints…frequently…fly to pieces like glass as soon as anything comes that is contrary to their traditions."	Chapter 2

Doctrine; definitions/exploration of

Referenced site	Summary	Location used
https://en.wiki- quote.org/wiki/J._ Re uben_Clark	President J. Reuben Clark said real truth cannot be harmed by investigation.	Chapter 1
https://www.chur- chofjesuschrist.org/si/ questions/what-is-doc- trine	Church website response to the ques- tion: What is doctrine?	Chapter 4
https://www. newspapers.com/ clip/21138508/partial_ transcript_of_ap_inter- view_with/	Elder Dallin H. Oaks said he doesn't think "it's possible to distinguish between policy and doctrine."	Chapter 4
http://podcast.latterday- faith.org/031-what-is- doctrine	Podcast that discusses how all church doctrines have evolved and changed over time.	Chapter 4

* Visit www.gayldscrossroads.org/topical-index for active hyperlinks to these sources

https://www.chur-chofjesuschrist.org/si/questions/what-is-doc-trine	The church says that any teaching that has not been voted on by the whole church to be canonized can be known to be of God or not if we feel God's spirit testify of their truthfulness.	Chapter 7
https://www.fairmor-mon.org/wp-content/uploads/2012/02/What_is_ Mormon_Doctrine.pdf	"It is likely that the Lord has allowed (and will continue to allow) his servants to make mistakes."	

Doctrine; changes in that coincide with external forces

Referenced site	Summary	Location used
https://www.churchofje-suschrist.org/manual/doctrine-and-cove-nants-stories/chapter-31-the-word-of-wisdom-february-1833	Joseph Smith got the Word of Wisdom revelation after feeling compelled to pray because his wife, Emma, asked him to.	Chapter 8
https://en.wikipedia.org/wiki/1890 _Manifesto	The church stopped polygamy at time the U.S. government forced it to.	Chapter 8
http://www.lds- mor-mon.com/taxes_priest-hood.sht ml	Worry over the church potentially los-ing its tax-exempt status and end of the racial priesthood/temple ban in 1978.	Chapter 8
https://en.wikipedia.org/wiki/Civil_ rights _and_ Mormonism# NAACP _involvement	The threat of losing revenue from BYU sports programs and end of the racial priesthood/temple ban in 1978.	Chapter 8

* Visit www.gayldscrossroads.org/topical-index for active hyperlinks to these sources

https://www.sltrib. com/news/educa tion/2019/11/11/ two-science- societies/	In 2019, two science societies removed BYU job postings over the school's Honor Code ban on 'homosexual behavior'.	Chapter 8
https://soundcloud. com/mormonla nd/ college-administra- tor- examines-by- us-honor-code-rever- sal-on-lgbtq-issues-epi- sode- 129	Podcast discussion with Michael Austin, a BYU alumnus and executive vice president for academic affairs at the University of Evansville, a Methodist school in Indiana, about the possibility that, as BYU continues to prohibit gay dating on campus, the school and its students will become more and more alienated from the associations that they have traditionally relied upon for success	Chapter 8
https://www.sltrib. com/news/educa tion/2020/01/21/first- time-ever- byu-will/	BYU gave in to external pressure to allow same-sex couples to participate in ballroom dancing competition.	Chapter 8

Doctrine; possible paths for change in

Referenced site	Summary	Location used
https://www.dia- loguejournal.com/ wp- content/uploads/ sbi/articles/Dialog ue_V44N04_420.pdf	Dr. Taylor Petrey, Professor of Religion, explores how church doctrine could evolve to embrace eternal gay mar- riage. This article is a must-read for anyone trying to understand if it's pos- sible for church doctrine to change on gay marriage.	Chapter 5 Chapter 7

*   Visit www.gayldscrossroads.org/topical-index for active hyperlinks to these sources

https://mormon-lgbtquestions.com/	Excellent source for seeing the evolution of the church's doctrine on LGBTQ matters. Great arguments for why change is still needed. Exploring this site is a must for anyone seeking to understand LGBTQ issues in the church.	Chapter 3

Gay sexual orientation; church's position on cause of

Referenced site	Summary	Location used
https://newsroom.churchofjesuschrist.org/article/interview-oaks-wickman-same-gender-attraction	Elder Dallin H. Oaks said the church doesn't take a position on the cause of sexual orientation.	Chapter 3
https://www.churchofjesuschrist. org/topics/gay/	Official church site describing the church's position prohibiting same-sex sexual activity and calling for love of LGBTQ individuals. In the "Church Leaders" section, "same-sex attraction" is acknowledged to not be a choice.	Chapter 3
https://newsroom.churchofjesuschrist.org/article/statement-proposed-rule-sexual-orientation-gender-identity-change	First Presidency stated in 2016 that "The Church denounces any therapy that subjects an individual to abusive practices." This statement falls short of denouncing the idea that "non-abusive" conversion therapy can change someone's sexual orientation.	Chapter 8

* Visit www.gayldscrossroads.org/topical-index for active hyperlinks to these sources

| https://www.chur-chofjesuschrist.org/ study/general-confer-ence/2015/10/behold-thy-mother | Elder Jeffrey R. Holland said it's not reasonable to expect sexual orientation to change in this life. | Preface

Chapter 8 |

Gay sexual orientation;
church's position that it will go away upon death

Referenced site	Summary	Location used
https://www.fairmor-mon.org/answers/ Mormonism_and_gen-der_issues/Same-sex_ attraction	Site that quotes "multiple" church lead-ers teaching that gay sexual attraction will not exist after death.	Chapter 4
https://www.pbs.org/ mormons/inte rviews/ holland.html	Elder Jeffrey R. Holland said gay sexual attraction will not exist after death.	Chapter 4
https://newsroom. churchofjesuschr ist. org/article/inter-view-oaks- wick-man-same-gender-at-traction	Elder Dallin H. Oaks said gay sexual attraction will not exist after death.	Chapter 4
https://newsroom. churchofjesuschr ist. org/article/inter-view-oaks- wick-man-same-gender-at-traction	Elder Lance B. Wickman said gay sexual attraction will go away after this life.	Chapter 8

*   Visit www.gayldscrossroads.org/topical-index for active hyperlinks to these sources

Gay sexual orientation; scientific findings about

Referenced site	Summary	Location used
https://m.youtube. com/watch ?v= 8IHw9 DVI3hE (if pressed for time, start at the 30- minute mark and listen for 20 minutes there)	BYU microbiology professor (and former mission president), Dr. William Bradshaw, explains how sexual orientation is not a choice – that it is determined biologically (he specifically says it is determined by nature, not nurture).	Preface Chapter 3
https://en.wikipedia. org/wiki/Epige net-ic_theories_of_homo-sexuality https://www. sciencemag.org/news/ 2015/10/homo-sexuality-may-be-caused-chemical-mod-ifications- dna	Scientific studies say sexual orientation is not a choice. Epigenetic explanations for sexual orientation.	Chapter 3 Chapter 7 Chapter 8
https://kinseyinsti-tute.org/research/ publications/kinsey-scale.php	There is a spectrum of sexual orienta-tion.	Chapter 3
https://docs.goo-gle.com/book/d/ 15RtVqRQ5 KOey-c6i5Bzb NSprMpbJ CD6n99 VfpKirv_ F0/ mobilebasic	Physiological traits of gay individuals reflect some sexually dimorphic traits of their opposite sex rather than their same sex.	Chapter 3

*   Visit www.gayldscrossroads.org/topical-index for active hyperlinks to these sources

https://www. youtube.com/ watch?v=gssnz1W-Z3dU (if pressed for time, watch from the 14-minute mark through the 30-min-ute mark)	Historian and scholar, Dr. Greg Prince, explains how epigenetics causes sexual orientation and gender dysphoria.	Chapter 3
https://www. theguardian.com/ science/blog/2015/ jul/24/gay-genes-sci-ence-is-on-the-right-track-were-born-this-way-lets-deal-with-it https://www.nytimes. com/2019/08/29/ science/gay-gene-sex. html	While sexual orientation is primarily determined by epigenetics, science has shown that inherited genetic factors (as opposed to epigenetic factors) can explain about 25-30% of the differences between people in sexual orientation - and that sexual orientation cannot be changed. A 2019 comprehensive study shows that a third of the influence on whether someone has gay sex can come from inherited genetics (as opposed to epigenetics).	Chapter 3 Chapter 7
https://en.wikipedia. org/wiki/Hand edness	Other biological traits are determined through a similar mix of inherited genetics and epigenetics. For example, being right-handed or left-handed is caused 25% by inherited genetics and 75% from epigenetic changes occurring in utero.	Chapter 3
https://www.listen-learnandlove.org/ articles	A great summary of the science can be found under the section titled "Sexual Orientation is Not a Choice" on the website for Richard Ostler's "Listen, Learn, and Love."	Chapter 3

*   Visit www.gayldscrossroads.org/topical-index for active hyperlinks to these sources

https://en.wikipedia.org/wiki/ Homosexual_ behavior_ in_ animals	Same-sex sexual behavior in animals is widespread across many species and happens at around the same rate as humans report being LGBTQ.	Chapter 3
https://www.google.com/amp/s/www.telegraph.co.uk/science/2016/03/15/homosexuality-may-be- triggered-by-environment-after- birth/amp/	Some researchers have found after-birth epigenetic changes relating to gay sexual orientation. Evidence of such changes are not as prevalent as evidences of epigenetic changes in utero.	Chapter 3
https://www.ted.com/talks/dr_lisa_diamond_why_the_ born_this_way_argument_does_not_ advance_lgbt_equality?language=en	Dr. Lisa Diamond has noted that relying too much on scientific explanations for LGBTQ realities can actually hurt the cause of LGBTQ equality.	Chapter 3

Gay sexual orientation; pseudo-scientific view of

Referenced site	Summary	Location used
https://www.fairmormon.org/conference/august-2018/thinking-differently-about-same-sex-attraction	Lecture given by Dr. Jeff Robinson saying sexual orientation is like the ability to speak a language.	Chapter 7

* Visit www.gayldscrossroads.org/topical-index for active hyperlinks to these sources

Gay sexual orientation; why it exists in nature

Referenced site	Summary	Location used
https://psmag.com/ environment/wh y-are-there-gay-peo ple https://www.bbc. com/news/magazi ne-26089486	Studies show that gay sexual orientation may play a crucial role in ensuring genetic diversity to help a species thrive.	Chapter 4
https://www.nytimes. com/2019/11/26/ science/same-sex-be havior-animals. html?smid=fb-ny-times&smtyp=cur&f-bclid=IwAR02I-caFSsNayOmc-jcwdaaSat2RE_xSqa-TEU7uALxBvmg-1sALw_zUBibvA8	Study showing that sexuality/mating/ bonding in general originated in the earliest evolutionary stages of life on this earth, which was among cellular creatures that didn't have binary genders - both heterosexuality and homosexuality persist as simply natural expressions of mating/bonding/intimacy desires to this day.	Chapter 4
https://m.youtube. com/ watch?v=8I Hw9D VI3hE (starting at the 41:00 mark)	Dr. William Bradshaw, BYU Professor, explains how studies have shown that "in the maternal line of gay men, the mothers, and the grandmothers, and the great-grandmothers have more children."	Chapter 4

* Visit www.gayldscrossroads.org/topical-index for active hyperlinks to these sources

Gender (Transgender) and Intersex

Referenced site	Summary	Location used
https://www.chur-chofjesuschrist.org/topics/transgen-der/?lang=eng	Church website launched in February 2020 that states the church's position that someone's eternal gender is their biological sex at birth, encourages more love and understanding, and otherwise lays out the church's views on gender dysphoria.	Chapter 4
https://blogs.scientifi-camerican.co m/ voic-es/stop- using-pho-ny- science- to-justi-fy-transphobia/ - https://m.youtube.com/watch?v=kT0H-Jkr1jj4& feature=you-tu.be	Article and video explaining the science behind why biological sex is not a simple binary construct in humans.	Chapter 4
https://www.chur-chofjesuschrist.org/study/manual/general-hand-book/38-church-pol-icies-and-guide-lines?lang=eng#ti-tle_number118	Church General Handbook section that formally codifies that the church views someone's eternal gender to be their biological sex at birth, instructs church members to love and be sensitive toward transgender individuals, and contem-plates church membership restrictions for transgender individuals for any social, medical, or surgical gender transition steps they take.	Chapter 4
https://isna.org/faq/frequency/	1 in every 1,500 babies are born "so noticeably atypical in terms of genitalia that a specialist in sex differentiation is called in."	Chapter 4

* Visit www.gayldscrossroads.org/topical-index for active hyperlinks to these sources

https://onlinelibrary. wiley.com/doi/ abs/ 10.1002/ %28 SICI%291520 - 6300%28200003/ 04%2912%3A2 %3C151%3A%3 AAID- AJHB1 % 3E3.0. CO%3B2-F	1 in 60 babies are born with less visible, but still significant, biological character- istics of both sexes.	Chapter 4
https://archive.org / stream/Doctrine s- of-Salvation-volume-2- joseph- fielding- smith/ JFSDoctrines ofSalvationv 2_ djvu. txt	President Joseph Fielding Smith said peo- ple will exist without any gender at all in the lower degrees of heaven.	Chapter 4

Hope

Referenced site	Summary	Location used
http://www.ldsliving. com/-This-Is- the- Church-of-Happy- Endings- Elder-Hol- land-Gives-Powerful- Message-to-Gradu- ates/s/88339	Elder Jeffrey R. Holland said the church should be "the church of the happy endings."	Chapter 10

* Visit www.gayldscrossroads.org/topical-index for active hyperlinks to these sources

https://www.chur-chofjesuschrist.org/study/manual/the-pearl-of-great-price-student-manu-al-2018/the-articles-of-faith/articles-of-faith-1-5-13	Elder James E. Talmage said in 1899 that canon is still open and that "revelation, surpassing in importance and glorious fulness any that has been recorded, is yet to be given to the Church."	Chapter 4
https://www.chur-chofjesuschrist.org/study/manual/doctrines-of-the-gos-pel-student-manu-al/23-restoration	Elder Bruce R. McConkie said the "last word has not been spoken on any subject" and that "There are more things we do not know about the doctrines of salvation than there are things we do know."	Chapter 4

Love; importance of

Referenced site	Summary	Location used
https://www.amazon.com/Ill-Walk-Car-ol-Lynn-Pearson/dp/1423653955	Verse from picture book by author, poet and scholar, Carol Lynn Pearson: "If you don't love as most people do, Some people say your love's not true. But I won't, I won't!"	Dedication page
http://bitly.ws/8E33	Lowell Bennion, founder of the first food bank and homeless shelters in Utah describes the difficulty of walking by faith in darkness when called upon to do something that goes against the spirit and the heart and soul of the gospel.	Dedication page

* Visit www.gayldscrossroads.org/topical-index for active hyperlinks to these sources

https://www.facebook.com/emily.e.nelson.92/posts/ 1021 97263 31658 849	Excellent list of what is harmful vs. helpful to say to LGBTQ church members and their loved ones, compiled by Emily Nelson, a mother of a gay son and moderator of an online Latter-day Saint parents support group.	Chapter 2
https://archive.sltrib.com/article.php?id=5117754&i-type=CMSID	Debra Oaks Coe of the executive committee of the Utah Commission for LGBT Suicide Awareness and Prevention teaches that when an LGBTQ comes out, "especially a young person to a parent, they are not looking for you to agree. They are asking if they are still loved."	Chapter 2
https://www.churchofjesuschrist.org/church/news/elder-ballard-tackles-tough-topics-and-gives-timely-advice-to-young-adults	Elder M. Russell Ballard said church members need to do a better job at listening to and loving LGBT church members.	Chapter 3
https://www.fairmormon.org/blog/category/homosexuality#_ednref7	Elder Quentin L. Cook said the church should be at the forefront of loving and that families should not "exclude or be disrespectful of those who choose a different lifestyle as a result of their feelings about their own gender."	Chapter 3

* Visit www.gayldscrossroads.org/topical-index for active hyperlinks to these sources

https://www.chur- chofjesuschrist.org/ study/general-confer- ence/2012/10/pro- tect-the-children	Elder Dallin H. Oaks said young LGBTQ people are vulnerable and need loving understanding, not bullying or ostracism.	Chapter 3
https://drive.goo- gle.com/ open?id =1sk lAZf BlrG8 SnB7B8 9C f57gg1 7PXPQ_Z	Compilation by Richard Ostler, an influential LGBTQ ally and active/ faithful Latter-day Saint, of positive and loving quotes from church leaders on LGBTQ matters.	Chapter 3
https://ldsquotations. com/author/te rryl- and-fiona-givens/	Author and scholar, Fiona Givens, teaches that "sin is not an unalterable state we inhabit; it is a felt disharmony."	Chapter 4
https://religionnews. com/2016/07/ 20/ mormon-wom- en-fear-eter- nal- polyga- my-study-shows/	Author, poet and scholar, Carol Lynn Pearson, teaches that we need to stop expecting people to wait to be happy in heaven when doctrine causes them harm now: "We here on earth to make things better."	Chapter 4
https://www.chur- chofjesuschrist. org/study/manual/ the-pearl-of-great- price-student-manu- al-2018/the-articles- of-faith/articles-of- faith-1-5-13?lang=eng	Elder James E. Talmage taught that professions of godliness without love are worthless.	Chapter 10

*   Visit www.gayldscrossroads.org/topical-index for active hyperlinks to these sources

Marriage; God's approval of many different forms of

Referenced site	Summary	Location used
https://www.patheos.com/blogs/unreasonablefaith/2009/04/the-varieties-of-biblical-marriage/	There have been several forms of marriage endorsed by God in the Bible.	Chapter 6

Marriage (straight); as a commandment

Referenced site	Summary	Location used
https://www.churchofjesuschrist.org/study/manual/gospel-topics/marriage	The church teaches that heterosexual marriage is necessary to enter the highest degree of heaven.	Chapter 7
https://www.churchofjesuschrist.org/study/general-conference/2008/10/celestial-marriage	Elder Russell M. Nelson said straight marriage "is not only an exalting principle of the gospel; it is a divine commandment."	Chapter 7
http://www.goodhopemcc.org/spirituality/would-jesus-discriminate/456-jesus-said-some-are-born-gay-matthew-1910-12.html	Christ taught that gay people do not need to marry.	Chapter 7

https://www.churchofjesuschrist.org/study/ensign/1976/04/i-have-a-question/should-mentally-retarded-children-be-baptized	People with physical or mental disabilities are not expected by the church to be baptized or to marry.	Chapter 7
https://www.josephsmithpapers.org/paper-summary/letter-to-isaac-galland-22-march-1839/4	Joseph Smith taught that different life circumstances can justify varying degrees of applicability of the commandments: "God will not command any thing, but what is peculiarly adapted in itself, to ameliorate the condition of every man under whatever circumstances it may find him."	Chapter 7

Marriage (mixed-orientation)

Referenced site	Summary	Location used
https://www.churchofjesuschrist.org/study/ensign/1987/05/reverence-and-morality	President Gordon B. Hinckley said mixed-orientation marriage should not be seen as a "therapeutic step to solve" being gay.	Chapter 3

* Visit www.gayldscrossroads.org/topical-index for active hyperlinks to these sources

http://www.qrd.org/qrd/religion/judeo-christian/protestant-ism/mormon/mormon-homosexuality	Official church pamphlet said: "Marriage should not be viewed as a way to resolve homosexual problems. The lives of others should not be damaged by entering a marriage where such concerns exist." (*Understanding and Helping Those Who Have* *Homosexual Problems. Suggestions for Ecclesiastical Leaders*, 1992, p. 4.)	Chapter 3
https://www.churchofjesuschrist.org/topics/gay/videos/elizabeths-story?lang=eng	Elder Dallin H. Oaks said mixed-orientation marriage is not recommended as a "solution" for being gay.	Chapter 3
https://www.churchofjesuschrist.org/topics/gay/leaders?lang=eng	Elder D. Todd Christofferson says choosing to enter into a mixed-orientation marriage is a personal choice and not something on which the church maintains a uniform position.	Chapter 3
https://www.churchofjesuschrist.org/study/ensign/2007/10/helping-those-who-struggle-with-same-gender-attraction	Elder Jeffrey R. Holland said trying to force a mixed-orientation marriage is "not likely" to change gay sexual attraction and that such marriages have resulted in "broken hearts and homes."	Chapter 3

* Visit www.gayldscrossroads.org/topical-index for active hyperlinks to these sources

https://newsroom. churchofjesuschr ist. org/article/inter-view-oaks- wick-man-same-gender-at-traction	Elder Dallin H. Oaks said someone who is attracted to the same sex may appropriately marry a person of the opposite sex if they can suppress their same-sex feelings and have a "great attraction" to that person (i.e., bisexuals are okay marrying someone of the opposite sex).	Chapter 3
https://www.huffpost. com/ entry/ ga y-mormon- men- mar-riage_n_ 6464848	Study that shows that mixed-orientation marriages are 2 to 3 times more likely to end in divorce than uniform- orienta-tion marriages.	Chapter 2 Chapter 3
https://www. tandfonline.com/ doi/ a bs/10.1080/ 19359705. 2014. 912970	Study that shows people in mixed-ori-entation marriages report higher rates of depression and a lower quality of life.	Chapter 2 Chapter 3
http://joshweed.com/	Weed family story of a high profile failed mixed- orientation marriage.	Chapter 3
https://www.sltrib. com/news/educa tion/2019/12/08/ ed-smart-father/ https://www.nyda-ilynews.com/news/ national/ny-ed-smart-came-out-struggles-gay-acceptance-elizabeth-smart-20191210-qyd6dnbc 3vh6fdguwczh-3v44pm-story.html	Smart family story of a high profile failed mixed- orientation marriage.	Chapter 3

* Visit www.gayldscrossroads.org/topical-index for active hyperlinks to these sources

Myths about gay sexual orientation

Referenced site	Summary	Location used
https://www.splcenter.org/fighting-hate/intelligence-report/2011/10-anti-gay-myths-debunked	Great website with resources that debunk the following myths: • Myth #1: Gay men molest children at far higher rates than heterosexuals • Myth #2: Same-sex parents harm children • Myth #3: People become homosexual because they were sexually abused as children or there was a deficiency in sex-role modeling by their parents. • Myth #4: LGBT people don't live nearly as long as heterosexuals. • Myth #5: Gay men controlled the Nazi Party and helped to orchestrate the Holocaust. • Myth #6: Hate crime laws will lead to the jailing of pastors who criticize homosexuality and the legalization of practices like bestiality and necrophilia. • Myth #7: Allowing gay people to serve openly will damage the armed forces. • Myth #8: Gay people are more prone to be mentally ill and to abuse drugs and alcohol. • Myth #9: No one is born gay. • Myth #10: Gay people can choose to leave homosexuality.	Chapter 7

* Visit www.gayldscrossroads.org/topical-index for active hyperlinks to these sources

Parenting

Referenced site	Summary	Location used
https://www.youtube.com/watch?v=PyRA-ueeJNIY	BYU microbiology professor (and former mission president), Dr. William Bradshaw, hosts a video on embracing LGBTQ children.	Chapter 3
https://mormon-lgbtquestions.com/	Church-published tips for parents of LGBTQ children cited (including that they should not "blame" themselves).	Chapter 3
https://newsroom.churchofjesuschr ist.org/article/inter-view-oaks- wick-man-same-gender-at-traction	Elder Dallin H. Oaks said parents might be justified in not letting their adult gay children meet their friends or participate in family events in the same way as their other children.	Chapter 3
https://whatweknow.inequality.cor nell.edu/topics/lgbt-equal-ity/what- does-the-scholarly-research-say-about-the-wellbeing-of-children- with-gay-or-lesbian-parents/	There is an overwhelming scholarly consensus, based on over three decades of peer-reviewed research, that having a gay or lesbian parent does not harm children.	Chapter 8
https://en.wiki-pedia.org/wiki/LGB T_parenting	Parents being gay causes no harm to children. The American Academy of Pediatrics and all of the major professional organizations with expertise in child welfare have issued reports and resolutions in support of LGBTQ parental rights.	Chapter 8

*   Visit www.gayldscrossroads.org/topical-index for active hyperlinks to these sources

https://en.wikipedia.org/wiki/LGBT_parenting#cite_note-Stacey_Biblarz-33	Kids raised by gay couples are not more likely to self-identify as LGBTQ.	Chapter 8
https://www.churchofjesuschrist.org/study/ensign/2002/09/hope-for-parents-of-wayward-children	Parents of straight children who have left the church have hope that such children will nevertheless be saved in the highest degree of heaven with them. Parents of gay kids can't hope for that without it meaning their kids will need to have their sexual orientation switched after they die.	Chapter 10
https://www.churchofjesuschrist.org/study/ensign/1981/06/i-have-a-question/will-those-who-died-as-little-children-have-to-receive-baptism-at-some-future-time	Parents of deceased young children have the assurance that their kids will automatically make it to the highest degree of heaven.	Chapter 10
https://www.millennialstar.org/president-kimball-and-his-inactive-son/	President Spencer W. Kimball worsened his relationship with his non-believing son by repeatedly calling him to repentance.	Chapter 10
https://www.churchofjesuschrist.org/study/general-conference/2007/10/the-weak-and-the-simple-of-the-church	President Boyd K. Packer taught that personal revelation for our families is no less important than revelation received by church leaders for the church.	Chapter 10

* Visit www.gayldscrossroads.org/topical-index for active hyperlinks to these sources

| https://www.then-ation.com/article/archive/mormon-family-values/

http://www.lds-mormon.com/hardy.shtml | David and Carlie Hardy family story from late 1990s. Brother Hardy wrote a letter to Elder Boyd K. Packer outlining the still pertinent reasons why the church is damaging LGBTQ people and their families. | Chapter 10 |

Personal revelation

Referenced site	Summary	Location used
https://www.churchofjesuschrist.org/study/general-conference/2018/04/revelation-for-the-church-revelation-for-our-lives?lang=eng	President Russell M. Nelson taught: "Regardless of what others may say or do, **no one** can ever take away a witness borne to your heart and mind about what is true."	Chapter 5

Polygamy

Referenced site	Summary	Location used
https://www.churchofjesuschrist.org/study/general-conference/1998/10/what-are-people-asking-about-us?lang=eng	President Gordon B. Hinckley taught that after 1890, polygamy goes against the law of God (and so is a sin), with excommunication being the consequence of anyone in a polygamous marriage.	Chapter 4

---

*   Visit www.gayldscrossroads.org/topical-index for active hyperlinks to these sources

https://www.fairmor-mon.org/answers/ Mormonism_and_ polygamy/1835_Doc-trine_and_Cove-nants_denies_polyg-amy	The church actually changed its scrip-ture/canon to redefine marriage: to allow for polygamy.	Chapter 6
https://www. churchofjesus-christ.org/manual/ doctrine-and-cov-enants-student-man-ual/section-132-mar-riage-an-eternal-cov-enant	Joseph Smith knew polygamy was going to be instituted as early as 1831 – even though that contradicted existing scrip-ture that said only monogamy was allowed in the church.	Chapter 6
https://www.tem-plestudies.org/ bringhurst-newell-g-section-132-of-the-lds-doctrine-and-cov-enants-its-complex-contents-and-contro-versial-legacy/	Current interpretation of Section 132 of Doctrine & Covenants, to address eternal marriage generally, is not consistent with the textual emphasis on, and historical context of, polygamy.	Chapter 6
See multiple refer-ences where cited in Chapter 6.	19th century prophetic/apostolic state-ments that polygamy is required for the highest degree of heaven and/or is better than monogamy.	Chapter 6

* Visit www.gayldscrossroads.org/topical-index for active hyperlinks to these sources

https://www.fairmormon.org/answers/Mormonism_and_polygamy/Brigham_Young_said_that_the_only_men_who_become_gods_are_those_that_practice_polygamy#cite_note-10	Brigham Young discussed polygamy being required for the highest heaven.	Chapter 6
http://bitly.ws/8HXJ	The First Presidency and apostles stated in an 1891 petition to the President of the United States that the church previously taught that polygamy was a necessity for exaltation.	Chapter 6
https://archive.org/stream/Mormon Doctrine1966/Mormon-Doctrine19 66_djvu.txt https://en.wikipedia.org/ wiki/ Mormonism_ and_ polygamy	Elder Bruce R. McConkie said "Obviously the holy practice [of plural marriage] will commence again after the Second Coming of the Son of Man and the ushering in of the millennium."	Chapter 6
https://www.amazon.com/Ghost-Eternal-Polygamy-Haunting-Hearts/dp/0997458208	Book by author, poet and scholar, Carol Lynn Pearson. She writes about the idea that because church leaders haven't actually denounced the idea of polygamy in heaven, current church doctrine is essentially just putting a pause on polygamy.	Chapter 6

* Visit www.gayldscrossroads.org/topical-index for active hyperlinks to these sources

https://religionnews. com/2016/07/20/ mormon-wom- en-fear-eternal- polyg- amy-study-shows/	The vast majority of women in the church dread the idea that they will be a plural wife for eternity.	Chapter 4
https://www.fairmor- mon.org/answers/ Mormonism_and_ polygamy/Brigham_ Young_said_that_ the_only_men_who_ become_gods_are_ those_that_prac- tice_polygamy#Questi on:_Is_plural_mar- riage_required_in_ order_to_achieve_ exaltation.3F	Several quotes from past apostles and prophets, and statements in manuals published by the church, indicate that polygamy is not required for exaltation.	Chapter 4
https://www.gregtrim- ble.com/what-every- mormon-really-needs- to- know-about-po- lygamy/	Essay arguing that church teachings are clear that no one will be forced to practice polygamy in heaven.	Chapter 4

*   Visit www.gayldscrossroads.org/topical-index for active hyperlinks to these sources

Proclamation on the Family

Referenced site	Summary	Location used
https://www.chur-chofjesuschrist. org/study/manual/ the-family-a-procla-mation-to-the-world/ the-family-a-procla-mation-to-the-world	The church's proclamation that describes doctrinal understandings on gender roles, marriage, and family.	Chapter 4 Chapter 5
https://rationalfaiths. com/from- ami-ci-to-ohana/	Timeline of events around when the church's family proclamation was issued and the church's involvement as an amicus curiae party in an early court case in Hawaii dealing with legalizing gay marriage.	Chapter 5
https://www.chur-chofjesuschrist.org/ study/general-con-ference/1995/10/ stand-strong-against-the-wiles-of-the-world?lang=eng	President Gordon B. Hinckley did not describe the family proclamation as a new revelation when he introduced it to the church in 1995. Rather, he said it was "a declaration and reaffirmation of stan-dards, doctrines, and practices relative to the family which…have repeatedly [been] stated throughout [the church's] history."	Chapter 5
https://archive. sltrib.com/article.ph p?id=50440474&i-type=CMSID	President Boyd K. Packer's use of the term "revelation" to describe the family proc-lamation in a General Conference talk was corrected.	Chapter 5

* Visit www.gayldscrossroads.org/topical-index for active hyperlinks to these sources

https://www.deser-et.com/faith/202 0/4/5/21208843/ church- proclama-tions-history-mor-mon- lds-latter-day-saints-gordon-b- hinckley-rus-sell-m-nelson https:// en.wikipedia.org/wiki/ The_ Family:_A_ Proclamation_to_the_ World#cite_note-16	The church has issued five other "proc-lamations" over the course of its history.	N/A

Prophets; inspiration and fallibility of

Referenced site	Summary	Location used
https://www. churchofjesus-christ.org/study/ new-era/2001/07/ words-of-the-proph-et-the-spirit-of-opti-mism?lang=eng	President Gordon B. Hinckley said "I am not asking that all criticism be silenced. Growth comes of correction."	Preface
https://www.chur-chofjesuschrist.org/ study/general-confer-ence/2013/10/come-join-with-us?lang=eng	Elder Dieter F. Uchtdorf said church leaders have made mistakes that are not in harmony with doctrine.	Preface

* Visit www.gayldscrossroads.org/topical-index for active hyperlinks to these sources

https://www.chur-chofjesuschrist.org/ study/general-confer-ence/2013/04/lord-i-believe?lang=eng	Elder Jeffrey R. Holland said the Lord has only ever had imperfect people through whom to do His work, including apostles.	Preface
https://www. churchofjesus-christ.org/study/ ensign/1979/08/ the-debate-is-over?lang=eng https://www.fairmor-mon.org/archive/ publications/when-the-prophet-speaks-is-the-thinking-done	"When the prophet speaks, the debate is over" is an extension of the original phrase "When the prophet speaks, the thinking has been done," which was an unauthorized statement that President George Albert Smith privately renounced after it was first published in a church magazine in 1945.	Preface
http://www.mormon-press.com/ezra-taft-benson-and-politics https://archive.sltrib. com/story.php?ref=/ lds/ci_14287116	Elder Ezra Taft Benson was reprimanded and asked to apologize by President Spencer W. Kimball for giving his 1980 talk titled "Fourteen Fundamentals in Following the Prophet" in which he essentially says the living prophet is more important than scripture and should be followed even in political matters because he cannot lead us astray.	Preface
http://www.eugeneen-gland.org/wp-content/ uploads/2012/07/ BRM-to- EE-Feb-80-Combined.pdf	Elder Bruce R. McConkie wrote that "Prophets are men and they make mis-takes. Sometimes they err in doctrine."	Chapter 2

*   Visit www.gayldscrossroads.org/topical-index for active hyperlinks to these sources

https://archive.org/ stream/Mormon Doc-trine1966/Mormon-Doctrine19 66_djvu. txt	Elder Bruce R. McConkie taught that General Authorities may or may not be authorities in doctrinal knowledge or the receipt of the promptings of the Spirit.	Chapter 2
https://www.facebook. com/ beyond the-blockpodcast/ videos/ 758569211 567124	Clever, one-minute video by scriptorian, podcaster, entertainer and social justice advocate, James C. Jones, enacting how Peter had to be told three times by the Lord before believing the gentiles could receive the gospel (see Acts 10:10-15).	Chapter 2
https://www.fair-mormon.org/blog/ 2014/11/25/liv-ing-fallibility	The church believes that prophets can make mistakes.	Chapter 5
https://www. fairmormon.org/ answers/Mormon-ism_and_doctrine/ Prophets_are_not_ infallible#Question:_ Were_Biblical_proph-ets_infallible.3F	Comparison of the mistakes/fallibility of Biblical prophets to those of mod-ern prophets.	Chapter 5
https://www. goodreads.com/ quotes/171150-if-i-do-not-know-the-will-of-my-father	Brigham Young said he sometimes taught, even in his official capacity as the presiding authority over the church, according to his own discretion, not divine revelation.	Chapter 5

* Visit www.gayldscrossroads.org/topical-index for active hyperlinks to these sources

https://www.fairmor-mon.org/answers/ Mormonism_and_ doctrine/Proph-ets_are_not_infalli-ble#cite_note-13	Elder Charles W. Penrose said the President of the Church, when speaking to the Church in his official capacity, is NOT infallible.	Chapter 5
https://en.wiki-pedia.org/wiki/ Lost_116_pages	God can have a back-up plan already in place to make up for the mistakes that prophets make.	Chapter 5
https://www.fairmor-mon.org/answers/ Mormonism_and_ doctrine/Proph-ets_are_not_infalli-ble#cite_note-16	Elder Boyd K. Packer said "Even with the best of intentions, [Church government] does not always work the way it should. Human nature may express itself on occa-sion, but not to the permanent injury of the work."	Chapter 5
https://www.fairmor-mon.org/answers/ Mormonism_and_ doctrine/Proph-ets_are_not_infalli-ble#cite_note-15	Elder Dallin H. Oaks said "We are often left to work out problems without the dic-tation or specific direction of the Spirit. That is part of the experience we must have in mortality."	Chapter 5
https://www.youtube. com/watch?v =2lKQrYUE3yc	Prophets and apostles can contradict each other, even within short periods of time. This video shows that in the context of whether we should be okay with the nick-name "the Mormon Church."	Chapter 5

* Visit www.gayldscrossroads.org/topical-index for active hyperlinks to these sources

https://en.wikipedia.org/wiki/Interracial_marriage_and_The_Church_of_Jesus_Christ_of_Latter-day_Saints	The church banned white church members who married Black individuals from entering a temple into at least the 1960s and recommended against any interracial marriages in official publications into the 2000s.	Chapter 5
https://www.sixteensmallstones.org/debunking-that-quote-about-brigham-youngs-greatest-fear/	Brigham Young said he worried about people not asking for themselves whether their leaders are led by God.	Chapter 5
https://speeches.byu.edu/talks/russ ell-m-nelson/love-laws-god/	President Russell M. Nelson says people can learn for themselves whether the church's leaders are truly prophets and apostles.	Chapter 5
https://www.churchofjesuschrist.org/study/general-conference/2018/04/revelation-for-the-church-revelation-for-our-lives	President Russell M. Nelson said "good inspiration is based upon good information" (so can new scientific discoveries about gay sexual orientation result in better inspiration?)	Chapter 6
https://www.fairmormon.org/answers/Criticism_of_Mormonism/Websites/MormonThink/Blacks_and_the_Priesthood	Elder Bruce R. McConkie said new revelation makes prior prophetic statements worthy of forgetting.	Chapter 6 Chapter 10

https://www.google.com/amp/s/prophetsseersandrevelators.wordpress.com/2015/06/01/the-calling-of-an-apostle/amp/	President Hugh B. Brown describes a "charge to the apostles" that every newly called apostle receives from the President of the church pursuant to which each new apostle agrees to speak his mind freely in private but to portray as his own opinion in public whatever position the majority of the apostles maintain.	Chapter 6
https://www.churchofjesuschrist.org/si/questions/what-is-doctrine https://www.fairmormon.org/wp- content/uploads/2012/02/What_is_Mormon_Doctrine.pdf	The church says that any teaching that has not been voted on by the whole church to become canon can be known to be of God or not if we feel God's spirit testify of their truthfulness. "It is likely that the Lord has allowed (and will continue to allow) his servants to make mistakes."	Chapter 7

*   Visit www.gayldscrossroads.org/topical-index for active hyperlinks to these sources

Psychological harm;
from non-LGBTQ affirming positions

Referenced site	Summary	Location used
https://getd.libs.uga. edu/pdfs/simmons_ brian_w_201712_ phd.pd http://mormons-buildingbridges. org/wp-content/ uploads/2019/10/ 2019092 8-U-of-U-MBB-Pre-sentation-SIM-MONS-FINAL. pptx - https://oatd.org/ oatd/ record?rec ord =handle%5C %3A10724% 5C%2F3 8227	Peer-reviewed, 2017 academic study showing that church teachings on marriage, family, gender, and sexuality cause PTSD symptoms for nearly 90% of LGBTQ Latter-day Saints.	Preface Chapter 2 Chapter 8 Chapter 10
https://www.tandfon-line.com/doi/full/10. 1080/13811118. 2020.1806159 https://drive.google. com/ file/d/ 1zN s8K5nNP w4SQx-PchOuc_ PFH0f0Q 3kIq /view?us-p=drivesdk	Peer-reviewed 2020 academic study showing that (i) lesbian, gay and bisexual (LGB) Utahns are over 4.5 times more likely to have recently thought about suicide and nearly 10 times as likely to have attempted suicide than heterosexual Utahns, and (ii) rates of suicidal thinking and suicide attempts among LGB Utahns was around three times higher than the rates among LGB non-Utahns living in the U.S., Canada and Europe	Preface Chapter 2 Chapter 8

*   Visit www.gayldscrossroads.org/topical-index for active hyperlinks to these sources

https://www.tandfonline.com/ doi /a bs/ 10.1080/ 1550428X. 2020. 1800545 ? journal Code= wgfs20 https://drive.google.com/ file/d/ 18n KkeahLsu NXA56l Yoy 95rfL PtzVG 0aB/ view? usp =drivesdk	Synthesized compilation of all published and non- published empirical research on Latter-day Saint LGBTQ psychological and interpersonal functioning.	Chapter 8
https://www.facebook.com/groups/ mormons building bridges/ permalin k / 25179 907 7496 8435/	Peer-reviewed study showing that religious teachings that define gay sexual behavior as sinful result in psychological damage and depression.	Chapter 10
https://en.wikipedia.org/ wiki/ Suicide_ among_ LGBT_ youth	LGBTQ youth have a higher rate of suicide than other youth.	Preface
https://www. ncbi.nlm.nih. gov/ pmc /articles/ PMC3721024/	It has been clinically proven that lack of hope causes depression.	Chapter 2
http://www.withoutend.org/ reactio ns-the-policy- november-2015/	Collection of stories compiled by historian and scholar, Clair Barrus, of families negatively affected by the church's November 2015 policy excluding kids with gay parents from being baptized.	Chapter 3

*   Visit www.gayldscrossroads.org/topical-index for active hyperlinks to these sources

https://www.kuer. org/ post/ can-lds- church-be-blamed- utah-s-lgbt- suicides# stream/ 0 https://en.wiki- pedia.org/ wiki/ Suici de_ among_ LGBT _youth	Debate about the causality between church teachings regarding gay sexual orientation and suicide	Chapter 8
https://en.m.wikipe- dia.org/ wiki/LG BT _Mormon_ suicides	Research has shown that church teachings that gay sexual orientation will be "cured" in the afterlife have led many gay Latter- day Saints to engage in suicidal ideation or to attempt or die by suicide.	Chapter 2 Chapter 8
https://www. sltrib.com/opin- ion/co mmen- tary/2019/11/02/jus- tin-utley- darkness-is/	Personal story of mental health harm because of the church's teachings about gay sexual orientation.	Chapter 8
https://www.wash- ingtonpost.com/ outlook/2019/12/19/ anti-lgbt- discrimi- nation-has-huge-hu- man- toll-research- proves-it/	Studies showing not granting LGBTQ individuals equal rights in all areas of life effects real and significant harm.	Chapter 8

*   Visit www.gayldscrossroads.org/topical-index for active hyperlinks to these sources

https://www.theguardian.com/world/2019/nov/14/suicide-rates-fall-after-gay-marriage-laws-in-sweden-and-denmark https://www.upworthy.com/legalizing-gay-marriage-has-caused-a-dramatic-drop-in-lgbt-suicide-rates	Studies showing legalizing gay marriage may result in a decrease in suicide rates.	Chapter 8
https://bostonchildstudycenter.com/ptsd/?fbclid=IwAR1 W7K83a0U WkPUzRkm 7ftA-Jx6mIcWzyZdRa wcwm51 jXlroq7F-wx ZKZJ9a0	Besides PTSD, another psychological category of harm that studies are showing LGBTQ individuals exposed to non-affirming ideologies experience is "traumatic invalidation."	Chapter 10

Scriptures; lack of prohibition of gay marriage (Bible's "clobber" passages)

Referenced site	Summary	Location used
https://www.nbcnews.com/feature/ nbc-out/christian-pastor-reframes- scripture-used-against-lgbtq-community-n673471	Book written by Christian pastor, Colby Martin, that explains why the Bible verses often used to condemn gay marriage are interpreted incorrectly.	Chapter 5

*   Visit www.gayldscrossroads.org/topical-index for active hyperlinks to these sources

https://www.face-book.com/ stan. mi tchell.58/ posts/ 3135281 313206 974 https://www. forgeonline.org/ blog/2019/3/8/what-about-romans-124-27	Firsthand account of research revealing that modern translations of the Bible that use the word "homosexual" incorrectly do so and that the translators knew of their error but failed to correct it.	Chapter 5
https://www.gay-church.org/homo-sexuality-and-the-bi-ble/the-bible-christi-anity-and-homosex-uality/ **https://medium. com/@adam-nich olasphillips/ the-bible-does-not- condemn-ho-mosexuality- seri-ously-it-doesn-t- 13ae949d6619** **http://www.wouldje-susdiscrimin ate. org/biblical_evi-dence.html** **https://www. rmnetwork.org/new rmn/wp- content/ uploads/2016/09/ Booklet-about-Ho-mosexuali-ty-and-the- Bible-Sept.-2016.pdf**	Sites where Christian pastors and com-mentators explain how the scriptures that many people say prohibit gay sexual behavior of any kind can more accurately be interpreted to allow for gay marriage.	Chapter 5

*   Visit www.gayldscrossroads.org/topical-index for active hyperlinks to these sources

https://beyondthe-blockpodcast.c om/ episodes/the-lon-gest-clobber- pas-sage-s1!0cdef	Great podcast episode where a gay convert to the church (who is a Bible scholar and theologian by training) explains how Bible scriptures don't condemn gay marriage.	Chapter 5
https://www.reddit. com/r/latterdaysaints/ comments/1zdsbd/ the_old_testa-ment_doesnt_prohib-it_homosexuality/	Scholar, Dr. Hugh Nibley, said the pri-mary sin of Sodom and Gomorrah was actually greed and that they lacked com-passion and hospitality (it wasn't gay sexual behavior).	Chapter 5

Scriptures promoting equality
(just some favorites, not a comprehensive list)

Referenced verse/site	Summary	Location used
2 Nephi 26:33	All are alike unto God.	Chapter 4 Chapter 6
https://www.amazon. com/Book- Mor-mon-Least- These/ dp/1948218232/ ref=tmm_pa p_swatch_0?_encod-ing=UTF8&qi d=&sr=	Rev. Dr. Fatimah Salleh and Margaret Olsen Hemming comment on the use of merism in 2 Nephi 26:33 "as a rhetorical device in which two ends of the spectrum are named as a way to encompass the entire spectrum in between."	Chapter 4
Mosiah 4:26	Minister to people according to their wants, not church leader's assessment of their wants or needs.	Chapter 2

*   Visit www.gayldscrossroads.org/topical-index for active hyperlinks to these sources

Mosiah 18:8-9	Comfort those who stand in need of comfort.	Chapter 2
Matthew 25:40	Inasmuch as ye have done it unto one of the least of these, ye have done it unto Christ.	Chapter 4
John 13:34-35	Love one another, as Jesus loved us.	Chapter 4
Acts 10:34-35	God is no respecter of persons.	Chapter 4 Chapter 7
1 Corinthians 13:13	Faith, hope, and love are enduring attributes; love is paramount.	Chapter 4
1 Timothy 5:20-21	Do not prefer one before another, doing nothing by partiality.	Chapter 4
1 Peter 2:7	"…the builders …tossed aside the stone that turned out to be the most important one of all." (Contemporary English Version)	Chapter 10
1 John 4:20	Those who do not love a brother or sister whom they have seen, cannot love God whom they have not seen.	Chapter 4

Sexual relations; importance of within marriage

Referenced site	Summary	Location used
https://speeches.byu.edu/talks/jeffr ey-r-hol-land/souls-sym-bols- sacraments/	Elder Jeffrey R. Holland teaches that marital sex is a sacred act that increases our ability to love our spouse in a unique way.	Chapter 4

*   Visit www.gayldscrossroads.org/topical-index for active hyperlinks to these sources

https://www. churchofjesus-christ.org/study/ensign/1982/10/the-gospel-and-romantic-love?lang=eng	Elder Bruce C. Hafen quotes Elder Boyd K. Packer's book, "Eternal Love," in which Elder Packer says: "No experience can be more beautiful, no power more compelling, more exquisite [than romantic love]."	Chapter 4
https://www.chur-chofjesuschrist.org/study/manual/gos-pel-topics/birth-con-trol	The church's website says, "Sexual relations within marriage are not only for the purpose of procreation, but also a means of expressing love and strengthening emotional and spiritual ties."	Chapter 5
https://journals. sage-pub.com/ doi/fu ll/ 10.1177/ 0956797 617691 361	Study showing that regular sexual intimacy is an important part of spousal emotional closeness and overall marital happiness.	Chapter 4
https://newsroom. churchofjesuschr ist. org/article/heaven	Church teaching that the nature of family relationships will be the same in heaven as they are here. The same "sociality" will exist there as it does here.	Chapter 4

Spiritual procreation

Referenced site	Summary	Location used
http://emp.byui.edu/ satterfieldb/qu otes/ Intelligence%20 and%20Spirit. html (Abraham 3:22; Doc-trine & Covenants 93:29, 33-34)	Canonized Latter-day Saint scripture, as interpreted by numerous prophets and apostles, seems to teach that a human spirit is created by shaping/organizing a pre- existing "intelligence" into a spirit/ human soul	Chapter 6

* Visit www.gayldscrossroads.org/topical-index for active hyperlinks to these sources

https://www. dialoguejournal. com/wp-content/ uploads/sbi/ articles/Dialogue_ V44N04_420.pdf	Dr. Taylor Petrey, Professor of Religion, explores how church doctrine could evolve to embrace eternal gay marriage. This article is a must-read for anyone trying to understand if it's possible for church doctrine to change on gay marriage.	Chapter 5 Chapter 7
https://en.wikipedia.org/wiki/Genesis_1:1	The idea the earth was created out of nothing was not something the original writers of the Bible proposed.	Chapter 6
https://scholarsarchive.byu.edu/ cgi/viewcontent. cgi?article=1626&context=msr	The original text of the Book of Genesis supports JosephSmith's teaching that the creation of the earth was done through the organizing of existing matter.	Chapter 6
https://www. churchofjesus-christ.org/study/ ensign/1982/06/ christ-and-the-creation (Abraham 3:22-24)	The church teaches that "Elohim [the Father], Jehovah [Christ], Michael [Adam], a host of noble and great ones – all these played their parts" in creating the earth.	Chapter 6
https://www.churchofjesuschrist. org/study/manual/ gospel-topics/spirit-children-of-heavenly-parents	The church teaches all people are "literally" children of Heavenly Parents and that we have inherited divine potential from Them.	Chapter 6

*   Visit www.gayldscrossroads.org/topical-index for active hyperlinks to these sources

https://www.chur-chofjesuschrist. org/church/news/ new-young-wom-en-theme-class-name-and-struc-ture-changes-an-nounced?lang=eng	The revised Young Women theme announced in October of 2019 includes the mention of Heavenly Parents (not just Heavenly Father).	Chapter 6
https://www. churchofjesus-christ.org/study/ ensign/2002/04/the-father-and-the-son	Even though Christ was not involved in forming our spirits, we can still refer to Him as our "Father" (because he is the father of our salvation, among other things).	Chapter 6
https://medium. com/neodotlife/sa me-sex-reproduc-tion-artificial- gam-etes-2739206aa4c0	Science is finding ways to allow gay couples to reproduce biologically.	Chapter 4 Chapter 6

*   Visit www.gayldscrossroads.org/topical-index for active hyperlinks to these sources

Staying in the church

Referenced site	Summary	Location used
https://www.sunstonemagazine.com/ why-i-stay-2/	Author, poet, and scholar, Carol Lynn Pearson, says God is where love is, which she sees in gay relationships and in the church (which is why she stays in the church). She also stays because she believes in growing where we are planted spiritually. She says she's able to stay in the church because she does "not stay in concepts that [she does] not accept." She also says: "Our church provides a perfect opportunity for me to create love in places where it appears to be lacking."	Chapter 10
https://mormonquotes.wordpress.c om/2014/10/02/ be-spiritually- independent/	Former General Relief Society Presidency member, Chieko N. Ozaki encouraged church members to have the spiritual independence to be the best church members they can—in their own ways.	Chapter 10
https://www.churchofjesuschrist.org/ study/manual/teachings-joseph-smith/ chapter-22?lang=eng	The Prophet Joseph Smith taught that we can embrace truth without being limited by "the creeds…of men…when that truth is clearly demonstrated to our minds, and we have the highest degree of evidence of the same."	Chapter 10
https://bit.ly/2TksPK9	President Joseph F. Smith taught that people can stay in the church even if they don't believe in all its teachings.	Chapter 10

* Visit www.gayldscrossroads.org/topical-index for active hyperlinks to these sou·

| https://www.josephsmithpapers.or g/paper-summary/discourse-8- april-1843-as-reported-by-william- clayton-b/3 | Joseph Smith taught that it is inconsistent with "Latter-day Saintism" to kick people out of the church just because they don't believe in certain teachings of the church. | Chapter 10 |

Suicide

Referenced site	Summary	Location used
http://www.russel-lyanderson.com/mormons/basic/doctrines/suicide_e om.htm	President Spencer W. Kimball taught that suicide is a sin and a terrible criminal act.	Chapter 7
https://www.chur-chofjesuschrist.org/study/manual/doc-trine-and-principles/doctrine-and-prin-ciples	Current church teachings leave the eternal effects of suicide ambiguous.	Chapter 7
https://www.kuer.org/post/can-lds-church-be-blamed-utah-s-lgbt- sui-cides#stream/0 https://en.wiki-pedia.org/ wiki/ Suicide_ among_ LGBT _youth	Debate about the causality between church teachings regarding gay sexual orientation and suicide	Chapter 8

*   Visit www.gayldscrossroads.org/topical-index for active hyperlinks to these sources

https://en.m.wikipe-dia.org/ wiki/ LGBT _Mormon_ suicides	Research has shown that church teachings that gay sexual orientation will be "cured" in the afterlife have led many gay Latter-day Saints to engage in suicidal ideation or to attempt or die by suicide.	Chapter 8
https://latterday-saintmag.com/is- lat-ter- day-saint- the-ology- responsible-for-lgbt- suicides/? fbclid=IwAR0F5E rowdn EgoXQSP-kLAmZFEIIxVs AgNLV yQMd-nP4A1 8lapw-3gx cShBNp8	May 2020 Meridian Magazine article argu-ing church teachings do not contribute to LGBTQ church member suicides (no studies are sourced in the article to back up this claim).	Chapter 8
http://www.johndeh-lin.com/researc h/ https://athenaeum. libs.uga.edu/ han dle/1 0724/ 38227 https://familyproject. sfsu.edu/	Numerous published, peer-reviewed stud-ies show church teachings and family dis-approval cause trauma for most LGBTQ church members and are contributing factors in their suicidality.	Chapter 8
https://rationalfaiths. com /utahs- escalat-ing- suicide-crisis-lds-lgbtq- despair/	Statistics showing increases in suicides in Utah coincide with time periods in which the church was actively engaged in anti-LGBTQ rights campaigns.	Chapter 8

*   Visit www.gayldscrossroads.org/topical-index for active hyperlinks to these sources

https://www.fairmormon.org/answers/Mormonism_and_gender_issues/Same-sex_attraction	Site that quotes "multiple" church leaders teaching that "same-sex attraction" will not exist after death.	Chapter 4
https://www.churchofjesuschrist.org/study/manual/god-loveth-his-children/god-loveth-his-children?lang=eng	Church pamphlet/article that says gay sexual attraction will not exist after death.	Chapter 4
https://www.pbs.org/mormons/interviews/holland.html	Elder Jeffrey R. Holland said gay sexual attraction will not exist after death.	Chapter 4
https://newsroom.churchofjesuschrist.org/article/interview-oaks-wickman-same-gender-attraction	Elder Dallin H. Oaks said gay sexual attraction will not exist after death.	Chapter 4
https://newsroom.churchofjesuschrist.org/article/interview-oaks-wickman-same-gender-attraction	Elder Lance B. Wickman said gay sexual attraction will go away after this life.	Chapter 8

* Visit www.gayldscrossroads.org/topical-index for active hyperlinks to these sources

Sustaining leaders

Referenced site	Summary	Location used
https://www.sltrib. com/religion/20 19/12/15/can-latter- day-saints/	Professor Patrick Mason says respecting church teachings while holding a different perspective is the "epitome of sustaining."	Chapter 7
https://www. churchofjesus- christ.org/study/ new-era/2001/07/ words-of-the-proph- et-the-spirit-of-opti- mism?lang=eng	Elder Gordon B. Hinckley said: "I am not asking that all criticism be silenced. Growth comes of correction…Wise is the man who can acknowledge mistakes pointed out by others and change his course."	Preface

Temple ordinances; sealings

Referenced site	Summary	Location used
https://religionnews. com/2019/01/ 03/ major-changes- to-mormon- tem- ple-ceremony-espe- cially-for- women/	Changes in temple ceremonies have been done to reflect progressive change (i.e., improvements for women).	Chapter 6
https://www.dia- loguejournal.com/ wp- content/uploads/ sbi/articles/Dialog ue_V34N0102_87. pdf	Many people (men and women) have been sealed to church leaders with whom they had no family relationship.	Chapter 6

*   Visit www.gayldscrossroads.org/topical-index for active hyperlinks to these sources

https://scholarsar-chive.byu.edu/cgi /viewcontent.cgi?ar-ticle=1625&co ntex-t=byusq	Many men not related to each other have been sealed to one another directly (in a father-son-type relationship) under the "law of adoption."	Chapter 6
https://en.wikipe-dia.org/wiki/Law_of_adoption_(Mor-monism)	LGBTQ activists asked the church in the 1970s to allow for gay civil unions (using the "law of adoption" doctrine/practice as an analogous argument)	Chapter 6
https://interpreter-foundation.org/ne ws-an-invitation-to-thank-dr- rich-ard-bushman/	The doctrine of sealing may have more to do with uniting all of humanity together, through priesthood and sacred covenants, than with binding individuals as roman-tic couples.	Chapter 6
https://www. churchofjesus-christ.org/topics/ plural-marriage-in-kirtland-and-nau-voo&old=true	The church recognizes that the way Joseph Smith taught the doctrine of sealing was more expansive than how it is currently taught today.	Chapter 6
https://www.chur-chofjesuschrist.org/ manual/members-guide-to-temple-and-family-history-work/chapter-7-pro-viding-temple-ordi-nances	A deceased woman can be sealed to mul-tiple deceased men.	Chapter 6

* Visit www.gayldscrossroads.org/topical-index for active hyperlinks to these sources

Terminology

Referenced site	Summary	Location used
https://en.wikipedia.org/wiki/Gay	Proper use of LGBTQ terminology.	N/A
https://www.churchofjesus-christ.org/study/ensign/1995/10/same-gender-attrac-tion?lang=eng, 1995	President Oaks taught in 1995 that we should refrain from using gay and lesbian as nouns to identify people. But in 2019, he used *LGBT* repeatedly in General Conference.	Chapter 4

Women quoted

I wish more women were quoted in this book. However, because this book analyzes church doctrine, which has only ever been officially declared by men (prophets and apostles) in our church, almost all quotes/citations included in this index come from men. I have added this list of women here to highlight their contributions and to create a space for me to express my hope that women's voices will someday become allowed to declare doctrine as well.

Name	Summary	Location used
Debra Oaks Coe	When an LGBTQ person comes out, they are not asking for agreement, they're asking if they're still loved.	Chapter 2
Christina Dee	Book endorsement	Cover pages
Judy Dushku	Book endorsement	Cover pages
Rachel Held Evans	"Faith is about following the quiet voice of God without having everything figured out ahead of time."	Chapter 10

* Visit www.gayldscrossroads.org/topical-index for active hyperlinks to these sources

Fiona Givens	Sin is disharmony with God's love.	Chapter 4
Jody England Hansen	It is more reasonable and ethical to not believe in harmful theology than to cling to every word of church leaders.	Chapter 10
Margaret Olsen Hemming	Commentary on 2 Nephi 26:33	Chapter 4
Marci McPhee	Book editor; *Jesus' First and Last Message*	Editor's Foreword
Emily Nelson	Excellent list of harmful vs. helpful things to say to LGBTQ people and their loved ones	Chapter 2
Chieko Okasaki	We should have the spiritual independence to be the best church members we can—in our own ways.	Chapter 10
Blaire Ostler	Describes as genocide the idea that LGBTQ identity will be completely wiped out in heaven.	Chapter 4 Favorite Resources
Carol Lynn Pearson	Book endorsement. Numerous quotes from various articles and books she has authored (see above references in this index).	Dedication page Chapter 4 Chapter 6 Chapter 10 Favorite Resources Path Forward
Sarah Quincy	Book endorsement	Cover pages
Jana Riess	Cited articles on President Oaks' talk and on temple recommend questions.	Chapter 4 Chapter 8

*   Visit www.gayldscrossroads.org/topical-index for active hyperlinks to these sources

Sandra Rogers	"When we are fully obedient to the first commandment, we cannot help but obey the second."	Chapter 4
Fatimah Salleh	Commentary on 2 Nephi 26:33	Chapter 4
Cheryl Smith	Facebook post that prompted this entire book.	Chapter 1

ABOUT THE AUTHOR

Evan Smith is an active Latter-day Saint. He was born in the church and grew up in Murray, Utah. He served a full-time mission in California from 1994-1996 and then married his wife, Cheryl, a year later. They received their undergraduate degrees together from Brigham Young University in 2000, and Evan later received his law degree from the University of Toronto in 2003. He has been a practicing corporate attorney in Boston ever since. He and Cheryl have four children and call a small town 35 miles south of Boston home. Evan has served in the church as a stake institute teacher, high councilor, branch president, bishop, early-morning seminary teacher, and counselor in a stake presidency. He loves backcountry snow skiing and can still (sometimes) land a backflip behind a boat on a wakeboard. He is a first-time writer.

ABOUT THE EDITOR

Marci McPhee grew up in Texas, where she joined the church at age 16. After graduating from Brigham Young University and spending twelve years as a fulltime mom, she began her career in higher education. In 2009-10, Marci took a year-long leave from Brandeis University in the Boston area to volunteer as an English teacher in the Marshall Islands in the Pacific. Marci has served as stake and ward Primary president, stake Relief Society board member, ward Relief Society president, early-morning seminary teacher and institute teacher. She's a founding writer of PrimaryinZion.wordpress.com, editor of *Sunday Lessons and Activities for Kids* (Walnut Springs Press, 2015), co-editor of *Girls' Camp: Ideas for Today's Leaders* (Walnut Springs Press, 2016), and editor of *Fifty Five Days of Faith* (Mulberry Books, October 2018). After 43 years in the Boston area, Marci now lives in San Antonio, Texas.

marcimcpheewriter.com